WHAT WORKS: RESEARCH INTO PRACTICE: BRIDGING THE GAP IN COMMUNITY CORRECTIONS

D1241711

FOUNDED 1870

ICCA

EDWARD R. RHINE, PH.D.
AND DONALD G. EVANS, EDITORS

Mission of the American Correctional Association
The American Correctional Association provides a professional organization for all individuals and groups, both public and private, that share a common goal of improving the justice system.

American Correctional Association Staff

Harold W. Clarke, President
James A. Gondles, Jr., CAE, Executive Director
Gabriella Daley Klatt, Director, Communications and Publications
Alice Heiserman, Manager of Publications and Research
Jeannelle Ferreira, Associate Editor
Xavaire Bolton, Graphics and Production Associate

Printed in the United States of America by Gasch Printing, LLC, Odenton, MD

ISBN: 978-1-56991-268-3

This publication may be ordered from:
American Correctional Association
9050 Junction Dr.
Annapolis, MD 20701
1-800-222-5646, ext. 0129

For information on publications and videos available from ACA, visit our Web site at: www.aca.org.

Contact ICCA's Web site at: http://www.ICCAWEB.org.

TABLE OF CONTENTS

Foreword
James A. Gondles, Jr., CAE vii

Introduction
Continuing the Commitment: Using Academic Research to Inform the Practice of Community Corrections
Edward R. Rhine, Ph.D. ix

Section 1:
Offender Assessments Across the Generations

Chapter 1

Assessment of Offenders and Programs: A Fifteen-Year Update
D. A. (Don) Andrews, Ph.D. 3

Chapter 2

Reaction Essay—An Update on Offender Assessment
David Simourd, Ph.D., C. Psych. 53

Section 2:
Behavioral Health in Special Needs Offenders

Chapter 3

An Integrated Perspective on the Prevalence, Diagnosis, and Treatment of Behavioral Disorders in Correctional Populations
Norman G. Hoffmann, Ph.D. 61

Chapter 4

Reaction Essay—The Need for a Unifying Vision
  on Offender Disorders

    Gerald D. Shulman, M.A., M.A.C., FACATA 83

Chapter 5

Law and Disorder: The Case Against Diminished Responsibility

    Nancy Wolff, Ph.D. 97

Chapter 6

Reaction Essay—Diminished Responsibility as a Systems Issue

    Charley Flint, Ph.D. 155

Section 3:
Correctional Treatment, Behavioral Management, and Community Supervision

Chapter 7

Effective Correctional Treatment: What Is the State of the Art?

    Marilyn Van Dieten, Ph.D.
    David Robinson, Ph.D. 165

Chapter 8

Reaction Essay—Challenges of Bringing Evidence-Based
  Practices into the Mainstream of Community Corrections

    William D. Burrell 213

Chapter 9

Behavioral Management Strategies in Correctional Settings

    Faye S. Taxman Ph.D. 221

Chapter 10

Reaction Essay—Guiding Principles for Implementing
Case Management

Marilyn Van Dieten, Ph.D. 251

Section 4:
Families and Communities:
Natural Support Systems for Offenders

Chapter 11

Families, Community, and Incarceration

Donald Braman, J.D., Ph.D. 273

Chapter 12

Reaction Essay—Turning Our Attention to Families:
A Natural Resource for Improving Reentry Outcomes

Carol Shapiro 301

Section 5:
Civic Engagement, the Community, and Reentry

Chapter 13

Doing Good to Make Good:
Evaluating a Civic-Engagement Model of Reentry

Gordon Bazemore, Ph.D.
Rachel Boba, Ph.D. 315

Chapter 14

Reaction Essay—Making Restorative Justice the Norm

Phyllis Lawrence, J.D. 359

Epilog
In Pursuit of Effective Community Corrections
   Donald G. Evans 377

About the Authors 387

Index 399

FOREWORD

I am proud to once again be co-publishing a book with the International Community Corrections Association (ICCA). Our seventh publication together, *Research into Practice* is a bit different from the six others ACA has published with ICCA previously. Each of the major papers in this volume has a connected paper that is a reaction to it. These reaction papers provide the reader an opportunity to see the main issues that were raised in some–quite technical presentations and get another viewpoint on the topics—often from practitioners.

The editors of this volume, Don Evans and Edward Rhine, are veterans in the field of community corrections and research-based practice. The concepts of a "what works" agenda may sometimes be difficult to understand, but these essays detail their essential elements. They explain not only what works but what does not work and why. If we are to decrease the prison population and the large numbers of those on probation and parole, it is incumbent on us to understand how to structure our programs and responses to offenders employing the framework of best practice and outcome measurement.

ACA is committed to providing useful resources for those working in corrections to improve the safety and effectiveness of our correctional facilities and programs. We also have a commitment to the education of corrections professionals to promote the most effective use of scarce resources to carry out the mission and goals of correctional agencies. This text and many of the other publications of the Association may be used in college courses and for the required continuing training of those already in the correctional system.

I hope our partnership with ICCA continues to thrive and address issues relevant to practitioners and researchers. Collaboration that leads to examination and discussion of issues affecting corrections professionals and the populations we oversee can only lead to positive outcomes.

James A. Gondles, Jr., CAE
Executive Director,
American Correctional Association

INTRODUCTION

CONTINUING THE COMMITMENT: USING RESEARCH TO INFORM THE PRACTICE OF COMMUNITY CORRECTIONS

Edward R. Rhine, Ph.D.

For many years, the International Community Corrections Association (ICCA) has demonstrated a laudable commitment to bringing the results of academic research to practitioners by sponsoring a research conference as an integral part of its annual "What Works" proceedings. Since 1993, ICCA has targeted varied issues and vexing challenges that confront the field of community corrections––if not corrections more generally—through hosting presentations by a variety of noteworthy individuals from Canada, the United States, and elsewhere across the world. A result of this thinking by some of the best minds in the field has been the growing literature emphasizing "what works" for offender rehabilitation.

The research papers in this volume evolved from the 2005 and 2006 Research Conferences of ICCA in Atlantic City, New Jersey, and Norfolk, Virginia. They cover a wide array of topics germane to community corrections practitioners, and those with a more general interest in the criminal justice system. The presentations address the assessment of offenders, correctional treatment and programming, principles that drive effective case management, strategies and promising modalities for dealing with behavioral and mental health disorders in correctional populations and in the larger arena of criminal justice, and families, communities, and offender reentry.

A reaction essay is provided to each of these contributions from authors well-versed in community corrections. The respondents offer insights and observations for the reader to consider. Several of the rejoinders reflect on the research literature pertinent to the original paper; others discuss the broader policy implications, while some present enhancements to the model that has been introduced. Regardless of the particular focus, the responses serve to augment and continue the dialog that began during the ICCA Research Conference.

Offender Assessments Across the Generations

The first research paper by Dr. Don Andrews, "Assessment of Offenders: A Fifteen Year Update," offers a rigorous and informed accounting of the evolution of offender assessments, especially since the path-breaking work begun by the author and several of his Canadian colleagues in the early 1990s. Dr. Andrews notes that the field has witnessed significant progress across time as first-generation (subjective) assessments gave way to second-generation (actuarial, mechanical) assessments to third-generation (criminogenic needs assessments) and eventually to fourth-generation tools. These fourth-generation assessments are the primary focus of this chapter. Dr. Andrews provides a rich discussion of how offender assessment today, if it is to be at the cutting edge of what research now demonstrates, must systemically incorporate the correctional treatment principles associated with risk, needs, and responsivity. This means that the results of such assessments must be fully integrated into intake, treatment planning, and service delivery in a manner that shapes and guides offender case management.

The reaction essay by Dr. David Simourd provides a cogent summary of the major themes covered by Dr. Andrews, highlighting essential findings associated with each. The themes include advances in correctional knowledge, the predictive validities of assessment instruments, general risk/need assessment instruments, the practical utility of risk, needs, responsivity principles, the vital connection of agency links and support for these principles, and the challenges they continue to confront. Dr. Simourd closes by noting that for more than thirty years Dr. Andrews has been one of the giants in the field, advancing knowledge of correctional rehabilitation through theoretical and research-grounded work.

Diagnosis, Prevalence, and Behavioral-Health Conditions in Special Needs Offenders

In a compelling paper, "An Integrated Perspective on the Prevalence, Diagnoses and Treatment of Behavioral Health Disorders in Correctional Populations," Dr. Norman Hoffmann considers mental health and substance use among adult and juvenile populations and the screening and diagnostic tools for estimating these conditions. Screening tools offer a probability estimate of the risk for a given condition, but must be distinguished from a diagnostic assessment, which provides a more comprehensive foundation for determining whether the condition is present. Dr. Hoffmann goes on to caution against confounding substance dependence (a "distinct, chronic, and severe condition") and substance abuse (a situational or transient condition) arguing they are independent and quite distinct from each other. He points out that the prevalence rates for mental health and substance use disorders across all correctional populations suggest the need for integrated and substantial clinical services during and subsequent to incarceration.

In terms of youth, Dr. Hoffmann notes that a majority of adolescents processed through the system of juvenile justice show symptoms of co-occurring, multiple mental health and substance-use disorders that can be properly assessed and the youth referred to appropriate services. On the adult side, one of his more significant findings is that female offenders demonstrate a higher prevalence and greater severity of substance dependence than their male counterparts.

In his response, Jerry Shulman begins by further highlighting the consequences associated with the continuing confusion between substance abuse and dependence. He elaborates on Dr. Hoffmann's discussion of the use of screening and diagnostic assessments of substance use and mental health disorders and the need for treatment given the very high incidence of such disorders across the criminal justice system. His rejoinder includes an informative accounting of these issues relative to male and female offenders in the system of juvenile justice.

In the next research paper, "Law and Disorder: The Case Against Diminished Responsibility," Dr. Nancy Wolff seeks to unravel the costs and consequences of fragmentation and disorganization between the criminal justice and behavioral health systems, and the pressing need for more clearly delineated roles and enhanced cross-system coordination. She highlights the rates of prevalence and causal connections pertaining to mental and substance-use illnesses, treatment, and criminal deviance within correctional settings and during the offender's return home to the community. Dr. Wolff calls for a better understanding of the causal pathways when mental and substance-use illnesses co-occur with criminal behavior. Her comprehensive chapter illuminates the need for these separate but interlocking "systems" to clearly allocate responsibilities in a coordinated manner across a continuum properly sequenced relative to the sanctioning and treatment process of the offenders.

Dr. Charley Flint's response, "Diminished Responsibility as a Systems Issue," begins by questioning who is being talked about when it comes to considering the mentally ill. She notes that the system is designed to address the problems they present, and the all too frequent misguided societal response. Flint points to "a bit of class bias" in social science research suggesting that the seriously mentally ill experience lives of chaos rooted within communities characterized by poverty and high unemployment. She concurs with Wolff that the interlocking systems responsible for addressing the complex issues associated with the processing of such offenders should not be granted diminished responsibility for achieving outcomes that contribute to the public good.

Correctional Treatment, Behavioral Management, and Community Supervision

Most practitioners are aware of the enormous growth of the "What Works" literature over the past several decades and its implications for rehabilitative programming. Far fewer are conversant with the more recent dialog on evidence-based practice as an increasingly important trend in community corrections. Drs. Van Dieten and Robinson present an incisive overview of treatment effectiveness and chart the evolution of the "What Works" movement toward evidence-based practice in their chapter, "Effective Correctional Treatment: What Is the State of the Art?" They cite recent meta-analyses demonstrating that programs incorporating the principles of effective correctional treatment may exert a recidivism-reduction impact within the range of 10 to 30 percent or even more—if the programs are of high quality reflecting compliance with such principles. These findings are fully consistent with those of Andrews, noted above.

The authors point out that the quality of implementation exerts a sizeable moderating impact on the effectiveness of correctional programs. Lower-effect sizes are associated with mediocre to poor program implementation. Drs. Van Dieten and Robinson provide a compelling translation of this literature. They focus on its implications for supervision case management, noting that this issue has all too often been "omitted from the research agenda." Their chapter concludes by describing a four-stage model for supervision, "Effective Case Work," that combines the principles of risk, need, and responsivity with motivational interviewing techniques.

William Burrell presents an incisive rejoinder entitled "The Challenges of Bringing Evidence-Based Practices into the Mainstream of Community Corrections Practice." He observes that the leaders and managers in the field are now at a crossroads relative to advancing the state of practice in offender supervision. Burrell argues that probation and parole agencies have struggled for more than thirty years with defining their mission and purpose. He calls for the unequivocal adoption and application of evidence-based practices with a sustained focus on four key areas: organizational mission and philosophy, organizational infrastructure, line personnel, and staff supervision. He closes by showing how the recent work of Dowden and Andrews (2004) on "Core Correctional Practices," combined with the strategies developed by Drs. Van Dieten and Robinson, might be used to establish the components of a practical toolbox to guide probation and parole case management.

These issues are further addressed within an innovative framework in a research paper by well-known scholar Dr. Faye Taxman, "Behavioral Management Strategies in Correctional Settings." Dr. Taxman presents a behavioral-management approach to supervision that integrates law enforcement and social work goals. Her model incorporates principles and interventions targeting actions and behaviors, not the attitudes or values of individuals (the assumption is that prosocial changes along these dimensions will follow). A behavioral-management approach presumes that the probation or parole officer is a facilitator of offender change, albeit still performing the functions of case manager. The officer, however, must receive organizational training and support in establishing a different kind of relationship (rapport) with offenders committed to guiding problem-solving and reinforcing change in a prosocial direction.

Dr. Taxman draws from a research foundation to shape her behavioral-management principles and carefully crafted strategies. She addresses the functions of case management (that is, assessment, case planning, treatment/service delivery, and compliance management), and the environment in which these transactions with offenders occur. Her discussion concludes by showing how to translate case management into behavioral management through changes in the organization's environment. The end goal is to foster law-abiding behavior of offenders under supervision.

In her response, Dr. Van Dieten turns to research summarizing what can be learned from the field of mental health relative to case management. She develops five core or guiding principles for the implementation of integrated case management across correctional agencies, drawing on Taxman's model, findings from the "What Works" literature, and her earlier discussion of the mental health literature. Both Drs. Taxman and Van Dieten agree that to be effective in engaging offenders in constructive prosocial change, the model that is adopted must foster the development of natural systems of support in the community that extend beyond the period of supervision or criminal justice system involvement.

Families and Communities:
Natural Support Systems for Offenders

Dr. Donald Braman's research, called "Families, Community, and Incarceration," shines a spotlight on the impact of mass incarceration on family life in urban America. He provides the results of a rich ethnography over the course of three years, focusing on the experiences of thirty families' interaction with the criminal justice system in the District of Columbia. His work examines the damaging consequences for offenders suffering from addiction, removed from their families through incarceration for often minor drug-related charges, returned upon release to parole, and frequently reimprisoned for violating the conditions of their supervision. With depressing frequency, his account reveals a cycle that ends in either the offender's death or a lengthier prison term. Dr. Braman also provides penetrating insights on how criminal sanctions presently act like a hidden tax on poor and minority families, adversely affecting their material and financial circumstances across generations, and the norms of trust and mutual responsibility so essential to sustaining the fabric of family life.

Dr. Braman argues that at the "going rate" of mass incarceration, family and community bonds have become far more detached, creating social, moral, and cultural impoverishment. He then offers three policy suggestions that have implications for community corrections, including the urgency of replacing talk of rehabilitation with offender accountability, the need to view offenders not as individuals, but as embedded within a web of social relationships, and the value of "progressives" engaging in a sustained dialog with conservatives about crime and punishment. He believes community corrections practitioners are uniquely positioned to embrace and act on all three recommendations.

In her eloquent rejoinder, Carol Shapiro discusses "Turning Our Attention to Families: A Natural Resource for Improving Reentry Outcomes." She, too, argues that the unit of analysis must shift from the individual to the family. Like Braman, she offers a contextual vision of the family as a natural support system, stating that if change is to occur within and outside the criminal justice system, families must be viewed not as repositories of pathology, but as parts of social networks that offer human capital and expertise to their members. Shapiro offers innovative methods for tapping into existing workforces in corrections, families, and others to identify effective strategies for strengthening the well-being of families.

Civic Engagement, the Community, and Reentry

Dr. Gordon Bazemore, a highly regarded scholar and advocate for restorative justice, draws on a formidable body of research in presenting a model and protocol for a "civic engagement" approach to offender reentry. The chapter "Doing Good to Make Good: Evaluating a Civic Engagement Model of Reentry," co-authored with Dr. Rachel Boba, points to a notable disconnect in the strategies designed to be supportive of reentry. Present strategies do not address the impact of the community as an independent variable (affecting the capacity of offenders to reintegrate successfully) or as a dependent variable (to be acted upon in terms of community-focused interventions). With but few exceptions, the authors argue that the approaches taken to reentry fail to incorporate a vision of the community as the ultimate destination of the "reentry journey," one that has the potential to infuse social capital through capacity building and receptivity as offenders return home.

Drs. Bazemore and Boba develop their model with a particular emphasis on the role of civic service tied to restorative justice principles and practices. The model draws on social science research centering on identity transformation, life-course criminology, and social-disorganization theory. The authors place a strategic emphasis on community service to accomplish three goals focusing on reducing existing community barriers for persons subject to correctional supervision, redefining the image of ex-offenders, and growing the capacity and receptivity of communities in providing tangible support and assistance as they return home. Drs. Bazemore and Boba develop an evaluation protocol to assess the model. They close by cautioning that the legitimization of punishment and the ascendancy of a "culture of retribution" now informing crime and justice policy present daunting challenges to the adoption of their approach.

Phyllis Lawrence provides a response supportive of restorative justice theory and practice in "Making Restorative Justice the Norm."

An experienced practitioner in working with victims and offenders for many years, Lawrence compares the broad framework of restorative justice with the adversarial process of criminal justice. Accenting the shortcomings of the latter, she proposes a systemic alternative calling for the infusion of restorative justice values at the core of a new agency that would focus on connecting victims and offenders. She discusses how this new agency would work and gives case guidance to all the actors (for example, victims, offenders, judges, probation officers, police, and prosecutors). According to Lawrence, restorative processes may be configured to ensure that victims feel included and empowered in many millions of cases now resulting in convictions without their input.

Looking Ahead

Each year the Research Conference adds an informative dimension to the proceedings of the International Community Corrections Association. This volume recognizes the importance of capturing the expertise and wisdom of those who present research papers for distribution to an audience far beyond those in attendance. The collection of research papers and reaction essays that follow are intended to serve as the inaugural foundation of what will become a regular and jointly sponsored publication by the International Community Corrections Association and the American Correctional Association. Forthcoming research conferences will provide subsequent editions to this monograph. In doing so, they will continue to offer timely contributions to the impressive and dynamic literature encouraging the translation of knowledge and research into evidence-based policy and practice across community corrections.

SECTION I:

OFFENDER ASSESSMENTS
ACROSS THE GENERATIONS

Assessment of Offenders and Programs: A Fifteen-Year Update*

1

D. A. (Don) Andrews, Ph.D.
Department of Psychology
Carleton University
Ottawa, Ontario, Canada

* An invited paper presented at the opening Research Plenary of the International Community Corrections Association (ICCA) Annual Conference, November 7-10, 2005, Atlantic City, New Jersey, "Making 'What Works' Work: Practical Application of Evidence-Based Practice." This paper draws on Andrews, Bonta, and Wormith (2006), and portions of it were presented at conferences in Kingston, Ontario (Correctional Psychology Conference, 2004), Midland, Ontario (Forensic Mental Health Conference, 2005), and at several CPAI-2000 and LS/CMI training sessions in 2004-05 (Saskatoon, Saskatchewan; Toronto, Ottawa, and North Bay, Ontario). Much of the paper is represented in Andrews and Bonta, 4th edition (2006).

Fifteen years have passed since the statements of Andrews, Bonta, and Hoge (1990) and Andrews, Zinger et al. (1990) on the correctional treatment principles of Risk, Need, and Responsivity. With those papers, the very valuable and traditional corrections-based concepts of "risk" and "need" continued as principles governing supervision, security level, and custody, but also were transformed into principles of human service. Level-of-supervision issues remain very important, but now, additionally, risk/need assessments have clinical value. Clinically, risk assessments have to do with who should receive treatment (higher-risk cases), and assessments of dynamic risk factors inform the selection of intermediate targets of change (reduce criminogenic need if you are interested in the objective of reduced re-offending). The responsivity and additional principles are outlined in Table 1, on the next page.

Inspection of Table 1 reveals that the number of principles associated with Risk, Need, and Responsivity have increased over the years. A notable addition is the expansion of the need principle with attention to the breadth of the criminogenic needs targeted. Another is the expansion of general responsivity through specific attention to staff relationship and structuring skills. Another is the focus on the management and organization aspects of integrity in program delivery. Note, too, that strength factors are now considered with reference to both prediction and individualized case planning. Each of these factors will be developed further in this paper.

Andrews, Bonta, and Wormith (2006) explored the recent past and near future of Risk, Need, and Responsivity assessment and applications. This author builds on that paper here and uses this opportunity to present related matters in greater detail than was possible earlier. At the first International Community Corrections Association (then called IARCA) "What Works" conference in 1993, James Bonta (1996) noted that the gap between first-generation assessments (1G: subjective assessment, professional judgment, or listening to your gut) and the second generation (2G: actuarial/mechanical) was huge while the gap between the second generation and the third generation was a mere fifty years (from 1928 to 1979).

Third-generation assessments systematically introduced criminogenic need assessment. Now, in only about twenty years, fourth-generation assessments are upon us with systematic Risk, Need, and Responsivity assessment from intake through case closure, and with full-blown case management with treatment planning and treatment follow-up.

Table 1. Principles of Effective Human Service in Justice Contexts

Psychology Theory:	Base program on an empirically solid theory (general personality and cognitive social-learning theory recommended)
Human Service:	Introduce human service into the criminal justice context
Risk:	Match intensity of service with risk level of cases
Need:	Target criminogenic needs (for reduced re-offending)
General Responsivity:	Employ behavioral, social learning, and cognitive-behavioral strategies
Specific Responsivity:	Match the mode and strategies of service with the learning styles, motivations, strengths, personality, and bio-demographics of offenders
Professional Discretion:	Deviate from recommendations for specified reasons
* Breadth (or Multimodal):	Target a number of criminogenic needs relative to noncriminogenic needs
* Strength:	Assess strengths to enhance prediction and specific responsivity effects
* Staff Practices:	The effectiveness of intervention is enhanced by high-quality relationship skills in combination with structuring skills (core correctional practices)
* Community-Based:	Community-based services are preferred but, if residential or institutional, the other principles still apply
* Management and Organizational Concerns:	Promote the selection, training, and clinical supervision of staff according to Risk, Need, and Responsivity. Build social and organizational systems and cultures that promote cognition and skills supportive of effective practice.

* Principle added or significantly augmented since Andrews et al. (1990). See Andrews (2001) for full statement of the principles.

This paper will underscore the value of enhancing adherence to Risk, Need, and Responsivity. The LS/CMI was designed to do just that through facilitating the linkages among assessment, treatment planning, and treatment delivery. On the other hand, the newer Correctional Program Assessment Inventory (CPAI-2000, Gendreau and Andrews, 2001) assesses programs, staff, and management in terms of actual levels of adherence at the program and agency level. That program and agency-level information may guide enhanced Risk, Need, and Responsivity adherence. The validities of these instruments and others will be reviewed as we move through this paper.

For illustrative purposes, Table 2 outlines the sections of the fourth-generation Level of Service/Case Management Inventory (LS/CMI: Andrews, Bonta, and Wormith, 2004). The great promise of fourth-generation instruments is to enhance adherence with Risk, Need, and Responsivity, thereby enhancing protection of the public from recidivistic crime. Note both a narrowing of risk/need assessment through a tight focus on the eight major factors as well as a broader sampling of personal problems with criminogenic potential and a history of violence. The instrument helps to structure case planning and service delivery in a manner consistent with Risk, Need, and Responsivity adherence.

Table 2. Example of Fourth-Generation Assessment: Level of Service/Case Management Inventory (LS/CMI)

Authors: D. A. Andrews, James Bonta, and Stephen Wormith (2004)

Publisher: MHS Multi-Health Systems

1. General Risk/Need Factors: Direct assessment of the central eight (see Table 5) including a new subscale aimed at the antisocial personality pattern. This section also provides an opportunity for ratings of case strengths.
2. Specific risk/need factors: Personal problems with criminogenic potential and an expanded survey of a history of antisocial behavior with particular reference to sexual offending, nonsexual violence, and diverse activities such as terrorism and impaired driving
3. Prison experience: Survey of past and current prison history along with barriers to release
4. Social, health, and personal well-being: Diverse factors from immediate financial issues through accommodation, health, low self-esteem, domestic violence, and being abused (in the past or currently, in the domains of sex, emotion, and neglect)
5. Specific responsivity: This section notes stages of motivation, anxiety, gender, ethnicity/culture, mental disorder, psychopathy, and so forth.
6. Professional discretion: Reasons for deviations from the recommended interventions are recorded
7. Risk/need summary and professional override
8. Risk/need profile
9. Program placement decision
10. Case management plan: Criminogenic, and noncriminogenic need areas targeted, special responsivity cosiderations
11. Progress record, criminogenic, and noncriminogenic need areas
12. Case closure

continued on next page

Positive Features	• Well-validated risk/need scores • Assessment of need areas that are strongly linked with positive outcomes when targeted • Assessments of change have been linked with enhanced predictive validity • Assessments of need have been linked with alternative measures of domains • Provides opportunity to validate targeting of noncriminogenic needs • Establishes opportunity to validate major hypotheses about specific responsivity • Case management software is available • Youth version is available (Hoge and Andrews, 2002) • Keyed to both community and institutional corrections • Brief actuarial violence scale in preparation • Acute dynamic risk survey in planning stage • Evidence that prison workers' access to risk information increased transfers to community alternatives to incarceration • Incorporates elements that have been associated with enhanced public protection at the agency level
Issues	• Establishing validity in regard to specific responsivity • Agency-level comparisons of Fourth Generation LSI with other Fourth-Generation systems* • Role at the time of sentencing

* Some other fourth-generation systems: The classic and original Wisconsin system (now known as CAIS and available from NCCD). Information at www.nccd-crc.org/nccd_main.html; COMPAS. Information at www.northpointeinc.com; OIA. Correctional Service Canada (Motiuk, 1997).

The sub-scores of program or agency-level assessment with the CPAI-2000 are outlined in Table 3. Through interviews, reviews of files and documents, and direct observation, a CPAI assessment of a program is a direct measure of level of adherence with Risk, Need, and Responsivity.

Table 3. Scorable Content of the Correctional Program Assessment Inventory (CPAI) – 2000 (Gendreau and Andrews, 2002)

A. (Section A is not scored)

B. Organizational Culture: A ten-item survey of clarity of goals, ethical standards, harmony, staff turnover, in-service training, self-evaluation, and agency outreach.

C. Program Implementation/Maintenance: A ten-item survey of the context within which the program was initiated, of value congruence with stakeholders, piloting, maintenance of staffing and credentials, qualifications of managers and staff with specific attention to selection, training, and clinical supervision with a focus on key skills and attitudes.

D. Management/Staff Characteristics: A seventeen-item survey of management and staff experience, training, skill levels, and attitudes and beliefs regarding treatment services.

E. Client Risk/Need Practices: A twelve-item survey of adherence to the principles of Risk, Need, and Responsivity assessment.

F. Program Characteristics: A twenty-two-item detailed survey of adherence to the Risk, Need, and Responsivity principles with an emphasis on breadth of targeting, general responsivity, and relapse prevention.

G. Core Correctional Practice: A forty-five item survey of observed elements of core correctional practice including relationship skills and the structuring skills of problem solving, modeling, reinforcing, and skill building.

H. Interagency Communication: A seven-item survey of brokerage, referral, advocacy, and coordination.

I. Evaluation: An eighteen-item survey of in-program and post-program research and monitoring activity.

This review of progress and challenges is organized as follows. First, Risk, Need, and Responsivity advances reflect the knowledge base in the psychology of criminal conduct. Theoretical, empirical, and applied progress in the last fifteen years has been described as "revolutionary" within the psychology of criminal conduct (Andrews et al., 2006). "Revolutionary" or not, we will see that progress has been impressive. Second, the mean-predictive-criterion-validity estimates of the best researched assessment instruments are reviewed. Third, the validity of general correctional risk/need instruments is compared with instruments from forensic mental health with all of the latter's very costly and perhaps unnecessary emphasis on pathology and mental disorder as assessed by mental health professionals. Fourth, developments in understanding the utility of Risk, Need, and Responsivity principles are summarized, including work on specific responsivity. Fifth, studies with the Correctional Program Assessment Inventory (CPAI) (Gendreau and Andrews, 2002) are described that link agency-level Risk, Need, and Responsivity adherence to agency-impact on recidivistic crime. Finally, we review the promise and challenge of proposed alternatives to Risk, Need, and Responsivity.

Development Within the Psychology of Criminal Conduct

Theoretical Understanding. General personality and social psychological perspectives are now everywhere in efforts to understand variation in the criminal behavior of individuals (Andrews and Bonta, 2003; McGuire, 2004). The dominant personality factors are recognized as (1) weak constraint/low self-control and (2) negative emotionality or the disagreeableness that accompanies feeling mistreated. The dominant social psychology is social learning/social cognition theory; thus, general personality and social learning/cognition approaches (GPSLs) of criminal conduct are now dominant. Table 4 is an effort to recognize some of the many scholars who have contributed to general personality and social learning/cognition approaches and Risk, Need, and Responsivity (see Andrews and Bonta, 2003, and/or McGuire, 2004, for specific references).

Table 4. Contributions to a General Personality and Social Learning/Cognitive Perspective on Crime

Freud: The structure of personality (id, ego, superego)	Psychological maturity as strong self-control, stable familial affection, and social productivity
The Yale School	The birth of social learning theory through (1) the integration of psychoanalysis, behaviorism, and sociology/anthropology and (2) the specification of frustration aggression (Dollard, Doob, Miller, Mowrer, and Sears)
Glueck and Glueck (1950)	Identified the major risk/need factors recognized today while placing lower-class origins, personal distress, and psychopathology in the weak risk category
Sociologists who recognized the importance of human diversity relative to social location	Travis Hirschi, Michael Hindelang, Edwin Sutherland and Donald Cressey, Ron Burgess and Ron Akers; Ron Akers, Robert Agnew, Francis Cullen, Walter Reckless, Graham Sykes and David Matza
Some behavioral, social learning, and social-cognitive psychologists	I. Azen and M. Fishbein; Neil Azrin; Albert Bandura and R. H. Walters; Albert Bandura; Roy Baumeister; Leanord Berkowitz; Carver and Scheiver; Donald Meichenbaum; Walter Mischel; Gerald Patterson; Rutter; B. F. Skinner
Meta-analytic contributions to prediction and/or treatment	Don Andrews; James Bonta; Craig Dowden; Paul Gendreau; Claire Goggin; Karl Hanson; Mark Lipsey
Developmental criminologists	Rolf Loeber; David Farrington; Terri Moffit

continued on next page

Practical assessment instruments	The Wisconsin group (S. C. Baird, B. J. Bemus, R. C. Heinz, G. Arling); Donald Gottfredson, P. Hoffmann, J. Nuffield; Robert Hare; Marnie Rice, Grant Harris, Vernon Quinsey, Catherine Cormier; Don Andrews, James Bonta, Robert Hoge, Steve Wormith
Some general personality and social learning/cognitive approaches and perspectives	Robert Agnew, et al. (2002); Ron Akers (1977, 1998); Don Andrews and James Bonta (1994, 2003); Albert Bandura (1977, 1997, 2001); Ronald Blackburn (1993); Hans Eysenck (1977); Scott Hengeller, Sonia Schowenwald et al. (1998); Walter Mischel and Y. Shoda (1995); Gerry Patterson (1993); Richard Jessor and Shirley Jessor (1977)

Empirical Understanding of Risk/Need Factors. Meta-analyses of the risk/need factors have greatly clarified knowledge of major and minor risk/need factors. Table 5 presents a narrative summary of the findings that have influenced the structure of two new LSIs (YLS/CMI: Hoge and Andrews, 2002; LS/CMI: Andrews, Bonta, and Wormith, 2004).

Table 5. Major Risk/Need Factors and Promising Intermediate Targets for Reduced Recidivism

History of Antisocial Behavior. Early and continuing involvement in the number and variety of antisocial acts in a variety of settings.
Dynamic need: build up noncriminal alternative behavior in risky situations.

Antisocial Personality Pattern. Adventurous pleasure seeking, weak self-control, restlessly aggressive.
Dynamic need: build problem-solving skills, self-management skills, anger management and coping skills.

Antisocial Cognition. Attitudes, values, beliefs and rationalizations supportive of crime and cognitive emotional states of anger, resentment, and defiance. Criminal/reformed criminal/noncriminal/prosocial identity.
Dynamic need: reduce antisocial cognition, recognize risky thinking and feeling, build up alternative less risky thinking and feeling, adopt reform/anticriminal identity.

Antisocial Associates. Close association with criminal others and relative isolation from anti-criminal others, immediate social support for crime.
Dynamic need: reduce association with criminal others, enhance association with anti-criminal others.

Family/Marital. Two key elements are nurturance/caring and monitoring/supervision.
Dynamic need: reduce conflict, build positive relationships, and enhance monitoring and supervision.

School/Work. Low levels of performance and satisfactions in school and/or work.
Dynamic need: Enhance performance, rewards, and satisfactions.

Leisure/Recreation. Low levels of involvement and satisfactions in anti-criminal leisure pursuits.
Dynamic need: Enhance involvement, rewards, and satisfactions.

Substance Abuse. Abuse of alcohol and/or other drugs.
Dynamic need: reduce substance abuse, reduce the personal and interpersonal supports for substance-oriented behavior, enhance alternatives to drug abuse.

Table 6. The Correlation (r) Between Criminal Behavior and the Central Eight, Personal Emotional Distress and Lower-Class Origins: Mean Estimates from Eight Meta-Analyses

1	2	3	4	5	6	7	8
History of Antisocial Behavior							
.21p	.38p	.16	.26	.35	.22	.28	.16
Antisocial Personality Pattern							
		.18	.19	.31	.12	.34	.33
Antisocial Attitudes							
.22p	.48p	.18	nt	.21	nt	.15	.36
Grand Mean of Big Four Risk/Need Mean Estimates (.26, 95% CI: .22/.30, n=24)							
Family/Martial							
.18	.20	.10	.19	.16	.10	.14	.33
Education/Employment							
.12	.28	.13	.19	.28	.04	.17	.21
Substance Abuse							
nt	nt	.10	.06	.24	.11	.22	.06
Leisure/Recreation							
nt	nt	nt	nt	.21(9)	nt	nt	nt
Grand Mean of Moderate Risk/Need Mean Estimates (.17, 95% CI: .13/.20, n=23)							
Lower Class Origins							
.06	.05	.05	.10	nt	.00	nt	nt
Fear of Official Punishment (Deterrence)							
.08	.07	.05	nt	.14	-.04	.02	-.08
Verbal Intelligence							
nt	nt	.07	.11	nt	nt	.01	nt
Grand Mean of Minor Risk/Need Mean Estimates (.03, 95% CI: -.02/.08 n=16)							

Notes on Table 6.

Table 6 is a quantitative summary of eight meta-analyses on the issues of risk/need factors. Each and every meta-analysis used the Pearson *r* as the measure of strength of association between assessments and criminal behavior.

The meta-analytic studies: One: Gendreau, Andrews, Goggin, an Chanteloupe (1992). Andrews and Bonta (2003, 75-76). Two: Simourd and Andrews (1994). Three: Gendreau, Little, and Goggin (1996). Four: Lipsey and Derzon (1998). Five: Prepared for this paper from data in Andrews, Bonta, and Wormith (2004). Six: Bonta et al. (1998); Seven: Hanson and Morton-Bourgon (2004). Eight: Dowden and Andrews (1999ab); Andrews and Bonta (2003, 310).

Figure 1. Comparison of Recidivism Rates on Effect Size, r= .65 - .35 = .30

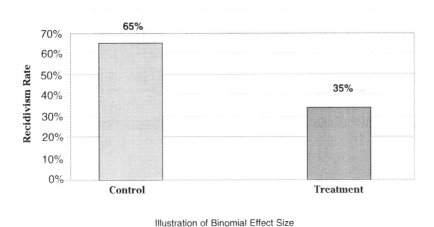

Illustration of Binomial Effect Size
Display (r)

Figure 1 illustrates how the *r* may be interpreted with the Binomial Effect Size Display. Briefly, the difference in the recidivism rate of one group from the recidivism rate of another group is the Pearson *r*. The *r* may also be called an Effect Size, reflecting the magnitude of the association between one variable and some other variable. In Figure 1, the recidivism rate for the higher risk group is .65, and it is .35 for the lower risk group. Thus, the effect size estimate (or the *r*) is .65 minus .35 = .30.

Returning to the overall pattern of results, apart from Leisure/ Recreation, which was assessed only in LSI studies (Column 5 of Table 6), there is deep and broad research support for the classification of major, moderate, and minor risk/need factors (and hence for the classification of criminogenic and noncriminogenic needs as more promising and less promising intermediate targets of change). The grand means of the major, moderate, and minor risk/need sets (.26, .17, and .03, respectively) were significantly different from each other (p < .01). It is handy to refer to the major set as the "big four" and the combined major and moderate factors as the "central eight."

Meta-analyses are also sorting out important theoretical issues. For example, it is becoming clear that both personality factors (such as low self-control) and social learning variables (such as attitudes and associates) are required to maximize predictive accuracy (Pratt and Cullen, 2000). Moreover, as noted above, it appears that at least two fundamental dimensions of personality are involved at the personal level of analysis (Miller and Lynam, 2001). One dimension is often called weak constraint or low conscientiousness (lack of persistence, impulsiveness, weak planning). The other dimension is often called negative emotionality or low agreeableness (hostile, spiteful, self-centered, indifferent to others, antagonistic).

Empirical Understanding of Effective Correctional Treatment. Since 1990, there have been more than thirty meta-analytic reviews of the correctional treatment literature (McGuire, 2004: Table 6.2). Inspection of Figure 2 reveals that adherence with each of risk, need, and general responsivity was associated with greater mean reductions in recidivism than was non-adherence to the principles (the sample of 374 tests of treatment was expanded upon by Dowden [1998]; see Andrews and Bonta [2003], Chapter 7).

Inspection of Figure 3 reveals that the overall level of adherence to Risk, Need, and Responsivity was associated with increasingly positive mean-effect sizes (from -.02 for complete nonadherence through .26 for full adherence).

We also now know that the validity of the risk principle has been underestimated because so few primary studies actually report treatment effects sorted according to risk levels of the cases (Andrews and Dowden, 2006). There are, however, clear limits to the risk principle: The principle only holds when programs are otherwise in adherence with the human service principles of need and general responsivity. Delivering nonbehavioral programs that target self-esteem and fear of official punishment will not work with either lower risk or higher risk cases.

Figure 2. Mean Effect Size by Adherence to Principles (k = 374)

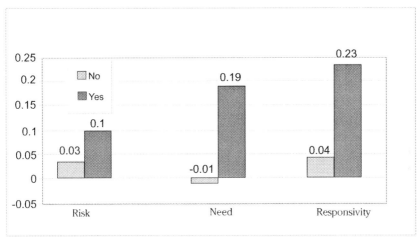

Mean Effect Size (r) by
adherence with Principles
(based on Dowden sample)

Figure 3. Mean Effect Size by Adherence to Risk, Need, and Responsivity

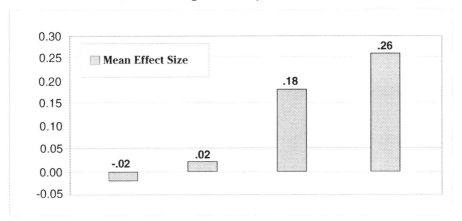

The validity of the need principle has also been underestimated because original tests did not consider the full breadth of differences in the number of criminogenic needs targeted and the number of noncriminogenic needs targeted. The strength of the full breadth measure of adherence to need is illustrated in Figure 4 where mean effect sizes are actually negative when the targets of change are predominately noncriminogenic needs, and decidedly positive when targets of change are predominately criminogenic needs.

The power of adherence with general responsivity can be enhanced by building specific worker relationship and structuring skills (Dowden and Andrews, 2004) into the program. The relationship skills include respectful and caring communication. The structuring skills include the modeling and reinforcement of anticriminal attitudes, values, and beliefs.

Figure 4. Mean Effect Size by Criminogenic-Noncriminogenic Needs

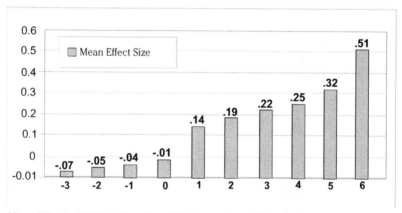

Mean Effect by Relative Targeting of Criminogenic and Noncriminogenic Needs

Attending to the integrity of program implementation is another way of enhancing the effects of Risk, Need, and Responsivity adherence (Andrews and Dowden, 2005). Indicators of integrity include the selection, training, and clinical supervision of staff with reference to key relationship and structuring skills. Other indicators are the monitoring of service delivery and of gains on the intermediate targets of change. The meta-analytic evidence suggests that many indicators of integrity are associated with positive treatment effects but only with programs that adhere to Risk, Need, and Responsivity (Andrews and Dowden, 2005). The mean correlation with effect size of eight integrity indicators for non-Risk, Need, and Responsivity programs was a nonsignificant .02

(95 percent CI: -.06/.10; computed from the effect sizes reported in the above-noted study).

In dramatic contrast, the mean correlation with effect size of nine integrity indicators for programs in adherence with Risk, Need, and Responsivity was .14 (95 percent CI = .03/.16). This finding is stunning. The management and organizational concerns of staff selection, training, supervision, and program monitoring appear to be of zero value in reducing recidivism unless the program adheres to the principles of Risk, Need, and Responsivity.

Simple Predictive Criterion Validity Estimates by Assessment Generation

Table 7 (on the next page) is a summary of meta-analytic surveys of the predictive validity of various risk/need assessment instruments (the particular meta-analytic surveys are identified in Andrews et al., 2006). The sad performance of the judgment calls of forensic mental health professionals is relatively dramatic (mean r of only .10 in predicting general recidivism) but quite consistent with the performance of unstructured judgment in a variety of spheres of activity (Grove, Zald et al., 2000). What is not so well appreciated in forensic mental health settings is the validity of correctional standards such as the Salient Factors Score (SFS) and the Wisconsin risk scale. In predicting general recidivism, they shine even compared to Hare's (1990) PCL-R (considered to be the "gold standard" in forensic mental health circles). LSI-R and the new LS/CMI General Risk/Need score are also yielding quite decent mean r estimates in the prediction of general recidivism.

Given the high level mean performance of general criminality scales in the special cases of work with sex offenders and mentally disordered offenders, the most prudent conclusion is that there is as yet little evidence to suggest that the simple predictive validity of the best-validated of the second-generation instruments is less or more than the best-validated of third- and fourth-generation instruments. A weakness of the meta-analyses is that several prominent instruments (in particular COMPASS and some of the CAIS scales) are not represented in the meta-analyses because the relevant data is not readily available or reflects multiple-regression solutions without cross-validation with fresh samples.

Table 7. Mean Predictive Criterion Validity Estimates (*r*) from Meta-Analytic Studies by Generation: Based on Andrews, Bonta, and Wormith (2006: Table 2)

Measure	Recidivism	
	General	Violence
First Generation (Clinical Judgment)		
	.10	.13
Second Generation (Actuarial/ Mechanical with emphasis on historical)		
General criminality scales	.42	.39 Sex/MD offenders
SFS	.26	
Wisconsin	.31	
SIRS	.36	
PCL-R	.27	.27
VRAG		.39
Third Generation (Mechanical with attention to dynamic risk factors)		
LSI-R	.36	.25
Fourth Generation (Mechanical with structured case planning and follow-up)		
LS/CMI General Risk/Need	.41	.29

However, the mean validity estimates are very respectable for general recidivism (.41) and for the prediction of serious recidivism resulting in incarceration (.37). These are what we would expect of an assessment across all of the central eight domains.

Obviously, this author is pleased with the relative performance of the LS/CMI General Risk/Need as summarized in Table 8. The prediction of violence yields the mean estimate of .29.

Table 8. Predictive Criterion Validity Estimates (*r*) for LS/CMI General Risk/Need (from Andrews, Bonta, and Wormith, 2004)

Study sample (N)	Recidivism		
	General	**Violence**	**Incarceration**
Andrews (1995)			
Probation (561)	.44	.26	.39
Incarceration (692)	—	—	.34
Rettinger (1998)			
Probation/Incarceration	.63	.44	—
Rowe (1999)			
Inmates (340)	.40	.30	.38
Girard (1999)			
Probation/Incarceration	.39	.28	—
Nowicka-Sronga (2004)	.40	.24	—
Raynor (2001)			
Mixed (700)	.37	—	.37
Mills et al. (209)	.39	.26	
Simourd (166)	.24	.22	.39
Mean	.41	.29	.37
CI	.32-.50	.22-.35	.35-.40

The information in Table 8 will illustrate the issue of variation in validity estimates that may be found from study to study. We need to recognize that the validity of assessments with any instrument may vary under some circumstances. The quality of the manuals may be an issue, as is user access to manuals, and of course, the training and ongoing clinical supervision of users (Lowenkamp, Latessa, and Holsinger, 2004).

The outstanding estimates in Table 8 are based on the Rettinger (1998) estimates of .63 for general recidivism and .44 for violent recidivism. Jill Rettinger knows the LSI inside and out. She has much experience working with the files of correctional agencies, and in addition to having access to LSI forms completed by correctional professionals, she had full access to an intensive semi-structured supplementary interview that was conducted by independent researchers. Generally, validity estimates will approach their upper limit when skilled assessors have ready access to multiple sources of information on the key risk/need variables.

Additionally, in that study of female offenders, a long follow-up period was involved so that the women had sufficient opportunity to demonstrate their antisocial behavior. The quality of assessment of the criterion (or outcome variable) also influences the magnitude of the predictive validity estimate in a positive manner (the ROC analyses yielded an AUC of .87 for general recidivism and .86 for violence).

The Rettinger study contrasts dramatically with that of Holtfreter, Reisig, and Morash (2004). The authors report a pitiful validity coefficient (*r*) for the LSI of less than .20. The outcome variable, however, was not officially recorded crime over a lengthy follow-up period but self-reported rule violations over a very short, six-month, follow-up period. Thirty-seven women who were "official" recidivists during this follow-up period were not available for interview (because they were AWOL or incarcerated). Hence, thirty-seven known recidivists were not counted as "recidivists" and, indeed, were dropped from the sample altogether. Even a measure of poverty did better than the LSI, and access to poverty-related services had a dramatic impact on self-reported recidivism. Perhaps financial difficulties were functioning as an acute dynamic risk factor (see discussion of dynamic assessment below).

The dynamic issue raises another major concern in evaluating the predictive validity estimates of pre-service assessments. Researchers must pay attention to when the assessment was conducted relative to service delivery. Services that adhere to Risk, Need, and Responsivity principles will greatly reduce the predictive validity of intake (pre-service) assessments. What is required in treatment-rich agencies is a post-service re-assessment that is examined in relation to subsequent offending (see dynamic assessment later in this essay).

Forensic Mental Health Assessments: A Special Case?

The validity coefficients for the VRAG stand out from all other tests sampled in the meta-analyses in the matter of predicting violence. VRAG studies also contributed to the impressive overall prediction of violence within the specialized samples.

In Table 9, (on page 24) VRAG items are sorted into the central eight categories (as previously reviewed in Table 5). The non-VRAG items tabled are characteristics that also linked with violent re-offending in the forensic mental health construction sample but were not selected for inclusion in VRAG. Multiple-regression findings determined item selection. That is, the single strongest predictor variable was first selected and then, after statistical controls for the first, the next strongest predictor variable was selected, and so on, until the minimum number of items are selected that maximize the multiple correlation coefficient.

First, note how data sources (in this case, forensic mental health) shape what information is even considered. Nothing was coded or reported from the domains of antisocial associates or leisure recreation. Nothing was selected from the domains of school/work or antisocial attitudes. The minor risk/need category has the second largest number of items and three items were selected. Those three were DSM-III schizophrenia, serious victim injury on the index offense, and female victim of the index offense. Each of these was scored as protective factors, that is, being schizophrenic, having seriously injured the victim, and injuring a girl or woman were associated with low rates of violent recidivism. Three elements of antisocial behavioral history made it in, being younger at the time of the index offense, nonviolent offense history, and failure on prior conditional release. The major contributor was the Hare PCL with any DSM personality disorder also contributing. Two family/marital items were selected (separated from parents by fifteen years of age and never married). Alcohol abuse was also selected.

The content of the VRAG earns far less than an "A" rating by general personality and social learning/cognition approaches/Risk, Need, and Responsivity standards, and yet outperforms the LSI and other instruments in the prediction of violence. Several possibilities exist. One, general personality and social learning/cognition approaches/Risk, Need, and Responsivity standards are incorrect or at least do not apply in the analysis of the criminal behavior of the mentally ill. Two, giving VRAG such high status is premature in that the data are not all in as yet. Three, something else is also operating here, and we have just not figured it out.

This author does not want to consider number one (at least not yet). Let us consider number two and do so from a variety of positions. First, there are a number of correctional instruments consistent with general personality and social learning/cognition approaches/Risk, Need, and Responsivity that performed well in the prediction of violent and serious recidivism. The results of these studies have just not made their way into the meta-analyses as yet.

Table 9. The Major and Minor Risk/Need Factors in the Forensic Mental Health Construction Sample for VRAG (*VRAG item)

History of Antisocial Behavior

* Age at index offense (negative)
* Nonviolent offense history
Childhood behavior problems (DSM-III)
Arrested before age sixteen
Escaped from an institution

* Failure on prior conditional release
Childhood aggression
Admissions to correctional institutions
Previous violent offense
Violent offense history

Antisocial Personality Pattern
*Hare PCL
Impulsivity score (DSM-IIII, ASP)
Level of Service Inventory (LSI) General propensity for rule violations

* Any DSM-III Personality Disorder
Elevated MMPI Pd

Antisocial Attitudes
Pro-criminal values

Attitudes unfavorable to convention

Antisocial Associates
Nothing coded or reported from this domain

School/Work
Suspended/expelled from school
Longest period of unemployment
(negative)

Highest grade achieved (negative)
Ever fired from job (ns)

Family/Marital
* Separated from parents (by 15 years)
Parental criminal history
Lived alone

*Never married
Parental alcoholism

Leisure/Recreation
Nothing coded or reported from this domain

Substance Abuse
*Alcohol abuse

Minor Risk/Need Factors
SES of parents (ns)
Previous psychiatric admissions (ns)
* DSM-III Schizophrenia (negative)
* Female victim, index offense (negative)
Victim knew offender (negative)
Sexual motive for index offense

Parental psychiatric history (ns)
IQ (ns)
* Serious victim injury, index (negative)
Violent Index offense (negative)
Weapon used in index offense (negative)

24

For example, the decidedly second-generation Offender Group Reconvic-tion scale (OGRS) was clearly a better predictor than clinical scales in a large sample of mentally disordered offenders, and it does not include any mental health information. Similarly, Gregg Gagliardi and associates (2004) report that "stock correctional variables" functioned very well in forecasting the recidivism of mentally ill offenders. Loza and Green (2003) and Kroner and Mills (2001) also show that correctional instruments may outshine or do at least as well as some forensic clinical instruments. Girard and Wormith (2004) reveal that use of the violent history items from section two of LS/CMI in combination with Antisocial Pattern yields validity estimates equal to or greater than the VRAG mean estimate. Similarly, Barnoski and Aos (2003) enhanced the predictive validity of the LSI by broader sampling of indicators of violent and serious prior offending. All in all, the relative value of correctional risk assessment and forensic mental health risk assessment is not yet settled.

Taking yet another look at the VRAG content, it is not clear that the PCL-R is necessary to its success. Quinsey and company (1998) note that a simple nonclinical checklist of early antisocial behavior (the CATS) can replace the PCL-R. We expect that a similar checklist could replace the multiple psychiatric diagnoses now required to score "any DSM personality disorder." Could a formal diagnosis of "schizophrenia" not also be dropped? Seriously, how necessary is it that the weak predictors of serious injury and female victim are allowed to enter as protective factors?

If the PCL-R may be replaced by a simple nonclinical checklist in the VRAG, perhaps it also could be replaced by nonclinical assessment of selected fundamental dimensions of personality. Miller and Lynam (2003) present the intriguing position that psychopathy represents extreme scores on four of the big five of personality, in particular low agreeableness and low conscientiousness. It is beginning to appear that the expense associated with forensic mental health assessments may be questioned on the basis of the impressive validity of lower cost general personality and correctional assessments.

Consideration of the mediators of a psychiatric diagnosis and the crime link is very fruitful. Substance abuse, one of the central eight, is an obvious candidate, as is antisocial cognition in that "believing the world is a hostile place and one must act first for self-protection" is supportive of crime. Delusional or not, diagnosed or not diagnosed, symptomatic or not symptomatic, attitudes, values, and beliefs supportive of crime are predictive of crime (Andrews and Bonta, 2003). In addition, whether identified by a mental health professional or by a community corrections worker, substance abuse predicts criminal behavior.

A closing point in this section has to do with the extraordinary attention paid to simple predictive criterion validity estimates in the forensic mental health tradition. Apart from variation in levels of supervision and security, what follows from the mental health assessment? Medication to control symptoms, perhaps, but what are the other targets? Search the VRAG for suggestions of intermediate targets. We will discuss psycho-pathy as a responsivity factor below.

Students of this author, colleagues, and this author like to say that the PCL-R saved forensic mental health from its sad performance in the arena of clinical judgment. We add that VRAG lifted the whole of the psychology of crime (forensic and correctional) into respectability around the prediction of violence. We now, however, are promoting general personality and social learning/cognition approaches and Risk, Need, and Responsivity vary widely, including within forensic mental health. We also continue to try to attend to the evidence.

Dynamic Validity

Paul Gendreau, Tracy Little, and Claire Goggin (1966) provided a great service to the field when they stressed the point that many of the best predictors of criminal recidivism were dynamic factors, factors capable of change (see Figure 5). Still, very few studies actually employ multi-wave longitudinal designs and report the incremental validity of re-assessments over and above that yielded by the original assessment. This information (still largely missing) is crucial to the valid identification of criminogenic needs (recall Figure 4).

Figure 5. Gendreau, Little, and Goggin (Criminology, 1996)

• Antisocial Attitudes	.19(29)
• Antisocial Associates	.18(27)
• Antisocial Personality	.18(62)
• Antisocial Behavioral History	.16(245)
• Criminogenic Need	.15(175)
• Educational/Vocational Achievement	.15(27)
• Lower Class Origins	.06(24)
• Personal Distress	.05(64)
• Lower Intelligence	.07(31)

Overall Personal Noncriminogenic Needs

Figures 6 and 7 summarize the mean effect sizes yielded by studies that targeted various criminogenic and noncriminogenic needs. Powerful data are presented there, but the truth is that showing that the setting of certain targets is associated with variation in successful rehabilitation is not the same as showing that actual gains and/or losses are associated with variation in recidivism (and that evidence we do not yet have).

Figure 6. Mean Effect Size by Specific Needs Targeted: Criminogenic Needs (overall mean effect = .08)

• Antisocial Cognition	.21(78)
• Self-Control Deficits	.22(59)
• Antisocial Associates	.21(51)
• Family Process	.29(30)
• Individualized Matching	.21(61)
• School/Work	.15(88)
• Substance Abuse	.11(36) *ns*

Figure 7. Mean Effect Size by Specific Needs Targeted: Noncriminogenic Needs (overall mean effect= .08)

• Fear of Official Punishment	-.05(43)
• Personal Distress	.08(101) *ns*
• Physical Activity	.18(62) *ns*
• Conventional Ambition	.16(245) *ns*
• Overall Personal Noncriminal	.15(175)
• Overall Interpersonal Noncriminal	.01(45)

Figure 8. Third Generation and Fourth Generation Increase in *r* square

• LSI-R (Andrews and Robinson, 1984)	294%
• LSI-R (Raynor, 2004)	293%
• OIA Need (Law, 2004)	282%
• OIA Risk, Need, Acute (Brown, 2004)	159%

Second-generation instruments offer little in the way of guiding adherence with the need principle. Such guidance has always been a feature of the LSI, and particularly so with the LS/CMI, wherein both criminogenic and noncriminogenic are sampled and case management protocols are presented. Figure 8 provides a few examples of the gains in predictive accuracy that are possible with re-assessments of dynamic variables.

Doubling and nearly a tripling of explained variance may be expected, but a careful meta-analytic review of the predictive validity of change scores is required. The Brown (2004) data are particularly interesting because she included not only the LSI-type of criminogenic needs but also fast-changing acute dynamic factors such as immediate negative emotionality and immediately stressed interpersonal relationships. The latter gets closer to the emotions, circumstances, and interpretations of the immediate situation of action (or what we used to call the "psychological moment"). This author is looking forward to the advances that appear so promising in the work of Ed Zamble and Vern Quinsey (1997), Vern Quinsey and additional colleagues (1997), and Karl Hanson and Andrew Harris (2000).

In the context of case planning and service delivery, for adherence to Risk, Need, and Responsivity, we expect appropriate targeting and, with appropriate intervention, achievement of intermediate gains. This is what the LS/CMI is intended to support. Figure 9 illustrates expected outcomes by risk, by targeting, and by intermediate gain. These data were collected in a probation agency for young offenders where the YLS/CMI was created. Note that the mean number of new convictions is reduced when appropriate intermediate targets are set and achieved, and this was particularly the case among higher risk young offenders. Figure 9 illustrates the type of data analyses that will be possible within agencies that adopt fourth-generation assessment systems.

Figure 9. Mean Number of New Offenses by Service

Intake	Appropriate Targets Set and Achieved		
Risk/Need	No	Yes	Eta
Higher	1.94	0.50	.29
Lower	0.70	0.55	.06
Overall	1.18	0.54	.18

Specific Responsivity

Unlike the principles of risk, need, and general responsivity, the principle of specific responsivity has not been the focus of a meta-analysis and, indeed, has not been widely studied.

Thus, we stand by and reiterate the Andrews, Bonta, and Hoge (1990) list of responsivity factors and encourage exploration of the classic differential-treatment systems through a series of tests of hypotheses reflecting some combination of cognitive/interpersonal maturity as well as interpersonal anxiety, weak social support for change, and antisocial personality pattern (see Table 10). The latter has been driven forward by the publication of the PCL-R and by Risk, Need, and Responsivity interpretations of psychopathy (Andrews and Bonta, 2003, 378-380; Simourd and Hoge, 2000; Wong and Hare, 2005). Pat Van Voorhis (1994) has greatly clarified the field by proposing a limited number of personality profiles that integrate the multiple traditional systems.

Gender, age, ethnicity, and mental illness are other potentially major responsivity considerations. The gender example is particularly compelling because of the specificity with which some feminists have critiqued Risk, Need, and Responsivity (to be reviewed below). Covington and Bloom (1999) in particular have offered a number of women-specific treatment recommendations (see Table 11). As we recommend in the case of psychopathy, we think it helpful to classify those recommendations according to their criminogenic-need implications (selection of appropriate intermediate targets of change) and their responsivity considerations (selection of appropriate modes and styles of service and of behavior-change strategies). As just a preliminary step, Table 11 indicates those intermediate targets of change and those intervention strategies that are/are not compatible with general personality and social learning/cognition approaches/Risk, Need, and Responsivity. For example, almost all responsivity considerations are judged compatible with general personality and social learning/cognition approaches/ Risk, Need, and Responsivity. On the other hand, not all of the recommended intermediate targets are compatible with general personality and social learning/cognition approaches/Risk, Need, and Responsivity. Of course, nothing in our system demands that noncriminogenic not be targeted although the balance is thought to be very important (recall Figure 5, and see Figures 15 and 16, later in this report).

Table 10. Principles of Specific Responsivity

Cognitive/interpersonal skill level. (Combination of empathy, interpersonal maturity, self-regulation skills, verbal intelligence.) Styles and modes of service that are verbally and interpersonally demanding and depend upon self-regulation, self-reflection, and interpersonal sensitivity should be used only with very high-functioning persons.

Interpersonal anxiety. Avoid both interpersonal confrontation and very intense interpersonal exchanges.

Antisocial personality pattern. In total, and in isolation, the personality elements of the antisocial personality pattern suggest not only risk (intensive supervision and service) and criminogenic needs (multiple), but also specific responsivity issues.

Low anxiety, low empathy, shallow emotion, manipulative, use high structure including monitoring and supervision and wide-open communication among involved service and control staff.

Sensation-seeking: program novel and exciting opportunities and events.

"Acting out" is reliably rewarded/low motivation for change: be sure treatment is readily accessible, employ outreach that is part of the total environmental surround.

Weak social support for change. Neutralize antisocial associates, structure active exposure to others who model and reinforce real alternatives to antisocial styles of thinking, feeling, and acting.

Gender. Provide gender-responsive services.

Age. Employ developmentally appropriate services.

Ethnicity/cultural considerations. Use cultural appropriateness.

Mental disorder. Address needs specific to disorder.

Case Management Classification. Use the Wisconsin "responsivity" classification system.

* **Motivation.** Match services according to stages of change.
*Additions to the Andrews, Bonta, and Hoge (1990) list.

Table 11. Specific Treatment Recommendations for Women Assigned to Need and Responsivity Considerations (Based on Recommendations of Bloom, 1999; Bloom and Covington, 2001; Covington, 2000; Covington and Bloom, 1999)

NEED: Promising Intermediate Areas of Change

Expansion and Growth of Self:
Develop knowledge of sources of self-esteem; knowledge of the effects of sexism, racism, and stigma on sense of self
Develop own sense of self
View substance abuse as a "self-disorder"
* Address roles of mother, professional, wife, partner, daughter, offender
Understand poor self-image and history of trauma and abuse
Integrate outer selves (roles) with inner selves (feelings, thoughts, attitudes)

Relationships:
Explore roles in family of origin; myths of motherhood; relationships with mother; relationship histories, including possible violence
* Explore decisions about building healthy support systems
Understand substance abuse as maintaining relationships with a drug-abusing partner or managing pain of abuse
* Recognize unhealthy, illusory, or unequal relationships with partners, friends, and family

Sexuality:
Explore sexuality, body image, sexual identity, sexual abuse, and fear of sex when clean and sober
Deal with sexual dysfunction, shame, fear, and/or trauma
View substance abuse as pain management

Spirituality:
Introduce concepts of spirituality, prayer, and meditation and show how they relate to healing and recovery in relation to transformation, connection, meaning, and wholeness
* Decision making (ORID): objective observation to establish facts; reflective emotional reactions; interpretive assessment of meaning and impact
Decisive identification of actions or decisions
* Express and contain negative emotions appropriately
* Develop empowerment through skill building
* Substance abuse
* Enhance quality of relationships at home, school, work, and at leisure

continued on next page

Table 11. Specific Treatment Recommendations for Women Assigned to Need and Responsivity Considerations (Based on Recommendations of Bloom, 1999; Bloom and Covington, 2001; Covington, 2000; Covington and Bloom, 1999) (*continued*)

* Question unhealthy relationships
* Discuss disability-related issues
Note appearance and overall health and hygiene
* Develop life plan

RESPONSIVITY:
Mode, style, influence strategies, service practices
Use women-only groups and individual sessions with female helper
* Staff model healthy relationships
* Create a community with a sense of connection
* Do not use the clinical model
* Emphasize safety
* Emphasis on connecting: mutual respect
* Build on strengths
Attend twelve-step programs
* Employ some psycho-educational methods
* Emphasize raising and exploring issues
* Use the least-restrictive environment

* Compatible with Risk, Need, and Responsivity

There have been very interesting developments in the domains of motivational interviewing and stages of change. Inspection of Table 12 on page 34 reveals particular motivational interviewing strategies linked with particular stages of change. The examples come from Miller and Rollnick (2002) and DiClemente and Velasquez (2002). This author and his colleagues are so impressed by motivational interviewing that it is now considered a core correctional practice in which all correctional workers should be trained and which should be a routine focus of clinical supervision (Gendreau and Andrews, 2002).

The Spirit of Motivational Interviewing: collaboration, evocation of possibilities, autonomy. General Principles: Express empathy (acceptance, reflective listening, ambivalence is normal); Develop discrepancy (client presents arguments for change; discrepancy between behavior and important personal goals/values); Roll with resistance (avoid arguing for change; resistance is not directly opposed; new perspectives invited not imposed); Support self-efficacy (support belief in the possibility of change: "I know what to do, and I know how to do it." Counselor's belief in clients' ability to change is important).

Assessment of Programs and Agencies

The field has available a number of instruments that will allow the sorting of offenders according to risk of recidivism and a more limited number of instruments that will assist in selecting appropriate intermediate targets of change. There are a number of traditional personality-based specific responsivity systems with their associated assessment approaches (as reviewed fifteen years ago: Andrews, Bonta and Hoge, 1990; Andrews and Bonta, 2003: Chapter 6; Van Voorhis, 1994). But does adoption of these instruments and adherence with the principles summarized in Table 1 lead to reduced re-offending?

The CPAI was developed to assess ongoing or proposed programming for its potential in reducing re-offending. Aleksandra Nesovic (2003) conducted detailed psychometric explorations of the CPAI and provides convincing evidence of high levels of inter-rater reliability in both questionnaire- and interview-based assessments of programs (at least .96: see Figure 10).

Figure 10. Reliability of CPAI (Nesovic, 2003)

- Questionnaire
  Total Score
        I-R   .96
        IC   .88
- Interview
  Total Score
        I-R   .98
        IC   .85
- Inter-form (Q and I): .80 (Total Score)
  Mean Q slightly higher than mean I ($p < 10$)

Table 12. Specific Responsivity: Stages of Change and Motivational Interviewing

Stages of Change	Motivational Interviewing Focus
Precontemplation:	
Reluctance	Use reflective listening, summarizing, and affirming to explore the situation.
Rebellion	Roll with resistance; do not argue; agree that change cannot be forced upon one; encourage menu of options.
Resignation	Instill hope; explore barriers; encourage small steps; build self-efficacy.
Rationalization	Use empathy and reflective listening; encourage mapping of pros and cons; do not argue.
Contemplation	Use accurate information on the risky behavior; map pros and cons; summarize; use affirmation; increase self-efficacy.
Preparation:	
Develop an Acceptable and Realistic Plan	Listen; reflect on the pros and cons.
Action:	
Implement the Plan	Listen and affirm.
Maintenance:	
Relapse—a "slip" is not failure	Return to earlier stages.

Effect Size by CPAI Score

Similarly, internal consistency reliability estimates were high (at least .85). Inter-form agreement was not perfect but was high (.80). Scoring programs according to the descriptions provided in research reports demonstrated the predictive value of adherence to Risk, Need, and Responsivity as measured with the CPAI. Inspection of Figures 11 and 12 reveals the correlation of CPAI sub-scores and total scores with effect size estimates.

Figure 11. Correlations with Effect Size: M-A by Nesovic (2003)

• Implementation	.15*
• Assessment	.44**
• Program	.46**
• Staff	.32**
• Evaluation	.29**
• (Section G: CCP)	(.44**)
• Total Tx	.52**
• Total	.50**

Figure 12. Mean Effect Field by CPAI Score

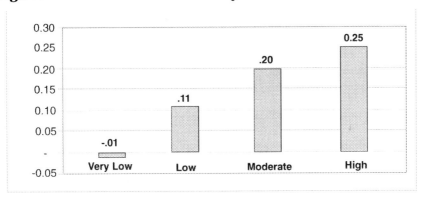

Figures 13-15 illustrate the wide applicability of the CPAI through demonstrations of the correlation of CPAI scores with effect size under a variety of justice settings, and by type of offender, type of research design, and type of programs.

Figure 13. Mean Effect Size and CPAI Tx Score Eta by Setting and Offender Type

• Community (.60)/Institution (.44)
• Restorative (.77)/Retributive (.51)
• Justice Staff (.49)/Other Staff (.57)
• Female (.60)/Male (.51)
• Ethnic Minority (.53)/Majority (.50)
• Violent Offenders (.54)/Nonviolent (.50)
• Young Offenders (.52)/Adult (.51)

Figure 14. Mean Effect Size and CPAI Tx Score Eta by Quality of Primary Studies

- Random Assign (.58)/Nonrandom (.46)
- Attribution Problem (.49)/No problem (.62)
- Internal Evaluator (.50)/External (.40)
- Small Sample (.59)/Large Sample (.45)
- Short Follow-up (.59)/Long Follow-up (.54)
- Atheoretical (.54)/Theoretical (.48)

Figure 15. Mean Effect Size and CPAI Tx Score Eta by Type of Program (Targets)

- Antisocial Attitudes (.28) Anger/SC (.30)
- Family (.59) Antisocial Associates (.45)
- Substance Abuse (.48) Academic (.52)
- Vocational/Employment (.65)
- Self-Esteem (.71) Physical Training (.65)
- Conventional Ambition (.78)

Mean Effect Size and CPAI Treatment Score ETA— A Measure of Covariation

Regardless of context, the predictive validity of the CPAI was apparent. Figure 16 shows how negative the mean effect sizes were for programs that targeted low self-esteem and were not otherwise in adherence with Risk, Need, and Responsivity. It also, very tentatively, suggests that there may be some crime-prevention potential of self-esteem programs that are otherwise in adherence with Risk, Need, and Responsivity.

Figure 16. Self-Esteem Programs: Mean Effect Size by CPAI Score

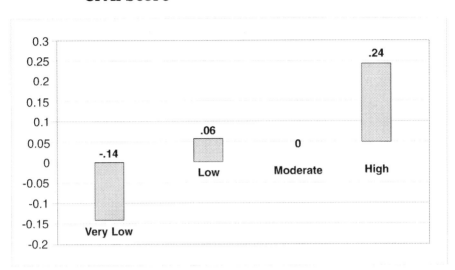

Major news comes from the University of Cincinnati and the CPAI work of Ed Latessa (presentations in North Bay, Ontario, 2004) and Chris Lowenkamp (2004) in their studies of halfway houses and community-based correctional agencies in Ohio (see Figure 17, thanks to the University of Cincinnati researchers for their generous permission to use their figures).

Figure 17. Recent Study of Community Correctional Programs in Ohio

- Largest study of community-based correctional treament facilities ever done (Latessa and Lowenkamp)
- Total of 13,221 offenders—37 halfway houses, and 15 community-based correctional facilities were included in the study.
- Two-year follow-up conducted on all offenders
- Recidivism measures included new arrests and incarceration in a state penal institution
- Also examined program characteristics

Source: Ed Latessa and Chris Lowenkamp (2004)

Inspection of Figures 18-22 reveals how agency-level adherence with Risk, Need, and Responsivity is associated with enhanced public protection. This is the type of evidence the field has been waiting for. In the "real world" of day-to-day correctional practice the evidence is that agencies that adopt and employ standardized risk/need assessment instruments are having greater crime reduction effects than are non-adopting agencies. Agencies that adhere to Risk, Need, and Responsivity are enhancing public protection to a greater extent than are agencies not in adherence with Risk, Need, and Responsivity. A next step is to introduce experimental control over Risk, Need, and Responsivity adherence at the program and agency level.

Figure 18. Relationship Between Proportion of Criminogenic Programming and Treatment Effect

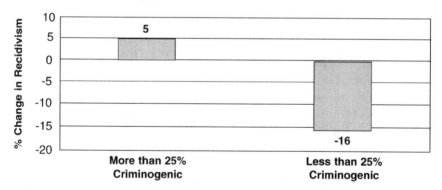

Figure 19. Relationship Between Treatment Model and Treatment Effect

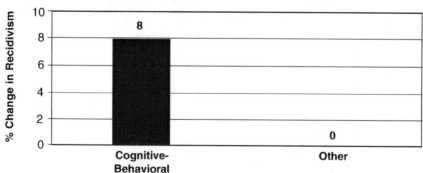

Figure 20. Relationship Between Role Playing and Treatment Effect

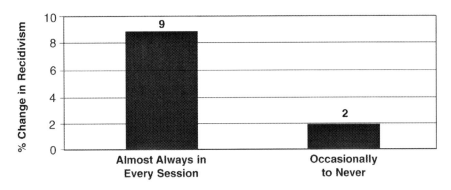

Figure 21. Relationship Between Treatment and Supervision

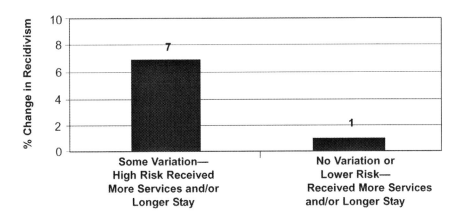

Figure 22. Relationship Between Significant Factors and Treatment Effect for Halfway Houses (Lowenkamp)

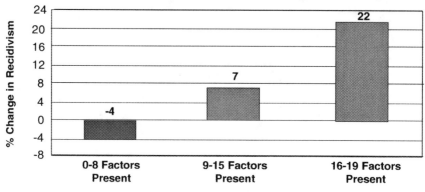

Source Lowenkamp, 2004

By way of summary, Figure 23 reveals that adherence with risk/need assessment principles and with general responsivity was correlated with effect size in both the meta-analysis and the agency-level projects. The overall correlation of CPAI score and effect size was moderate to strong in both projects. In this author's opinion (but he bows to the University of Cincinnati experience if they object to this interpretation), the importance of CPAI validities in the .40 to .50 range is particularly noteworthy because, overall, the effects of the ongoing "real world" services were not very great and, in fact, were often negative. Basically, the effects were positive only for those agencies that were adhering to Risk, Need, and Responsivity.

Figure 23. CPAI Correlation with Effect Size

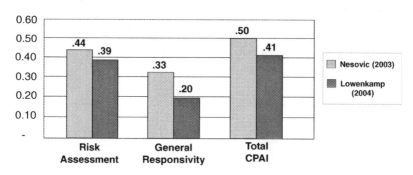

Source Lowenkamp, 2004

At the agency level, it is very important that integrity is maintained, even when some of the best-validated programs are being implemented. In the state of Washington, Functional Family Therapy was an utter failure with less competent therapists involved and a success with more competent therapists delivering the program (Barnoski, 2004).

Similarly, the quality of implementation determined the success of Aggression Replacement Therapy. Multisystemic Family Therapy was so poorly implemented that it was a total failure in Washington. It is beginning to appear that the implementation and operation of all programs, including those that shine on paper, should be subject to assessments of adherence to Risk, Need, and Responsivity and associated principles. It is not by chance that the new CPAI-2000 includes a direct observation component monitoring the relationship and core structuring skills of workers in interaction with offenders.

Feminist, Critical Criminological, and Clinical Psychological Challenges to Risk, Need, and Responsivity

Table 13 provides a set of near quotes from some feminists and from some critical criminologists that range from mild skepticism in regard to prediction, through charges of immorality and discrimination, and to outright expressions that human diversity as it relates to criminal conduct is limited to class, ethnicity, gender, and age. In fact, the available evidence in regards to general personality and social learning/cognition approaches and Risk, Need, and Responsivity appears quite contrary to the charges.

Table 13. Some Feminist and Critical Criminological Criticisms of Risk, Need, and Responsivity

1. Skepticism regarding the ability to predict recidivism.
2. The psychology of criminal conduct and Risk, Need, and Responsivity do not care enough about poverty, gender, and race/ethnicity (favored variables of critical criminology).
3. "Risk" reflects a white, middle-class male norm.
4. "Risk" really reflects age, race, class, and gender.
5. Risk, Need, and Responsivity-based classification is immoral, inefficient, subjective, and discriminatory (as opposed to classification based on age, race, class, and gender; or to professional judgment; or to what?).
6. Risk, Need, and Responsivity-based treatment does not work with girls and women (or with blacks, or with the poor, or with the emotionally distressed, or with. . . : "Nothing works").
7. Risk, Need, and Responsivity-based classification and/or treatment is not as valid or as powerful as the alternative (what alternative?).
8. Victimization causes crime.
9. Offenders should be offered healing rather than correctional treatment.
10. It is more important to meet the noncriminogenic needs of women than it is to focus on criminogenic needs.

Look at the LSI evidence in regard to age, gender, and social class in Figures 24 and 25. Recidivism rates are increasing with LSI risk/need for men and women, younger and older, regardless of their welfare status. Moreover, LSI risk/need completely eliminates the predictive validity of gender and poverty and almost all of the predictive validity of age. Not shown in a table, but any contribution of a history of victimization to the prediction of recidivism is totally understandable through the contributions of victimization to LSI risk/need (Lowenkamp, Holsinger, and Latessa, 2001; Rettinger and Andrews, 2006). In other words, some of the preferred variables in feminist and critical criminological theory have virtually no incremental validity relative to the central eight in the prediction of criminal recidivism.

Inspect the evidence regarding adherence with Risk, Need, and Responsivity and effect size with male and female offenders (Figure 26). Studies with girls and women are few in number, but the pattern of results suggests that adherence to Risk, Need, and Responsivity is important in the reduction of criminal recidivism. To our knowledge, there is no evidence to the contrary in the controlled-outcome literature.

Figure 24. LSI and Recidivsm by Offender Age, Gender, and Socio-Economic Status (A 1997)

	Very low	Low	Medium	High
YW	.00 (8)	.14 (7)	.29 (7)	.80 (5)
AW	.07 (29)	.01 (20)	.41 (17)	.75 (4)
YM	.13 (24)	.34 (32)	.64 (44)	.92 (13)
AM	.10 (90)	.18 (110)	.45 (128)	.61 (23)
Low SES	.09 (11)	.25 (24)	.47 (78)	.77 (22)

Figure 25. LSI (4) x Age (2) x Gender (2) x Reliance on Welfare (2) in Relation to Recidivism (Three-Year Post-Probation Follow-Up) N=561

• Overall correlation of LSI with recidivism	.44
• With controls for age, gender, poverty	.40
• Contributions of gender and poverty with controls for LSI	*ns*
• Contribution of age reduced to a minor one	.11

Figure 26. Risk, Need, and Responsivity Adherence and Effect Size by Gender

• Level of Adherence				Corr w
None	Low	Med	High	ES
Women				
• .02 (14)	.03 (10)	.17 (09)	.36 (12)	.57
Men				
• -.02 (110)	.02 (96)	.18 (75)	24 (48)	.56

There is very real fear among some feminist scholars that risk/need assessment may result in the over-classification of female offenders. Indeed, this is a fear in working with male offenders as well. A careful balancing of static risk, dynamic risk, and noncriminogenic need is required. A key here is to be careful not to sample weak-risk factors and not to sample noncriminogenic needs in assessing for purposes of allocating levels of supervision and/or security classification. Over-classification may be avoided by focusing on the major risk factors, considering strengths as a positive, and being sure that the weak-risk factors are not allowed to contribute. The latter, of course, include seriousness of the current offense, personal emotional distress, and abuse history. Recall from Table 2 that assessments with LS/CMI carefully sample an array of social, health, and personal well-being issues, but do so explicitly as noncriminogenic factors that do not contribute to the risk assessment score.

The clinical psychological challenge for Risk, Need, and Responsivity comes from the "Good Lives Model" of Tony Ward and colleagues (2003). Some of the criticism is right on the mark, and some is simply misplaced. For example, they say the psychology of criminal conduct is not holistic. Definitions of "holistic" are sometimes slippery, but the psychology of criminal conduct is obviously open to the potential importance of the biological, the personal, the interpersonal, the community, and the immediate situation of action (Andrews and Bonta, 2003). Indeed, LS/CMI assessments explore strengths and a number of other issues extending well-beyond the central eight risk factors. They say that Risk, Need, and Responsivity is based on a "rational choice" model of human behavior, but the underlying general personality and social learning/cognition approaches recognize personally mediated control, interpersonally mediated control, and relatively automatic or nonmediated control.

They say that "need" is not defined as it usually is in psychology and that is correct. "Need" in Risk, Need, and Responsivity refers to changeable problematic circumstances, as in the correctional rather than psychological tradition. This author looks forward to seeing how the introduction of psychological definitions of "need" may enhance prediction and/or treatment effectiveness.

The Good Lives Model is said to be a positive perspective as opposed to the negativity of Risk, Need, and Responsivity. This author thinks they are correct. Risk, Need, and Responsivity (and associated assessment instruments such as LS/CMI) now formally incorporate "strength" factors that may assist in protecting individuals from the risk factors. Strengths also may function as specific responsivity factors as in "develop a service plan that builds on the strengths of the case."

The major point of the proposed model is to suggest that the enhancement of psychological well-being may contribute to reduced recidivism. They wish to view rehabilitation programs as programs aimed at enhancing well-being. We look forward to research on the Good Lives Model that actually deals with the constructs of risk, responsivity, and, in particular, with the crucial issue of the targeting of criminogenic and noncriminogenic need. Recall Figure 4 wherein a failure to emphasize the targeting of criminogenic needs was associated with increased re-offending. Then again, recall Figure 16, wherein, there is the possibility that even programs that target enhanced self-esteem may reduce re-offending if the program is otherwise in adherence with Risk, Need, and Responsivity. Risk, Need, and Responsivity does not rule out the targeting of noncriminogenic targets, but, if an objective is reduced recidivism, Risk, Need, and Responsivity does demand that the balance of targets be favorable to reduced re-offending.

Looking forward to Good-Lives-based service and research, a caution must be raised around the ethical and professional issues. Increasingly, it is expected that professionals will employ research-supported approaches to assessment and treatment. Secondly, there are very real issues with respect to the objectives and power of the justice system. Does the justice system have the right to intervene with non-criminogenic issues? Why would the health and welfare systems not be called upon to deal with such issues with both offenders and nonoffenders?

Generally, Risk, Need, and Responsivity research and service and Good Lives research and service must be evaluated with reference to common standards: That is, the ethical, legal, decent, just, cost-effective, and humane pursuit of reduced victimization through human service delivery in the least onerous context.

Conclusions

1. General Personality and Social Learning/Cognition perspectives are the dominant theories of crime. They have earned that status through clear theoretical outlines, research evidence of ability to predict and influence criminal behavior, and extraordinary applied contributions.

2. The meta-analytic evidence and recent agency-level studies with the Correctional Program Assessment Inventory support the value of adherence to the human service principles of Risk, Need, and Responsivity.

3. Correctional risk/need assessment instruments perform well and may exceed the validity and utility of forensic mental health assessments.

4. Particular strengths of fourth-generation instruments relate to the possibility of enhancing adherence with the principles of effective human service by identifying risk levels, identifying criminogenic and noncriminogenic need areas, identifying specific responsivity issues, and structuring service from planning through case closure.

5. Research on specific responsivity may be on the verge of great gains because of developments in personality assessment, in Motivational Interviewing and Stages of Change, and the intellectual and political energy associated with gender and ethnicity issues.

6. Risk, Need, and Responsivity knowledge and technology may continue to be underused and of reduced value if the problems of implementation and integrity are not better addressed. Prompts for adherence may be built into assessment and case management instruments themselves and, at the agency-level, through ongoing assessments that monitor adherence—in particular the performance of direct-contact workers and the quality of the support provided by management.

7. Criticism of Risk, Need, and Responsivity from clinical psychology promises that Risk, Need, and Responsivity may be strengthened by linkages with psychological definitions of human need. In the process, however, care must be taken to insure the ethical pursuit of goals of enhanced personal well-being does not inadvertently become criminogenic.

8. Criticisms of Risk, Need, and Responsivity from some feminists and some critical criminologists suggest that the critics are more interested in demographic variables and in the reduction of social inequality than in building an empirically defensible psychology of criminal conduct and crime prevention. One can work on both without destroying one or the other as long as there is respect for human diversity and for evidence.

References

Andrews, D. A. 2001. Principles of Effective Correctional Programs. In L. L. Motiuk and R. C Serin, eds., *Compendium 2000 on Effective Correctional Programming*. Ottawa: Correctional Services of Canada, pp. 9-17.

Andrews, D. A., and J. Bonta. 1995. *The Level of Service Inventory-Revised*. Toronto: Multi-Health Systems.

___. 2003. *The Psychology of Criminal Conduct*, 3rd ed. Cincinnati: Anderson.

Andrews, D. A., J. Bonta, and R. D. Hoge. 1990. Classification for Effective Rehabilitation: Rediscovering Psychology. *Criminal Justice and Behavior*, 17, 1952.

Andrews, D. A., J. Bonta, and S. J. Wormith. 2004. *The Level of Service/Case Management Inventory (LS/CMI)*. Toronto: Multi-Health Systems.

___. 2006. The Recent Past and Near Future of Risk/Need Assessment. *Crime and Delinquency*, 52, 7-27.

Andrews, D. A. and C. Dowden. 2006. Risk Principle of Case Classification in Correctional Treatment: A Meta-Analytic Investigation. *International Journal of Offender Therapy and Comparative Criminology.* 50(1), 88-100.

___. 2005. Managing Correctional Treatment for Reduced Recidivism: A Meta-Analytic Review of Program Integrity. *Legal and Criminological Psychology.* 10, 173-187.

Andrews, D. A., C. Dowden, and J. L. Rettinger. 2001. Special Populations Within Corrections. In J. A. Winterdyk, ed., *Corrections in Canada: Social Reactions to Crime*. Toronto: Prentice-Hall, pp. 170-212.

Andrews, D. A. and D. Robinson. 1984. *The Level of Supervision Inventory: Second Report*. (Report to Research Services). Toronto: Ontario Ministry of Correctional Services.

Andrews, D. A., I. Zinger, R. D. Hoge, J. Bonta, P. Gendreau, and F. T. Cullen. 1990. Does Correctional Treatment Work? A Psychologically Informed Meta-Analysis. *Criminology*, 28, 369-404.

Barnoski, R. 2004. *Outcome Evaluation of Washington State's Research-Based Programs for Juvenile Offenders*. Olympia Washington: WSIPP.

Barnoski, R. and S. Aos. 2003. *Washington's Offender Accountability Act: An Analysis of the Department of Corrections' Risk Assessment*. Olympia, Washington: Washington State Institute for Public Policy.

Bonta, J. 1996. Risk-Needs Assessment and Treatment. In A. T. Harland, ed, *Choosing Correctional Options That Work: Defining the Demand and Evaluating the Supply.* Thousand Oaks, California: Sage, pp. 18-32.

Bonta, J., M. Law, and R. K. Hanson. 1998. The Prediction of Criminal and Violent Recidivism among Mentally Disordered Offenders: A Meta-Analysis. *Psychological Bulletin,* 123, 123-142.

Brown, S. L. 2003. *The Dynamic Prediction of Criminal Recidivism: A Three-Wave Prospective Study 1995-2002.* Unpublished doctoral dissertation, Queen's University, Kinston, Ontario, Canada.

Clements, C. B. 1996. Offender Classification: Two Decades of Progress. *Criminal Justice and Behavior,* 23, 121-143.

Covington, S. S. and B. Bloom. 1999. *Gender-Responsive Programming and Evaluation for Women in the Criminal Justice System: A Shift from What Works? To What Is the Work?.* Paper presented at the 51st Annual Meeting of the American Society of Criminology, Toronto, Canada.

DiClemente, C. C. and M. M. Velasquez. 2002. Motivational Interviewing and the Stages of Change. In W. R. Miller and S. Rollnick, eds., *Motivational Interviewing, Second Edition.* New York: Guilford Press, pp. 201-216.

Dowden, C. 1998. A Meta-Analytic Examination of the Risk, Need and Responsivity Principles and Their Importance Within the Rehabilitation Debate. Unpublished MA thesis. Department of Psychology, Carleton University, Ottawa.

Dowden, C. and D. A. Andrews. 1999. What Works for Female Offenders: A Meta-Analytic Review. *Crime and Delinquency.* 45 (4), 438-452.

___. 2004. The Importance of Staff Practices in Delivering Effective Correctional Treatment: A Meta-Analysis of Core Correctional Practices. *International Journal of Offender Therapy and Comparative Criminology.* 48(2), 203-214.

Gagliardi, G. J., D Lovell, P. D. Peterson, and R. Jemelka. 2004. Forecasting Recidivism in Mentally Ill Offenders Released from Prison. *Law and Human Behavior,* 28 (2), 133-155.

Gendreau, P. and D. A. Andrews. 2001. *The Correctional Program Assessment Inventory–2000 (CPAI 2000).* University of New Brunswick, Saint John, New Brunswick.

Gendreau, P., C. Goggin, and P. Smith. 2002. Is the PCL-R Really the "Unparalleled" Measure of Offender Risk? A Lesson in Knowledge Cumulation. *Criminal Justice and Behavior,* 29, 397-426.

Gendreau, P., T. Little, and C. Goggin. 1996. A Meta-Analysis of the Predictors of Adult Offender Recidivism: What Works! *Criminology,* 34, 575-607.

Girard, L. and J. Wormith. 2004. The Predictive Validity of the Level of Service Inventory-Ontario Revision on General and Violent Recidivism among Various Offender Groups. *Criminal Justice and Behavior*, 31, 150-181.

Gray, N. S., J. Taylor, R. J. Snowden, S. MacCulloch, H. Phillips, and M. J. MacCulloch. 2004. Relative Efficacy of Criminological, Clinical, and Personality Measures of Future Risk of Offending in Mentally Disordered Offenders: A Comparative Study of HCR-20, PCL: SV, and OGRS. *Journal of Consulting and Clinical Psychology*, 72, 523-531.

Grove, W. M., D. H. Zald, B. S. Lebow, B. E. Snitz, and C. Nelson. 2000. Clinical Versus Mechanical Prediction: A Meta-Analysis. *Psychological Assessment*, 12, 19-30.

Hannah-Moffat, K. and M. Shaw. 2001. *Taking Risks: Incorporating Gender and Culture into the Classification and Assessment of Federally Sentenced Women in Canada.* (Policy Research Report). Ottawa, Ontario: Status of Women Canada.

Hanson, R. K. and M. T. Bussière. 1998. Predicting Relapse: A Meta-Analysis of Sexual Offender Recidivism Studies. *Journal of Consulting and Clinical Psychology*, 66, 348-363.

Hanson, R. K., and A. J. R. Harris, 2000. Where Should We Intervene? Dynamic Predictors of Sexual Offense Recidivism. *Criminal Justice and Behavior*, 27, 6-35.

Hanson, R. K. and K. Morton-Bourgon. 2004. *Predictors of Sexual Recidivism: An Updated Meta-Analysis.* (User Report 2004-02). Ottawa: Public Safety and Emergency Preparedness Canada.

Hare, R. D. 1990. *The Hare Psychopathy Checklist-Revised.* Toronto: Multi-Health Systems.

Hemphill, J. F. and R. D. Hare. 2004. Some Misconceptions about the PCL-R and Risk Assessment: A Reply to Gendreau, Goggin, and Smith. *Criminal Justice and Behavior*, 31, 203-243.

HM Prison Service and National Probation Directorate. 2001. *The Offender Assessment System: User Manual.* London, England: Home Office.

Hoffman, P. B. 1994. Twenty Years of Operational Use of a Risk Prediction Instrument: The United States Parole Commission's Salient Factor Score. *Journal of Criminal Justice*, 22, 477-494.

Hoge, R. D. and D. A. Andrews. 2002. *Youth Level of Service/Case Management Inventory (YLS/CMI).* Toronto, Ontario: Multi-Health Systems.

Hollin, C. R. 2002. Risk-Needs Assessment and Allocation to Offender Programmes. In J McGuire, ed. *Offender Rehabilitation and Treatment: Effective Programmes and Policies to Reduce Re-Offending.* Etobicoke, Ontario: John Wiley and Sons, pp. 309-332.

Holtfreter, K., M. D. Reisig, and M. Morash. 2004. Poverty, State Capital, and Recidivism among Women Offenders. *Criminology and Public Policy*, 3, 185-209.

Jesness, C. F. 1988. The Jesness Inventory Classification System. *Criminal Justice and Behavior*, 15, 78-91.

Kroner, D. G. and J. F. Mills. 2001. The Accuracy of Five Risk Appraisal Instruments in Predicting Institutional Misconduct and New Convictions. *Criminal Justice and Behavior*, 28, 471-489.

Law, M. 2004. *A Longitudinal Follow-Up of Federally Sentenced Women in the Community: Assessing the Predictive Validity of the Dynamic Characteristics of the Community Intervention Scale.* Unpublished doctoral dissertation, Carleton University, Ottawa, Ontario, Canada.

Lerner, K., G. Arling, and S. C. Baird. 1986. Client Management Classification Strategies for Case Supervision. *Crime and Delinquency*, 32, 254-272.

Link, B. G., H. Andrews, and F. T. Cullen. 1992. The Violent and Illegal Behavior of Mental Patients Reconsidered. *American Sociological Review*, 57, 275-292.

Lipsey, M. W. and J. H. Derzon. 1998. Predictors of Violent or Serious Delinquency in Adolescence and Early Adulthood: A Synthesis of Longitudinal Research. In R. Loeber and D. P. Farrington, eds., *Serious and Violent Juvenile Offenders: Risk Factors and Successful Interventions.* Thousand Oaks, California: Sage, pp. 86-105.

Lowenkamp, C. T. 2004. *Correctional Program Integrity and Treatment Effectiveness: A Multi-Site, Program-Level Analysis.* Unpublished doctoral dissertation, University of Cincinnati.

Lowenkamp, C. T. and E. J. Latessa. 2002. *Evaluation of Ohio's Community Based Correctional Facilities and Halfway House Programs.* Technical Report. University of Cincinnati.

Lowenkamp, C. T., E. J. Latessa, A. M. Holsinger. 2004. Empirical Evidence on the Importance of Training and Experience in Using the Level of Service Inventory-Revised. National Institute of Corrections, U.S. Department of Justice. *Topics in Community Corrections*, 49-53.

Loza, W. and K. Green. 2003. The Self-Appraisal Questionnaire. *Journal of Interpersonal Violence,* 18, 781-798.

Maruna, S., T. P. Lebel, N. Mitchell, and M. Naples. 2004. Pygmalion in the Reintegration Process: Desistance from Crime through the Looking Glass. *Psychology, Crime, and Law*, 10, 271-182.

McGuire, J. 2004. *Understanding Psychology and Crime: Perspectives on Theory and Action.* Berkshire, England: Open University Press.

Miller, J. D. and D. R. Lynam. 2001. Structural Models of Personality and Their Relation to Antisocial Behavior: A Meta-Analytic Review. *Criminology*, 29(4), 765-798.

___. 2003. Psychopathy and the Five-Factor Model of Personality: A Replication and Extension. *Journal of Personality Assessment,* 81 (2), 168-178.

Miller, W. R. and S. Rollnick. 2002. *Motivational Interviewing,* 2nd ed. New York: Guilford Press.

Motiuk, L. L. 1997. Classification for Correctional Programming: The Offender Intake Assessment (OIA) Process. *Forum on Corrections Research,* 9, 18-22.

Motiuk, L. L., J. Bonta, and D. A. Andrews. 1990. *Dynamic Predictive Criterion Validity in Offender Assessment.* Paper presented at the Canadian Psychological Association Annual Convention, Ottawa.

Nesovic, A. 2003. *Psychometric Evaluation of the Correctional Program Assessment Inventory (CPAI).* Unpublished doctoral thesis. Carleton University, Ottawa, Ontario, Canada.

Northpointe. 1996. COMPAS [Computer Software]. Traverse City, Michigan: Northpointe Institute for Public Management, Inc.

Pratt, T. and F. T. Cullen. 2002. The Empirical Status of Gottfredson and Hirschi's General Theory of Crime: A Meta-Analysis. *Criminology,* 38, 931-964.

Quinsey, V. L., G. Coleman, B. Jones, and I. F. Altrows.1997. Proximal Antecedents of Eloping and Reoffending Among Supervised Mentally Disordered Offenders. *Journal of Interpersonal Violence,* 12, 794-813.

Quinsey, V. L., G. T. Harris, M. E. Rice, and C. A. Cormier. 1998. *Violent Offenders: Appraising and Managing Risk.* Washington, D.C.: American Psychological Association.

Raynor, P., J. Kynch, C. Roberts, and S. Merrington. 2000. *Risk and Need Assessment in Probation Services: An Evaluation.* Home Office Research Study No. 211. London, England: Home Office.

Rettinger, L. J. 1998. *A Recidivism Follow-Up Study Investigating Risk and Need Within a Sample of Provincially Sentenced Women.* Unpublished doctoral dissertation, Carleton University, Ottawa, Canada.

Rigakos, G. S. 1999. Risk Society and Actuarial Criminology: Prospects For A Critical Discourse. *Canadian Journal of Criminology,* 41, 137-151.

Simourd, D. J. and R. D. Hoge. 2000. Criminal Psychopathy: A Risk-and-Need Perspective. *Criminal Justice and Behavior,* 27, 256-272.

Stouthamer-Loeber, M., R. Loeber, E Wei, D. P. Farrington, and P .O. H. Wikström. 2002. Risk and Promotive Effects in the Explanation of Persistent Serious Delinquency in Boys. *Journal of Consulting and Clinical Psychology,* 70, 111-124.

Swanson, J. W., R. Borum, M. S. Swartz, and J. Monahan. 1996. Psychotic Symptoms and the Risk of Violent Behavior in the Community. *Criminal Behavior and Mental Health*, 6, 309-329.

Van Voorhis, P. 1994. *Psychological Classification of the Adult Male Prison Inmate.* Albany, New York: State University of New York Press.

Ward, T. and M Brown. 2004. The Good Lives Model and Conceptual Issues in Offender Rehabilitation. *Psychology, Crime and Law,* 10, 243-257.

Ward, T. and C. Stewart. 2003. Criminogenic Needs and Human Needs: A Theoretical Model. *Psychology, Crime, and Law*, 9, 125-143.

Webster, C. D., K. S. Douglas, D. Eaves, and S. D. Hart. 1997. *The HCR-20: Assessing Risk for Violence (Version 2)*. Burnaby, BC: Simon Fraser University.

Webster, C. D., G. T. Harris, M. E. Rice, C. Cormier, and V. L. Quinsey. 1994. *The Violence Prediction Scheme: Assessing Dangerousness in High Risk Men.* Toronto: University of Toronto Centre of Criminology.

Wong, S. and R. D. Hare. 2005. *Guidelines for a Psychopathy Treatment Program.* Toronto: Multi-Health Systems.

Zamble, E., and V. L. Quinsey. 1997. *The Criminal Recidivism Process.* New York, NY: Cambridge University Press.

Zinger, I. 2004. Actuarial Risk Assessment and Human Rights: A Commentary. *Canadian Journal of Criminology and Criminal Justice*, 46, 607-621

REACTION ESSAY— AN UPDATE ON OFFENDER ASSESSMENT

2

David Simourd, Ph.D, C. Psych.

ACES, Inc.
Kingston, Ontario, Canada

To say Don Andrews has had an impact on corrections may be a gigantic understatement. He and his colleagues have been actively involved in the correctional rehabilitation movement for more than thirty years and have fundamentally changed correctional practice. Dr. Don Andrews has authored numerous research articles and developed, with Dr. Jim Bonta, a standardized risk/need assessment instrument. However, one of his most influential works was the 1990 article co-authored with Dr. Jim Bonta and Dr. Robert Hoge entitled "Classification for Effective Rehabilitation: Rediscovering Psychology." This seminal article described the rehabilitation framework of the principles of Risk-Need-Responsivity, which are the backbone of all correctional practice today. Anyone who has not read this article is encouraged to do so to appreciate the many unsung details of Risk, Need, and Responsivity. Even veteran readers of this article should reread it periodically to reinforce the flavor of what we are trying to achieve in corrections.

Times change, though, and the corrections field must keep pace with the many advances. Don Andrews has kept pace with advances in corrections, and he treated participants at the 2005 annual conference of the International Community Corrections Association in Atlantic City, New Jersey to new insights.

Dr. Andrews' presentation covered six main themes: (1) advances in correctional knowledge, (2) predictive validities of assessment instruments, (3) general risk/need assessment instruments, (4) practical utility of Risk, Need, and Responsivity principles, (5) agency links to Risk, Need, and Responsivity principles, and (6) challenges to Risk, Need, and Responsivity.

Advances in Correctional Knowledge

The theoretical and empirical foundations of Risk, Need, and Responsiv-ity are based on the General Personality and Social Learning/ Cognition perspective on criminal conduct. The essence of the General Personality and Social Learning/Cognition is that a variety of assimilated factors become active at the "psychological moment" of a criminal act. The General Personality and Social Learning/Cognition is based on a range of theoretical and empirical phenomena developed from such areas as psychoanalysis, social learning theory, criminology, and behaviorism. The General Personality and Social Learning/Cognition also draws on the early juvenile delinquency research, and more recent developmental criminologists. Considerable scientific knowledge has accumulated during the past several years, and Don presented an overview of this information that supports the General Personality and Social Learning/Cognition and Risk, Need, and Responsivity.

In presenting updated information supportive of Risk, Need, and Responsivity, Don dedicated significant time to advancements in our empirical knowledge of the common risk factors for criminality. Much of the Risk, Need, and Responsivity is based on empirical evidence derived from meta-analytic literature reviews. This is the most common research review procedure in the social and medical sciences in which separate primary studies are combined to show an overall effect. In 1990, Dr. Andrews described the "Big Four" criminal risk factors—antisocial pattern, antisocial attitudes, antisocial companions, and behavioral history.

Dr. Andrews has expanded the "Big Four" to the "Central Eight," which includes the big four plus issues related to: social relations, social achievement, leisure pursuits, and substance abuse. Don presented persuasive research showing the relationship among the 'major' and 'minor' criminal risk variables. Major risk factors (for example, the big four) are those variables that are strongly linked to criminal behavior whereas minor risk factors (for example, lower social class, fear of punishment, personal distress, and verbal intelligence) are those variables that are weakly related to criminal behavior. Don presented data that shows the correlation between the major risk variables and recidivism range between r = .17 and r = .43, with an average of r = .26. The same correlations between minor risk variables and recidivism range between r = -.17 and r = .04, with an average of r = .04. The negative correlation indicates that recidivism actually increased. Even those who are unfamiliar with statistics can appreciate that the average correlation is stronger for the major risk factors than the minor risk factors. In all, these data show that focusing on the right stuff is critical to improving the behavior of offenders.

A significant element of Risk, Need, and Responsivity is the delivery of effective interventions to offenders. Dr. Andrews presented data that has accumulated since 1990 that concerns the relationship between adhering to Risk, Need, and Responsivity principles and reductions in recidivism. The effect size (as measured by the correlation coefficient) for programs that adhere to Risk, Need, and Responsivity was r = .26 whereas the effect size for programs that do not adhere to Risk, Need, and Responsivity was r = -.02. What this means is that programs that adhere best to Risk, Need, and Responsivity reduce the recidivism potential of offenders by a considerable degree. Programs that fail to adhere to Risk, Need, and Responsivity have very little effect on reductions of recidivism and, at worst, can actually increase offender recidivism.

Although information showing the relationship of Risk, Need, and Responsivity adherence and Risk, Need, and Responsivity nonadherence is eye opening, more stunning was information on staff training and supervision. Dr. Andrews presented research showing that staff issues are virtually unrelated to reductions in recidivism unless they operate in programs that adhere to Risk, Need, and Responsivity. In other words, the best trained and supervised staff will be largely ineffective in reducing the criminal potential of offenders *unless* they are involved in programs that attend to the 'what works' principles.

Predictive Validities of Assessment Instruments

Since 1990, there has been tremendous growth in criminal-risk-assessment instruments. This is important because one of the core Risk, Need, and Responsivity principles is an accurate understanding of offender risk and need factors. Dr. Andrews presented research evidence that some correctional risk-assessment instruments are better than others from the point of view of showing stronger empirical links to recidivism. He also showed that clinical judgments are weakly related to reoffending (r = .10) compared to risk-assessment instruments (r = .26 to r = .46). A key point is that increased correlations to recidivism are found among those assessment instruments that cover the main risk/need factors, are administered by well-trained staff, who have quality information upon which to rate offender risk/need attributes.

General Risk/Need Assessment Instruments

After showing the empirical evidence on the importance of using quality risk/need assessment instruments, Dr. Andrews raised the question of whether there is a need for specific assessment instruments for those offenders suffering from mental health difficulties who are in conflict with the law. He described the background to the *Violence Risk Appraisal Guide* (Quinsey, Harris, Rice, and Cormier, 1998) and applauded its development and use in forensic mental health. In fact, he claims that the *Violence Risk Appraisal Guide* (VRAG) "elevated the psychology of crime into respectability." However, he offered compelling theoretical and empirical arguments that the underpinnings of the *Violence Risk Appraisal Guide* are rooted in the General Personality and Social Learning/Cognition. In addition, the application breadth of quality risk/need assessment instruments suggests that there is no particular need for assessment instruments specific to mental health.

Practical Utility of Risk, Need, and Responsivity Principles

For most people working in corrections, the world is neither theoretical nor empirical—it is practical. Don attended to the concerns of the frontline correctional worker when he discussed the change potential of offenders and commented on ways change can be enhanced. Dr. Andrews highlighted an often-overlooked finding from the meta-analysis risk-factor research (specifically, that of the 1996 Gendreau et al., study) that demonstrated dynamic and static-risk variables have equal predictive accuracies. Most frontline correctional workers likely have a fundamental belief that offenders can change, and Don confirms this belief by reinforcing the notion of attending to dynamic risk factors.

Dr. Andrews also recognized that one of the least attended of the Risk, Need, and Responsivity principles is that of responsivity. Responsivity relates to the idiosyncratic skills/attributes/characteristics of offenders that can facilitate change. These factors range from cognition (empathy, self-management, and so forth), through ethnicity (cultural sensitivity) to motivation (level of readiness for change). Particular reference was made to the concept of Motivational Interviewing, a technique designed to enhance client awareness of his/her issues and the need for change.

Agency Links to Risk, Need, and Responsivity Principles

Dr. Andrews noted that the corrections field has made significant strides in the development of appropriate assessment instruments and clinical sensitivities to techniques to reduce recidivism. However, it is the combination of Risk, Need, and Responsivity principles and the application of these principles in the 'real world' that produce the greatest reductions on recidivism. Agencies must offer a comprehensive approach that combines all contemporary knowledge to be effective. The Correctional Programs Assessment Inventory (CPAI; Andrews and Gendreau) was developed to assess the degree to which agencies conform to the Risk, Need, and Responsivity principles and deliver "effective" programs. A key component of the CPAI is that programs may appear "on paper" to be attending to contemporary practices but, in fact, are not in the "real world." According to Dr. Andrews, failure to achieve congruence between the treatment model and the action limits success on the part of the agency and offender.

Challenges to Risk, Need, and Responsivity

The Risk, Need, and Responsivity principles have been around for more than fifteen years and are widely accepted and integrated into numerous correctional agencies. Having the leading expert on this information speak about this at the ICCA convention was almost like Dr. Andrews was speaking to the converted. However, Don reminded participants that there exist those who question the theory, research, and practical application of Risk, Need, and Responsivity. Some of these challenges are based on skepticism concerning the predictive research or on ideological grounds. Dr. Andrews counters these challenges with a reminder that the Risk, Need, and Responsivity principles are based on theories and empirical findings from various social science disciplines and that Risk, Need, and Responsivity can apply to a wide range of offender groups.

In summary, Dr. Don Andrews has had a dramatic impact on corrections for many years. He continues to support the "ethical, legal, decent, just, cost-effective, and humane pursuit of reduced victimization through human service delivery in the least onerous context." He does this through updates to the Risk, Need, and Responsivity principles as advances in knowledge occur. The field of corrections has benefited greatly from his contributions, and participants at the 2005 ICCA convention were treated to a world-class presentation.

References and Suggested Readings

Andrews, D. A. and J. Bonta. 2006. *The Psychology of Criminal Conduct*, 4th ed. Cincinnati, Ohio: Anderson Publishing.

Andrews, D. A., J. Bonta, and R. D. Hoge. 1990. Classification for Effective Rehabilitation: Rediscovering Psychology. *Criminal Justice and Behavior*, 17, 19-52.

Gendreau, P., T. Little, and C. Goggin. 1996. A Meta-Analysis of the Predictors of Adult Offender Recidivism: What Works! *Criminology*, 34, 575-607.

Quinsey, V. L., G. T. Harris, M. E. Rice, and C. A. Cormier.1998. *Violent Offenders: Appraising and Managing Risk*. Washington, DC: American Psychological Association.

SECTION 2:

BEHAVIORAL HEALTH IN SPECIAL NEEDS OFFENDERS

An Integrated Perspective on the Prevalence, Diagnosis, and Treatment of Behavioral Disorders in Correctional Populations

Norman G. Hoffmann, Ph.D.
Evince Clinical Assessments
Waynesville, North Carolina

3

Background and Issues

While there have been numerous attempts to determine the prevalence of mental health and substance use disorders over the past decade, drawing clear conclusions or estimating service needs is restricted by methodological limitations. Many studies focus only on selected areas or on those with the most severe conditions. Methodological weakness also limits the extent to which one can be assured that the various reports accurately determine true prevalence. Frequently, the measures used are inadequate for distinguishing conditions with similar symptoms such as unipolar depression versus bipolar disorder or substance abuse from substance dependence.

From a clinical perspective, studies assessing only one condition (for example, alcohol dependence) or a family of conditions (such as severe mental illnesses) are insufficiently informative to determine the extent of needs or to formulate estimates of the type and extent of services required to address the conditions or reduce the likelihood of their influence on criminal recidivism (for example, relapse to alcohol or other drug dependence resulting in crimes related to the addiction).

Various studies have documented that antidepressants and/or cognitive-behavioral therapies are effective in the treatment of unipolar depression (DeRubeis, Hollon, Amsterdam et al., 2005). However, if the individual exhibiting symptoms of a depressive episode actually suffers from a bipolar illness, the long-term prognosis is poor unless mood-stabilizing medications are employed. Similarly, substance dependence is distinct from abuse, and the necessary services and expectations for treatment goals for long-term recovery differ.

Pragmatic limitations cause many prevalence studies to rely on screening procedures rather than the more extensive assessments required for making definitive determinations. Screening procedures might provide a relatively good approximation if the error rates for false-positives and false-negatives are relatively equal and the condition in question is relatively prevalent. However, confounding screening with diagnostic determinations can result in serious errors in the estimated prevalence, not to mention determination of service needs.

For example, one relatively recent estimate for alcohol dependence relied on the **C**ut down, **A**nnoyed, **G**ulity, and **E**ye Opener (CAGE) as the screening tool to estimate the prevalence of alcohol abuse and dependence (Mumola, 1999). The CAGE was referred to as a "diagnostic instrument," which it is not. However, given the frequent confusion between screening and diagnostic tools, this error is quite understandable. Even clinicians and researchers often confuse the two functions in their reports.

Screening tools provide a probability estimate concerning risk for a given condition; a diagnostic tool provides comprehensive evidence for whether or not the condition is present. In the case of the report in question, the criterion of three positive responses of the possible four was used as an indication of alcohol abuse or dependence. Such a threshold for the CAGE is likely to produce a high false-negative rate for dependence, not to mention abuse, which has a much lower threshold for problems. Fortunately the report also provides percentages for the other thresholds so that one could explore the findings in greater detail.

This report will use data derived from routine clinical evaluations of individuals in both juvenile justice and adult corrections systems in identifying behavioral health conditions likely to require clinical services. Implications of the findings in terms of the types and durations of services both within institutions and in the community will be discussed. By considering both juvenile and adult populations, issues concerning the possible continuation of problems into adult life will be explored along with their implications for criminal recidivism.

Several key points will be illustrated by the analyses. One of the most ubiquitous errors is to consider substance abuse and dependence as similar or equivalent conditions. The case will be made that for a given substance, dependence is a distinct, chronic, and severe condition distinguishable from abuse, which is more likely to have consequences of a narrower scope and more likely to be situational or transient. The two conditions should be addressed as independent and distinct conditions. A second point is that in the absence of legal concerns about self-incrimination, properly structured interviews can provide an excellent initial identification of problems for a vast majority of cases. The essential feature is that the assessment must use appropriate techniques and directly assess the current diagnostic criteria.

Finally, routine assessments for co-occurring conditions are not only feasible and practical, they are essential, especially for adolescent populations. The time and resources required for the identification of mental health and substance use disorders is almost insignificant when compared to the costs resulting from the failure to identify and treat these conditions.

Adolescent Populations

The need for consistent assessment of and services for multiple co-occurring problem areas including learning difficulties, victimization, mental conditions, and substance use disorders has been acknowledged for some time (Mears, 2001). Conducting comprehensive assessments may be limited by time, costs, and legal concerns. Recent developments in the assessment of adolescents facilitate routine identification of mental health and substance use disorders. Such assessments can be used not only by mental health and addictions professionals, but also by juvenile justice staff for initial screenings. Screening and assessment tools range from a six-item question set for identifying risk for substance dependence to structured interviews capable of providing initial documentation for a variety of conditions.

Ideally, screens should be short, inexpensive, and easy to use. Staff members who are not clinical professionals are often in the best position to use a screen and alert professional staff or consultants when sufficient indications of problems are detected. Even more comprehensive interviews, such as the one used to collect the data discussed here, can be designed so that technicians or nonclinical staff can collect considerable amounts of information to be passed on to clinicians with the expertise to make final determinations.

Under no circumstance should any instrument "make a diagnosis" or "determine" a decision regarding an individual. Only qualified professionals with access to all information including official records, reports by family and other collateral sources, history information, and tests and personal interview data are in the position to determine diagnoses and make life-altering decisions. The algorithms used in analyzing the following data should be considered as a research tool. In clinical practice, determinations would be preliminary, or tentative, pending verification by a qualified professional.

Samples and Procedures

The juvenile justice data reviewed here were drawn from the juvenile justice system in the state of Maine. Data from a total of 597 consecutive cases (519 males and 78 females) from the state's two detention centers and several drug courts were available for analysis. The drug court diversion cases consisted of 101 individuals (84 males and 17 females) who were similar in terms of demographics and clinical severity for common mental health conditions. The total sample will be considered here since it represented all consecutive cases coming to the attention of juvenile authorities in the state during the data collection period.

Clinical staff from the agency contracted to assess all adjudicated and diversion adolescents used the PADDI (Practical Adolescent Dual Diagnostic Interview) to ensure uniform assessment of substance use disorders and other common mental health conditions including major depressive and manic episodes, various anxiety disorders, conduct disorder, and oppositional defiant disorder (Estroff and Hoffmann, 2001). The content of the PADDI items are designed to address the major elements of the DSM-IV-TR diagnostic criteria (American Psychiatric Association, 2000). The PADDI interview also covered dangerousness to self or others and victimization (physical, sexual, and emotional abuse). Although interview times varied depending upon the extent of positive findings, most interviews were completed within forty-five minutes.

Clinical staff created anonymous data forms by covering or obscuring all personal identifiers on the original interview booklets and photocopying the completed forms. The data were then entered and verified into an Excel file that was imported into Statistical Package for the Social Sciences (SPSS). Previous published reports covered initial portions of the current database and documented the prevalence and severity of common conditions seen in this juvenile population (Abrantes, Hoffmann, Anton, and Estroff, 2004; Abrantes, Hoffmann, and Anton, 2005).

Two areas of research currently underway involve an exploration of the combinations of conditions found in the juvenile justice population and associations among the types of maltreatment, or victimization experiences (physical, sexual, and emotional abuse), and various behavioral health conditions. These studies are not yet published, but in the submission process.

In addition to the juvenile justice data, a convenience sample from various treatment programs will be considered for comparison. The clinical sample consists of 161 males and 269 females treated in several residential programs throughout the United States. As with the juvenile justice data, programs provided anonymous forms in exchange for analyses that provided statistical information about their populations. Unlike the juvenile justice data, the clinical sample is less rigorous in terms of consecutive admissions, but it does provide a perspective for the juvenile justice data. Findings from the initial cases in the clinical sample have been published elsewhere (Hoffmann, Bride, MacMaster, Abrantes, and Estroff, 2004), but are updated here for the current sample. The intent is not to perform a rigorous comparison between the juvenile justice and clinical populations. Rather, the point of including the clinical cases is to illustrate that co-occurring conditions are common in diverse high-risk adolescent populations whether they be in the justice or treatment systems.

Before delving into the indications for specific mental health and substance use disorders, a brief description of the juvenile justice sample will provide a context for the clinical findings. When asked about the nature of their offenses, the majority of juveniles (58 percent) indicated theirs was a nonviolent offense, and 23 percent acknowledged a violent offense. Substances were reported to be a primary issue in 35 percent of cases. Multiple responses were permitted so that the totals do not sum to 100 percent. Because the data are anonymous, we cannot verify the reports, but it would appear that nonviolent and drug-related offenses accounted for the majority of individuals.

Ethnic Composition and Educational Issues

The ages of the juveniles ranged from thirteen to eighteen, but 85 percent were between the ages of fifteen and seventeen. The average age was 16.3 (SD = 1.04). Almost nine out of ten were white (88 percent), and Native Americans (4 percent) were the only minority with more than ten cases. This contrasts dramatically with the clinical sample where whites constituted only about two-thirds of the sample with Native Americans (17 percent) and African-Americans (11 percent) representing the largest minority groups.

Educational attainment and learning problems were common in both groups. While 75 percent of the juvenile group was over the age of sixteen, fewer than 40 percent had passed beyond the eighth grade, and almost one in five reported having had serious reading difficulties. About half had been in special classes. The statistics for the clinical sample show that 42 percent had been in special classes and 23 percent had significant reading difficulties. Clearly educational problems and the need for some remedial education will be an issue for a substantial proportion of juvenile justice cases.

One additional indication of the level of problem prevalence is the fact that 36 percent of the juvenile cases and 33 percent of the clinical cases were on some type of medication within two weeks of the evaluation. An additional 28 percent and 34 percent of the cases in the two groups, respectively, reported having been on some type of prescription prior to that time. Unfortunately, the nature of the medications is not captured in the electronic data. Still, the apparently high prevalence of medication prescriptions for an adolescent population suggests previous attempts to address medical or mental health problems.

Table 1. Proportion of Cases with Positive Indications for Behavioral Health Conditions Health Conditions

Condition	Males		Females	
	Juvenile Justice n = 519	Clinical n = 161	Juvenile Justice n = 78	Clinical n = 269
Major depression current *	16 %	16 %	37 %	30 %
Major depression lifetime	26 %	26 %	59 %	47 %
Manic episode current *	11 %	17 %	22 %	14 %
Manic episode lifetime	20 %	31 %	31 %	21 %
Bipolar syndrome **	8 %	9 %	15 %	12 %
Multiple hallucinations ***	4 %	9 %	12 %	18 %
Post-Traumatic Stress Disorder	16 %	23 %	40 %	47 %
Panic Attacks	10 %	11 %	22 %	24 %
Conduct Disorder	80 %	89 %	76 %	80 %
Substance Dependence	67 %	78 %	78 %	95 %
Four or more current [†]	13 %	14 %	30 %	34 %
Two or more current [†]	65 %	78 %	80 %	87 %

* Current is defined as either currently present or occurring within the past two months

** Reporting clear depressive and manic episodes.

*** Both auditory and other types of hallucinations in the absence of substance use, falling asleep, or awakening

† Seven conditions are included; lifetime depression and mania, and bipolar syndrome are excluded.

Clinical Findings

Diagnostic results on some of the more prevalent conditions among the males and females are presented in Table 1. To be considered positive for the affective and anxiety diagnoses, an individual had to respond positively to items addressing the minimum DSM-IV-TR criteria for the respective diagnosis. In the case of manic and major depressive episodes, the condition was considered current if symptoms were present within the past two months and was considered lifetime if the last episode was prior to that timeline. Substance dependence rather than substance abuse was counted as a positive for the purpose of the table and count for the number of diagnoses present. Hallucinations, especially auditory ones, may be an indication of serious mental illnesses. To be considered positive for this analysis, the individual had to report auditory hallucinations and at least one other type of hallucination unrelated to substance use or experienced while going to sleep or awakening.

Conduct disorder is the most prevalent diagnostic indication for both the juvenile justice and clinical samples followed by substance dependence. What is truly remarkable is the finding that approximately a third of the females in both samples have positive indications for four or more of the seven areas under consideration. Clearly the norm is for co-occurring conditions since a majority of both genders in both samples reported positive indications for at least three of the seven conditions included in this analysis.

Even if conduct disorder and substance dependence are ignored, a third of the juvenile justice males and two-thirds of the females have indications for one or more conditions. Approximately one in seven males and more than a third of the females have symptoms indicating two or more conditions. The prevalence of multiple conditions for the juvenile justice cases are only several percentage points lower than those for the clinical sample.

Features of Substance Dependence

Perhaps no area of behavioral health has generated more controversy and confusion than the substance use disorders. Confounding abuse with dependence is seen throughout the scientific literature and in a variety of societal and policy domains. Noting the abuse versus dependence distinctions for alcohol, Hasin and colleagues (1997, 217) have gone so far as to state that, "Abuse actually showed a greater level of differentiation from dependence than from the no diagnosis group." Other studies have also revealed distinct clinical profiles for alcohol dependence versus abuse and that the two can be readily distinguished in the vast majority of cases if appropriate inquiries are employed (Hoffmann, DeHart, and Campbell, 2002; Hoffmann and Hoffmann, 2003).

In the case of adolescents, arguments have been raised questioning the appropriateness of applying the adult criteria to adolescents. While caution must be exercised in considering a substance use disorder diagnosis in the context of adolescent experimentation and risk taking, the dependence syndrome as made operational by the PADDI produces a clear differentiation of dependent individuals from either abuse or no diagnosis for the vast majority of cases. Not only do those who are dependent manifest problem patterns comparable to adults, the temporal factors also suggest sufficient time for the development of a dependence syndrome.

Among the juvenile justice cases with complete data on substance use disorders, only 10 percent have no diagnostic indications; 3 percent report symptoms compatible with past abuse or dependence but deny use in the past twelve months; 2 percent are diagnostic orphans in that they report some indications of dependence, but do not meet formal criteria for either abuse or dependence; 16 percent meet abuse criteria, and 68 percent meet criteria for dependence.

One way to conceptualize the severity or scope of problems associated with substance abuse or dependence is the number of positive findings for the seven dependence and four abuse criteria of the DSM-IV-TR. Of the 393 juvenile justice cases meeting dependence criteria, only 10 percent are positive on only three dependence criteria; as contrasted to the 60 percent who are positive for at least six of the seven criteria. Approximately 65 percent of the dependent cases endorse at least half of the eighteen PADDI items pertaining to dependence.

Furthermore, 85 percent of the dependent cases are also positive for at least three of the abuse criteria, and a clear majority of cases are positive on most of the individual abuse items. In short, those who meet dependence criteria tend to manifest convincing evidence for the disorder. As will be discussed in the section on International Perspectives (see Table 5), the substance-dependent adolescents in the juvenile justice system had severity profiles comparable to those of adult prison inmates.

In contrast, the abuse-only cases demonstrate a restricted scope of problems. Of the ninety-two cases meeting abuse criteria, 81 percent endorsed no more than two of the four abuse criteria and only 5 percent were positive on all four criteria, as compared to 60 percent of the dependent cases. Only 9 percent of the abuse cases endorsed five or more of the individual abuse items as compared to 78 percent of the dependent cases. These data would be compatible with those of Hasin and colleagues who questioned the legitimacy of the abuse diagnosis in adults and suggested little differentiation from those technically meeting abuse criteria and those with no diagnosis (Hasin, Van Rossem, McCloud, and Endicott, 1997). However, as with their findings, individuals meeting dependence criteria reveal a very distinct and substantive syndrome of problems.

The duration of misuse and problems for the dependent cases further reinforces the argument that adolescents can develop substance dependence by fifteen to eighteen years of age. The majority of dependent individuals report the first use to intoxication or high on or before the age of twelve, and more than 60 percent report the first problem as a consequence of substance use by the age of fourteen. On average, 4.4 years have elapsed between the first intoxication and the time of the evaluation. The first problem emerged an average of 2.3 years ago. The median times from first intoxication/high and first problem to the evaluation are four and two years, respectively. The adolescents acknowledge that someone considered their substance use a problem on average 1.4 years before the current evaluation. It is conceivable that earlier detection and effective services could have avoided the behaviors resulting in juvenile justice involvement for some of these individuals.

Maltreatment History

Diagnostic considerations are not the only issues identified by the structured PADDI interview. Maltreatment in the form of physical, sexual, and emotional abuse also is covered. The questions used reflect definitive abuse and, therefore, may tend to underestimate prevalence of milder forms of maltreatment. A positive finding for physical abuse requires that the individual was struck so hard that marks were left, a bone was broken, or emergency medical attention was warranted. Sexual abuse as used here requires unwanted physical contact or coercion into sexual activity. Emotional abuse is defined as being humiliated or ridiculed over a period of time.

Slightly more than 50 percent of the males and 69 percent of the females in the juvenile justice system reported some type of maltreatment. Almost 20 percent of males and 40 percent of females reported multiple types of abuse. Thirty-two percent of the males and 38 percent of females reported physical abuse. Emotional abuse rates were also similar for the males and females with prevalence of 44 and 50 percent, respectively. However, as would be expected, sexual abuse rates differed considerably with only 10 percent of males reporting such abuse compared to a third of the females. Not surprisingly, maltreatment tends to be correlated with reports of various affective and anxiety disorders such as post-traumatic stress disorder and panic attacks.

Service Needs

Clearly, the service needs for adolescents in the juvenile justice system are substantial and varied. Prevalence rates for a variety of behavioral health conditions among the juvenile justice population rival those seen in clinical populations. This is not surprising since a Congressional survey of juvenile facilities found that two-thirds of the facilities surveyed hold youths who are awaiting treatment in the community (U.S. House, 2004).

Indications of substance dependence are compelling, as are symptom profiles for some of the more chronic and severe affective and anxiety disorders. For substance dependence, well over half of the males and almost three out of four females appear to require substantial treatment services. Substance-dependent adolescents may require some periodic treatment services as adults since dependence is a chronic condition involving the potential of relapse. The prevalence of mental health conditions also suggests the need for ongoing services that may extend into adult life. For example, even if only half of the adolescents identified as being at risk for a bipolar disorder actually required medication, the findings indicate that at least one in twenty of the adolescents in the juvenile justice system require ongoing medication and might need assistance in managing their condition as adults.

Summary

In summary, the findings are consistent with other reports that indicate the majority of adolescents entering the juvenile justice system manifest symptoms of multiple mental health and substance use disorders. The findings also show that a suitable structured interview can provide a practical means of detecting problem cases for referral to appropriate professionals. Based on these clinical findings, the service needs are extensive and involve addressing not only mental health conditions and substance dependence, but also may need to deal with other areas such as victimization and educational/learning difficulties. Investment in such services can pay handsome returns on the treatment investment in evidence-based services. The question is whether this society is willing to invest in its youth.

Adult Populations

To the extent that adolescents in juvenile justice eventually enter the adult correction systems, we would expect to see equally high rates of co-occurring conditions in adult systems as well. This would be particularly true for those individuals with chronic conditions such as substance dependence or bipolar disorder when the underlying behavioral health conditions may contribute to criminal activity or behaviors resulting in contact with law enforcement.

The data for the following discussion were derived from more than 7,000 routine assessments of adult inmates by staff employed by the Minnesota Department of Corrections. Counselors used an automated version of the SUDDS-IV (Substance Use Disorder Diagnostic Interview-IV) adapted for use with inmate populations (Hoffmann and Harrison, 1995). The software for the administration of the SUDDS-IV was loaded onto laptop computers to facilitate consistent evaluations within the correctional institutions and generate individual reports of findings. Aggregated data captured by the automated assessments were stripped of personal identifiers and used for routine analyses and for the production of routine statistical reports.

Rather than repeat the exploration seen in the juvenile justice cases in an adult population, this section of the paper will use detailed data from the substance use disorder assessment in a state prison population to illustrate several points. First, we will extend the discussion, that for a given substance, the DSM-IV-TR diagnosis of dependence typically is markedly distinct from abuse.

Then, we will explore ethnic and gender differences and similarities in terms of prevalence and dependence severity for various substances. In general, we will make the case that in correctional populations, staff will see differences of both prevalence and severity between genders within an ethnic group, and ethnic differences greater for prevalence than severity. A brief discussion of quick screening for substance dependence will highlight the practicality of routine screening. Then, we will discuss implications for problem identification and service needs among adult inmates.

Substance-Specific Abuse versus Dependence

Data from the juvenile justice and adolescent clinical samples clearly suggested a distinct general differentiation between abuse and dependence as defined in the current diagnostic criteria. Several studies have documented the distinctions between alcohol abuse and alcohol dependence (Hasin et al., 1997; Hoffmann and Hoffmann, 2003). Extending the exploration of differences between abuse and dependence reveals similar findings for other drugs as well.

As can be seen in Table 2, those meeting dependence criteria for a given substance typically far exceed the minimum DSM-IV-TR requirements. This is particularly true for cocaine and opioid dependence, where fewer than 10 percent meet only the minimum of three positive criteria. For all substances considered except marijuana, the majority of cases are positive for at least six of the seven dependence criteria. The lower rate of positive criteria for marijuana may be due to several factors. One is that marijuana-dependent persons do not tend to act out or engage in risky behaviors, as may be the case with alcohol or stimulants. Also, behaviors and symptoms related to heavy marijuana use may not be identified as such. However, even for marijuana, dependence emerges as a distinct syndrome with relatively few cases meeting only minimal dependence criteria.

Table 2. Proportion of Adult Inmates with Positive Criteria Given a Diagnosis of Dependence

Diagnosis	Number of Positive Dependence Criteria				
	3	4	5	6	7
Alcohol dependence N = 2,265	16 %	15 %	15 %	18 %	36 %
Marijuana dependence N = 1,389	22 %	22 %	19 %	17 %	20 %
Cocaine dependence N = 854	9 %	11 %	15 %	25 %	40 %
Stimulant dependence N = 1007	12 %	12 %	15 %	21 %	40 %
Opioid dependence N = 183	5 %	12 %	10 %	16 %	57 %

In contrast, those with an abuse diagnosis for a given substance tend not to have such a distinct syndrome defined by a broad variety of problem areas. Table 3 provides the contrast between abuse and dependent cases in terms of positive findings on the abuse criteria. For most substances, the majority of abuse-only cases are positive for one or, at most, two of the abuse criteria. Fewer than 5 percent of abuse cases are positive for all four abuse criteria as contrasted to the dependent cases. Except for marijuana, approximately 40 percent of the individuals meeting dependence criteria for a given substance are also positive for all four of the abuse criteria as well. The patterns seen in the abuse criteria further support the argument that abuse and dependence diagnoses emerge as distinct syndromes.

The number of individual items endorsed by dependent individuals also shows the extent of differences between abuse and dependence. For example, more than half of the alcohol-dependent individuals provided positive responses to at least ten items relating to the dependence criteria and a similar proportion had six or more positive responses on the abuse items. In contrast, only 39 percent of the alcohol-abuse cases were positive for more than two of the abuse items.

Clearly, abuse and dependence as defined by the DSM-IV-TR emerge as distinct syndromes. In most cases, the two are clearly distinguishable with the use of a thorough diagnostic interview. Dependent inmates accounted for a disproportionate proportion of various negative events prior to incarceration including repeatedly driving under the influence, violence related to use, risky sexual behaviors, and so forth (Hoffmann, 2002). Dependence not only is distinct from abuse, it also tends to be the more chronic condition with a more guarded prognosis (Shuckit, Smith, and Landi, 2000; Shuckit, Smith, Danko, Bucholz, Reich, and Bierut, 2001).

Table 3. Proportion of Adult Inmates with Positive Criteria Given A Diagnosis of Abuse the Diagnosis Indicated

Diagnosis		Number of Positive Abuse Criteria				
		0	1	2	3	4
Alcohol abuse	N = 1,193	--	38 %	37 %	21 %	4 %
Alcohol dependence	N = 2,265	2 %	8 %	15 %	31 %	44 %
Marijuana abuse	N = 936	--	56 %	33 %	9 %	2 %
Marijuana dependence	N = 1,389	4 %	15 %	27 %	32 %	22 %
Cocaine abuse	N = 303	--	65 %	25 %	9 %	1 %
Cocaine dependence	N = 854	1 %	5 %	15 %	38 %	41 %
Stimulant abuse	N = 255	--	56 %	23 %	20 %	1 %
Stimulant dependence	N = 1,007	1 %	5 %	13 %	29 %	52 %
Opioid abuse	N = 30	--	63 %	25 %	9 %	3 %
Opioid dependence	N = 183	3 %	9 %	13 %	37 %	38 %

Gender Comparisons

In general, female inmates have both a higher prevalence of dependence and a greater severity. This is one of the most striking differentials in this inmate population. The proportion of cases positive for abuse or dependence on the more prevalent substance categories are provided in Table 4. Overall, 52 percent of males and 70 percent of females are dependent on one or more substances. The most common substance of dependence is alcohol; however, for the female inmates, cocaine and stimulants rival the prevalence rates seen for alcohol. Not only are the females more likely to be dependent than the males, the dependence is more likely to involve a variety of drugs. Almost a third of the females and 22 percent of the males are dependent on more than one substance.

When severity of dependence is considered, women tend to manifest somewhat greater severity in terms of the number of positive-dependence criteria. There is a general trend for women to be positive on more of the dependence criteria when dependent on a given substance. A significantly greater level of dependence for women is seen for alcohol (p < .0001) and for stimulants (p < .004).

It appears that women in the state correctional facilities in Minnesota not only are more likely to be substance dependent, but also tend to have greater severity. For many of these inmates, their substance-use disorders will preclude being able to resume productive lives without substantial treatment and other support services. Logically, treatment would begin while incarcerated and continue upon release into the community.

Ethnic Comparisons

As with gender, substantial prevalence differentials are noted among the ethnic groups; however, when controlling for gender, no statistically significant differentials are seen for severity. A greater proportion (49 percent) of Native American male inmates is dependent upon alcohol as compared to other males (an average of under 30 percent). Similarly, Caucasian males are more likely to be dependent upon stimulants (21 percent) as compared to a prevalence of less than 10 percent for the other ethnic groups. African-American males are more likely to be dependent on cocaine (15 percent) compared to less than 10 percent for other males.

However, when considering severity indications in terms of the number of positive-dependence criteria, the ethnic differentials tend to be statistically nonsignificant when viewed within each gender. While there is a general trend for greater severity in those ethnic groups with a higher prevalence of dependence for a given substance, the differentials are not statistically significant given the very large sample sizes.

While females tend to exhibit greater levels of severity, ethnic differentials for males and females tend not to generate remarkable differences. In other words, for either gender, once a group of individuals meet criteria for dependence, the average level of severity is likely to be similar among the ethnic groups analyzed here.

Table 4. Prevalence of Diagnoses by Gender of Adult Inmates

Substance	Males N = 6,881			Females N = 801		
	No Diagnosis	Abuse	Dependence	No Diagnosis	Abuse	Dependence
Alcohol	55 %	16 %	29 %	60 %	10 %	30 %
Marijuana	69 %	13 %	18 %	77 %	7 %	16 %
Cocaine	87 %	4 %	9 %	65 %	5 %	30 %
Stimulants	85 %	3 %	12 %	74 %	2 %	24 %
Opioids	98 %	<1 %	2 %	90 %	1 %	9 %
Any Diagnosis	27 %	21 %	52 %	22 %	8 %	70 %

International Perspective

Data on co-occurring conditions was collected on 155 consecutive admissions to two prisons in the United Kingdom. The data collection involved the use of the CAAPE (Comprehensive Addiction and Psychological Evaluation), a structured interview covering seven areas of Axis I, six areas of Axis II, and substance use disorders (Hoffmann, 2000). A senior clinician administered the interview for all newly admitted inmates. Data from the interviews were entered into anonymous Excel computer files and analyzed using the same general statistical procedures as the other databases.

One of the two British facilities is designed for younger male offenders and the other for males perceived to have likely behavioral health issues. Thus, the statistics from these facilities will not be as representative of the general population as those from the juvenile justice and state prison systems previously discussed. However, the data do provide a perspective on the relative frequency of problems within the higher risk segments of the British correctional system, and they also show how different instruments employed with different populations reveal similar syndromes with regard to substance dependence.

As with the adult males in the Minnesota state system, alcohol accounted for the highest prevalence of dependence with 57 percent meeting dependence criteria. However, unlike the state inmate group, cocaine was the next most prevalent dependence diagnosis with 48 percent of the high-risk British inmates being positive for this substance. The next most prevalent substances of dependence were marijuana (37 percent) and heroin (26 percent). Both of these rates were much higher than the United States sample, but it must be remembered that the British sample is drawn from a higher risk population.

Given the nature of the facilities, the prevalence of mental health conditions is not surprising. Among the Axis I conditions, post-traumatic stress disorder (49 percent) and depression (26 percent) are among the more prevalent. However, 22 percent of these inmates reported manic episodes not related directly to drugs. Interestingly, the rates for major depressive and manic episodes are not that dissimilar from the indications derived with the PADDI in adolescent populations.

As would be expected, the criteria for antisocial personality disorder are met by most (83 percent), which is also similar to the conduct disorder prevalence among the adolescent males. Other common Axis II conditions for the British inmates include borderline and obsessive-compulsive personality disorder, each with a prevalence of 39 percent. One must remember that the Axis II obsessive-compulsive disorder involves much more manipulation and controlling of others and is less internally focused than the Axis I obsessive-compulsive disorder.

Despite the differences in populations and instruments employed to determine the various conditions, there are some remarkable similarities with respect to substance dependence. Given a diagnosis of substance dependence, the severity as indicated by the number of positive dependence criteria is remarkably similar across the three populations: juveniles, state prison inmates, and British inmates.

Table 5. Number of Positive Dependence Criteria for Dependent Cases

Instrument and Sample	Number of Positive Dependence Criteria				
	3	4	5	6	7
PADDI/Juvenile Justice N = 393	10 %	12 %	19 %	19 %	40 %
SUDDS-IV/State Inmates N = 4,155	12 %	14 %	16 %	20 %	38 %
CAAPE/United Kingdom N = 124	5 %	7 %	15 %	36 %	37 %

Table 5 provides a comparison of severity given substance dependence. For the SUDDS-IV and CAAPE data, the substance with the greatest severity is selected and compared with the generic findings from the PADDI. For each population, the vast majority of individuals meeting dependence criteria exceed the minimal requirements for the condition. Approximately 40 percent of the cases in each population are positive for all seven of the dependence criteria. Almost 60 percent of the adolescents and state inmates are positive for at least six of the seven criteria. The British inmates are a particularly high risk population where more than 70 percent are positive for at least six criteria. Clearly, substance dependence produces a distinct profile for the majority of cases when a detailed interview is employed to explore substance use disorders.

Quick Screening

A variety of brief screening instruments have been developed to detect substance use disorders. The UNCOPE Screen, a six-item screen, has been validated on both arrestees (Hoffmann, Hunt, Rhodes, and Riley, 2003) and inmate populations (Campbell, Hoffmann, Hoffmann, and Gillaspy, 2005). Figure 1 provides the items in this freely available screen. Unlike some screens, the UNCOPE Screen identifies risk for alcohol as well as other drug dependence, and it can be embedded in a questionnaire or administered orally in the context of an interview.

The UNCOPE Screen has been validated using simple cut-scores for identifying risk for substance dependence as well as ROC (receiver-operating characteristics) analysis. Reasonable sensitivity (probability of correctly identifying a dependent individual) and specificity (correctly identifying those who are not dependent) have been found by considering those who respond positively to three or more of the six items as being at risk for dependence (Hoffmann, Hunt, Rhodes, and Riley, 2003). Obviously, the probability of dependence increases as the number of positive responses increases. The receiver operating characteristics analyses suggested that the proportion of time a positive diagnosis will be correctly identified was about .90 (Campbell, Hoffmann, Hoffmann, and Gillaspy, 2005). Recent analyses of the juvenile justice data confirms that the UNCOPE also appears to be an efficient screen for adolescent populations as well (Urofsky, Seiber, and Hoffmann, 2005).

Figure 1. The UNCOPE Screen

U - Have you spent more time drinking/using than intended? **(Unintended Use)**

N - Have you ever **neglected** usual responsibilities because of using?

C - Have you ever wanted to **cut down** on drinking/using?

O - Has anyone **objected** to your drinking/use?

P - Have you found yourself thinking a lot about drinking/use? **(Preoccupied)**

E - Have you ever used to relieve **emotional distress**, such as sadness, anger, or boredom?

Given the availability of this and other screens, routine substance use disorder screening of individuals in both juvenile and adult populations is practical. Unlike diagnostic evaluations, which typically require 45 minutes or more, a brief screen for substance dependence can be done in a matter of a few minutes.

The breadth of conditions in mental health makes screening for these conditions more problematic. However, routine screens for major affective disorders and the more prevalent anxiety disorders can be done with brief instruments as well (for example, Hoffmann, and Estroff, 2000).

Screening is an important aid in detecting mental health and substance use disorders, but it must not be confused with a diagnostic assessment. A screen provides a probability estimate of risk; a diagnostic assessment must be comprehensive enough to document the basis for a diagnosis when present and the negative findings to ensure against a false-positive diagnosis. In any case, only professionals with the appropriate expertise can determine whether one has or does not have a given condition. No instrument used in isolation should ever be considered as the sole diagnostic determination. The professional, who can integrate information from all sources, is in the position to make diagnoses or life-altering decisions.

Overarching Findings and Issues

Several conclusions can be reached which span the various instruments and populations used in the analyses undertaken here. First, sufficient screening instrumentation is available to assist in routine screening for all individuals entering either the juvenile or adult correctional system. This is particularly true for substance use disorders. Second, a variety of detailed, structured interviews exist to ease assessment of those at risk for behavioral health disorders so that relatively routine assessments can be made in most settings. Technicians or other trained paraprofessionals often can conduct structured interviews for review by appropriate professionals. Third, the prevalence of mental health and substance use disorders in all correctional populations suggest substantial needs for clinical services.

Effective clinical services are likely to make positive contributions to the management of inmates and detainees, but also may contribute to reductions in criminal recidivism in a substantial proportion of cases. Such services are not a luxury, but rather a necessity if societies are to reduce the prevalence and impact of criminal behaviors related to behavioral health conditions.

Given the complexity of conditions seen, comprehensive and integrated clinical services are indicated. This is especially true for adolescent populations where co-occurring conditions are definitely the norm rather than the exception. However, among high-risk adult correctional populations, the prevalence of co-occurring conditions also speaks to the need for integrated services.

Chronic conditions, such as substance dependence and bipolar disorder, suggest that at least some juveniles and adults will require services and assistance in the management of their conditions on a protracted basis. For adolescents, such services will extend into adult life. For the more chronic conditions, life-long management of the disorders will be required for optimal outcomes. These chronic conditions are no different than other chronic medical disorders such as diabetes and hypertension, where ongoing care and management are expected.

The extent of problems among women is of particular concern since many of these individuals will be responsible for children in their care and often will be single parents when returning to the community. Programs to address their needs can benefit not only the former inmates, but also their children.

Society needs to approach the assessment of behavioral health and delivery of appropriate and effective services not from an entitlement, but from a return-on-investment perspective. The potential returns for effective services to address behavioral health disorders among both adolescent and adult offenders can provide financial and societal benefits far in excess of the costs of service delivery.

References

Abrantes, A., N. G. Hoffmann, R. Anton. 2005. Prevalence of Co-occurring Disorders Among Juveniles Committed to Detention Centers. *International Journal of Offender Therapy and Comparative Criminology*, 49(2), 179-193.

Abrantes, A., N. G. Hoffmann, R. Anton, and T. W. Estroff. 2004. Identifying Co-Occurring Conditions in Juvenile Justice Populations. *Youth Violence and Juvenile Justice*, 2(4), 329-341.

American Psychiatric Association. 2000. *Diagnostic and Statistical Manual of Mental Disorders, Fourth Edition, Text Revision.* Washington, DC: Author.

Campbell, T. C., N. G. Hoffmann, T. D. Hoffmann, and J. A. Gillaspy. 2005. UNCOPE: A Screen for Substance Dependence among State Prison Inmates. *The Prison Journal*, 85(1), 7-17.

DeRubeis, R. J., S. D. Hollon, J. D. Amsterdam, R. C. Shelton, P. R. Young, R. M. Salomon, J. P. O'Reardon, M. L. Lovett, M. M. Gladis, L. L. Brown, and R. Gallop. 2005. Cognitive Therapy Vs Medications in the Treatment of Moderate to Severe Depression. *Archives of General Psychiatry,* 62(4):409-416.

Estroff, T. W. and N. G. Hoffmann. 2001. PADDI: *Practical Adolescent Dual Diagnosis Interview.* Smithfield, Rhode Island: Evince Clinical Assessments.

Hasin, D., R. Van Rossem, S. McCloud, and J. Endicott. 1997. Alcohol Dependence and Abuse Diagnoses: Validity in Community Sample of Heavy Drinkers. *Alcoholism: Clinical and Experimental Research,* 21, 213-219.

Hoffmann, N. G. 2000. CAAPE: Comprehensive Addiction and Psychological Evaluation. Smithfield, Rhode Island: Evince Clinical Assessments.

___. 2002. *Annual Report 2001: Diagnosis of Substance Use Disorders.* Report prepared for the Minnesota Department of Corrections. Smithfield, Rhode Island: Evince Clinical Assessments. Online source: www.doc.state.mn.us//publications/pdf/substanceuse disorder 2002annualreport.pdf

Hoffmann, N. G., B. E. Bride, S. A MacMasters, A. M. Abrantes, and T. W. Estroff. 2004. Identifying Co-Occurring Conditions in Adolescent Clinical Populations. *Journal of Addictive Diseases,* 23(4), 41-53.

Hoffmann, N. G., S. S. DeHart, and T. C. Campbell. 2002. Dependence: Whether a Disorder or a Disease, It is Not a "Concept." *Journal of Chemical Dependency Treatment,* 8(1), 45-56.

Hoffmann, N. G. and T. W. Estroff. 2000. Emotional Health Inventory. Waynesville, North Carolina: Evince Clinical Assessments.

Hoffmann, N. G. and P. A. Harrison. 1995. SUDDS-IV: *Substance Use Disorder Diagnostic Schedule-IV.* Smithfield, Rhode Island: Evince Clinical Assessments.

Hoffmann, N. G. and T. D. Hoffmann. 2003. Construct Validity for Alcohol Dependence as Indicated by the SUDDS-IV. *Journal of Substance Use and Misuse,* 38 (2), 293-306.

Hoffmann, N. G., D. E. Hunt, W. M. Rhodes, and K. J. Riley. 2003. UNCOPE: A Brief Substance Dependence Screen for Use with Arrestees. *Journal of Drug Issues,* 33 (1), 29-44.

Mears, D. P. 2001. Critical Challenges in Addressing the Mental Health Needs of Juvenile Offenders. *Justice Policy Journal,* 1(1), 40-59.

Schuckit, M. A., T. L. Smith, G. P. Danko, K. K. Bucholz, T., Reich, and L. Bierut. 2001. Five-Year Clinical Course Associated with DSM-IV Alcohol Abuse or Dependence in a Large Group of Men and Women. *American Journal of Psychiatry,* 158(7):1084-1090.

Schuckit, M. A., T. L. Smith, and N. A. Landi. 2000. The Five-Year Clinical Course of High-Functioning Men with DSM-IV Alcohol Abuse or Dependence. *American Journal of Psychiatry*, 157 (12). 2028-2035.

Urofsky, R. I., E. Seiber, and N. G. Hoffmann. 2005. UNCOPE Evaluation of a Brief Screen for Detecting Substance Dependence among Juvenile Justice Populations, *Journal of School Counseling*.

U.S. House of Representatives. 2004. Incarceration of Youth Who Are Waiting for Community Mental Health Services in the United States. Retrieved August 2006 from http://www.house.gov/reform/min/pdfs_108_2/pdfs_inves/pdf_health_mental_health_youth_incarceration_july_2004_rep.pdf

Zywiak, W. H., N. G. Hoffmann, and A. S. Floyd. 1999. Enhancing Alcohol Treatment Outcomes through Aftercare and Self-Help Groups. *Medicine and Health/ Rhode Island* 82 (3), 87-90.

REACTION ESSAY— THE NEED FOR A UNIFYING VISION ON OFFENDER DISORDERS

4

Gerald D. Shulman, M.A., M.A.C., FACATA
(Fellow of the American College of Addiction Treatment Administrators)
President Shulman and Associates
Training and Consulting in Behavioral Health
Jacksonville, Florida

Introduction

The prior chapter by Dr. Hoffmann makes important contributions to the field with his description of the assessment issues, particularly the confusion between screening and diagnostic assessment, between substance abuse and substance dependence and the confusion among some of the mental health diagnoses. He notes the importance of the high prevalence of substance use and/or mental health disorders in both the juvenile and adult justice populations, which leads us to a consideration of interventions which may reduce initial encounters with the justice system, lower recidivism, and include issues of successfully completing probation or parole.

Dr. Hoffmann comments about the failure to distinguish between two DSM-IV-TR diagnoses: "substance abuse" and "substance dependence" (American Psychiatric Association, 2000). As he so aptly points out, these terms are used interchangeably, confounding the two different diagnoses in the scientific literature, clinical settings, and in societal and policy domains.

Figure 1. The DSM-IV-TR Diagnostic Criteria for Substance Dependence (Used with permission of the American Psychological Association)

A maladaptive pattern of substance abuse leading to significant impairment or distress as manifested by at least three of the following within a 12-month period:

1. Tolerance to the substance as defined by: (a) a need for marked increased amounts of the substance to achieve intoxication or the desired emotional and physical effect, (b) markedly lowered effect with continued use of the same amount of the substance.
2. Withdrawal, as manifested by either of the following: (a) the characteristic withdrawal symptoms for the substance concerned or (b) the same (or chemically similar) substance is taken to relieve or avoid withdrawal symptoms.
3. The substance is often taken in larger amounts or over a longer period of time.
4. There is a persistent desire or unsuccessful attempt to reduce or control substance abuse.
5. Large amounts of time and effort are expended in activities designed to obtain the substance (e.g., visiting multiple doctors or traveling long distances), use the substance, or recover from its effects.
6. Important social, occupational, or recreational activities are avoided because of substance abuse.
7. The substance abuse is continued despite knowledge of having a persistent physical or psychological problem that is caused or exacerbated by the substance.

Figure 2. The DSM-IV-TR Diagnostic Criteria for Substance Abuse (Used with permission of the American Psychological Association)

A. A maladaptive pattern of substance use which leads to significant impairment or distress and is displayed by at least one of the following in a 12-month period:

   1. Recurrent substance use that results in a failure to fulfill obligations at school, work, or home. This may take the form of repeated absences, poor work performances, neglect of children or household duties, or substance-related absences for significant social events.

   2. Recurrent substance abuse in situations in which it is hazardous to personal health or the health of others, for example, driving a car or operating machinery while under the influence of the substance.

   3. Recurrent substance-related legal problems, for example, arrests for substance-related disorderly conduct.

   4. Continuation of substance abuse despite ongoing social or interpersonal problems caused or exacerbated by the effects of the substance, for example, frequent arguments with spouse or partner about consequences of intoxication.

B. The symptoms do not meet the criteria for Substance Dependence.

"Substance abuse" also is used as a term inclusive of both abuse and dependence as in SAMHSA's *National Directory of Drug and Alcohol Abuse Treatment Programs* (2005) and even further, the acronym "SAMHSA" stands for *Substance Abuse* and Mental Health Administration. While some of this confusion results from the inappropriate use of these diagnostic terms, the extent of the confusion leads to speculation that at least part of the problem may exist in the construction of the criteria themselves.

To meet diagnostic criteria for substance dependence (Figure 1), an individual would have to meet a minimum of three of the seven criteria while for substance abuse (Figure 2), meeting one of the four criteria is required. As Dr. Hoffmann pointed out, for juveniles, the number of positive criteria they need to meet for abuse is only one or two of the four while for dependence, 60 percent were positive for at least six of the seven criteria. For adults, the pattern is similar. The distinction between abuse and dependence is very important in many arenas, including criminal justice. Abuse tends to be situational while dependence is a chronic disorder increasing the likelihood of a continuation of the criminal behavior if not addressed.

There is a significant difference between Use, Intoxication, Abuse, and Dependence when dealing with psychoactive drugs. *The International Classification of Disease*, 10th ICD-10 edition (2000) has a diagnosis of *Harmful Use* described as "a pattern of psychoactive substance use that is causing damage to health. The damage may be physical (as in cases of hepatitis from the self-administration of injected psychoactive substances) or mental (for example, episodes of depressive disorder secondary to heavy consumption of alcohol)" but no diagnosis of *Substance Abuse*. Since there is a greater level of differentiation of abuse from dependence than from dependence and no diagnosis (Hassin, Van Rosem, McCloud, and Edicott, 1997), consideration should be given to a review of the DSM-IV-TR Substance Use Disorders criteria with the possibility of combining in the four abuse and seven dependence criteria to equal a total of eleven criteria, and increasing the diagnostic threshold to four or even five of the criteria.

While important, there is a caveat to this discussion. The association of criminal behavior with substance use may be just that, an association that does not automatically infer causation. There are those offenders, often individuals with antisocial values if not diagnosable as having an antisocial personality disorder, whose criminal behavior while associated with substance use (for example, alcohol or drug-affected at the time of the arrest) is not the result of the substance use.

Enrolling such offenders in prison-based or post-release addiction treatment will not directly affect their criminal behavior except to make them "better criminals" since the substances will no longer affect their criminal activities negatively. A screening instrument, the Behaviors and Experiences Inventory (Hoffmann, Mee-Lee, and Shulman, 2005), documents reading issues;

a history of sexual, physical, and emotional victimization; and indications of Attention-Deficit/Hyperactivity Disorder (ADHD), Conduct Disorder, and Antisocial Personality Disorder (ASPD). These conditions are unlikely to improve as a result of addiction treatment and help to discriminate between those offenders whose criminal behavior is a direct result of their substance use and those for whom substance use is incidental to their criminal behavior.

Figure 3. CRAFFT

A Brief Screening Test for Adolescent Substance Abuse*

	YES	NO
C - Have you ever ridden in a **CAR** driven by someone (including yourself) who was "high" or had been using alcohol or drugs?	____	____
R - Do you ever use alcohol drugs to **RELAX**, feel better about yourself, or fit in?	____	____
A - Do you ever use alcohol/drugs while you are by yourself, **ALONE**?	____	____
F - Do your family or **FRIENDS** ever tell you that you should cut down on your drinking or drug use?	____	____
F - Do you ever **FORGET** things that you did while using alcohol or drugs?	____	____
T - Have you gotten into **TROUBLE** while you were using alcohol or drugs?	____	____

* Two or more "yes" answers suggest a significant problem.

In addition to Dr. Hoffmann's comment that, "Ideally screens should be short, inexpensive, and easy to use" are two other characteristics that set screening instruments apart from more comprehensive assessments. They are that screens can be self-administered and/or administered in groups. An appropriate screen for both adults and adolescents as found in Dr. Hoffmann's paper is the UNCOPE (Hoffmann, 1999). What is gaining favor for adolescents is the CRAFFT (Children's

Hospital Boston, 2001), which, like the UNCOPE Screen, is a six-item screen that covers both alcohol and other drugs (Figure 3).

While the focus of Dr. Hoffmann's paper was on the assessment of substance use disorders, as he so accurately points out, the existence of mental health disorders is also a major contributing factor to criminal behavior. Without assessment and treatment of such conditions, the continuation of criminal behavior is predictable. Once again, we have to keep in mind the difference between screening and diagnostic assessment. There are clearly more available mental health screening tools for adolescents than adults, and among these are the three most commonly used:

1. Massachusetts YSI-2 (Massachusetts Youth Screening Instrument–Version 2): Developed by Grissom and Barnum (2003) as a self-report measure for those entering the juvenile justice system with thoughts, feelings, and behaviors indicative of mental health problems;
2. POSIT (Problem-Oriented Screening Instrument for Teenagers): Developed by Rahdert (1991) as a brief self-report screening to identify troubled youths' problems in psychosocial functioning requiring further assessment;
3. CAFAS (Child and Adolescent Functional Assessment Scale): Developed by Hodges (1990) to assess youth's everyday psychosocial functioning across school, home, community, and work settings.

The author's recommendation for a more comprehensive assessment of mental health problems among adolescents is the PADDI, Practical Adolescent Dual Diagnosis Interview developed by Estroff and Hoffmann (2001), which assesses for substance use and mental health disorders.

Screening adults for a broad range of mental health disorders is problematic due to the number of possible conditions and the variability in terms of presentation within a given diagnosis or diagnostic category. This situation makes it virtually impossible to do a global screen for all possible problems, and most adult screening instruments screen for a single disorder, for example, depression. One solution is to screen for the more prevalent conditions or those of primary interest. Another approach is to use observational indications to guide screening. Using this approach, staff would look at the individual's cognition, affect, and behavior (an easy mnemonic is CAB). For example, if the individual affected appears depressed or anxious, screening for depression or anxiety may be indicated. Similarly, if the individual's behavior is unusual, screening for psychosis or intoxication may be indicated.

Because of this great variety of different mental health disorders, instruments which assess for a broader range of mental health disorders are the more comprehensive assessment such as the MMPI (Minnesota Multiphasic Personality Interview) or the MCMI-III (Millon Clinical Multiaxial Inventory-III). Because of the time commitment involved in administering, scoring, and interpreting for a professional clinician, these tools cannot be considered screening instruments.

The high incidence of substance use and mental health disorders in a justice population raises the issue of universal screening and the objection to "giving a diagnosis to adolescents who will carry it for the rest of their lives." President Bush's New Freedom Commission on Mental Health (2003) recommended screening for co-occurring mental and substance use disorders and, with integrated treatment strategies, they also recommend screening for mental disorders in primary health care, across the life span, and connecting to treatment and supports. If we believe that substance use and mental health disorders are really that, disorders or diseases, why would we not screen for them as we do for other disorders like hypertension and diabetes?

Some oppose universal screening in that it will inappropriately stigmatize people as mentally ill, start people on an unnecessary life-long course of medication, and harm our basic freedoms. However, once individuals, particularly adolescents, become part of the criminal justice system, they are even more stigmatized, and if universal screening can help them avoid that consequence, then the screening appears to be more of a benefit. Lehrman (2006) cites horror stories as a result of the implementation of the Commission's recommendation, but these are more the result of poor instrument selection and inappropriate response to the results rather than a basic flaw in the concept.

If we are to consider routine screening, why make it universal? We have learned from child welfare that if the screening is not universal, minorities and economically disadvantaged individuals are selected for screening with much more frequency than others.

An important consideration is a response to those individuals who do not meet diagnostic criteria for a substance use or mental health disorder but nonetheless have problems that might have led to criminal behavior. For example, an adolescent might not meet criteria for Conduct Disorder or an adult for Antisocial Personality Disorder, but the person might but have problems with anger management and impulse control. These individuals are often overlooked because of the absence of a formal diagnosis, but if these problems are not addressed, the individuals are likely to recidivate.

In this author's experience as a clinical psychologist performing assessment on male felons in the Pennsylvania State Prison System (1961-1962), more than 60 percent of the inmates assessed would not have been incarcerated if it were not for their drinking; yet, most of these men would not have been diagnosable as either having alcohol abuse or dependence. The combination of low intellectual capacity, impaired judgment, and inability to appropriately manage their anger and control their impulses with even small amounts of alcohol led them to commit some illegal act.

Dr. Hoffmann points out that educational attainment and learning problems were common in both justice and clinical adolescent populations. Twenty percent had serious reading difficulties, and about half had been in special classes. The absence of a high school diploma or GED has proven to be associated with relapse to substance use in adults (Mee-Lee, Shulman, Fishman et al., 2001). It would appear that an investment in prison-based educational services for both adolescents and adults would be a prudent strategy.

The clinical findings comparing juvenile males and females raise a most interesting issue. With the exception of conduct disorder (in both justice and clinical populations) and manic episode lifetime (clinical population), the incidence of behavioral-health problems is higher for all diagnostic categories in females than males. Especially notable is the fact that the incidence for females who have four or more behavioral health conditions is more than twice what it is for males. The explanations for these findings are critically important if we are to reduce the number of female juveniles who end up in the justice system and reduce recidivism among those who do. While the literature has not been able to provide definitive answers, a number of suggestions require further research.

The gender disparity in the number of arrestees has led some (Tiet et al., 2001) to propose a "gender paradox," whereby the gender group less likely to be disordered has a more severe form or presentation of the disorder. Another and similar explanation for the discrepancy in rates of mental health disorders by gender is the "relative deviance" hypothesis. This suggests that girls are far less likely to demonstrate behaviors that lead to incarceration and that when they do, such behaviors likely represent a higher level of psychopathology (Stewart and Trupin, 2003).

Anxiety disorders are significantly more common in girls who are younger at first referral, and more are charged with a violent offense even though the incidence of conduct disorders is higher for boys than girls (Wasserman et al., 2005). This suggests that antisocial girls will be more impaired across co-occurring dimensions than antisocial boys and, therefore, may have more elevated mental health problems.

Even more compelling is the issue of childhood abuse, particularly sexual abuse and its sequelae. Up to 92 percent of incarcerated girls have experienced one or more forms of physical, sexual, or emotional abuse before entering the juvenile justice system. More than 65 percent have been beaten or burned at least once, and 45 percent have been raped. Girls exposed to violence on an ongoing basis are prone to self-abusive behavior, depression, mental illness, drug use, and suicide. In one sample of female juvenile offenders, 70 percent had been exposed to some sort of trauma, and 65 percent had experienced symptoms of post-traumatic stress disorder (PTSD) (Physicians for Human Rights, 2006).

A substantial proportion of female delinquents report a history of physical and sexual abuse. In another study of youth incarcerated in Virginia for violent offenses, 51 percent of the girls evidenced a documented history of sexual abuse, and 35 percent a history of physical abuse, levels which were significantly higher than those reported for boys.

Sexual abuse can provide a dangerous pathway to criminal activities, substance use, and mental health disorders (Loper, 2000). The possible resulting substance abuse is a particular concern because it is a major risk factor for delinquency. Substance abuse often co-occurs with conduct disorder (particularly with boys) and depression (particularly with girls and juveniles who have been the victims of sexual abuse).

The rate of mental illness in girls who are offenders is two to three times that found in boys who are offenders (Lexcen and Redding, 2000). In this study, 68 percent of girls reported a history of sexual abuse, and 73 percent reported a history of physical abuse.

The Report on Women in Criminal Justice (Law Enforcement Assist-ance Administration, 1998) states that in many instances of offense, young women may be acting out as a means of self-protection in response to life-threatening conditions. The underlying cause of female juvenile delinquency has been reported to be family problems, including sexual and/or physical abuse in the home. It is not surprising, therefore, that most female juvenile offenders report that their first arrest was for running away from home to avoid physical and sexual abuse.

National statistics showed that eight million girls, or one out of four, are sexually abused before age eighteen. Statistics pertaining to the incidence of physical or sexual abuse and/or exploitation in the backgrounds of delinquent female juvenile offenders vary from a low of 40 percent to a high of 73 percent. Girls are much more likely than boys to be victims of sexual abuse, especially family-related abuse (Chesney-Lind, Sheldon, and Joe, 1996). The abuse and exploitation of young girls should be viewed as a major and pervasive public health threat and as a primary precursor to the development of mental health disorders and involvement in the criminal justice system.

While the causal relationship between female childhood and adolescent sexual abuse and involvement in the criminal justice is clear, the original question concerned the greater degree of mental health problems among girls than boys in the justice system. When looking at the odds ratios for sexually abused (by intercourse) females before age sixteen to have developed a mental health disorder (National Institute on Drug Abuse, *NIDA Notes*, 2002), the research indicates that women who experienced any level of childhood sexual abuse (nongenital, genital, and intercourse) were three times more likely than unabused girls to report drug dependence as adults. The odds ratios for developing alcohol abuse ranges from 2.42 to 4.01, drug dependence 2.83 to 5.70, major depression 1.37 to 3.14, generalized anxiety disorder 1.48 to 2.94, and two or more disorders, 1.61 to 5.47, depending on the type of sexual abuse (Table 1).

Dr. Hoffmann also determined that women in the corrections system are more likely than men to be substance dependent, to be dependent on more than one substance, and to have a greater severity of dependence as demonstrated by the greater number of dependence criteria met.

Table 1. Association of Childhood Sexual Abuse with Drug Dependence and Psychiatric Disorders

	Nongenital	Intercourse	Any Sexual Abuse
Drug Dependence	2.83	5.70	3.09
Alcohol Dependence	2.42	4.01	2.80
Major Depression	1.37	3.14	2.80
General Anxiety Disorder	1.48	2.94	1.89
Two or More Disorders	1.61	5.47	2.58
$n = 1,411$			

Conclusion and Recommendations

It is clear that a majority of juvenile and adult females present to the criminal justice system with a variety of behavioral health problems, if not diagnosable substance use and mental health disorders. What can be done to reduce or reverse this process, seeking an outcome in which females can avoid an initial or repeat encounter with the justice system? This would seem to encompass two different approaches, although both would share similar elements. The first would be "prevention" (keeping them from becoming part of the system) and the second would be reducing the rate of recidivism.

Prevention

A strategy for at-risk girls would include the following components (Law Enforcement Assistance Administration, 1998):

- A strong basic education component that combines academic instruction in reading, language arts, and mathematics with positive social training;
- A component that enables girls to obtain the skills and knowledge to take charge of their lives;
- A component that enables girls to acquire a positive self-image, increase their understanding of themselves and the roles they play in the community, and appreciate their responsibilities as productive citizens;
- Universal screening for substance use and mental health disorders, and available treatment, when indicated;
- In the absence of universal screening, development of profiles of girls likely to become involved in the criminal justice system by identifying important factors (for example, a history of abuse) and provide appropriate interventions to reduce the likelihood of that occurring.

Reduction of Recidivism

A strategy for already-incarcerated females should include at minimum:

- Development of gender-specific programs as required by the 1992 Reauthorization of the Juvenile Justice Delinquency Prevention Act;
- All youth should be screened and referred for further evaluation, assessment, and treatment by mental health and substance abuse professionals (National Mental Health Association, 1998);
- Other appropriate services as listed among the prevention recommendations.

References

American Psychiatric Association. 2000. *Diagnostic and Statistical Manual of Mental Disorders, 4th Edition, Text Revision*. Washington, DC: Author.

Chesney-Lind, M., R. G. Sheldon, K. A. Joe. 1996. Girls, Delinquency and Gang Membership. *Gangs In America, 2nd Edition*. Sage Publications: Thousand Oaks, California

Children's Hospital Boston. 2001. *CRAFFT*. Center for Adolescent Substance Abuse: Boston, Massachusetts.

Estroff T. W. and N. G. Hoffmann. 2001. *PADDI: Practical Adolescent Dual Diagnosis Interview*. Smithfield, Rhode Island: Evince Clinical Assessments.

Grissom, T. and R. Barnum. 2003. *MAYSI-2: Massachusetts Youth Screening Instrument – Version 2*. Professional Resource Press: Sarasota, Florida.

Hassin, D., R. Van Rosem, S. McCloud, and J. Edicott. 1997. Alcohol Dependence and Abuse Diagnoses: Validity in Community Sample of Heavy Drinkers. *Alcoholism: Clinical and Experimental Research*, 21, 213-219.

Hodges, K. 1990. *CAFAS: Child and Adolescent Functional Assessment Scale*. Functional Assessments Systems: Ann Arbor, Michigan.

Hoffmann, N. G., G. Mee-Lee, and G. D. Shulman. 2005. *BEI: Behaviors and Experiences Inventory*. Waynesville, North Carolina: Evince Clinical Assessments.

Hoffmann. N. G. 1998. *UNCOPE*. Waynesville, North Carolina: Evince Clinical Assessment. Law Enforcement Assistance Administration. 1998. Women in Criminal Justice: A Twenty Year Update: Special Report. Washington, DC: U.S, Department of Justice.

Lehrman, M. D. 2006. The Dangers of Mental Health Screening. *Journal of American Physicians and Surgeons*, 11(3), 80-82.

Lexcen, F. and R. E. Redding. 2000. Mental Health Needs of Juvenile Offenders. *Juvenile Justice Fact Sheet*, Institute of Law, Psychiatry and Public Policy, University of Virginia: Charlottesville, Virginia.

Loper, A. B. 2000. Female Juvenile Delinquency: Risk Factors and Promising Interventions. *Juvenile Justice Fact Sheet*, Institute of Law, Psychiatry and Public Policy, University of Virginia: Charlottesville, Virginia.

Mee-Lee, D., G. D. Shulman, M. J. Fishman, et al., eds. 2001. *ASAM Patient Placement Criteria for the Treatment of Substance-Related Disorders, Second Edition, Revised*. American Society of Addiction Medicine: Chevy Chase, Maryland.

National Institute on Drug Abuse. 1991. *POSIT: Problem Oriented Screening Instruments for Teenagers*. Bethesda, Maryland: Author.

___. NIDA Notes. 2002. *Childhood Sexual Abuse Increases Risk for Drug Dependence in Adult Women.* Bethesda, Maryland: Author.

National Mental Health Association. 1998. *Position Statement: Children with Emotional Disorders in the Juvenile Justice System.* Alexandria, Virginia: Author.

Physicians for Human Rights. 2006. *Unique Needs of Girls in the Juvenile Justice System.* Cambridge, Massachusetts: Author.

President's New Freedom Commission on Mental Health. 2003. *Achieving the Promise: Transforming Mental Health Care in America: Final Report.* SAMHSA. Washington, DC. www.mentalhealthcommission.gov/contactus.html.

Rahdert, E. 1991. *POSIT: Problem Oriented Screening Instruments for Teenagers.* National Institute on Drug Abuse: Bethesda, Maryland:.

Stewart, D. G. and E. W. Trupin. 2003. Clinical Utility and Policy Implications of a Statewide Mental Health Screening Process for Juvenile Offenders. *Psychiatric Services,* 54, 377-382.

Substance Abuse and Mental Health Services Administration. 2005. *National Directory of Drug and Alcohol Abuse Treatment Programs.* Rockville, Maryland: Author.

Tiet, Q. Q., G. A. Wasserman, R. Loeber, L. McReynolds, L. S. Miller. 2001. Developmental and Sex Differences in Types of Conduct Problems. *Journal of Child and Family Studies,* 24, 406-426.

Wasserman, G. A. Larkin, S. McReynolds, S. J. Ko, L. M. Katz, J. R., Carpenter. 2005. Gender Differences in Psychiatric Disorders at Juvenile Probation Intake. *American Journal of Public Health,* 95(1), 131-137.

World Health Organization. 1990. *International Classification of Disease, 10th Edition.* Geneva, Switzerland: Author.

Law and Disorder: The Case Against Diminished Responsibility

5

Nancy Wolff, Ph.D.
Center for Mental Health Services and Criminal Justice Research
Edward J. Bloustein School of Planning and Public Policy
Rutgers, The State University of New Jersey

For every disorder, there is a socially appropriate response. For biological or emotional disorders–when people are seen as "sick"—we expect them to seek care and medical professionals to provide it. For social disorders, we expect the police and criminal justice system to respond. When the nature of the disorder is clear, so too is the socially appropriate response. Yet, when biological disorders such as mental and substance-use illnesses co-occur with criminal deviance, the appropriate mix of responses becomes less clear. This ambiguity emerges in part because social and psychological disorders may coincide without being causally related, and in part because responses from the mental health and criminal justice systems may interfere with one another unless they are appropriately sequenced and responsibility suitably allocated.

Assigning responsibility (and blame) for criminal deviance among persons with serious mental illnesses has been sharply debated ever since the doors of public mental hospitals began to open in the late 1950s (Abramson, 1972; Whitmer, 1980; Weiner, 1984). Responsibility has been attributed to the individual (Lamb, 1982), the treatment system (Bachrach, 1987), the criminal justice system (Bittner, 1967), public policy (Grob, 1994), and the public (Bachrach, 1979; Wahl, 1995). For persons with substance use illnesses, responsibility and blame were attributed to the individual and his/her poor decision making and moral character, until the mid 1980s when substance use was "medicalized" (Hora et al., 1999). While the dominant patterns of responsibility and blame have shifted over time, inadequate treatment is now most frequently portrayed as the primary culprit (Lamb et al., 2004; Nolan, 2003).

As a consequence, efforts to decarcerate persons with behavioral-health problems invariably stress a two-pronged approach: enhanced behavioral-health treatment and improved coordination between the criminal justice and behavioral-health systems. Behavioral-health treatment, preferably in the community, is expected to yield both improved behavioral health and reduced crime, simultaneously enhancing a preferred set of behavioral-health and justice outcomes, which combine together to reduce criminal deviance and enhance public safety and individual welfare.

This two-pronged approach is easy to purvey to policymakers and the public. It seems humane. It evokes the promise of all the psychopharmacological advances from recent decades. It is compatible with persisting images of people with mental illness. And, it allows the criminal justice system to retain its primarily punitive focus, which has largely displaced notions of rehabilitation over the past twenty-five years. Yet, in reality, the effectiveness of this strategy depends critically on whether inadequate treatment for behavioral-health problems is the primary cause of criminal deviance. Its success depends on whether behavioral health and criminal justice have the sort of "systems" that can be coordinated and directed to cooperate in ways that facilitate cross-system objectives.

This paper explores these assumptions and identifies implications when they are not met. The first part of the paper describes the prevalence of behavioral-health problems within correctional settings and summarizes the literature on the connection among mental and substance use disorders, treatment, and criminal deviance. The criminal justice process is described in the second part, focusing on how persons "flow" through sixteen distinct stages; each point representing an opportunity for identifying and engaging persons with mental and substance use illnesses with treatment. The notion of "appropriate" diversion is also discussed in this section. The next section describes the characteristics and structure of medical and behavioral-health treatment in correctional settings and for those making the transition back to the community. The fourth section describes several lessons from the literature on the effectiveness of diversion and explores the challenges associated with enhancing coordination among various parts of the criminal justice system as well as the connections between these components and the behavioral-health system. The paper concludes with a set of recommendations that follow from this assessment.

Mental and Substance Use Illnesses in the Criminal Justice System

Concern about the presence of persons with behavioral-health problems in correctional settings began in the early 1960s, and was featured prominently in the discussions leading up to the report of the President's Commission on Law Enforcement and Administration of Justice (1967).[1] In the early 1970s, the social phenomenon of incarcerating persons with mental illness was given the moniker of "criminalization," and its triggering mechanisms were changes in civil-commitment criteria and the inadequacies of the mental health system (Abramson, 1972).

Clinicians and administrators within correctional settings throughout the 1970s and 1980s provided anecdotal accounts of the "large" numbers of persons with mental illness in jails and prisons, and the negative consequences associated with their presence in these settings (Whitmer, 1980; Wilberg et al., 1989). Researchers also began to document a significant presence of mental illness in particular criminal-justice settings (Swank and Winder, 1976; Whitmer, 1980). It was frequently said during the 1990s that the nation's largest jails (for example, Los Angeles' Jail and Rikers Island) had become the largest mental health providers in the country.

The putative trans-institutionalizing of persons with mental illness from mental institutions to correctional institutions was seen as a direct result of underfunded mental health policies and a fragmented community-based service system, in combination with more restrictive civil-commitment criteria (Lamb et al., 2004). It was also consistent with the hydraulic balance used to describe the relationship between the mental health and criminal justice systems, suggesting that when one system expands, the other contracts (Penrose, 1939).

Because there was little reliable scientific evidence available on the prevalence of mental illness in jails and prisons, anecdote and rhetoric dominated much of the "criminalization" discussion in the 1980s and 1990s. Surveys of particular prisons[2] conducted in the early 1980s placed the estimates of serious mental illness within a range of 6 to 8 percent, with rates more than doubling to 15 to 20 percent if those likely to need mental treatment for more acute symptoms, such as situational depression, during their incapacitation were included (Jemelka et al., 1989). Prevalence estimates of mental illness in jail settings varied from 3 to 50 percent, depending on the sample design (Lamb and Weinberger, 1998; Teplin, 1983, 1990).

While there was a surfeit of estimates, methodological limitations associated with these studies cast considerable doubt on their quality, as well as their "generalizability." In the absence of reliable prevalence evidence, policy and practice discussions recycled and stalled until the late 1990s. Proposals to decarcerate on therapeutic grounds, however, began to gain traction after the release of the Bureau of Justice Statistics' report on the prevalence of mental illness in correctional settings. This report estimated that approximately 16 percent of all persons in jails and prisons report having either a mental disorder or an overnight in a psychiatric facility (Ditton, 1999). Sixteen percent of the correctional population translates into nearly 300,000 persons who are in active need of mental treatment while detained and after release. It is further estimated that approximately two-thirds of these individuals were under the influence of alcohol or drugs at the time of the offense (Ditton, 1999). Generally speaking, substance-use history is equally common among all state prisoners, independent of their mental health status. Nearly 60 percent of all state prisoners report using substances in the month prior to offending (Mumola, 1999).

While few interested parties are fully satisfied with the Bureau of Justice Statistics' prevalence estimate, it was large enough in magnitude, and consistent enough with expectations, to motivate a policy response. This is not to suggest, however, that the prevalence of mental- and substance-use illnesses in correctional settings is known with any degree of certainty. A rigorous epidemiological study of the prevalence of mental- and substance-use illnesses in correctional settings, modeled on the prevalence studies of the general population in the United States (Kessler et al., 2001) and the correctional and general population in the United Kingdom (Office of National Statistics, 1998), is needed here. Nonetheless, most advocates, policymakers, and researchers are willing to advance policy initiatives to compel the decarceration process based on estimates that enumerate more than a quarter of a million people with a mental illness.[3]

Information about the magnitude of need can be effective at motivating action, but is not sufficient for determining how best to respond. Information is also needed on the nature of the criminal behavior leading to incarceration, the relationship between the criminal behavior and the mental disorder, and the connection between disordered behavior and mental-health treatment.

Nature of Criminal Behavior among Persons with Mental Illness

Criminologists often use a "wedding cake" model to characterize the prevalence of different types of criminal activity (Walker, 1985). At the base are large numbers of petty crimes, including trespassing, disorderly conduct, suspicious person, public intoxication, shoplifting, and minor assaults. These crimes result in misdemeanor charges and are handled in courts of limited jurisdiction. The second layer includes felonies that are considered less serious in nature and are typically committed by first-time offenders or between people who are familiar with each other. These charges are often dismissed or involve negotiated pleas resulting either in probation or some form of intermediate sanctions. Serious, typically violent, felonies are reflected in the next layer, which is considerably smaller in size. Examples of these crimes include murder, manslaughter, rape, aggravated assault, robbery, burglary, and so forth. Celebrity cases are the top layer and include cases involving well-known individuals or crimes sensationalized by the media.

Crimes for which persons with a mental illness are charged fall into all four layers.[4] Their offenses, like those of persons without a mental illness, are most often petty violations, but sometimes involve nonviolent and violent felonies (Clark et al., 1999; Ditton, 1999; Lewis et al., 1991; Teplin, 1985; Torrey et al., 1992; Schuerman and Kobrin, 1984; Wolff et al., 1997). The distribution of these offenses varies by correctional setting (Ditton, 1999). In jail settings, less serious offenses predominate—the most frequent are property offenses (31 percent), violent offenses (30 percent), petty offenses (23 percent), and drug offenses (15 percent). By contrast, in state prison settings, violent offenses are more prevalent (53 percent), followed by property offenses (24 percent), drug offenses (13 percent), and petty crimes (10 percent). The fourth layer involves crimes committed by persons with a mental illness that are violent and involve a public official (for example, a political or civic leader) or innocent bystander (for example, a stranger on a train platform), and become sensationalized by the media (Wahl, 1995).

Studies describing the criminal justice contact of persons with a serious mental illness typically draw data from people who are connected to treatment settings. In part because these settings differ in character, data on criminal activity also vary, but the overall pattern tends to replicate the distribution found in most jails. Studies report police contact rates in the 69 to 83 percent range,[5] and arrest rates in the range of 18 to 40 percent (Clark et al., 1999; Wolff et al., 1997; Lewis et al., 1991). In the Clark et al. study, the majority of arrests were for theft (14 percent), substance abuse offenses (15 percent), disorderly conduct (12 percent), assault (11 percent), domestic violence (9 percent), and criminal trespass (6 percent). The ACT clients in the Wolff et al. study were more likely to be arrested for a probation violation (18 percent), public disturbance (22 percent), failure to pay (9 percent), and battery (12 percent). Of the 313 mental health patients in the Lewis et al. study, sixty were arrested during an eighteen-month period. Roughly one-fifth of the arrested group was charged with a felony, and less than half were violent felonies. An arrest for criminal damage, trespass, disorderly conduct was more common among this group.

In an effort to dispel the notion that mental disorder and criminal deviance are inextricably linked, mental health services researchers have developed classification schemes describing crime types and their relationship to mental illness. Lewis et al. (1991), who used a sample of 129 patients with criminal histories, identified three clusters of offender types. The first cluster commits nuisance offenses (for example, public intoxication and trespass) and their involvement in crime is considered a "by-product of their illness."

The second cluster engages in survival crimes (for example, petty theft, panhandling) because they are poor. Cluster three includes repeat offenders who committed serious crimes (for example, burglary, and assault). These individuals have "criminal histories [that] are indistinguishable from those of 'normal' criminals . . . [and] their mental disorder seems incidental or secondary to their criminality" (Lewis et al., 1991, 119). Hiday (1999) developed a similar three-level classification scheme for offenders with mental illness. The first group in her taxonomy commits "survival crimes" such as shoplifting or criminal trespassing. These individuals are often homeless and likely to have co-occurring substance abuse problems. The second group commits acts of violence as a result of their psychiatric symptoms. The third group commits a variety of crimes that are principally motivated by antisocial tendencies, not mental disorder.

Both of these classification schemes have a wedding cake design but by attributing cause to the criminal behavior, crime types are classified in ways that differ from the layers developed by criminologists. Nonetheless, these classification schemes convey the notion that people with mental illness commit different types of offenses for different reasons, and only some are directly related to psychiatric symptoms.

Yet, because of their simplicity, these schemes have limited ability to profile people with mental illness who are arrested and incarcerated. The nature and types of disorder among these individuals is much more socially and historically complex than is suggested by these schemes. In reality, crimes are committed by people who may have co-occurring substance abuse problems, seizure disorders, traumatic brain injuries, antisocial tendencies, histories of juvenile delinquency, learning disabilities, anger management problems, histories of sexual and physical trauma, as well as reside in poor, disorganized communities—all of which are likely to influence disordered behavior (see the text box on the following page). These characteristics of the individual are often lost in the elegance of simple classification schemes and, as a consequence, the details needed to inform policy and practice are not revealed in part because a narrow therapeutic lens is being applied.

Profiles of Incarcerated Persons with Mental Illness

Person A

Male inmate in his early forties diagnosed with schizoaffective disorder, antisocial personality disorder, and polysubstance abuse. He has a long history of drug and alcohol abuse. He has had multiple admissions to psychiatric hospitals while in the community and an extended admission to a forensic hospital during incarceration. His criminal history predates puberty. He has been incarcerated on and off for more than twenty years for violent crimes. He has committed more than twenty institutional infractions and has spent more than five years in administrative segregation for assaults and failure to obey. He has an explosive temper.

Person B

Female inmate in her early twenties diagnosed with depression and substance abuse. She has no prior history of psychiatric hospitalizations or suicide attempts. Her involvement with outpatient mental health treatment began at age twelve for behavioral difficulties at home. As a child she was sexually and physically abused. She has a moderate drug problem and poor anger management skills. She is serving her first prison sentence for drug distribution and has returned to prison on a parole violation.

Person C

Male inmate in his early twenties diagnosed with schizoaffective disorder and borderline personality disorder. He engages in self-mutilation and has attempted suicide several times, including while incarcerated. He has a history of emotional and mental health problems, family rejection, school behavioral problems, and homelessness. His first psychiatric hospitalization began after entering the correctional system, and includes three admissions to a forensic psychiatric facility. He has a history of being noncompliant with medications. He is currently serving a four-year sentence for robbery, attempted murder, and aggravated assault. He has a juvenile record and has violated conditions of probation. Institutional infractions include multiple charges of self-mutilation, destroying government property, and possession of a weapon.

Relationship Between Criminal Behavior and Mental Disorder

Two competing narratives can be found in the literature linking crime and mental illness. The first contends that mental illness does not cause criminal behavior, the second that only treatment can effectively deter criminal deviance among people who have serious mental disorders. There is considerably more evidence in support of the former claim than the latter.

People with mental illness who are not actively psychotic are equally as likely to engage in violence as their counterparts in the community *without* mental illness (Monahan et al., 2002). Some persons with serious mental illness do, during psychotic episodes, manifest their illness in ways that place themselves or others at risk of physical injury (Hodgins, 2001; Lindquist and Allebeck, 1990; Link et al., 1992; Swanson et al., 1996). But, such cases are relatively uncommon and would represent a relatively small layer in any classification scheme.

Offending behaviors by persons with mental illness, like people without mental illness, are more typically predicted by a variety of socioeconomic, lifestyle, and historical factors (American Psychiatric Association, 1998; Brill and Malzberg, 1962; Campbell et al., 1994; Monahan and Steadman, 1983; Stein and Diamond, 1985; Zitron et al., 1976) each exerting a separate impact on the probability to (re)offend. Most of the people with mental illness who are criminally active do not meet conditions for civil commitment at the time of arrest (Lamb and Grant, 1982; Lamb et al., 2004). Mentally ill individuals in jails are likely to have been homeless in the year before their arrest (30 percent), unemployed (53 percent), and under the influence of alcohol or drugs at the time of arrest (65 percent) (Ditton, 1999).

Connection between Disordered Behavior and Mental Health Treatment

Mental illness is overrepresented in prisons and jails (Ditton, 1999; Jemelka et al., 1989; Regier et al., 1990). Because there is no evidence that mental illness is the principal or proximate cause of offending behavior, there is little reason to expect that treatment alone would prevent such behavior.[6]

There is evidence showing that individuals enrolled in programs embodying the best clinical practices (assertive community treatment and integrated treatment models) continue to have encounters with the police, and a sizable minority is arrested (Clark et al., 1999; Wolff et al., 1997). For example, 75 percent of the persons with severe mental illness who were actively treated by an assertive community treatment program had encounters with the criminal justice system over a year's time.[7] Clients with the most frequent and serious contacts (all of whom had been arrested) had received, during that year, the most expensive and intensive mental health treatment (Wolff et al., 1997).

So, if evidence is lacking that mental illness is a proximate cause for criminal activity, how did this become such an influential narrative in mental health policy? The foundation of logic can be traced back to the early writings of Leona Bachrach (1979; 1982) and Richard Lamb (1982). Talbott and colleagues (1986), for example, in describing "young chronics," distinguished between the noncompliance behavior of the individual and that of the mental health system. In the case of the former, they described individuals who resisted their illness and either dropped out or refused treatment, and as a consequence often decompensated in ways that resulted in either civil commitment or criminal events. Non- compliance behavior on behalf of the individual was identified as the cause of subsequent decompensation and disordered social behavior.

Following this logic, if individuals were compliant with treatment (particularly, the medication regime), disordered behavior would be prevented (in other words, there would be no motivation for deviant behavior). At a minimum, to test this logic sequence, we would need to know how many people with serious mental illness were not compliant with treatment at the time of their contact with the police. Yet, even with this information, it would not be evident whether or to what extent other factors such as substance or alcohol use, public perceptions of behavior, or poverty were affecting decision making and behavior. Whether the deviant behavior, in these cases, is goal-directed (rational) or illness-centered (irrational) is an empirical issue, and not one modeled by a unidirectional and simple logic path, but rather one modeled on a decision tree structure with many possible branches.

Treatment-compliance behavior, however, is not strictly dependent on the behavior of the persons with mental illness. The therapeutic process is a partnership and depends on the behavior of the client/patient and the provider/system delivering the services. Acknowledging this duality, Talbott and Bachrach developed the notion that the treatment system may be noncompliant. It may be noncompliant in the sense that the level of services available are inadequately related to local need; the type of services are inappropriate in that they do not reflect best practices or the needs of the particular individual; services are cumbersome to access and/or geographically inaccessible; the delivery of services are not sensitive to cultural differences among clients; and the providers are unresponsive to "difficult" clients.

Disorder within the behavioral-health system and its failure to respond to the needs of persons with mental illness was the central focus of the President's *New Freedom Commission Report* (2003). Here, the logic suggests that if the disorder within the behavioral-health system were cured or rehabilitated, one of the negative performance indicators attributed to system disorder, the social disorder among persons with serious mental illness, would be eliminated.

It is reasonable to hypothesize that failure to respond by the treatment system may be a source of social disorder. Yet, we need more compelling evidence prior to accepting this hypothesis as fact. Particularly, we would need to know why people who had contact with the police were not engaged in treatment. Was it because the system was not responsive, or that the client was not responsive, or some combination of both? Also, for those who were engaged in treatment and in contact with the criminal justice system, what did their relationship with the treatment system look like? How responsive was the system and the client to treatment in the previous months leading up to the encounter?

What is perhaps most troubling about the discussions linking criminalization and decarceration is the tendency to assume that for persons with mental and substance use illnesses there is but one cause for their deviance—illness—and one cure, behavioral-health treatment. This effectively reduces the public image of people with mental and substance use illnesses to the illness itself. Yet, for everyone else (who are not mentally ill or substance users), there are well over a dozen theories describing possible determinants of their criminal behavior, linking it to economic, biosocial, psychological, or social structural factors, along with a variety of forms of conflict (Akers, 2000). Each of these theories captures some aspect of the individual and/or community that might trigger criminal deviance, and thus identifies a variety of ways in which that deviance might be avoided or mitigated.

Reducing people to their mental or substance use illnesses narrows our vision about how society could respond most effectively to their criminal deviance. Therapeutic spin, while perhaps unlocking the doors to the jails and prisons, not only artificially restricts the range of causes and solutions to a set of clinical interventions; it also has the undesirable side-effects of reinforcing the stigma that persists for people with mental and substance use illnesses. And, it reinforces the public and policymakers' perception that community-based treatment is failing by attributing all criminal behavior to clinical failures.

Considerably less attention has focused on the social-system dynamics (or context) surrounding the disordered behavior of persons with mental and substance use illnesses, although criminologists focus centrally on social context in explaining criminal behavior for the general population (Agnew, 1985; 1992; Sampson and Groves, 1989; Shaw and McKay, 1942; 1969; Wilson, 1987; Wolfgang et al., 1972). For example, it is well known within the mental health services field that many persons with serious mental illness live chaotic lives and reside in impoverished communities (Burt et al., 2001; Dennis et al., 1991; Durham, 1989; Federal Task Force, 1992).

Inner city areas in particular are characterized by crime and offer few legitimate options. We also know that unemployment is high among persons with serious mental illness (reaching as high as a 90 percent level for persons with schizophrenia) (*President's New Freedom Commission*, 2003). Being poor with lots of unstructured idle time and living in areas characterized by crime is a recipe for deviant outcomes—like trespassing, vagrancy, theft, drug distribution and possession, and other crimes related to deprivation.

The connection among the lack of economic opportunity, perceived or actual unfairness, and crime was prominently featured in the report of the *President's Commission on Law Enforcement and Administration of Justice* (1967). The Commission noted that "people who, though declared by the law to be equal, are prevented by society from improving their circumstances even when they have the ability and the desire to do so, are people with extraordinary strains on their respect for the law and society" (President's Commission, 1967, 6). Furthermore, the report states that "society has not devised ways for ensuring that all its members have the ability to assume responsibility." And, then drawing the connection between poverty and crime, the Commission stressed that "warring on poverty, inadequate housing, and unemployment, is warring against crime" and that "every effort to improve life in America's 'inner cities' is an effort against crime" (President's Commission, 1967, 6).

Todd Clear, reviewing the *Commission's Report* thirty years later, reiterated that "the centerpiece of the Commission's agenda was rehabilitation—-not the old, 'failed,' medical model based on crime as mental illness, but the newer idea of reintegration based on the view of blocked opportunity for legitimate participation in society" (1998; p. 5). Many of these themes were raised in the *President's New Freedom Commission Report* (2003), although here the language emphasized "recovery," not rehabilitation.

The Criminal Justice System and Process

People with mental and substance use illnesses have frequent encounters with the police, who serve as the "gatekeepers" to the criminal justice system. Whether these encounters warrant an arrest, prosecution, and sentencing depends on the discretion of the police, prosecutors, and judges. This section begins by describing the formal and informal action of the criminal justice system and concludes with a discussion of the appropriateness and inappropriateness of invoking the criminal justice system and its process in cases involving persons with mental illness.

The Criminal Justice Process: Sixteen Points of Intervention

The criminal justice system will be described as a sequential process into which people "flow" if their behavior is identified as deviant in the community, the police are contacted, an arrest is made, and adjudication is pursued. Sixteen points of intervention are identified within four stages of the criminal justice process. These points of intervention can be thought of as points of leverage through which concerns about mental and substance use illnesses could shape the practices of actors within the criminal justice system. Barriers to intervening at these points will also be highlighted in this discussion.

The criminal justice system is comprised of three discrete subsystems—police, courts, and corrections—and employs approximately 2.3 million people within 55,000 public agencies (Bauer and Owens, 2004). Of the $167 billion spent on criminal justice in 2001, 43 percent was for police, 34 percent for corrections, and 23 percent for the courts. State and local governments are the principal sources of funding for criminal justice services, with local governments assuming primary responsibility for police protection (70 percent) and the state, for corrections (63 percent). Criminal justice expenditures grew on average 8 percent per year between 1982 and 2001, representing more than a four-fold increase from $36 billion in 1982 to $167 billion in 2001 (Bauer and Owens, 2004).

While it is customary to refer to these 55,000 public agencies nested inside police, courts, and corrections as a *system*, it is not so in terms of perspective, funding, organization, or operations. The different elements of the system are funded in diverse and inconsistent ways, and simple labels such as *police, the courts*, and *corrections* fail to convey its organizational complexity and diversity. Indeed, it is more common to refer to the criminal justice system as a non-system (Freed, 1970; Skoler, 1977). Fragmentation exists at the organizational level, with the system being divided first into three subsystems (police, courts, and corrections), which may be separated by jurisdiction (federal and state) and branch of government (executive and judicial) (Figure 1). The subsystems have very different legal mandates, performance expectations, and accountability standards. Moreover, the leadership within these subsystems may be elected or appointed through a political process.

Figure 1. Description of the Criminal Justice System

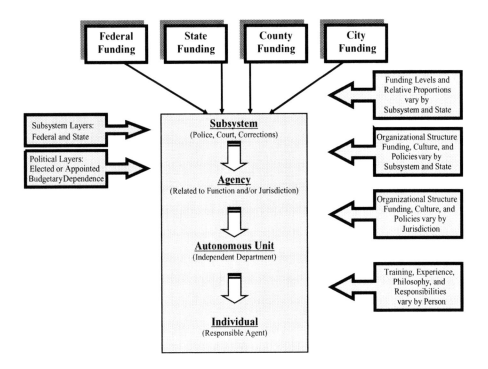

These subsystems are further divided into separate agencies. Agencies within and between the subsystems differ in terms of their philosophies and goals, the standards guiding their actions (for example, "probable cause" for police but "reasonable doubt" for prosecutors), and policies as defined by strategy and priorities. The agencies may be further subdivided into independent departments performing specialized functions within a particular jurisdiction. How individuals in each agency execute their responsibilities is conditioned by their training, experience, philosophy, and local context.

Organizational fragmentation is exacerbated and perpetuated by diverse funding sources, which come from federal, state, county, and city budgets. Funding not only comes from different sources but is also attached to different legal mandates. For example, funding may emanate from the same source (say, county government) but be allocated to agencies that perform independent functions (such as the jail and the district attorney's office).

In addition, within a subsystem (say the court), some parts are funded by the state (for example, judges in Michigan), while others are funded by the county (for example, clerk of court, administrator's salaries, and general operating expenses, again in Michigan), but this varies considerably from state to state. All the organizational levels, however, are similar in the sense that they depend on outside sources for revenues, which ties their accountability to budgetary decision makers and, in some senses, the voting public. It is for this reason that these agencies are careful to stylize their behaviors and reputations to the preferences of their funding sources.

Another layer of fragmentation tied to principles of federalism relates to the variation in organizational and funding by state and local jurisdiction within the state. What exists as a criminal justice system has evolved piecemeal and without any central organization or coordination at the national, state, or county level. As noted by the 1967 *President's Commission*:

> The entire system represents an adaptation of the English common law to America's peculiar structure of government, which allows each local community to construct institutions that fill its special needs. Every village, town, county, city, and State has its own criminal justice system, and there is a Federal one as well. All of them operate somewhat alike. No two of them operate precisely alike. (*President's Commission*, 1967, 7)

Yet, even this characterization assumes too much structure, because within these jurisdictions the actors within the three subsystems have different objectives and are motivated by different norms. This leads Patrick V. Murphy to comment that:

> the most readily observed characteristic of the American criminal justice process is its disarray. What is supposed to be a system of criminal justice is really a poorly coordinated collection of independent fiefdoms, some ridiculously small, which are labeled police, courts, corrections, and the like. This diagnosis was true in 1967 when the President's Commission on Law Enforcement and Administration of Justice discerned the outline of what should be a workable productive system of criminal justice. That diagnosis, equally true today, is easy to make; the challenge is to discover and chart useful routes toward coordination of criminal justice, whose hallmarks are harmony, effectiveness, and indeed justice. (Skoler, 1977, xvii)

While there is no formal or consistent organizational structure unifying the "system" (Freed, 1970; Skoler, 1977), it is functionally integrated through a sequential process of arresting, prosecuting, sentencing, incapacitating, and releasing with supervision, which activates agencies within each of the subsystems in a systematic and structured fashion (*President's Commission*, 1967). These subsystems are connected by serial functions, whereby one subsystem's "output" (for example, arrest) becomes another system's "input" (prosecution). Because of these serial connections, mutual interdependencies exist. A change in behavior by one subsystem (for example, police arrest more people) has consequences downstream (in other words, increased census of jails and prisons, growing caseloads for prosecutors and defense attorneys, more people on parole or community supervision). For this reason, it is most instructive to see criminal justice as a process, both to understand how it functions and where interventions might most readily engage persons with mental and substance use illnesses.

This process is characterized by four stages: community, police, court, and corrections. Sixteen potential points of intervention are nested within these stages (see Figure 2). In describing each stage, the focus will be on its organization and functions, the key decision makers, and the scope of their discretion, as well as the impact of their choices on how people engage in the criminal justice process. Definitions of intervention options with reference to practice examples are provided in text boxes in each of the four stages.

Figure 2. Critical Points of Intervention and Related Referral Options

Non-Community Settings		16 Critical Points of Intervention		Community Setting
Residential Treatment	Action Taken ←	**Community Process** **Crisis Line/ Drop-in Center** **Hospitals**	No Action Taken → Action Taken	**Outpatient** Treatment
Crime or Incident				
Jail with or without Treatment	Action Taken ←	**Police Process** **Initial Contact** **Investigation** **Arrest** **Custody**	No Action Taken → Action Taken → Discretionary Release	**Emergency Assessment**
Jail with or without Treatment	Detained ←	**Court Process** **Charging** **Preliminary Hearing** **Arraignment** **Bail/Detention** **Plea Negotiations** **Adjudication** **Sentencing**	Charges Dropped → Bailed → Not Guilty Guilty/Plea	with or without Supervision or Treatment
Jail or Prison with or without Treatment	← Action Required	**Correctional Process** **Confinement** **Release** **Revocation**	→	with or without Supervision or Treatment

Stage 1: The Community. Deviance occurs in communities and is defined by them. Seeing a disheveled person talking to himself will be interpreted differently if this person is placed in a suburban community, a small or midsize town, or an inner city. Labels of "suspicious" or "scary" are assigned in large part based on the reactions of community residents. Behaviors or appearances that disturb residents and excite their fears in some areas, motivating public action, may become normalized elsewhere. How a community responds to deviance is likely to depend on a host of factors, including local norms and expectations of behavior, the prevalence of social disorganization and cultural heterogeneity within the community, the history, the prevalence, and the nature of crime in the area, and its social capital (Morenoff et al., 2001; Skogan, 1990).

Whether people connect disordered behavior to crime and to the community's welfare has been the focus of several criminologists. Wilson and Kelling (1982) related the public's thinking about disorder, crime, and fear to "broken windows," which were both metaphors and symbols of frayed neighborhood norms. They argued that "if a window in a building is broken and is left unrepaired, all the rest of the windows will soon be broken . . . One unrepaired broken window is a signal that no one cares, and so breaking more windows costs nothing" (Kelling, 1982, 31). It follows that evidence of uncontrolled (and perhaps sanctioned) social disorder—public drinking, drug dealing, loitering, panhandling, and tolerating vagrancy—signals that the community is at an elevated risk for crime and economic decline.

Skogan (1990), testing the broken windows theory, found that disorder foreshadows serious crime and economic decline within communities. The broken windows theory suggests that the best way to preserve and protect the social and economic welfare of a community is to stop social disorder at its first sign (Kelling and Coles, 1997). But, this presumes that there is some social and economic welfare within the community to protect from erosion.

Whether or not one accepts broken windows as a reliable marker for community norms, it seems clear that how a community reacts to perceived disorder depends on its perception of alternative interventions and its assessment of which option will perform in a reliable and reasonable fashion. Options might include contacting a relation of the person (assuming that the distressed person is known to the community), calling a crisis-intervention line or community-help service (assuming they exist), or calling the police. If only the police option exists, then it becomes the default option. Yet, even then, the community's propensity to involve the police will depend on their perceived role in the sort of problem solving that is typically described under the rubric of "community policing." Communities that see the police in these terms will contact them to deal with observed deviance. Other communities, however, may not respond to disorder by contacting the police because they are seen as hostile to the welfare of the community and the individuals who reside there.

Pre-Charge Diversion

With or without police involvement, the community, represented by a family member, friend, or concerned citizen, could inform a mental health facility, through a crisis line or other referral mechanism, that there is a distressed individual in need of mental health attention. A mobile team then could be dispatched to the scene. Alternatively, a citizen could transport the distressed individual to a crisis or treatment center for evaluation.

Example: New York City has twenty-three mobile crisis teams responding to concerns about the psychiatric well-being of people in the community. Referrals are received directly from the public, including the police, and may be routed through LifeNet, a 24/7 mental-health-emergency-crisis line, providing assessment and referral services at no cost. These services are funded by the Mental Health Association of New York City, Inc. and the New York City Department of Health and Mental Hygiene, and are coordinated with the New York City Police Department.

Stage 2: The Police. Police are the gatekeepers to the criminal justice process. The police process includes contact, investigation, arrest, and custody, each representing an intervention point. At each point, the police choose to take action or not, and they may engage a variety of other agencies existing within or outside the community. The responding officer gives the initial incident definition. In looking at a situation, the police choose to socialize, "medicalize," or criminalize an incident. That is, the officer might determine that no laws have been broken and that the party or parties to the incident simply require calming, guiding, and warning. In other cases, the incident may involve someone who is acting erratically and in ways that cannot be calmed, suggesting that the person needs medical treatment. Alternatively, the incident may involve situations where the officer observes a behavior that is in clear violation of the law, warranting an arrest.

In many cases, there are likely to be gray areas where the observed incident sits on the boundary between law breaking and erratic, potentially law-breaking behavior, which could be interpreted as a medical problem or a crime. Factors affecting this choice are likely to include the availability of options other than jail, the capacity of the local jail, the relative efficiency of non-jail options to jail processing, the "publicness" of the behavior, the culture of local policing, the expectations of the community, the officer's and community's history with the individual and others exhibiting similar types of behavior, as well as other social and contextual dynamics that are unique to that officer, police department, and local area (Bittner, 1967; Riksheim and Chermak, 1993; Teplin, 1985).

While police have considerable discretion in their interpretation of criminal deviance, their decisions must fit within the broader culture of the agency to which they are assigned. Police agencies are organized around each locality's law enforcement priorities and social norms. The culture of the agency may define the style of policing in ways that emphasize maintaining order ("watchmen"), enforcing the laws ("law enforcement professionals"), or servicing the community ("social worker") (Cole and Smith, 1996). Also, agencies may have explicit policies that guide the management of situations involving people with special needs, such as mental illness (Council of State Governments, 2002). These policies might include defining how these individuals are to be engaged and what happens to them once in custody. Policies may be standardized through enhanced training of all officers on the force or a specialized unit.

"Medicalizing" the officer's interpretations of incidents involving persons with mental illness is challenging for several reasons. First, police officers are not clinicians and, for this reason alone, are not likely in the quick of the incident to determine and attribute biological disorder to social disorder. Specialized training might help identify individuals who are actively psychotic but generally will be less useful in distinguishing among cases where mental illness may be either managed through treatment or disguised by individual choice.

Second, professional and organizational variation is common among police officers and agencies. Attempting to standardize their interpretations of special needs may reveal and heighten philosophical differences that polarize officers and agencies regarding the relative balance between the social control and social service functions of the police. Variation in police culture may be in part driven by the structural variation within the subsystem itself. There are approximately 18,000 law enforcement agencies across the United States; some agencies have more than a thousand officers (1 percent), others have only one (5 percent), and most have ten or fewer (47 percent) (Hickman and

Reaves, 2003). Size may matter to the extent that individual discretion has greater expression if organizational control is diminished by scale.

Another reason why officers may be reluctant to medicalize incidents relates to uncertainty. There are three types of uncertainty relevant to this context. The first concerns professional uncertainty—the officer is not confident that he/she is interpreting or discerning biological behavior correctly. Erratic behavior may be caused by drugs, alcohol, or rage, not schizophrenia or bipolar disorder. The lines separating these various causes are not always bright even to clinicians with years of clinical training. By contrast, the law is less gray and, as a consequence, the officer is more certain about what qualifies as criminal behavior. The second type of uncertainty concerns the officer's efficiency and effectiveness. Taking a person to a medical facility (for example, emergency, inpatient, or outpatient) might be expected to involve more "down time" and less certainty that the individual will be detained, compared to the criminal justice processing route. Greater certainty about how much time it will take and what will happen through arresting (for example, no more calls from neighbors on this shift) may not only be more efficient, from the officer's perspective, but also more effective from a social control perspective.

Yet, while the officer might control the entry into the criminal justice process, there is no certainty that the individual will be prosecuted, which concerns the last type of uncertainty. The discretion and control of the police officer ends at the booking desk, at which time discretion moves to the prosecutor. Police learn, over time, which cases will be prosecuted and what evidence is needed for prosecution. If cases involving charges of petty crimes, including trespassing, disorderly conduct, suspicious persons, public intoxication, shoplifting, and minor assaults, are not being prosecuted, officers learn that this is not the way to handle incidents that involve these types of behavior, encouraging them to consider alternative processing options.

Deferred Prosecution Diversion

The prosecutor, in negotiations with defendants and/or their legal representative, agrees to suspend prosecution after charging on the condition that the defendant participates in an intervention, such as treatment. Charges are held in abeyance for a defined period of time and are then dismissed if the intervention condition is satisfied; otherwise, the charges are reactivated.

Example: The Tazewell, Illinois County State's Attorney's office oversees a Deferred Prosecution Program, which supervises nonviolent adult misdemeanor and first felony offenders. The State's Attorney's office screens offenders, and those selected must complete a voluntary period of supervision, which may include restitution, counseling, or community service, as well as drug testing. Successful completion results in dismissal; failure results in formal prosecution.

Stage 3: The Court. While police may be gatekeepers to the criminal justice system, prosecutors control the flow of people immediately past the gate. Prosecutors, who are elected or appointed officials, are affiliated with attorney's offices of the district, state, or commonwealth. These offices are organized at the county level and are estimated to include more than 2,300 offices employing nearly 27,000 chief and assistant attorneys (DeFrances, 2002).

In general, prosecutors have virtually unlimited discretion in the decision to charge an individual with a crime (in other words, pursue prosecution). Their decision to charge is influenced by the nature of the evidence evaluated in terms of its likeliness to meet standards of reasonable cause and whether the charge itself warrants the court's time. They may choose not to pursue the case because the case lacks merit or because the prosecutor's office has an explicit or implicit policy against prosecuting cases involving certain types of charges. By not pursuing the charges, the case is dismissed.

If, on the other hand, charges are pursued, the prosecutor again has control over the number and types of charges to be filed; the conditions for setting bail, whether plea bargaining will be considered; and the parameters for sentencing. In essence, the prosecutor determines whether the individual gains access to and moves through the criminal justice system or is released. Yet, even after charges are filed, the prosecutor retains the discretion to reduce or dismiss the charges (referred to as a notation of *nolle prosequi*).

The mission and norms of the prosecutor's office are derived from its legal responsibility of enforcing the laws of the state. Prosecutors act on behalf of the people by prosecuting those suspected of breaking the law, and in so doing, they serve as the organizational link between the police and the courts. Determining whether a crime has been committed and is worthy of prosecution is determined within the context of the local interpretations of the law and policies guiding the stringency with which these laws must be enforced. Cole (1997, 164) notes that "the prosecutor can individualize justice in ways that will benefit the accused, the victim, and society. When the offense involves conduct arising from mental illness, the prosecutor may believe that some form of psychiatric treatment is needed, rather than punishment."

Some reformers propose altering the norms of prosecutorial practice by having these attorneys define just outcomes by weighing more heavily the consequences for the well-being of the offender (Nolan, 2003). Prosecutors, however, may be reluctant to embrace principles of therapeutic jurisprudence, in which they individualize justice in accordance with their notions of what is most appropriate for the individual, if the risk to public safety is calculated to be too high or too uncertain. If these assessments by prosecutors are based predominately on individual or collective impressions of persons with mental illness as being irrational and unpredictable, it would be reasonable to expect them to pursue criminal justice processing in an effort to minimize risks that could have political consequences.

There are two separate and important issues here. First, the prosecutor may not have a reasoned and balanced assessment of the potential for effective treatment or whether such treatment is available within their jurisdiction. What prosecutors know about mental illness per se or about the delivery system within their communities is unclear. Second, since the chief prosecutor in each jurisdiction is typically elected, the public's perception of dangerousness may influence the prosecutor's decisions to consider individualizing justice in ways that favor treatment alternatives to prosecution. Research has shown that there exists an "unrealistically elevated fear of violence about persons with mental illness and a strong desire to maintain social distance from these individuals" (Link et al., 1999, 1332).

To the extent that prosecutors' assessments are guided by limited or discriminatory impressions of illness, it remains safer for prosecutors to advance cases involving mental illness through the criminal justice process, where more information will eventually be revealed about the alleged crime, situational factors surrounding the incident, and any possible role played by the illness itself. The feasibility of deferred prosecution is likely to be enhanced if perceptions of risk approach actual or reasonable risk levels. This is likely to occur only if prosecutors have a more informed understanding of mental illness, the local treatment system's capacity, and the factors motivating deviance among persons with serious mental illness.

Overall, less than 10 percent of cases activated by the prosecutor are adjudicated by trial. The vast majority of misdemeanor charges, involving the court of limited jurisdiction, are processed in assembly-line fashion. Charges are read by the court clerk, a guilty plea is entered, and the judge assigns a sentence, usually a monetary fine, probation, community service, or time served. "Lower court judges are more interested in responding to 'problems' than to formally defined 'crimes.' They seek to use their discretion to impose sentences that will fit the needs of the offender and the community, rather than simply imposing the sentences provided by law" (Cole and Smith, 1996, 243). In cases involving charges of a more serious nature, such as felonies, the trial court is still infrequently engaged. Instead, the prosecutor, defense attorney, the judge, and other court personnel work together in "courtroom workgroups" with the goal of negotiating plea arrangements or other alternative resolutions in lieu of a trial (Eisenstein and Jacob, 1977; Nardulli et al., 1988).

The dynamics and norms within these work groups, and between prosecutors and defense attorneys in general, are shaped by the legal culture in that local area. Culture, in this context, refers to the usual way in which cases are advanced, court personnel interact with each other and share standardized information and penalties for crimes. In general, communities have standards that determine the customary and reasonable "price" for particular crimes (usually referred to as the "going rate") (Heumann, 1997). Plea negotiations, for example, might include a condition of inpatient or outpatient treatment in lieu of other sanctions or a sentence of probation supervision coupled with a condition of treatment.

Judges strive to ensure that the adjudication process is legal and fair. They preside over preliminary hearings, arraignment hearings, trials, and sentencing hearings, and participate in "out-of-court" negotiations with prosecutors and defense attorneys on issues related to pleas and sentencing. In cases involving trials, the philosophy and sentencing style of the judge can influence the decisions of the prosecutor and defense attorney upstream. In particular, if the judge has a reputation for leniency in cases involving certain types of charges, prosecutors may choose to either dismiss the charges altogether or to pursue a different set of charges. Similarly, the stringency of a judge's sentencing style is likely to encourage plea negotiations in lieu of trial.

Judges, collectively or individually, could signal their preferences regarding the prosecution of persons with mental illness by either informally or formally revealing their views on the inappropriateness of prosecuting and incarcerating persons with mental illness, or sending the same message, indirectly, through their sentencing. Policymaking representatives of the court, such as the chief justices and state court administrators may, through bodies such as the Conference of Chief Justices or Conference of State Court Administrators, draft specific resolutions on policies such as diversion and the specialty roles of courts (Conference of Chief Justices, 2000). These policy statements open the way for nontraditional court processing, which might include specialized courts that hear cases relating to particular problems, such as drug addiction, mental illness, domestic violence, driving while under the influence, and so forth.

As with policing, there are advantages and disadvantages to concentrating specialized knowledge in particular actors. In general, specialization makes sense when all cases relating to a particular problem can be assigned to an expert judge. Otherwise, expertise is concentrated in a fraction of the cases, while generalist judges continue to process the remainder of cases without the benefit of expert knowledge. These judges may not be sensitive to issues involving mental illness or the treatment system. The behavior and philosophy of individual judges and the policies of the leadership within the court structure inadvertently signal to the other actors upstream and downstream whether certain issues or problems are relevant to the criminal justice process. The failure of judges to understand these issues may cause the court to underuse its power to connect people to treatment in correctional settings and the community, or to inadequately value the efforts expended on behalf of the defense attorney and other advocates to find treatment for the person instead of incarceration.

Specialty Court Diversion

Defendants who participate in these specialty courts are offered the option of treatment or jail. By choosing treatment, they may forgo criminal processing altogether, or undergo criminal processing but forgo criminal sentencing. Problem-solving courts have specialized dockets and are represented by a collaborative, nonadversarial team, including the judge, prosecuting attorney, defense attorney, and a mental-health-system representative. The court supervises compliance with treatment.

Example: The Brooklyn, New York, Court recruits defendants with mental illness charged with nonviolent felonies or misdemeanors with likely jail sentences. The court holds the client and the system responsible for compliance with treatment conditions through a process of judicial monitoring that enhances accountability and cross-system communication and coordination.

Stage 4: Corrections. Judges control the doors to the jails and prisons as well as the gates to the community. Through sentencing, they determine whether the individual will be placed on probation (community supervision) or incapacitated in jail (for a sentence less than a year) or prison (for a sentence of a year or more).

Parole boards, which may be independent of the state department of corrections, assess the prisoner's readiness for release prior to the completion of the assigned sentence. Those who are determined "ready" or who have a mandatory condition of release are then released under the supervision of parole.

The primary responsibility of corrections, whether supervision occurs in the community or a correctional setting, is security and public safety. Prisons and jails, however, are also constitutionally required to provide medical treatment to inmates with medical needs (Haney and Specter, 2003; Metzner, 2002). Judges have the authority to stipulate conditions of treatment during incarceration and if released to the community (Wolff, 2002, 2003).

Organizationally, the corrections system is Byzantine; some parts are centralized, while others are highly decentralized; some parts are coordinated, while other parts are independent; some parts push to decarcerate, while others push to reincarcerate. The prevailing balance among these complex interactions varies across states and localities. Yet, there is some order to the system. Incapacitation is the primary function of prisons and jails.

Each state has its own state prison system, as does the federal government. Local jurisdictions, cities, municipalities, and counties operate and fund temporary holding facilities ("lockups") and jails. There are roughly 3,200 small, short-term lockups, maintained by local police and municipalities, used to hold people awaiting a bail hearing (Hickman and Reaves, 2003).

In general, jails, of which there are approximately 3,400, hold detainees who are either ineligible for or unable to make bail; convicted offenders awaiting sentencing; offenders with short sentences (less than a year); parolees or probationers awaiting a hearing on a technical violation; and state and federal inmates displaced by overcrowding (Stephan, 2001). At midyear 2003, the nation's prisons and jails held 2,078,570 persons—one in every 140 U.S. residents.[8] The proportion of U.S. citizens being incarcerated has been increasing annually—from a rate of 601 persons in custody per 100,000 U.S. residents in 1995 to 715 persons in custody per 100,000 residents in 2003 (Harrison and Karberg, 2004).

Probation and parole provide community supervision either instead of or following incarceration. In 2003, there were approximately 4.9 million adult men and women under some form of community supervision; 59 percent of whom were supervised by probation (Glaze and Palla, 2004). Each state has a probation department with units attached to a court district. The department itself may be administered by the state (centralized) or a local jurisdiction (decentralized). Some states have unified probation and parole departments. While most parole agencies are independent of the state department of corrections, some are unified.

The input-output sequencing of parole and probation differ. Probation works closely with the court, and its interactions start at sentencing, whereas parole works routinely with its state department of corrections; these relations are activated after a period of incarceration. The expectations and functions of probation and parole, however, are similar. In the case of probation, the court agrees, as a condition to sentencing, to exchange community placement for incarceration if the individual exhibits good behavior while in the community. Probation officers are responsible for ensuring that the individual's behavior conforms to the expectations of the court. The court retains the authority to revoke the individual's community status if appropriate standards of behavior are violated, as determined by the probation officer.

Parole, on the other hand, is granted as a reward for good behavior while incarcerated but is conditional on that behavior continuing while the individuals complete their sentences in the community.[9] Parole is granted with conditions, and it is the responsibility of the parole officer to ensure that these conditions are satisfied. Failure to adhere to the conditions of probation or parole results in a technical violation, which activates the revocation of community placement and a return to prison or jail. Revocation is especially common among parolees. In an average year, approximately one-third of new admissions to prisons result from a violation of parole conditions (Hughes et al., 2001). Nearly 16 percent of revocations are for some type of drug-related violation, such as a positive test for drug use or possession of drugs (Hughes et al., 2001).

Courts and parole boards often attach special conditions to community supervision orders. These special conditions take into account an individual's needs and risk level. The most common conditions require some form of therapeutic intervention such as inpatient or outpatient treatment or testing for drug or alcohol addiction, mental illness, or behavior problems (for example, anger management). Also, for those assessed to need closer or more intense supervision, the court or board, respectively, may require intensive probation supervision (IPS) or intensive supervision parole (ISP). This form of supervision is akin to intensive case management in that parole officers supervise smaller caseloads (ranging from fifteen to forty clients) and interact with the clients more frequently and instrumentally.[10]

Decision-making authority (and hence, power) rests with parole and probation officers once community supervision conditions have been specified. The expectations, however, of these officers are conflicting. On the one hand, they are agents of social control who monitor compliance with community conditions and initiate revocation of community privileges if behavior deviates from these conditions.

Reintegration Initiatives

Corrections, perhaps in cooperation with community-based agencies, develops and implements reentry plans for persons with mental illness. The goal of reentry planning is to ensure that treatment follows the individual once released from prison or jail. Reentry planning may be coordinated with parole supervision. Coordination here works only for persons released under the supervision of parole.

Example: The New Castle County, Delaware, reentry court focuses on repeat offenders who have been incarcerated for one year or more and have a community service requirement as a release condition. Case managers engage offenders prior to release. The goal is to develop and implement reentry-court plans. Case managers act as "service brokers," helping clients reintegrate post-release. The court and probation officers monitor reintegration efforts. Probation officers work closely with community police officers and the case managers to enhance monitoring.

Those who take a strict stance, identifying more violations and initiating more revocations, while ostensibly protecting the community, are more likely to engender strained relations with their clients. This adversarial relationship, however, is inconsistent with the expectation that parole and probation officers assist offenders in reentering the community. Asking for help with problems related to unemployment, drug addiction, and mental health requires trust. But, it is hard to maintain trust in probation or parole officers who treat any sign of aberrant behavior as a reason to return a person to jail or prison. Again, the balance between these two roles is influenced by training and local agency culture, which typically stress social control, as symbolized by the gun on the hip and badge on the shirt.

Defining and Justifying the Appropriateness of Diversion

A number of social critics and mental health advocates have posited that it is generally inappropriate to incarcerate persons with serious mental illness (Human Rights, 2003; Torrey et al., 1992).[11] This becomes the justification for interventions that "divert" these individuals to treatment and away from the criminal justice system. "Inappropriateness" in this context typically rests on claims about medical needs, undue hardships, or therapeutic justice. Common to these arguments is the notion that people with mental illness are in some way vulnerable and thus require special protections. For example, the medical need argument stresses that because illness is causing disorder, therapeutic intervention is required, not punishment. In a sense, the illness is making the person vulnerable to criminalization.

Forcing a connection between crime and illness, however, can itself be dysfunctional. Lewis (1953, 3) warns that "if crime and disease are to be regarded as the same thing, it follows that any state of mind which our masters choose to call 'disease' can be treated as a crime; and compulsorily cured." By attribution, inappropriateness defined by the disorder labels the illness and individual in ways that could foster psychological dysfunction. In particular, Wexler (1991, 20) refers to instances where "laws may, through . . . labels and attributions, lead persons to regard themselves as dysfunctional or as lacking in control."

Alternatively, it has been argued that incarcerating persons with mental illness imposes an undue hardship on them because jails and prisons are toxic environments, given their mental or emotional frailties (Carter, 1998; Human Rights, 2003; Kupers, 1999; Snow and Briar, 1990; Torrey et al., 1992). Few would dispute the assertion that incarceration imposes hardship on those who are incarcerated (indeed, some would say that is precisely the intent of incapacitation). This hardship can certainly have antitherapeutic consequences. However, the central question here is not whether incarceration imposes any antitherapeutic consequences, but whether the magnitude of these effects justifies treating this group differently from other offenders (who also may be depressed or otherwise damaged in prison settings) in terms of their criminal processing (Kupers, 2000).

In its bluntest form, this argument assumes that the hardship of incarceration on persons with mental illness is equal across all disorders (in other words, schizophrenia, bipolar, post-traumatic stress disorder, depression) and within each disorder group. It asserts that the hardships for those with mental illness are greater than those imposed on groups of people with other frailties, such as substance abuse disorders, cancer, AIDS, diabetes, or other chronic conditions (Wolff, 2002, 2003).

Claims about the putative inappropriateness of incarceration have also been justified on the grounds that therapeutic norms trump other societal values. In particular, therapeutic intervention is argued to be more important than punishment. This argument invokes the spirit of therapeutic jurisprudence, which as described by Wexler (1991, 8), is "the study of the role of law as a therapeutic agent. It looks at the law as a social force that, like it or not, may produce therapeutic or antitherapeutic consequences. Such consequences may flow from substantive rules, legal procedures, or from the behavior of legal actors (lawyers and judges)." The challenge, however, which these legal actors face, concerns properly balancing the different agency roles if and when they conflict. Winick (1996, 665) argues that "therapeutic jurisprudence has always suggested that therapeutic goals should be achieved only within the limits of considerations of justice," and moreover that the law "should be applied fairly, evenhandedly, and non-discriminatorily." It would follow then that justice should not be "blind" to therapeutic consequences but neither should it trump fairness.

Arguments in favor of special diversionary treatment of persons with mental illness are likely to have significant side effects. Claims that those with mental illness merit distinctive programs of diversion need to be eval-uated, not simply for their therapeutic consequences, but in terms of the other values upon which the criminal justice system is structured—most notably concepts of procedural fairness and evenhandedness. In particular, creating special classes of people who receive different (and preferential) forms of justice, in practice, distorts the principles of justice on which the criminal justice system rests.

As described by DiIulio (1993, 10), "doing justice" involves standards of fairness, defined horizontally and vertically, which include: (1) holding peo-ple accountable for their offenses; (2) ensuring due process protections; (3) treating equal offenders equally; and (4) treating unequal offenders and offenses differently. To do this kind of justice, there needs to be some polit-ical, social, and legal consensus regarding the relative weighting of punish-ment and rehabilitative/therapeutic goals, how differences in offenses and among offenders would enter into the balance, and how procedural justice and due process would be ensured in the calibration of "just" differences.

Overall, in terms of persons with mental illness, the appropriateness or inappropriateness of processing them through the criminal justice system cannot be determined in a vacuum, in a piecemeal fashion, or without con-sideration of the broader external effects on the individual, society, and the criminal justice system. At present, there are no guiding standards that determine when it is appropriate to divert people out of the criminal justice system (for cause or crime type), or under what conditions people with chronic illness should be treated differently in terms of being held account-able, punished, or coerced into treatment, with the notable exception of those who meet standards for diminished capacity (for example, not guilty by reason of insanity) or contagion (for example, tuberculosis).

Correctional Health Care

People incarcerated in prison or jail have a constitutional right to receive treatment consistent with standards set forth in *Estelle v. Gamble* (1974) and *Ruiz v. Estelle* (1980).[12] In recent years, standards for mental health care have been further defined by the National Commission on Correctional Health Care (2003) and the American Psychiatric Association (2000). In general, these standards include, but are not limited to, screening; evaluating; providing crisis intervention; preventing suicide; providing psychiatric medications, case management, therapy/counseling, special programs and housing units, and reentry planning. In addition to constitutional mandates and professional standards, the public expects that, through the incarceration experience, individuals will be rehabili-tated prior to their release.

The challenge here does not involve understanding the intent of the court, the standards for treatment, or the public's expectations but the difficulty in securing the funding necessary to support this level of care. Correctional dollars are allocated according to mission, and the primary mission of corrections, as defined by state and local jurisdictions and perceived by correction officials, is custody and security. Funding for correctional health is more or less a residual, that amount left over after custody needs are satisfied. Whether the residual is sufficient to provide appropriate treatment (inside the gate) and subsequently restore people to their communities (outside the gate) is unknown. In general, there is very little information available on correctional health care spending, and even less on its appropriateness relative to inmate need and public expec-tations. The estimates that are available pertain to prisons in large measure because prisons are centrally funded by the state, whereas jails rely on local funding sources.

Correctional Health Care Funding

As a whole, the state departments of correction spent approximately $2.5 billion on prisoner medical and dental care in fiscal year 1996, which repre-sented approximately 12 percent of the total operating expenditure (Metzner, 2002). States vary in their spending on correctional health care. For example, correctional health care spending as a percentage of total prison operation expenditures is estimated at approximately 20 percent for New Hampshire, Nevada, and Wyoming, compared to 5 to 6 percent for Nebraska, Iowa, and Oregon. The prison system in New Jersey reportedly spent 7.5 percent of its annual operating budget, or $62 million, on correctional health care in fiscal year 1996. This translates into roughly $2,300 per inmate per year, or $6.30 per day. Metzner, reporting data on mental health spending by sixteen state prison systems, estimated that these states spent, on average, 17 percent of their correctional health care budget on mental health services, with a range among states from 5.4 percent (Minnesota) to 42.7 percent (Michigan) (1992). Mental health spending represented roughly 18 percent of the correctional health care budget for New Jersey prisons in 2002.[13]

There are no formal estimates of the size of correctional health care expenditures for jails. Efforts to calculate these estimates are frustrated in part by the decentralization of jail administration and in part by the way in which budgetary authority is structured within the county and jail. Funding for mental health services provided by jails comes from a variety of sources, including state and local governments (Goldstrom et al., 1998). Slightly less than half of jails reported some funding from public mental health systems (Goldstrom et al., 1998).

In a recent study of New Jersey jails, for example, only a few administrators were knowledgeable about their facility's spending on health care (Wolff et al., 2002), a result that can be attributed to the budgetary process itself. Funding for correctional health care in New Jersey is allocated at the county level. All counties set total correctional budgets but differed in the discretion and proportions granted to jail administrators. In some counties, administrators had full discretion over the total corrections' budget, while other counties required administrators to set aside a defined proportion of the total budget for health care. In some cases, the health budgets were carved out and the freeholders either negotiated directly with private contractors or assigned this responsibility to another county agency (for example, the county department of health). Counties choosing the carve-out approach frequently did not involve local administrators in the negotiation process. Given the complexity associated with budgeting and the variation among counties in New Jersey, it was not too surprising that jail administrators were unaware of spending levels on health care. Those administrators who controlled the full correctional budget reported health care spending at about 10 percent of their operating budgets.

Provision of Behavioral-Health Services in Correctional Settings

Approximately 95 percent of state correctional facilities reported providing some form of mental health treatment to prisoners (Beck and Maruschak, 2001). It is customary for these facilities to screen for mental illness at intake (78 percent); assess psychiatric problems (79 percent); deliver round-the-clock mental health care (63 percent); provide therapy or counseling (84 percent); prescribe psychotropic medications (83 percent); and provide reentry assistance (72 percent). On average, one in eight prisoners in state prisons is engaged in structured counseling (about 80 percent of the prevalence estimate) and one in ten is receiving psychotropic medications (nearly 60 percent of prevalence estimate) (Beck and Maruschak, 2001).[14]

Considerably less substance use treatment was available to state prisoners. Roughly one in four state prisoners received any treatment for substance use problems, with a higher percentage (40 percent) receiving treatment if they reported drug use at the time of their offense (Mumola, 1999). The most common treatment received was self-help group/peer counseling.

Some departments of corrections are establishing mental health systems inside the prison and jail, often upon court order (*Brad H v. City of New York*, 2001; *C.F. v. Terhune*, 1999). For example, according to the consent decree associated with the *C. F. v. Terhune* class action suit brought against the New Jersey Department of Corrections on behalf of prisoners with mental health problems confined in New Jersey prisons, the New Jersey Department of Corrections was required to build a comprehensive psychiatric capacity and to coordinate mental health treatment post release (Cevasco and Moratti, 2001). The New Jersey prison system now provides comprehensive mental health treatment to special needs inmates in five types of locations: a forensic psychiatric hospital, stabilization units, residential treatment units, transitional care units, and outpatient care for those in the general population.

This tiered approach to mental health treatment delivery typically includes (1) an inpatient unit for specialized treatment at the prison or a forensic hospital; (2) an acute or stabilization unit for close observation by nursing staff and stabilization; (3) a residential treatment unit designed to house stabilized inmates for an extended period of time; (4) a transitional care unit for stepping down the level of monitoring and preparing the individual for reentry to the general population; and (5) outpatient treatment for those in general population (Lovell et al., 2001; Lovell and Jemelka, 1998). In addition to these units, prisons may also provide life skills, personality management (for example, anger management), and domestic violence counseling, as well as treatment for addiction and sexual offending. Drug treatment activities in a correctional setting typically include only some form of detoxification and education or self-help, particularly Alcoholics Anonymous and Narcotics Anonymous (Wilson, 2000).[15] Therapeutic communities may be available for the treatment of drug addiction, as well as co-occurring mental illness (Peters and Matthews, 2003).[16] These programs, plus mental health treatment, are delivered by psychiatrists, psychologists, nurses, social workers, and correctional counselors, with supervision provided by correctional officers.

The majority of jails also report providing some type of mental health treatment (Goldstrom et al., 1998; Stephan, 2001). They are most likely to provide screening at intake (78 percent), followed by psychotropic medication (66 percent), twenty-four-hour care (47 percent), routine therapy or counseling (46 percent), psychiatric evaluation (38 percent), and reentry assistance (35 percent) (Stephan, 2001).[17] On average, mental health services are being provided at a level that is roughly half the estimated need (16 percent). It is reported that one in twelve inmates in local jails received mental health therapy or counseling (53 percent of the estimated need) and psychotropic medications (56 percent of the estimated need) (Stephan, 2001). Similarly, slightly more than half (51 percent) of all jail inmates received some form of substance use treatment, but the percentage increases to 60 percent for convicted jail inmates who were using at the time of their offense (Wilson, 2000).

As part of the New Jersey Correctional Health Care Study (Wolff et al., 2002), jail respondents were asked about the care they provided to inmates with mental illness. The typical treatment plan for serious mental illness at the reporting jails always included medications. These plans also included other components but these varied among facilities. In general, inmates with serious mental illness had access to individual therapy at a majority of jails (60 percent), while few jails offered these inmates group therapy (33 percent), case management (25 percent), or support groups (13 percent). In general, inmates with serious mental illness who were stable were placed in the general population. Two of the seventeen jails reported having a special unit for inmates with acute psychiatric problems.

Most jails place inmates with acute psychiatric problems either in the infirmary, close observation holding units, intake units, or disciplinary units. Only the infirmary is medically staffed. Three jails reported placing inmates with acute psychiatric problems in the general population. Inmates with serious mental illness who are stable most often are placed in the general population. Seven of the seventeen jails reported having special "protective" units available for inmates with special needs, including stable mental illness. A minority of these units was exclusively for inmates with mental illness. Facilities with larger inmate populations were more likely to have special units or programs for persons with mental illness, although some-medium sized facilities had special programs while some larger facilities did not.

In describing the management of a "typical" case of mental illness, nearly 90 percent of respondents reported having access to "front-line" medications for the treatment of serious mental illness. Only two respondents indicated that they had access to formularies that did not include newer medications. Most respondents indicated that inmates with chronic conditions were maintained on the medications that they were taking in the community. However, it was reported that for some chronically ill inmates with longer expected stays, lower-cost medication regimes were frequently substituted. The cost of medications for serious mental illness was a leading concern among most respondents.

Mental Health Delivery System

Correctional health and mental health services are delivered by professional staff either employed by the facility or provided through contract with an outside agency. The outside contractors might be a large national organization, such as Prison Health Services, Inc (PHS) or Correctional Medical Services (CMS), a regional or local provider group, or an individual provider. Contracting arrangements are not uniform. A correctional facility might contract for medical services, mental health services, and addiction services separately. Or, alternatively, it might contract with a single managed care group for a comprehensive medical package after which this group carves out some particular services to regional or local providers or specialty groups. By contrast, the facility might provide some services in-house (say, medical services) but contract for specialty services (for example, mental health services). In addition to health and mental health services, facilities frequently contract for data, claims, and utilization management.

Although contracting is prevalent in the correctional health care field, very little evidence is available on the distribution and characteristics of the contracting process. According to information available on the websites of PHS and CMS, together they claim to be covering approximately 460,000 inmates located in 700 facilities (prisons and jails). Nearly 60 percent of jail jurisdictions report paying for contracted services either on a fee-for-service or on a per capita basis (Stephan, 2001).

Quality of care within correctional settings has not been measured or monitored in any systematic or rigorous fashion. Most often quality is associated with being accredited by the National Commission on Correctional Health Care, which certifies that certain management and delivery guidelines have been met regarding availability and types of treatment on site, staffing and training arrangements, governance, and legal requirements. The National Commission on Correctional Health Care accreditation "documents an efficient, well-managed system of health care delivery" (National Commission on Correctional Health Care, 2004).

Accreditation, however, does not address quality in terms of clinical process or outcomes. It is well known that structural measures are not suitable proxy measures for clinical quality in the delivery of health care (Institute of Medicine, 2000). Measures of process of care and recovery outcomes are crucial, yet this information is not available for correctional settings. To assess quality, at a minimum, information is needed on who gets the services (in other words, are treatments effectively matched to needs, how much unmet need is there) and how "treatment" is defined and maintained (for example, what does "psychotropic medication management" mean in terms of availability of medications, dosing, maintenance monitoring, and polypharmacy).

Challenges to Inter- and Intra-System Coordination

Like the mental health system, the criminal justice system is fragmented and highly decentralized. The performance of these systems is a product of their disorganization, and it is for this reason that coordination efforts have received considerable emphasis over the years (Wolff, 2002a, 2002b). It is important, however, to keep in mind that there is nothing new about the disorganization within these systems or in the efforts to coordinate them, individually or collectively. Dating back to the 1960s, efforts have been advanced to coordinate subsystems and across systems, and across settings. History shows that, in spite of the policy and its incentive mechanism, disorganization has persisted. These repeated failures suggest that past interventions have not been adequately sensitive to the dynamics within these two nonsystems that keep them independent and fractionalized.

To the extent that coordination initiatives can be effective, they must appeal to the interests of those who are directly involved in the exchange. This section begins with a brief review of the evidence on coordination initiatives and concludes with a discussion of the barriers to coordination with emphasis on how they work against coordination as it pertains to people with mental illness in the criminal justice system.

Coordination Initiatives and Their Effectiveness

Coordination initiatives have taken many forms. In the criminal justice system, there have been efforts to unify parts of subsystems, such as the trial courts, into a single administrative unit (Tobin, 1999). Other initiatives have been designed to encourage collaboration between the court and community with the goal of addressing particular types of problems within the trial courts' jurisdiction, such as domestic violence, handgun violence, drug use, and mental illness (Rottman et al., 1998). Recently, there have been a variety of initiatives intended to coordinate the actions of the criminal justice and mental health systems in responding to the special needs of persons with mental illness. The point of intervention varies; some programs intervene at the level of the police, while others focus on the jail or courts. Specific initiatives have been described in the academic literature (Goldkamp and Irons-Guynn, 2000; Lamb and Reston-Parham, 1996; Steadman et al., 1995; 1999; Wolff, 2002) and the *Consensus Project Report* (Council of State Governments, 2002).

Whether diversion programs are (cost) effective has been the focus of a number of evaluations. The extant evidence, however, is thin and, in most cases, lacks methodological rigor. In general, diversion programs, intervening at the point of the police, jail, or court, do engage people with mental illness and reroute them to mental health treatment, which is the primary objective of these programs. But, whether these interventions are better than other types of interventions is unclear in part because the study designs did not include a comparison group and in part because issues of selection bias are not accounted for in the analysis.

Moreover, these evaluations typically ignore the impact of the local context, such as police handling of deviance, funding of mental health and substance abuse treatment programs, evaluating crime rates, interpreting civil commitment criteria, and so forth. Also, outcomes are defined simplistically and include variables such as "received treatment" and "rearrested." What it means to receive treatment is unclear, as is the meaning of rearrest. For example, subjects may have contact with the police but avoid arrest because there are "diversion" arrangements in place.

Despite these methodological limitations, several lessons can be drawn from this literature. The first concerns the effect of social control. Many diversion interventions involve some form of social control, whereby the subject is closely supervised by an actor from the criminal justice system (for example, judge, probation/parole officer) or mental health system (for example, a caseworker). The research shows that increasing direct supervision within diversion models is positively correlated with reincarceration. Turner and Petersilia (1992) randomly assigned inmates leaving prison to an intensive supervision program or traditional supervision. After twelve months, 18 percent of those assigned to traditional supervision were reincarcerated, compared to 30 percent of those assigned to intensive supervision.

Research by Draine and Solomon on the assertive community treatment (ACT) model indicates that those receiving more intensive specialized forensic ACT were at greater risk for returning to jail than those getting less intensive services (Draine and Solomon, 1994; Solomon and Draine, 1995). A follow-up study found similar dynamics among individuals on probation and parole that had an intensive case manager (Draine and Solomon, 2001). It appears that service models focusing on monitoring and control increase the awareness of deviations from probation or parole conditions, which undermine efforts toward social integration or rehabilitation in the community.

The literature, however, affirms the promise of case management. Ventura et al. explored the impact of case management for people with mental illness leaving jail (1998). They found that case management was effective in reducing the likelihood of returning to jail. The case management program was jail based and promoted transition to community-based case managers. Examining differences between this case management program and the ACT team studied by Solomon and Draine raises important questions about the structure of services in incarcerated settings. The service in the Ventura et al. study was jail based and relied on existing services in the community. One of the key ingredients of a successful release program may be engagement inside the jail facility and/or a transition to existing services in the community as opposed to keeping specialized "forensic" service teams on the outside.

Pretrial diversion programs are expected to reduce the congestion within the criminal justice system. But some within the field have argued that these programs have the opposite effect because they widen the court's net by diverting people to supervision who ordinarily would not have been prosecuted (Binder and Geis, 1984). Precisely because diversion programs represent "tickets to treatment," police officers and district attorneys who might otherwise have dismissed these cases now have an incentive to keep them within the criminal justice system. Net widening has been found in evaluations of drug courts (Belenko, 2002) and other pretrial programs (Nuffield, 1997). If supply drives demand, building diversion capacity may serve to encourage its use in ways that will invite more supervised and perhaps punitive treatment.

Absent from the mental health services literature is any discussion of factors other than illness on the success of diversion, in spite of the fact that the ability to (re)integrate into society in prosocial ways depends on factors related to the availability of housing, employment, and crime-free neighborhoods. For example, the drug court literature shows greater success for participants who are employed compared to those who are unemployed (Belenko, 2002). Integrating criminological theory into the development of diversion programs involves incorporating the complexity of social and developmental factors, which might be related to both criminality and the course of mental illness. There is potential here for developing provocative and testable frameworks that blend theoretical insights from criminological research and mental health services research. Such frameworks can lead to new interventions, new research questions, and improved services to assist persons with mental illness who have encounters with the criminal justice system.

Barriers to Coordination

While there is limited evidence on the effectiveness of coordination efforts, such as diversion, there is strong political and social momentum behind the strategy of diverting people with mental illness out of the criminal justice system and better coordinating the mental health and criminal justice systems to facilitate diversion. Getting the approach to work, however, requires understanding the factors that currently reinforce disorganization within and between the two systems (Wolff, 2002a, 2002b).

Lack of Interest or Motivation. Coordination requires cooperation, and cooperation requires people to change their behavior in ways that accommodate the interests of others. Resistance often originates at the individual level because individuals within the units of mental health and criminal justice systems already have responsibilities that exceed their efficiency. In particular, dockets for judges and caseloads for parole and probation officers have increased over time, as census levels have been rising in jails and prisons.

It is obvious, given the numbers, why individual actors and agencies within the criminal justice system would be motivated to cooperate with the mental health system. Yet, the notion of cooperation here is typically framed in terms of a wholesale shifting, via diversion mechanisms, of people with mental illness back to the system that, from the perspective of their system's expertise, should have been providing services in the first place. While it is understandable why actors within the criminal justice system would want to shift responsibility back to the mental health system, it is equally understandable why the actors within the mental health system would be resistant, especially when they fear getting clients with histories of violence, like person A described in the earlier text box.

There are likely to be both costs and benefits to any exchange between the systems. Negotiating the terms of the exchange in responsibilities requires someone's time, of which no one perceives having a surplus. Scheduling meetings alone can seem to take too much time. Moreover, neither system rewards individuals for negotiating such arrangements, which dampens any individual or organizational motivation to reallocate time to achieve cross-unit or system coordination. Lack of time to build bridges and to negotiate the flow of people across them, as well as the lack of internal rewards, combine together to reinforce rigid boundaries between agencies and across systems.

Specialized Function and Competence. Systems tend to grow through specialization. As the demand for services expands, agencies, units, and individuals within the criminal justice and mental health systems have become more specialized in their responsibilities and their production styles, which serve to define professional boundaries. To be a professional within these specialized units, individual and group behavior must be in accordance with a particular set of role definitions. Deviating from professional norms not only risks disaffiliation but also the appellation of not being professional.

By contrast, performing within the limits of professional norms, individuals are more likely to be rewarded through promotion. Legal liability, especially related to malpractice and other forms of civil litigation for untoward outcomes related to misconduct, encourages compliance with professional standards of behavior. Strict conformity to professional norms, especially for officers with social control responsibilities, also promotes safety. In the criminal justice system, not following protocols can result in serious injury to the officer and the public.

For all these reasons, there is strong pressure for individuals to conform to the norms of their profession, and this pressure reinforces a sense of competency that is tied to specialized functions. Limiting their jobs to functions defined by protocols and reinforced by professional norms, training and experience, builds a sense of competency and mastery. Adding cross-disciplinary functions, such as therapeutic case management for parole officers, might be resisted at the individual level because these functions are in conflict with prevailing professional norms, require technical competencies that do not exist, or access to information that is unavailable or too costly to retrieve.

Risk Aversion. People are adverse to change, since the management of persons with mental illness often become front-page news. The names of agencies (for example, mental health program or correctional setting), along with the names of the responsible administrators (for example, CEO or warden) are listed prominently. And, in some cases, the names of individual providers are also mentioned. These events frequently trigger a response from advocates and advocacy organizations, often culminating in political pressure and litigation and more press coverage.

Many communities have experienced violent events that trigger moral panic or public outrage. In New Jersey, a recent murder of a person with mental illness in custody by another person with mental illness also in custody resulted in dozens of articles and letters to editors in local papers, a series of investigations of the jail, and draft bills to the legislature regarding diversion. In Washington State, the murder of a beloved, retired fire captain by a person with mental illness eventually led to a revision in the state's commitment statute and fueled the implementation of a mental health court, later dedicated in memory of the victim (Sims, 1999).

Such negative exposure can damage personal reputations and the public's confidence in its elected officials. Events like this grow in significance in the criminal justice system where people in authority are elected and agency budgets are determined within a political process. Because position can be gained, retained, and lost by media coverage, leadership within agencies is likely to view coordination through the lens of risk. Any bad event that can be traced to the individual or organization holds downside risk. For this reason, elected officials (and their operatives) can be expected to be averse toward activities that might bear negatively on their public image. For example, judges of mental health courts know they are one bad outcome away from extinction.

Likewise, risk aversion works against coordination from the perspective of mental health agencies and providers. They, too, do not want the negative press associated with a bad outcome. Providers can limit their risk exposure by avoiding complex and difficult patients. This creates incentives for providers to look for legitimate reasons to deny responsibility for these cases. This may involve claiming the person does not meet residency or service eligibility requirements, has not advanced through proper bureaucratic channels, is too dangerous, or is untreatable (Wolff, 2002c).

Individual Responsibility. Determining "service" responsibility for persons with co-occurring disorders, combined as mental health and addiction or behavioral health and criminal deviance, is left more to chance than to formal design. In most cases, responsibility is borne by the agency that has the lowest entry barriers, which in recent years has been the criminal justice system. In practice, no system has any interest in absorbing the full responsibility, and no system can be effective by assuming only partial responsibility.

The privatization movement within corrections and the mental health system has fostered fragmentation of responsibility. In correctional settings, there may be separate contracts among medical, mental health, and addiction services. Once these contracts shift and set responsibilities, each side of the contract can deflect responsibility to the other while inmates get lost in the bureaucratic shuffle. Furthermore, private providers on the "inside" often do not have connections to community-based agencies, making it more difficult for them to coordinate services at the point of release.

As a consequence, an organizational stalemate of sorts is likely to persist as long as there is a lack of clear guidance on who is responsible for what, how responsibility is shared when disorders co-occur, and how accountability will be measured and monitored. In the absence of clear lines of responsibility, individual actors will act in ways that seem efficient from their individual perspectives even though, when combined, they produce poorer system and social outcomes.

Recommendations

Embedded within the criminal justice and mental health system are incentives that encourage and reward independence, specialization, professionalism, and risk aversion, which combine to foster diminished responsibility. These incentives influence how agencies interact within their own system and with the units of other systems. In recent years, many recommendations and policies have been advanced to encourage collaboration between the mental health and criminal justice systems. But these recommendations and policies typically focus on program development, not incentives. These programs, however, are like fish swimming upstream—most will die swimming against the current. For coordination efforts to work, the current needs to change. For this reason, the recommendations here focus on rethinking the incentives that have historically perpetuated the practice of diminished responsibility.

Recommendation # 1: Create Clarity through Consistent Definitions

- Develop a classification system for defining (1) "pure" cases of biological and criminal disorder and (2) "blended" cases of biological and criminal disorder.

- Develop criteria for "appropriate" diversion to treatment that are integrated with the definitions of pure and blended disorders, as well as consistent with principles of horizontal and vertical equity and community-based standards of normalization.

Recommendation # 2: Develop "Coordination" as a Performance Goal

- Develop performance measures of coordination at the system, agency, program, and individual level.

- Develop interdisciplinary training on coordination, and provide training in integrated sessions with representatives from cross-system agencies and programs together.

Recommendation # 3: Encourage Coordination through Incentives

- Connect promotion, salary increases, and budgets to performance on coordination measures at the individual and program level. Add coordination measures to contracts with providers.

- Reward parole and probation officers for success in areas of social integration.

- Create incentives that encourage individuals on the ground level to investigate ways to facilitate appropriate diversion and to identify reasons why diversion succeeds or fails.

Recommendation # 4: Promote Change through Investment

- Create education programs for prosecutors and judges on mental illness, alternatives to criminal processing, and the structure of treatment options within the community.

- Develop "fast response" mechanisms within the court that provide information and options to judges or prosecutors considering decisions that will move individuals into the system for reasons related to unstable behavior or lifestyle.

- Develop shared information systems that facilitate the movement of information that is central to the effective management of illness and social integration.

Recommendation # 5: Integrate Funding and Services

- Blend housing, medical, and vocational funds and contract for "whole" services delivered by a single source.

- Establish a community services center that provides comprehensive health and social services, responds to concerns about disordered behavior in the community, and receives individuals appropriately diverted from police, prosecutors, courts, and correctional settings.

Endnotes

[1] This section focuses primarily on the connection among mental illness, treatment, and criminal deviance; connections that underpin the decarceration movement for persons with mental illness. Where possible, information about substance use is provided as it relates to this more general discussion. The connection among substance use, treatment, and crime is different in important ways, making it conceptually difficult to describe both together. For a concise review of the criminalization of substance use, as well as treatment in correctional settings, see Peters and Matthews (2003).

[2] In general, prisons and jails differ by the inmate's length of sentence; prisons hold people convicted of felonies who are serving sentences longer than a year, while jails hold people awaiting adjudication and those convicted of misdemeanors and serving sentences of a year or less.

[3] Large numbers of prisoners convicted of drug-related crimes motivated a similar decarceration trend in the late 1980s (see Nolan, 2003).

[4] A similar crime pattern exists for persons with a substance use illness (Bureau of Justice Statistics, 1994). However, for these individuals, activities related to the drug market are motivating a significant amount of the criminal behavior and violence. In particular, roughly 16 percent of convicted jail inmates reported committing their offense to get money to buy drugs (Wilson, 2000). Drug trafficking is correlated with violent crime (Bureau of Justice Statistics, 1994).

[5] The level is higher for studies with longer follow-up periods, which ranged from twelve to thirty-six months.

[6] This is not true for substance use. Substance use manifests itself in a uniquely criminal way. Drug addiction, for example, involves the use and abuse of illicit drugs, which are illegal. Trafficking in these substances is also illegal. Likewise, people with substance use addictions tend to engage in crime to support their habits (Wilson, 2000).

[7] Similar results were found by Clark et al. (1999).

[8] The majority (66 percent) of these were in state or federal prisons; the remainder in local jails.

[9] Inmates with mental illness have been found to serve longer sentences than their non-mentally ill counterparts (Harris and Dagadakis, 2004). This evidence is consistent with reports from correctional officials suggesting that inmates with mental illness are more likely to complete their full sentences in prison, meaning they are more likely to be released from prison without parole supervision.

[10] For more detail on these initiatives, see special issue of *Crime and Delinquency*, 36, January 1990.

[11] The argument to divert people with substance use illness to treatment in lieu of incarceration has focused more on the ineffectiveness of incarceration as a rehabilitation strategy and its expense (Nolan, 2003; Office of National Drug Control Policy, 2004).

[12] The courts have repeatedly rejected any notion of a constitutional right to substance abuse treatment or rehabilitation in correctional settings, except in cases of "deliberate indifference" (Peters and Matthews, 2003).

[13] These statistics were not available for mental health and substance use treatment, separately.

[14] Substance abuse treatment is provided by the majority of jails (73 percent), with larger jails being more likely to provide some form of drug treatment (Wilson, 2000). Treatment (in other words, detoxification units, group/individual counseling, and residential programs) was provided by approximately 43 percent of jail facilities. Nearly two-thirds of jails reported providing access to drug or alcohol education or self-help groups (Wilson, 2000).

[15] See Office of National Drug Control Policy Fact Sheet (2001) and National Institute on Drug Abuse Research Monograph, Number 118 (1991), especially chapters by Lipton et al., and Peters and May, as well as Peters and Matthews (2003), for a review of drug treatment in correctional settings.

[16] Edens et al. (1997) provide an overview of treatment programs for co-occurring disorders in correctional settings.

[17] Considerably higher service estimates were reported by Goldstrom et al. (1998). Based on a national jail survey conducted in 1993, they report the following service availability estimates in order of most common: crisis intervention (88 percent of jails), psychotropic medications (85 percent), mental health screening at booking (84 percent), follow-up evaluations (73 percent), formal therapy (66 percent), inpatient hospital care (64 percent), and case management services (64 percent).

References

Abramson, M. F. 1972. The Criminalization of Mentally Disordered Behavior. *Hospital and Community Psychiatry*, 3(4), 101-105.

Agnew, R. 1985. A Revised Strain Theory of Delinquency. *Social Forces*, 64, 151-167.

Agnew, R., H. R. White. 1992. An Empirical Test of General Strain Theory. *Criminology*, 30, 475-500.

Akers, R. L. 2000. *Criminological Theories*. Los Angeles: California: Roxbury Publishing Company.

American Psychiatric Association. 1998. Fact Sheet: *Violence and Mental Illness*. Retrieved January 15, 2002, from: http://www.psych.org/public_info/violence.pdf.

___. 2000. *Guidelines for Psychiatric Services in Jails and Prisons, Psychiatric Services in Jails and Prisons: A Task Force of the American Psychiatric Association, Second Edition*, Washington, DC: American Psychiatric Association

Bachrach, L. L. 1979. Planning Mental Health Services for Chronic Patients. *Hospital and Community Psychiatry*, 30(6), 387-393.

___.1982. Young Adult Chronic Patients: An Analytical Review of the Literature. *Hospital and Community Psychiatry*, 33, 189-197.

___. 1987. An Overview: Model Programs for the Schizophrenic Patient. In H. F. Lamb, ed., *New Directions for Mental Health Service: Number 35. Leona Bachrach Speaks, Selected Speeches and Lectures*. San Francisco: Jossey-Bass. pp. 13-27.

Bauer, L. and S. D. Owens. 2004. *Justice Expenditure and Employment in the United States, 2001*. U.S. Department of Justice, NCJ 202792.

Beck, A. J. and L. M. Maruschak. 2001. *Mental Health Treatment in State Prisons, 2000*. Bureau of Justice Statistics, NCJ 188215. Washington, DC: U.S. Department of Justice.

Belenko, S. 2002. The Challenges of Conducting Research in Drug Treatment Court Settings. *Substance Use and Misuse*, 37 (12 and 13), 1635-1664.

Binder, A. and G. Geis. 1984. Ad populum Argumentation in Criminology: Juvenile Diversion as Rhetoric. *Crime and Delinquency*, 30(4), 624-647.

Bittner, E. 1967. Police Discretion in Emergency Apprehension of Mentally Ill Persons. *Social Problems*, 14, 278-292.

Brad H v City of New York. 2001. 188 Misc. 2d 470; 729 N.Y.S.2d 348; 2001 N.Y. Misc. LEXIS 221.

Brill, H. and B. Malzberg. 1962. Statistical Report on the Arrest Record of Male Ex-Patients Released From New York State Mental Hospitals During the Period 1946-8. In *Criminal Acts of Ex-mental Hospital Patients* (Supplement No. 153). Washington, D.C.: American Psychiatric Association Mental Hospital Service.

Bureau of Justice Statistics. 1994. Fact Sheet: *Drug-Related Crime*. Report: NCJ-149286, Office of Justice Statistics, U.S. Department of Justice.

Burt, M. R., L.Y. Aron, E. Lee, and J. Valente. 2001. *Helping America's Homeless: Emergency Shelter or Affordable Housing?* Washington, DC: The Urban Institute Press.

Campbell, J., S. Stefan, and A. Loder. 1994. Putting Violence in Context. *Hospital and Community Psychiatry*, 45, 633.

Carter, J. H. 1998. Treating the Severely Mentally Ill in Prisons and Jails. *Forensic Examiner*, 7(3-4), 28-29.

Cevasco, R. and D. Moratti. 2001. New Jersey's Mental Health Program. In American Correctional Association, *The State of Corrections, Proceedings, American Correctional Association Annual Conferences, 2000*, Lanham, Maryland: American Correctional Association. pp 159-168.

C.F. v Terhune. 1999. 67 F. Supp. 2d 401, 1999, U.S. Dist. LEXIS 15677.

Clark, R. E., S. K. Ricketts, and G. J. McHugo.1999. Legal System Involvement and Costs for Persons in Treatment for Severe Mental Illness and Substance Use Disorders. *Psychiatric Services*, 50(5), 641-647.

Clear, T. R. 1998. Societal Responses to the President's Crime Commission: A Thirty Year Retrospective. In U.S. Department of Justice, Office of Justice Programs, *The Challenge of Crime in a Free Society: Looking Back, Looking Forward*. Washington, DC: U.S. Department of Justice.

Cole, G. F. 1997. Criminal Justice: *Law and Politics, Sixth Edition*. Belmont, California: Wadsworth Publishing Company.

Cole, G. F. and C. E. Smith. 1996. *Criminal Justice in America*. Belmont, California: Wadsworth Publishing Company.

Conference of Chief Justices and Conference of State Court Administrators. 2000. In *Support of Problem-Solving Courts*. Retrieved on August 29, 2004 from http://cosca. ncsc.dni.us/Resolutions/resolutionproblemsolvingcts.html.

Council of State Governments. 2002. *Criminal Justice/Mental Health Consensus Project*. New York: Council of State Governments.

DeFrances, C. J. 2002. *Prosecutors in State Courts, 2001*. Bureau of Justice Statistics, NCJ 193441, Washington, DC: U.S. Department of Justice.

Dennis, D. L., J. C. Buckner, and I. S. Lipton. 1991. A Decade of Research and Services for Homeless Mentally Ill: Where Do We Stand? *American Psychologist*, 46, 1129-1138.

Dilulio, J. J. 1993. Rethinking the Criminal Justice System: Toward a New Paradigm. In *Performance Measures for the Criminal Justice System*. Discussion Papers from the BJS-Princeton Project, NCJ-143505. Washington, DC: U.S. Department of Justice.

Ditton, P. 1999. *Mental Health and Treatment of Inmates and Probationers*. Bureau of Justice Statistics, NCJ 174463, Washington, DC: U.S. Department of Justice.

Draine, J. and P. Solomon. 1994. Jail Recidivism and the Intensity of Case Management Services among Homeless Persons with a Mental Illness Leaving Jail. *The Journal of Psychiatry and Law*, 22, 245-261.

____. 2001. The Use of Threats of Incarceration in a Psychiatric Probation and Parole Service. *American Journal of Orthopsychiatry*, 71, 262-267.

Durham, M. 1989. The Impact of Deinstitutionalization on the Current Treatment of the Mentally Ill. *International Journal of Law and Psychiatry*, 12, 117-131.

Edens, J. F., R. H. Peters, H. A. Hills. 1997. Treating Prison Inmates with Co-Occurring Disorders: An Integrative Review of Existing Programs. *Behavioral Sciences and the Law*, 15, 439-457.

Eisenstein, J. and H. Jacob.1977. *Felony Justice*. Boston: Little Brown.

Estelle v. Gamble. 1976. 429 U.S. 97.

Federal Task Force on Homelessness and Severe Mental Illness. 1992. *Outcasts on Main Street: A Report of the Federal Task Force on Homelessness and Severe Mental Illness*. Delmar, New York: National Resource Center on Homelessness and Mental Illness.

Freed, D. J. 1970. The Nonsystem of Criminal Justice. In J. S. Campbell, J. R. Shaid, and D. P. Stang, eds., *Law and Order Reconsidered: Report of the Task Force on Law and Law Enforcement to the National Commission on the Causes and Prevention of Violence*. New York, NY: Praeger Publishers, pp. 263-275.

Glaze, L. E. and S. Palla. 2004. *Probation and Parole in the United States*, 2003. U.S. Department of Justice, NCJ 205336, Washington, DC: U.S. Department of Justice.

Goldkamp, J. S. and C. Irons-Guynn. 2000. *Emerging Judicial Strategies for the Mentally Ill in the Criminal Caseload: Mental Health Courts in Fort Lauderdale, Seattle, San Bernardino, and Anchorage*. Crime and Justice Research Institute Monograph (NCJ 182504), Bureau of Justice Assistance.

Goldstrom, I., M. Henderson, A. Male, R. W. Manderscheid. 1998. Jail Mental Health Services: A National Survey. In R. W. Manderscheid and J. J. Henderson, eds., *Mental Health, United States, 2000*. Washington, D.C.: Government Printing Office. pp. 29-42.

Grob, G. N. 1994. *The Mad Among Us*. New York: Free Press.

Harris, V. and C. Dagadakis. 2004. Length of Incarceration: Was there Parity for Mentally Disordered Offenders? *International Journal of Law and Psychiatry*, 27, 387-393.

Harrison, P. M. and J. C., Karberg. 2004. *Prison and Jail Inmates at Midyear, 2003*. Bureau of Justice Statistics, NCJ 203947. Washington, DC: US Department of Justice.

Haney, C. and D. Specter. 2003. Treatment Rights in Uncertain Legal Times. In J. B. Ashford, B. D. Sales, and W. H. Reid, eds., *Treating Adult and Juvenile Offenders with Special Needs*. Washington, DC: American Psychological Association, pp. 51-80.

Heumann, M. 1997. Adapting to Plea Bargaining: Prosecutors. In G. F. Cole, ed., *Criminal Justice: Law and Politics, Sixth Edition*. Belmont, California: Wadsworth Publishing Company. pp. 177-195.

Hickman, M. J. and B. A. Reaves. 2003. *Local Police Departments, 2000*. Report of the U.S. Department of Justice, NCJ 196002, U.S. Department of Justice.

Hiday, V. A. 1999. Mental Illness and the Criminal Justice System. In A. Horwitz and T. Scheid, eds., *The Handbook for the Study of Mental Health: Social Contexts, Theories, and Systems*. Cambridge: Cambridge University Press. pp. 508-525.

Hodgins, S. 2001. The Major Mental Disorders and Crime: Stop Debating and Start Treating and Preventing. *International Journal of Law and Psychiatry*, 24, 427-446.

Hora, P., W. Schma, and J. Rosenthal. 1999. Therapeutic Jurisprudence and the Drug Court Movement: Revolutionizing the Criminal Justice System's Response to Drug Abuse and Crime in America. *Notre Dame Law Review*, 74, 439-555.

Hughes, T. A., D. J. Wilson, and A. J. Beck. 2001. *Trends in State Parole, 1990-2000*. Bureau of Justice Statistics, NCJ 184735. Washington, DC: U.S. Department of Justice.

Human Rights Watch. 2003. *Ill-Equipped: U.S. Prisons and Offenders with Mental Illness*. New York: Human Rights Watch.

Institute of Medicine. 2000. *Crossing the Quality Chasm: A New Health System for the 21st Century. Report of the Committee on Quality of Health Care in America*, Washington, DC: National Academy Press.

Jemelka, R., E. Trupin, and J. A. Chiles. 1989. The Mentally Ill in Prisons: A Review. *Hospital and Community Psychiatry*, 40(5), 481-491.

Kelling G. L., C. M. Coles. 1997. *Fixing Broken Windows: Restoring Order and Reducing Crime in Our Communities.* New York: Simon and Schuster.

Kessler, R. C., E. J. Costello, K. R Merikangas, and T. B. Usten. 2001. Psychiatric Epidemiology: Recent Advances and Future Directions. In R. W. Manderscheid and J. J. Henderson, eds., *Mental Health, United States*, 2000. Washington, D.C.: Government Printing Office. pp. 29-42.

Kupers, T. 1999. *Prison Madness: The Mental Health Crisis Behind Bars and What We Must Do About It.* San Francisco, California: Jossey-Bass.

Kupers, T. 2000. Beware of Easy Answers for the Mental Health Crisis Behind Bars. *Fortune News*, Fall, 1-5. Retrieved on January 21, 2002, from: http://www.fortune society.org/fall00-06.htm

Lamb, H. R. 1982. Young Adult Chronic Patients: The New Drifters. *Hospital and Community Psychiatry*, 33(6), 465-468.

Lamb, R. H. and R. W. Grant. 1982. The Mentally Ill in an Urban County Jail. *Archives of General Psychiatry*, 39, 17-22.

Lamb, H. R. and C. Reston-Parham. 1996. Court Intervention to Address the Mental Health Need of Mentally Ill Offenders. *Psychiatric Services*, 47, 275-281.

Lamb, R. H. and L. S. Weinberger. 1998. Persons with Severe Mental Illness in Jails and Prisons: A Review. *Psychiatric Services*, 49(4): 483-492.

Lamb, R. H., L. E. Weinberger, and B. H. Gross. 2004. Mentally Ill Persons in the Criminal Justice Perspectives. *Psychiatric Quarterly*, 75(2), 107-126.

Lewis, C. 1953. The Humanitarian Theory of Punishment. *Res Judicatae*, VI (June), 224-230.

Lewis, D. A., S. Riger, H. Rosenberg, H. Wagenaar, A. J. Lurigio, and S. Reed. 1991. *Worlds of the Mentally Ill.* Carbondale, Illinois: Southern Illinois University Press.

Lindquist, P. and P. Allebeck. 1990. Schizophrenia and Crime. A Longitudinal Follow-Up of 644 Schizophrenics in Stockholm. *British Journal of Psychiatry*, 157, 345-50.

Link, B., H. Andrews, and F. T. Cullen.1992. The Violent and Illegal Behavior of Mental Patients Reconsidered. *American Sociological Review*, 57, 275-292.

Link, B. G., J. C. Phelan, M. Bresnahan, A. Stueve, and B. A. Pescosolido. 1999. Public Conceptions of Mental Illness: Labels, Causes, Dangerousness, and Social Distance. *American Journal of Public Health*, 89, 1328-1333.

Lipton, D. S., G. P Falkin, and H. K. Wexler. 1991. Drug Treatment Services in Jails. In National Institute on Drug Abuse, *Drug Abuse Treatment in Prison and Jails. Research Monograph, Number 118*. Retrieved on August 29, 2004 from http://www.drugabuse.gov /pdf/monographs/download118.html

Lovell, D., D. Allen, C. Johnson, and R. Jemelka. 2001. Evaluating the Effectiveness of Residential Treatment for Prisoners with Mental Illnesses. *Criminal Justice and Behavior*, 28, 83-104.

Lovell, D. and R. Jemelka. 1998. Coping with Mental Illness in Prisons. *Family and Community Health*, 21, 54-60.

Metzner, J. L. 2002. Class Action Litigation in Correctional Psychiatry. *Journal of the American Academy of Psychiatry and the Law*, 30, 19-29.

Monahan, J. and H. Steadman.1983. Crime and Mental Disorder: An Epidemiological Approach. In N. Morris and M. Tonry, eds., Crime and Justice: *An Annual Review of Research*. Chicago, Illinois: University of Chicago Press. pp.145-189.

Monahan, J., H. J. Steadman, E. Silver, P. S. Appelbaum, P. C. Robbins, D. P. Mulvey, L. H. Roth, T. Grisso, and S. Banks. 2002. *Rethinking Risk Assessment: The MacArthur Study of Mental Disorder and Violence*. New York: Oxford University Press. pp. 31-32; 44-45.

Morenoff, J. D., R. J Sampson, and S. W. Raudenbush. 2001. *Neighborhood Inequality, Collective Efficacy, and the Spatial Dynamics of Urban Violence*. Research Report No. 00-451. Population Studies Center, Institute of Social Research, University of Michigan.

Mumola, C. J. 1999. *Substance Abuse and Treatment, State and Federal Prisoners*, 1997. Bureau of Justice Statistics, NCJ 172871. Washington, DC: U.S. Department of Justice.

Nardulli, P., J. Eisenstein, and R. Flemming. 1988. *Tenor of Justice: Criminal Courts and the Guilty Plea Process*. Urbana, Illinois: University of Illinois Press.

National Commission on Correctional Health Care. 2003. *Standards for Health Services in Prisons, Third Edition*. Chicago, Illinois: National Commission on Correctional Health Care.

___. 2004. *Introduction to Accreditation*. Retrieved on August 29, 2004 from http://www.ncchc.org/accred/

National Institute on Drug Abuse. 1991. *Drug Abuse Treatment in Prison and Jails. Research Monograph, Number 118*. Retrieved on August 29, 2004 from http://www. drugabuse.gov/pdf/monographs/download118.html

Nolan, J. L. 2003. Reinventing Justice: *The American Drug Court Movement.* Princeton, New Jersey: Princeton University Press.

Nuffield, J. 1997. *Diversion Programs for Adults*. Report JS4-1/1997-5: Public Works and Government Services Canada. Retrieved on August 27, 2004 from http://www.sgc.gc.ca.

Office of National Drug Control Policy. 2001. *Drug Treatment in the Criminal Justice System*. NCJ-181857. Retrieved on August 29, 2004 from http://www.whitehousedrug pol icy.gov/publications/factsht/treatment.

Office of National Statistics. 1998. *Psychiatric Morbidity among Prisoners in England and Wales*, London: The Stationery Office.

Penrose, L. S. 1939. Mental Disease and Crime: Outline of a Comparative Study of European Statistics. *British Journal of Medical Psychology*, 18, 1-15.

Peters, R. H. and C. O. Matthews. 2003. Substance Abuse Treatment Programs in Prisons and Jails. In T. J. Fagan and R. K. Ax, eds., *Correctional Mental Health Handbook*. Thousand Oaks, California: Sage Publications, Inc.

Peters, R. H. and R. May. 1991. Correctional Drug Abuse Treatment in the United States: An Overview. In National Institute on *Drug Abuse, Drug Abuse Treatment in Prison and Jails. Research Monograph, Number 118*. Retrieved on August 29, 2004 from http://www. drugabuse.gov/pdf/monographs/download118.html

President's Commission on Law Enforcement and Administration of Justice. 1967. *The Challenge of Crime in a Free Society*. Washington, D.C.: U.S. Government Printing Office.

President's New Freedom Commission on Mental Health. 2003. *Achieving the Promise: Transforming Mental Health Care in America*. Washington DC. www.mentalhealthcommission. gov/contactus.html

Regier, D., M. Farmer, D. Rae, B. Locke, S. Keith, L. Judd, and F. Goodwin. 1990. Comorbidity of Mental Disorders with Alcohol and Other Drug Abuse: Results From the Epidemiological Catchment Area. *Journal of the American Medical Association*, 264(19), 2511-2518.

Riksheim, E. and S. Chermak.1993. Causes of Police Behavior Revisited. *Journal of Criminal Justice*, 21, 353-382.

Rottman, D., H. S. Efkeman, and P. Casey. 1998. *A Guide to Court and Community Collaboration*. National Center for State Courts.

Ruiz v. Estelle, 503 F.Supp. 1265 (S.D. Tex. 1980)

Sampson, R. J. and B. G. Groves.1989. Community Structure and Crime: Testing Social-Disorganization Theory. *American Journal of Sociology*, 94, 774-802.

Schuerman, L. A. and S. Kobrin. 1984. Exposure of Community Mental Health Clients to the Criminal Justice System, Client/Criminal or Patient/Prisoner. In L. A. Teplin, ed., *Mental Health and Criminal Justice*. Beverly Hills, California: Sage Publications. pp. 87-138.

Shaw, C. and H. D. McKay. 1942. *Juvenile Delinquency and Urban Areas*. Chicago, Illinois: University of Chicago Press.
___. 1969. *Juvenile Delinquency and Urban Areas, Revised Edition*. Chicago, Illinois: University of Chicago Press.

Sims, R. 1999. King County Mental Health Court dedicated. Retrieved on August 29, 2004 from http://www.metrokc.gov/exec/news/1999/042999.htm

Skogan, W. 1990. *Disorder and Decline: Crime and the Spiral of Decay in American Neighborhoods*. Berkeley, California: University of California Press.

Skoler, D. L. 1977. *Organizing the Non-System*. Lexington, Massachusetts: Lexington Books.

Snow, W. H. and K. A. Briar. 1990. The Convergence of the Mentally Disordered and the Jail Population. *Journal of Offender Counseling, Services and Rehabilitation*, 15(1), 147-152.

Solomon, P. and J. Draine. 1995. One Year Outcomes of a Randomized Trial of Case Management with Seriously Mentally Ill Clients Leaving Jail. *Evaluation Review*, 19, 256-273.

Steadman, H. J., S. S. Barbera, and D. L. Dennis. 1995. A National Survey of Jail Diversion Programs for Mentally Ill Detainees. *Hospital and Community Psychiatry*, 45(11): 1109-1113.

Steadman, H. J., M. W. Deane, J. P. Morrissey et al. 1999. A SAMHSA Research Initiative Assessing the Effectiveness of Jail Diversion Programs for Mentally Ill Persons. *Psychiatric Services*, 50(12), 1620-1623.

Stein, L. I. and R. J. Diamond. 1985. The Chronic Mentally Ill and the Criminal Justice System: When to Call the Police. *Hospital and Community Psychiatry*, 36, 271-274.

Stephan, J. J. 2001. *Census of Jails*, 1999. Bureau of Justice Statistics, NCJ 196633. Washington, DC: U.S. Department of Justice.

Swank, G. and D. Winer. 1976. Occurrence of Psychiatric Disorders in a County Jail Population. *American Journal of Psychiatry*, 133, 1331-1333.

Swanson, J. W., R. Borum, M. S. Swartz, and J. Monahan. 1996. Psychotic Symptoms and Disorders and the Risk of Violent Behavior in the Community. *Criminal Behaviour and Mental Health*, 6(4), 309-329.

Talbot, J., L. Bachrach, and L. Ross. 1986. Noncompliance and Mental Health Systems. *Psychiatric Annals*, 16, 596-599.

Teplin, L. A. 1983. The Criminalization of the Mentally Ill. *Psychological Bulletin*, 94(1), 54-67.

___. 1985. The Criminality of the Mentally Ill: A Dangerous Misconception. *American Journal of Psychiatry*, 142(5), 593-599.

___. 1990. The Prevalence of Severe Mental Disorders among Male Urban Jail Detainees: Comparison with the Epidemiologic Catchment Area Program. *American Journal of Public Health*, 80(6), 663-669.

Tobin, R. W. 1999. *Creating the Judicial Branch: The Unfinished Reform*. National Center for State Courts.

Torrey, E. F., J. Stieber, J. Ezekiel, S. M. Wolfe, J. Sharfstein, J. H. Nobel, and L. M. Flynn. 1992. *Criminalizing the Seriously Mentally Ill*. Washington, D.C.: Public Citizens Health Research Group.

Turner, S. and J. Petersilia. 1992. Focusing on High-Risk Parolees: An Experiment to Reduce Commitments to Texas Department of Corrections. *Journal of Research in Crime and Delinquency*, 29, 34-61.

Ventura, L. A., C. A. Cassel, J. E. Jacoby, and B. Huang. 1998. Case Management and Recidivism of Mentally Ill Persons Released from Jail. *Psychiatric Services*, 49, 1330-1337.

Wahl, O. F. 1995. *Media Madness: Public Images of Mental Illness*. New Brunswick, New Jersey: Rutgers University Press.

Walker, S. 1985. *Sense and Nonsense about Crime*. Belmont, California: Wadsworth.

Weiner, B. A. 1984. Interfaces between the Mental Health and Criminal Justice System: The Legal Perspective. In L. A. Teplin, ed., *Mental Health and Criminal Justice*, London: Sage Publications, Inc., pp. 21-42.

Wexler, D. B. 1991a. An Introduction to Therapeutic Jurisprudence. In D. B. Wexler and B. Winick, eds., *Essays in Therapeutic Jurisprudence*. Durham: Carolina Academic Press. pp. 16-38.

___. 1991b. Putting Mental Health into Mental Health Law: Therapeutic Jurisprudence. In D. B. Wexler and B. Winick, eds., *Essays in Therapeutic Jurisprudence* Durham: Carolina Academic Press. pp. 3-15

Whitmer, G. E. 1980. From Hospitals to Jails: The Fate of California's Deinstitutionalized Mentally Ill. *American Journal of Orthopsychiatry*, 50, 65-75.

Wilberg, J. K., K. Matyniak, and A. Cohen. 1989. Milwaukee County Task Force on the Incarceration of Mentally Ill Persons. *American Jails*, III(2), 20-26.

Wilson, D. J. 2000. *Drug Use, Testing and Treatment in Jails*. Bureau of Justice Statistics, NCJ 179999. Washington, D.C: U.S. Department of Justice.

Wilson, J. Q. and G. L. Kelling. 1982. The Police and Neighborhood Safety. *Atlantic Monthly*. March, 29-38.

Wilson, W. J. 1987. *Truly Disadvantaged: The Inner-City, The Underclass and Public Policy*. Chicago, Illinois: University of Chicago Press.

Winick, B. J. 1996. The Jurisprudence of Therapeutic Jurisprudence. In D. B. Wexler and B. J. Winick, eds., *Law in a Therapeutic Key: Developments in Therapeutic Jurisprudence*. Durham: Carolina Academic Press. pp. 653 and 665.

Wolff, N. 2002. Courts as Therapeutic Agents: Thinking Past the Novelty of Mental Health Courts. *Journal of the American Academy of Psychiatry and the Law*, 30, 431-437.

___. 2002a. Public Management of Mentally Disordered Offenders: Part I. A Cautionary Tale. *International Journal of Law and Psychiatry*, 2(1), 15-28.
___. 2002b. Public Management of Mentally Disordered Offenders: Part II. A Vision with Promise. *International Journal of Law and Psychiatry*, 25(5): 427-444.

___. 2002c. Risk, Response and Mental Health Policy: Learning from the Experience of the United Kingdom. *Journal of Health Politics, Policy and Law*, 27(5), 801-832.

Wolff, N. 2003. Courting the Court: Courts as Agents for Treatment and Justice. In W. H. Fisher, ed., A Special Volume of *Research in Community and Mental Health on Community-Based Interventions for Offenders with Severe Mental Illness*. Oxford: Elsevier Science. pp. 143-197.

Wolff, N., R. J. Diamond, and T. W. Helminiak. 1997. A New Look at an Old Issue: People with Mental Illness and the Law Enforcement System. *The Journal of Mental Health Administration*, 24(2), 152-165.

Wolff, N., D. Plemmons, B. Veysey, and A. Brandli. 2002. Release Planning for Inmates with Mental Illness Compared with Those Who Have Other Chronic Illnesses. *Psychiatric Services*, 53, 1469-1471.

Wolfgang, M. E., R. M. Figlio, and T. Sellin. 1972. *Delinquency in a Birth Cohort*. Chicago, Illinois: Sage.

Zitron, A., A. Hardesty, E. Birdock, and A. Drossman. 1976. Crime and Violence among Mental Patients. *American Journal of Psychiatry*, 133, 142-149.

Reaction Essay— Diminished Responsibility as a Systems Issue

6

Charley Flint, Ph.D.

Professor of Sociology and Coordinator of Criminal Justice Programs
Department of Sociology, William Paterson University
Wayne, New Jersey

When this author first read the title of Nancy Wolff's paper, "Law and Disorder: The Case against Diminished Responsibility," she thought it was going to be an article discussing the issue of what to do with mentally ill persons who are convicted of criminal offenses. Dr. Wolff does discuss this issue in the first part. The author succinctly puts forth the arguments on this issue. There is the issue of who is responsible for criminal deviance among persons who are seriously mentally ill—from the individual to the systems of treatment and criminal justice.

This author now believes the shift is on inadequate treatment as the main reason for criminal deviance among persons with mental illness. And as a result, there is the effort to decarcerate persons with behavioral health problems. In many parts of the paper, Dr. Wolff includes persons with substance abuse problems with those persons with mental disorders. She then gives an overview of the two-pronged approach of enhanced treatment and improved coordination between the criminal justice and behavioral health systems.

When looking at her title, this reviewer, though not an expert in the least on this subject matter, but as a fellow practitioner, is confused. Just who is being talked about? Are we to assume that the diminished responsibility is with those who are mentally ill but have been convicted of criminal offenses? Or maybe it is the mental health system that failed at the attempt to deinstitutionalize those being held in institutions for the mentally ill. Or, maybe it is society for its "criminalization" of mental disorders? For too long, as Dr. Wolff points out, the general society has had the notion that mental disorders and criminal deviance are linked. In an effort to debunk this myth, we should be sure that we are not putting these individuals in harm's way.

Some parts of the paper read as if the author were arguing against the differential treatment of those who have committed crimes and are also suffering from mental illness. This author is concerned with the lack of "reliable scientific evidence on the prevalence of mental illness in jails and prisons" and the rhetoric that dominated the discussion of the criminalization of the mentally ill during the 1980s and 1990s.

Dr. Wolff does believe that the Bureau of Justice Statistics report of the late 1990s (Ditton, 1999), though somewhat problematic, was "large enough in magnitude, and consistent enough with expectations, to motivate a policy response." This response, she asserts, is to put forth initiatives to compel decarceration. A move she finds "troubling" in the discussions linking criminalization and decarceration is "the tendency to assume that for persons with mental and substance use illnesses there is but one cause for their deviance—illness, and one cure—behavioral health treatment." This is what some theorists refer to as a "master status." Many marginalized persons are labeled in this manner.

Her point is well argued, however, that this serves to reinforce the stigma associated with people with mental illness and may serve as a hindrance in creating appropriate ways of responding to their criminal deviance. Her presentation on the contextual nature of the "disordered behavior of persons with mental illness" is well presented, though this reviewer feels that, like most mainstream (read functionalist theories) of social science, it is a bit class biased.

For instance, she says "it is well known within the mental health services field that many persons with serious mental illness live chaotic lives and reside in impoverished communities. Inner city areas, in particular, are characterized by crime and offer few legitimate options. We also know that unemployment is high among persons with serious mental illness. Being poor with lots of unstructured idle time and living in areas characterized by crime is a recipe for deviant outcomes—like trespassing, vagrancy, theft, drug distribution and possession, and other crimes related to deprivation." She is correct in saying that this theory of deprivation is used to explain crime among the general population, and more attention should focus on this when explaining crime by those with mental disorders.

Those who use this theory should consider that the majority of the people in those areas do not commit crimes, and that persons who do not live in such areas also commit crimes. However, her point that the "connection among the lack of economic opportunity and other blocked opportunities" is well taken.

In the second part of the paper, Dr. Wolff shifts her focus to the systems that respond to deviant behaviors. The criminal justice system is charged with responding to criminal deviance and the mental/behavioral health system function is to respond to mental disorders. She argues that the criminal justice system is not a system but a process. Many in the criminal justice field describe it as both a system and a process. It is a system in that it is made up of three basic components (law enforcement, the courts, and corrections) that are interrelated.

The criminal justice system, as we have come to know it in the United States, may not be a system in the real sense of the word, but is an analytical concept. It is, as Dr. Wolff states, fragmented in terms of organization, funding, and jurisdiction. Each of the three components is furthered divided with varying functions. As one author (Schmalleger, 2003, p. 22) states "Agencies of justice with diversity of functions (police, courts, and corrections) and at all levels (federal, state, and local) are linked closely enough for the term 'system' to be meaningfully applied to them." It has been demonstrated time after time that what happens in one component will have some impact on one or all of the other parts.

Due to this interrelatedness, we use the terms "system." Regardless of whether we agree or disagree with the terms used, the author very aptly describes the different processes that individuals may go through once they enter the system. She presents the various options or diversion that can occur at each stage or step in this process and the problems and challenges that can arise, particularly as they relate to those with mental illness.

One of the major characteristics of the criminal justice system in this regard is the discretion of the functionaries at each stage; whether it is the police who decide to arrest or not arrest (as she says, they are the gatekeepers), the prosecutor who decides to indict or not, the judge who decides to incarcerate or not, or the parole board which decides to release or not.

Many factors can influence the decisions of the functionaries—legal factors as well as extralegal ones. These are sometimes referred to as *aggravating* and *extenuating factors*. Dr. Wolff discusses factors that may influence the discretion of functionaries who come in contact with people with mental illness. Though the list of factors discussed is expansive, there is another factor that is not discussed—the social status of individuals including race, ethnicity, and gender. Studies have documented that these are important factors when it comes to which option the police will take. Dr. Wolff's options of whether the police will "choose to socialize, medicalize, or criminalize an incident" are also impacted by the individual's status.

Many studies have looked at police discretion, but fewer have looked at the discretion of the prosecutors, who, Dr. Wolff states (and this author wholly agrees), "control the flow of people immediately past the gate." It is "the prosecutor who determines whether the individual gains access to and moves through the criminal justice system or is released." Her assessment of the response of the prosecutor to persons with mental illness who come into contact with the criminal justice system is an excellent critique. One problem she illuminates is the prosecutor's knowledge of mental illness per se and his or her knowledge of what treatment is available or the effectiveness of such treatment. This author is appalled at the number of times that prosecutors equate mental illness with what they call mental retardation.

Judges as functionaries of the court are imbued with some of the same faults as the prosecutors. They are not necessarily knowledgeable about mental illness, may be operating under preconceived notions of "the mentally ill as violent offenders," and are influenced by what Dr. Wolff calls the "legal culture" of the community. This, then, will be reflected in their sentencing patterns.

The last process deals with corrections. If incarceration is the sentencing option, institutions must accept whoever is sent to them. Parole and probation as sentencing options of the court are impacted by the guidelines set by the court. Parole boards, as subsystems of corrections, or as independent agencies, have some discretion in deciding if the offenders are ready to return to the community after they have served the minimum required time of incarceration. One factor that is considered when granting parole is good behavior while incarcerated. Persons with some mental disorders may have a difficult time footing this bill, and may be somewhat disadvantaged. Dr. Wolff notes that studies suggest that inmates with mental illness tend to serve longer sentences than their non-mentally ill counterparts and that they are more likely to complete their full sentences in prison, rather than under parole supervision. The stigma of being seen as "sick" and more dangerous than their counterparts is probably one of the factors that may explain why this is the case.

Probation and parole officers as functionaries in this stage are impacted by many of the same conditions as other functionaries in the system, but they also suffer from role conflict. They are expected to serve as an advocate for and assist their clients, but they also serve a policing function in that they are charged with monitoring whether their clients are complying with the conditions of release and if not, they can "send them back to the slammer." Again, the person on parole with mental illness may not be able to comply with the conditions (for example, gaining access to mental health services). He or she may not find that these services are culturally sensitive and gender specific and may not know how to relate this to his or her parole officer.

Dr. Wolff provides a critical assessment of the challenges within each component and lists appropriate suggestions for diversion or alternatives for each stage. Better coordination is needed among the components and the criminal justice system and the mental health field. More training of the functionaries in all stages is warranted when dealing with persons who have mental illnesses and who come in contact with the system. This training will not solve all the problems, but it will bring about an awareness that is sorely lacking in the present system that deals with criminal deviance.

Dr. Wolff's overview leaves the reader with a well-informed review of the arguments for and against diversion of persons with serious mental illness from incarceration. She concludes that at present there are no set standards for determining who should be diverted or under what conditions they should be diverted. She does point out there is the notable exception of those who meet the standard of diminished capacity or contagion. One might say that age is another exception. Children under a certain age are treated differently.

One wonders if persons are seriously mentally ill, how do we ascertain criminal liability? This author's understanding of what constitutes criminal behavior is behavior that is intentional and knowing. Are those who are seriously mentally ill capable of being clear about what they are doing? There are many factors to consider when answering the question of "What should we do when persons suffering from mental disorders come into contact with the criminal justice system?" Should they be treated differently than persons who are not deemed to be mentally ill? How do we balance fairness and accountability or treatment and punishment?

A large number of persons with mental disorders come into contact with the criminal justice system. Some are diverted from the system at various stages of the process, but some do find themselves incarcerated. According to the Human Rights Watch (2003) report, *Ill-Equipped: U.S. Prisons and Offenders with Mental Illness*, "Between two and three hundred thousand men and women in U.S. prisons suffer from mental disorders, including such serious illnesses as schizophrenia, bipolar disorder, and major depression." The report estimated 70,000 are psychotic on any given day. Drawing on interviews with correctional officials, mental health experts, prisoners and lawyers, they take a look at the issue of the mentally ill in prisons. They conclude that many who cannot get help in their communities are swept into the criminal justice system after they commit a crime. Prisons, whose primary function is incapacitation, are not intended for the mentally ill. Persons who are mentally ill and are convicted criminals have a right to decent standards of treatment for their illness. The report documents institutions which are making progress in this area, but it also shows that some institutions still do not accommodate the mental health needs of these individuals.

As mentioned elsewhere, many of the functionaries in the criminal justice system are not too knowledgeable about mental illness or those who suffer from these illnesses. Functionaries in the penal system, like security staff, may see the mentally ill as being difficult and disruptive (this is especially true in women's institutions where women in general are seen as being too difficult and too needy); their behaviors, such as self-mutilation, may be seen as "malingering," and they may be punished instead of given treatment.

For those who suffer from mental illness and find themselves in our penal institutions, mental health treatment is paramount. As the Human Rights Watch report (2003) concludes:

> Mental health treatment can help some people recover from their illness, and for many others it can alleviate its painful symptoms. It can enhance independent functioning and encourage the development of more effective internal controls. In the context of prisons, mental health services play an even broader role. By helping individual prisoners regain health and improve coping skills, they promote safety when the offenders are ultimately released.

Dr. Wolff presents the many challenges facing correctional health care, with the lack of adequate funding being one of the major challenges. Another is the lack of coordination between and within the criminal justice system and the mental health system. Those within these systems should pay heed to the recommendations that she puts forth for ending the "practice of diminished responsibility." And this author gets it. She is referring to the systems that are responsible for responding to social disorder when she talks about diminished responsibility. They, along with others such as researchers, are the usual suspects in this disorder that is caused by diminished responsibility.

References

Bureau of Justice Statistics. 1994. *Fact Sheet: Drug-Related Crime*. Report: NCJ-149286, Office of Justice Statistics, U.S. Department of Justice.

Ditton, P. 1999. *Mental Health and Treatment of Inmates and Probationers.* Bureau of Justice Statistics, NCJ 174463, Washington, DC: U.S. Department of Justice.

Human Rights Watch. 2003. *Ill-Equipped: U.S. Prisons and Offenders with Mental Illness*. New York: Human Rights Watch.

Schmalleger, Frank. 2003. *Criminal Justice Today*. Upper Saddle River, New Jersey: Prentice Hall.

Section 3:

Correctional Treatment, Behavioral Management, and Community Supervision

EFFECTIVE CORRECTIONAL TREATMENT: WHAT IS THE STATE OF THE ART?

7

Marilyn Van Dieten, Ph.D.
David Robinson, Ph.D.
Orbis Partners, Inc.
Ottawa, Ontario, Canada

Over the last two decades the "What Works" movement has instilled a sense of optimism regarding our ability to have an impact on criminal behavior. Through advances in this literature, a knowledge base has been constructed and continues to grow in support of rehabilitation as a viable means of reducing recidivism. By uncovering the common factors that characterize effective programs, researchers have provided us with important information to guide implementation efforts. In this paper, we present a brief review of the literature with an emphasis on the treatment methods and common factors that contribute to positive outcomes. We then will turn our attention to implementation and highlight some of the most frequently cited challenges and innovative practices designed to overcome them and to enhance positive outcomes. Finally, we will then look to the future and delineate some avenues that we believe beg to be explored and re-explored, both in practice and in research.

Introduction

Ironically, the origin of the "What Works" movement is frequently traced to reservations originally expressed about the efficacy of correctional treatment. For example, Robert Martinson's famous 1974 essay, *What Works? Questions and Answers about Prison Reform*, is often cited as a catalyst for the germination of the What Works movement. The definitiveness of this manuscript is heralded in its title, "Questions and Answers"! Today, we are less likely to admit that we have the "answers," even though the quality of the evidence appears more worthy of bold conclusions. Many readers will recall that after reviewing 230 studies of rehabilitation programs in criminal justice settings, Martinson and his colleagues concluded that *"with few and isolated exceptions the rehabilitation efforts that have been reported so far had no appreciable effect on recidivism"* (Martinson, 1974, 25). Given that 40 to 60 percent of the studies reviewed by Martinson reported some level of reduced recidivism, it was not long before treatment advocates were able to identify the conditions and characteristics of effective intervention programs and to offer empirical support for specific types of rehabilitation (Palmer, 1975; Gendreau and Ross, 1979; Andrews and Bonta, 2002).

A sustained interest in "What Works" has been attributed not only to advances in our understanding of effective offender rehabilitation but also to increased pessimism regarding the impact of sentencing options on recidivism (Day and Howells, 2002). Paul Gendreau focused on explicating the effects of criminal sanctions—especially the new brand of interventions he described as attempts to "punish smarter." His meta-analytic work (Gendreau, Little, and Goggin, 1996) summarized a large body of existing studies showing that intermediate sanctions, without correctional treatment, produced no reductions in recidivism. Ted Palmer (1975) made critical examinations of Martinson's research and helped focus the research field on identifying the subset of correctional treatment modalities that yielded successful outcomes. His 1995 paper brought increased focus to the various "nonprogrammatic" and practical issues that must be addressed in implementing effective programs.

There is now a significant body of research demonstrating that sanctions that do not include treatment are likely to have a detrimental effect on recidivism (McGuire, 2002). For example, researchers have concluded that judicial sanctions (including dismissal without warning, pre-adjudication measures, judicial dispositions such as probation, custody, and parole) that are delivered without treatment services are generally ineffective as methods of reducing re-offending (Hoge, 2001; Gendreau, Goggin, Cullen, and Andrews, 2000). In addition, "control" oriented interventions that became popular in the

1980s to support a "punishment works" agenda have proven ineffective. The rigorous evaluations conducted by Petersilia and MacKenzie clearly demonstrate that boot camps and intensive supervision, perhaps the best examples of the widely touted effective punishers, do not work unless participants are also engaged in treatment programs (Petersilia, 1998; MacKenzie et al., 2001).

Our current exploration of the treatment outcome literature confirmed that the rehabilitation potential of specific programs provides solid ground for continued optimism. This material has been so well-documented and summarized elsewhere that it seems unnecessary to review it again. However, it may be worth re-stating the findings, for which there is very high consensus, and reviewing the freshest contributions. A brief review of the treatment outcome literature will help set the stage for examining the future of treatment in corrections.

Review of Treatment Effectiveness: Moving from What Works to Evidence-Based Practice

"If one asks categorically, then, whether rehabilitative intervention works with . . . offenders, the answer is, essentially, yes." (Lipsey, 1999)

Systematic reviews, when properly executed with full scientific integrity, obviously provide the most reliable and comprehensive statement about what works. Few would disagree that presently the most compelling summaries review of the treatment literature include meta-analysis and cost-benefit analysis. Both have played a critical role in increasing our understanding of the literature and also moving the findings to practical implementation in the field.

"Meta-analysis" involves the synthesis of many studies that provide empirically derived and quantitative estimates (effect sizes) of the degree of association between treatments/interventions and reduced recidivism. Using meta-analysis, researchers combine the data from many single studies into one large study that provides a massive sample for testing various hypotheses about "what works" in reducing recidivism. For example, in their most impressive incarnations, meta-analyses can allow social science researchers to build samples of more than 50,000 subjects by combining many smaller studies involving samples of as few as thirty or forty offenders to as large as 1,000 or more offenders. The augmented sample size achieved by pooling the many individual studies allows researchers to gain much more confidence about their conclusions. It also furnishes enough statistical power not only to answer the question of whether or not treatment works, but also under what conditions effective treatments are most successful. A very appealing feature of meta-analysis is that it allows researchers to estimate more precisely the magnitude of the effect of treatment in reducing re-offending (for example, in percentage terms).

Given that the number of entries has grown so dramatically in recent years, we offer a list of the current body of meta-analyses in correctional treatment with considerable trepidation. We admit the risk of inadvertently overlooking the work of some of our colleagues and omitting the contributions that are most recent. However, we furnish a partial list of examples including general examinations of correctional treatments that provide solid contributions to the body of meta-analysis studies. Some of the studies provide very basic findings that have come to be replicated, while others are more innovative in method and in interpretation of results. The studies include more general examinations of correctional treatments as well as reviews of specific treatment modalities and interventions targeting particular offender groups. Our selections also have been guided by our reading of the theoretical and applied importance of the issues that have become the focus of meta-analysis studies. The following selective synopses refer to nine studies that have made significant contributions to the meta-analytic enterprise since 1990.

1. Andrews et al. (1990) used meta-analytic techniques in one of the first large samples of correctional studies. They used meta-analysis to test explicit hypotheses from a theory of effective correctional treatment. They provided evidence that programs delivered to high-risk offenders and that target criminogenic needs are most effective. In addition, they also identified programs that relied on social learning or cognitive-behavioral methods and which demonstrated more favorable outcomes.

2. Lipsey (1995) conducted meta-analysis on a large body of studies of interventions for juvenile delinquents. He concluded that rehabilitative techniques were generally effective in reducing recidivism and provided evidence that skills-based, particularly cognitive-based programs, were most promising. Lipsey also presented some of the earliest meta-analytic evidence to demonstrate that the quality of program implementation positively effected outcomes.

3. MacKenzie, Wilson, and Kider (2001) used meta-analytic techniques to assess the impact of boot camps based on thirty-two studies with randomized controlled experiments and quasi-experiments. They found no overall effect in reducing recidivism but cited evidence that a larger positive effect could be achieved if a counseling component were incorporated.

4. Petrosino, Turpin-Petrosino, and Finckenauer (2001) conducted meta-analysis to study the impact of the so-called Scared Straight programs whereby juveniles receive exposure to the reality of tough criminal sanctioning. They found that juveniles were at increased risk to engage in criminal activity after completing this type of intervention.

5. Cohen (1998) used cost-benefit analysis to evaluate the relative impact of different types of criminal sanctions for sex offenders. He concluded that treatment provides value for money and can be generalized to a variety of settings.

6. Lipsey, Chapman, and Landenberger (2001) used meta-analytic techniques to assess the impact of cognitive-behavioral treatment using fourteen studies selected for the quality of empirical methods. All but one showed a desirable effect on recidivism, and they found that programs delivered with better implementation procedures were about four times more effective than cognitive-behavioral treatment programs with lower lower-quality implementation.

7. Dowden and Andrews (2003) subjected the findings of thirty-eight studies on family interventions to meta-analysis and controlled for methodological rigor and characteristics of the intervention. They found that family interventions were effective in reducing juvenile recidivism when they were targeted to higher-risk cases and attended to offender responsivity issues (for example, skills-based programs based on social learning or cognitive-behavioral models).

8. Dowden, Antonowicz, and Andrews (2003) examined the contribution of relapse-prevention techniques to the reduction of recidivism using their large database of correctional treatment studies. While they found that relapse-prevention methods had less impact than some of the other techniques identified as effective in meta-analyses, such methods were helpful. In particular, involving family in relapse-prevention techniques, identifying offense chains, and attending to responsivity factors (for example, skills-based) contributed to higher effect sizes.

9. Dowden and Andrews (1999) extended their focus to a smaller group of twenty-six studies that specifically reported on treatment effectiveness for female offenders. The findings from this meta-analysis also confirmed that correctional programs delivered to female offenders produced effect sizes that were similar in magnitude to those produced in general offender samples. In addition, programs that adhered to the risk, needs, and responsivity principles yielded superior effects.

Results of these meta-analyses and other contributions that are not described in this paper show very convincingly that treatment can have positive effects on offender recidivism and a direct impact on public safety. The body of existing evidence also leads to the conclusion that the effects of programming generalize across different offender groups, including both adults and juveniles. We now have considerable evidence to suggest that some treatment programs have a direct impact on promoting public safety by reducing recidivism. The recidivism reduction impact of effective programs is usually within the 10 to 30 percent range. For most stakeholders within our field, this magnitude of effect is considered very positive. Through the meta-analyses and other review studies, there was also evidence that criminal sanctions contributed little if any to the critical work of reducing recidivism. In fact, in many instances, sanctions were associated with increased recidivism.

There also have been more specific findings that shed light on the conditions under which correctional treatment is most effective. One result that has been corroborated by several independent meta-analyses concerns the approach used by practitioners. Cognitive-behavioral skills and social-learning-based programs delivered to higher-risk offenders are most effective. Another finding points directly to the importance of what has emerged from these efforts—the quality of implementation. For example, a variety of indicators that tap quality components (for example, staff training, use of manuals, low drop-out rates, technical supervision and support, research involvement), and so forth have been pooled together in some of the meta-analyses. Results clearly indicate that the quality of implementation represents a very major moderating effect in determining the effectiveness outcome of correctional programs.

Two of the meta-analysis studies described above stand out as particularly important contributions in the effort to understand correctional treatment effectiveness. The 1990 study by Andrews and his colleagues and Lipsey's 1995 study helped push the field ahead by providing confidence that the "what works" model was legitimate. Both of these studies were large in scope, bringing together an impressive number of treatment studies with methodological rigor. These studies examined the effectiveness of treatment modalities and explored the moderating effects of theoretically relevant variables that were gaining attention from both researchers and practitioners. Moreover, their reports provided independent confirmation of major findings. For correctional program decision-makers and policy designers, the studies made it clear that the time had come to take up the challenge to introduce effective rehabilitative programs in a more deliberate way.

The work of Andrews and his colleagues was guided by specific hypotheses that emerged from Andrews' work on treatment and assessment, particularly in community corrections with adult and juvenile samples. The meta-analyses coded a number of factors that represented components in their theory about offender change. Specifically, the principles of risk, need, and responsivity were tested. With the meta-analytic data, the researchers supplied compelling evidence that programs were most effective when delivered to higher risk offender groups (in other words, the risk principle). They also showed that the programs demonstrating greater potential for risk reduction targeted characteristics of offenders known to have a criminogenic effect (in other words, the need principle). Finally, with respect to the treatment modalities, they found that programs that focused on skill-building techniques, borrowed from social learning models of behavior, and employed cognitive-behavioral methods were associated with the largest effect sizes. The meta-analysis also produced evidence that criminal sanctioning, on its own, did not produce significant effect sizes with respect to recidivism reduction.

With one well-executed empirical exercise, their meta-analysis provided very strong support for the risk, need, and responsivity principles. Now widely quoted and incorporated into a number of restatements of the tenets of research-based practice, these principles of risk, need, and responsivity have become standard correctional terminology wherever evidence-based practice is implemented. At about the same time the meta-analysis results were released, Andrews (Andrews, Bonta, and Hoge, 1990) and his colleagues published a formal statement of the principles, citing a number of studies from the assessment and treatment literature that supported their findings.

The other study that we view as seminal to the flurry of meta-analytic activity that followed in the last ten years is Lipsey's first study of juvenile programs. He examined a body of research in which he attempted to answer the question: "What Do We Learn from 400 research studies on the Effectiveness of Treatment with Juvenile Delinquents?" The findings of this study have been reported in several additional manuscripts including a helpful presentation of the results as well as re-analysis in Lipsey (1999). Lipsey was able to replicate the findings of Andrews and the general findings of the pre-1990 meta-analyses that produced significant effect sizes for correctional treatment. However, the detail of this work and the large sample on which it was based allowed Lipsey to explore additional moderator variables. He also was able to examine treatment effectiveness separately for non-institutionalized (in other words, community) and institutionalized juvenile programs.

Lipsey reported that for both groups, programs of longer duration that used interpersonal-skill-building approaches, individual counseling, and multiple services were most effective. Within the community sample, he found that higher-risk or more serious offenders showed the greatest gains from treatment. For both groups there was evidence that programs struggling with implementation issues (for example, dropouts) had lower effect sizes than programs with better implementation success. Another key finding concerned the phenomena whereby programs in which researchers were involved in implementation (for example, pilot or demonstration projects) had a much greater impact on recidivism. Lipsey discovered that greater research involvement contributed to larger effect sizes. This result previously regarded as an indication of research bias has subsequently been shown to be an important indicator of quality implementation. Other findings from this groundbreaking research related to the generalizability of the effect sizes across subgroups of the juvenile population. There were no significant differential or moderating effects for age, gender, or race. Within the institutionalized juvenile subgroup of studies, there were similar levels of program effectiveness regardless of whether participation was mandatory or voluntary.

There have been other major contributions to the meta-analytic agenda that also need to be mentioned. No review of the meta-analysis literature in corrections would be complete without reference to British researcher James McGuire's 2002 collection of writings: *What Works: Reducing Reoffending— Guidelines from Research and Practice*. The edited volume brought together contributions from major international players who contributed to the meta-analysis field or shaped theory and practice in correctional treatment. This collection profiled the consistency of research results and the number of program development areas that had emerged in recent years (for example, sex offending, substance abuse, and so forth). The collection also helped define "what works" as a catch phrase for innovative and effective practice in the field.

The Most Recent Meta-Analysis Findings

The newest contribution to the meta-analysis literature deserves more detailed description (Landenberger and Lipsey, 2005) because it crystalizes a number of issues that we now believe need to be addressed if the field is to move forward. This new study builds on the approach that Lipsey and his colleagues pioneered in previous meta-analyses and focuses specifically on cognitive-behavioral programs. The latest work might be considered a gourmet version of correctional treatment meta-analyses. Landenberger and Lipsey place cognitive-behavioral interventions under a meta-analytic microscope that permits them to explore issues that are critical for exploiting the potential of this modality with adult and juvenile offenders. It provides an in-depth exploration of a variety of moderator factors as applied to the effectiveness of cognitive-behavioral interventions with offenders. The study is both groundbreaking and exciting in terms of the new knowledge that it uncovers. While many of the findings have appeared in individual studies described above, the new work gives much greater clarity and detail about the issues that program designers need to focus on to maximize the impact of their interventions. We believe that these results can advance the field's search for "what works."

Landenberger and Lipsey focused on fifty-eight studies (including both experimental and quasi-experimental methods) that were selected from a larger body of investigations of cognitive-behavioral interventions for offenders. They employed stringent criteria for inclusion of studies in their meta-analysis database, culling the fifty-eight studies from a larger body of 1,070 studies that explored the question of the effectiveness of cognitive-behavioral treatments with this population. Inclusion criteria included the stringency of defining cognitive interventions and research methods that employed comparison groups that were equivalent (or equated using statistical controls) to the treatment groups. The researchers coded an extensive number of variables for the fifty-eight studies, including methodological indicators, type of treatment components (cognitive skills, cognitive restructuring, interpersonal problem-solving, social skills, anger control, moral reasoning, victim impact, substance abuse, behavior modification, relapse prevention, individual attention), recidivism type, dosage, offender risk level, implementation monitoring, staff training and experience, researcher participation, treatment setting, and adjunctive service components. By simultaneously controlling for a number of the moderating influences on program effectiveness, Landenberger and Lipsey attempt to estimate the potential recidivism-reduction effect of the most state-of-the-art implementation of cognitive-behavioral programs. Their projections allow us to look into the future and gain a glimpse of the potential returns on the implementation of a "perfect" program. What is most intriguing about their presentation of these findings is that the most promising results they project have actually been achieved by a number of the treatment programs comprising their meta-analysis.

In describing their results in the order of their presentation in this manuscript, Landenberger and Lipsey reported the following:

- Programs targeting moderate- to high-risk offenders produced higher effect sizes than those targeting offenders at lower risk.

- Treatment dose was positively correlated with effect size, with longer treatment hours associated with more positive outcomes.

- Researcher involvement in programs, implementation monitoring, and training for program delivery staff were positively correlated with effect size, while a high number of program dropouts signaled poorer outcomes.

- Cognitive-behavioral programs when combined with other services (for example, counseling, education) were more effective than programs delivered alone.

- Programs that incorporated the following components were most effective: cognitive restructuring, anger control, and individual attention, in addition to cognitive-behavioral programming.

It is also important to note that the authors found that the effect sizes were similar for males and females and for adult and juvenile offenders. While there was variation in the effect sizes across brand name programs (for example, Reasoning and Rehabilitation, Moral Reconation Therapy, Thinking for a Change), the differences were not statistically significant. Community programs appeared to be associated with a larger effect size; however, the effects were not significantly different from programs delivered in prisons. Overall, they found that there was a 25 percent reduction in recidivism associated with cognitive-behavioral programs. The mean recidivism rate for control groups was 40 percent compared to a mean of 30 percent for cognitive-behavioral treatment groups.

After identifying the strongest moderator factors, as listed above, Landenberger and Lipsey conducted a series of analyses aimed at controlling for the combined effects of the various factors. By examining each of the moderating factors simultaneously, the authors were able to develop a model that predicted the optimum effect size that might be expected when all of the moderator characteristics associated with increased positive effects were included in the model. In these analyses, some factors that were not significantly correlated with effect size when considered separately were found to be predictive in the composite model. Their analysis suggested that the "optimum" program would be delivered to higher-risk offenders with a high quality of treatment delivery. In addition, the program would include interpersonal problem-solving and anger control as central components and exclude victim impact and behavior-modification elements. This combination of effective components produced a recidivism reduction of 52 percent. Hence, when compared to the control group recidivism rate of 40 percent, the combination of these treatment components resulted in an average recidivism rate of 19 percent. They concluded: "This impressive effect is not a mathematical projection beyond what appears in the data." They go on to explain that programs that had achieved or exceeded this success rate were at the 82nd percentile within their distribution of effect sizes.

The results of this study provide very encouraging evidence that the current state of program development, particularly within the cognitive-behavioral realm, has advanced to the stage where recidivism can be reduced by more than 50 percent through offender participation in such high-quality programs. The research also points to very specific factors that should be incorporated into programs to augment the level of effectiveness, both in terms of implementation quality and the inclusion of specific active ingredients that appear to work best in cognitive-behavioral programs. Moreover, from the studies reviewed by Landenberger and Lipsey, there were a number of programs that met and exceeded the average effectiveness rate (52 percent reduction) reported for the full sample of fifty-eight studies.

Implementing Evidence-Based Programs

While the meta-analysis results are both impressive and encouraging, there are some sobering elements that were reflected in the results. That is, the newest research very clearly confirms that we must be vigilant about program integrity. However, attempts to study the implementation practices of correctional programs in the meta-analyses often lacked the detail necessary to quantify essential implementation factors. More detail for measuring program-integrity factors is needed in future evaluations of correctional treatments.

In 1999, Gendreau, Goggin, and Smith prepared a paper entitled, "The Forgotten Issue in Correctional Treatment: Program Implementation." The paper was extremely timely as it reminded program specialists on the treatment-delivery staff about the need to maintain fidelity to the treatment models. Contributors to the correctional treatment literature also have provided research and commentary on the various facets of program implementation quality that must be addressed (Dowden and Andrews, 1999; 2004; Marshall, 2005; Palmer, 1995). At a minimum, adequate training and follow-up with good supervision and monitoring of program delivery are essential.

The fact that meta-analysts have identified implementation quality as a consistently important moderator of treatment effectiveness indicates that there was sufficient variation in program quality to arrive at such conclusions. In other words, there were many programs within the correctional treatment databases that evidenced poor implementation procedures to a degree that was sufficient to negatively impact results. The sobering conclusion might be stated like this: "We have the technology but improper installation can render it useless!" There is something very frustrating about the realization that something as critical as recidivism reduction is in reach, but for many potentially effective programs, the positive effects will not be realized.

One of the most common techniques used to ensure treatment integrity is to monitor adherence to program manuals. Manual-based interventions have been advocated by many researchers (Wilson, 1998; Gendreau and Andrews, 2001) and have a number of advantages, including the potential for replication in other sites, an assurance that appropriate treatment targets will be addressed, and that clients are exposed to a full dosage of the prescribed intervention. But, manuals represent only one part of the treatment process. Staff may be very well versed in the program content of an effective program but lack the facilitative style and relationship skills that correlate with client outcome (Castonguay, Goldfried, Wiser, Rauer, and Hayes, 1996).

In fact, this may be particularly true for correctional clients who are mandated to treatment and unwilling to change. In a recent meta-analysis of Motivational Interviewing, Hettema, Steele, and Miller (2005) reported that the use of manuals actually contributed to negative outcomes with resistant clients. They identified one study where slavish reliance on a treatment manual actually increased resistance by pushing clients to address certain content before they were ready. After reviewing videotapes of therapists delivering a manual-based cognitive-behavioral program with sex offenders, Marshall (2005) cautioned program developers to avoid being overly detailed when writing treatment manuals as providers who depend on the manual are less likely to use facilitative skills and remain responsive to the offender's learning style. To date, the use of treatment manuals has not proven to be a significant independent predictor of effect size in meta-analyses. While treatment manuals are necessary to provide a blueprint for the delivery of treatment, characteristics of program delivery style and skill acquisition are also essential.

In their most recent meta-analysis of correctional treatment, Andrews and Dowden (Under Review) focus specifically on the issue of program integrity, rating a series of relevant dimensions from the extant literature:

1. Theoretical model
2. Selection criteria for workers
3. Provision of training
4. Provision of supervision
5. Availability of training manuals
6. Monitoring of service process or intermediate gain
7. Adequate dosage/exposure
8. New/fresh program
9. Small sample size
10. Involved evaluator

Despite missing data required to score some dimensions in many of the studies, there was sufficient detail to show that the ten indicators formed a composite that reliably correlated with effect size. Overall, the average number of program-integrity components reported for their sample of 273 was 3.46. Three indicators provided the strongest links to program effectiveness including the presence of an involved evaluator, staff selection, and small sample size.

Earlier meta-analyses exploring effective correctional treatment also confirmed that involving researchers in the design and/or delivery of service contributes to reductions in recidivism (Lipsey, 1999; Andrews and Bonta, 2002; Dowden and Andrews, 2000). As reviewed above, Landenberger and Lipsey (2006) demonstrated that involvement of researchers was one of the stronger correlates of effect size. In interpreting this effect, there have been apprehensions that researchers who participate in program implementations might skew the results in favor of their preferred models.

In the newest Dowden and Andrews' meta-analysis, evidence was presented to confront the potential bias of researcher involvement. They ran two separate sets of meta-analyses to better understand the impact of researcher bias. In the first set of analyses, studies coded as "appropriate" for meeting the key requirements of effective intervention were assessed to determine the impact of researcher involvement. The second set of analyses was conducted on treatment studies coded as "inappropriate" because of their failure to meet the principles of risk, need, and responsivity. The authors argued that if a true bias is present, the impact of researcher participation (or bias) would appear in both sets of studies. However, researcher involvement did not produce an effect on outcomes in the programs coded as "inappropriate treatment." In fact, within the pool of inappropriate treatments, the set of variables that included researcher involvement and other program integrity elements was negatively correlated with effect size. The results suggest that quality of implementation will not compensate for program modalities that do not reduce recidivism. Without the appropriate intervention, fidelity to a program model is likely to be irrelevant.

It is understandable that by having researchers involved, especially within the context of a pilot project, research study or program evaluation, there will be extra vigilance about program implementation. Andrews and Dowden found that when researchers were involved in implementation, the mean number of program integrity components was higher. However, these findings also raise some practical concerns for all of those involved in the implementation of effective programs. The magnitude of the findings on researcher involvement forces us to think about the day-to-day delivery of programs that are not conducted in settings where there are laboratory-like conditions and pureness of application. Many jurisdictions have equipped themselves with the training and delivery structure necessary to provide a menu of evidence-based correctional programs. Of course, thousands of offenders participate in these potentially effective programs every day. However, a pressing question concerns the extent to which those programs are delivered according to design, to the right offenders (for example, high risk), and with an adequate level of supervision to sustain positive results. We have seen many jurisdictions that have successfully implemented such a menu of programs while ensuring that a high-quality delivery infrastructure was in place to sustain effectiveness. However, we have also seen jurisdictions struggle to secure the necessary resources to maintain programs and ensure quality program delivery by skilled staff.

Recall that one of the three program-integrity components that showed the greatest independent contribution to predicting effect size in the most recent Andrews and Dowden study was related to staff selection. This finding brings attention to the concern that in some settings, program delivery staff may not, in fact, possess the requisite skills and characteristics appropriate for treatment delivery. In our program implementation and training work, we frequently observe this problem. In some cases, individuals, who may not have the optimum skill set, select themselves by volunteering for the training opportunities that are occasioned by the introduction of a new treatment program for offenders. In other cases, managers choose program delivery staff on the basis of criteria that may not be essential to doing a good job delivering effective programs, including seniority, pay level, or educational qualifications (for example, having a social science degree, and so forth). Our discussion below about practitioner characteristics associated with successful outcomes brings additional focus to the issue of staff selection. We believe there may be a set of identifiable skills or service orientations that should be considered in selecting treatment delivery staff, and we will discuss this in more detail below.

The final component linked to program integrity that was identified in the Andrews and Dowden meta-analysis is sample size. A number of agencies are introducing evidence-based practices across large jurisdictions and rolling out effective correctional treatment programs on larger scales. Many jurisdictions have devoted considerable effort to providing training and structuring their professional workforce to give greater attention to the work of program delivery. National programs are now available with training and implementation packages that have made it easier to mount large-scale implementation projects. However, among their body of studies, Andrews and Dowden found that appropriate programs with smaller samples (n<100) had larger effect sizes than appropriate programs with larger samples. We fear that these less promising results derived from larger-scale implementation efforts where program integrity becomes became more difficult to sustain. This hypothesis suggests that the smaller samples represented new implementations when the influence of researcher involvement, the effects of recent training, and the awareness of proper implementation protocol were more salient for program managers and had been more intense. This interpretation is consistent with our observations of jurisdictions which struggle with the challenges of implementing what works on an ongoing basis.

The field needs innovative, practical, and professional strategies to assist agencies in the challenging task of enhancing program integrity. Regarding the future, the evidence points to a clear need to develop strategies that jurisdictions can apply to monitor and increase the quality of implementation. Ongoing training and supervision are obvious components that need to be included. We recommend that the field continue to search for vehicles to achieve this end. Currently, there are a few exemplary practices that can be recommended to assist jurisdictions to address quality assurance. The field needs innovative, practical, and professional strategies to assist agencies in the challenging task of enhancing program integrity.

One mechanism that has been used by program providers to assess adherence to the principles of effective intervention is the Correctional Program Assessment Inventory (CPAI). Gendreau and Andrews developed the CPAI after closely examining the qualities and characteristics of exemplary programs (Gendreau and Andrews, 2001). Essentially, the CPAI is a structured instrument that is administered by certified staff who conduct site visits, examine program documentation, and observe delivery of program components. Programs are rated on a series of quality indicators (for example, professional training, staff selection, treatment components, use of assessment, and so forth) and correctional managers receive feedback aimed at how they can increase the quality and effectiveness of their programs. Latessa and Holsinger (1998) have conducted hundreds of CPAI evaluations across the United States. Results to date suggest that with notable exceptions, many programs do not comply with the principles of effective intervention. The experience of the CPAI has provided strong evidence to recommend that a standardized review process should be an integral component for all ongoing program-implementation efforts.

Another procedure established in national correctional systems in the United Kingdom and Canada is known as the correctional treatment accreditation process. Accreditation panels consisting of international experts have been successful in promoting greater rigor in the implementation of correctional programs in their jurisdictions. The panel reviews the program content and implementation process to ensure that new programs meet minimum standards of effectiveness to be recognized as an appropriate treatment within their correctional systems. Programs are responsible for furnishing a documentation package demonstrating their ability to meet requirements in a number of relevant programming domains. Included among the criteria are results from evaluations, or at a minimum, concrete research and measurement plans to assemble such evidence in the future.

Many of the standards identified within this certification process correspond to the factors that have been identified as significant in the meta-analyses we have reviewed. A panel of correctional treatment experts representing the academic and practitioner communities review each program submission and decide whether certification will be extended. Programs that fail to meet all of the criteria for certification status receive advice on how to correct program deficits. In some cases, programs are given provisional certification until certain conditions are met. Ongoing recertification by demonstrating maintenance of program integrity would be a logical next step in this accreditation process.

There are other mechanisms that promote program integrity around the issue of staff skills. Some national programs insist on a tenure of supervision for new program delivery staff to ensure that the program is being delivered as designed. Some programs also have initiated user group symposia (for example, video conferences) to explore quality control issues as they relate to ongoing program implementation. Other methods include staff certification, whereby program delivery staff must submit tapes of their program delivery for review by an authorized trainer. These techniques can be supported with ongoing training and the denial of certification, where necessary. Many program administrators perceive such mechanisms as obstacles to implementing and expanding their program reach. However, use of such efforts will result in more effective program delivery—and ultimately greater public safety.

The use of performance measurement to assess the impact of programs on individual offenders also should be a standard component for monitoring program integrity. At this stage in the evolution of our knowledge base in corrections, it is clear that all jurisdictions should be using standardized risk and need assessment as a prerequisite to the implementation of any other evidence-based practices. Client progress should be monitored on an ongoing basis to determine whether positive change is occurring. The use of dynamic risk/needs tools for reassessment purposes is essential to current day correctional practice. It is clear from all of the research we have reviewed that correctional managers must attempt to document their performance in promoting offender change. Currently, there are many assessment tools in use that are primarily static in focus and provide little in the way of measurement properties that allow for dynamic reassessment. However, dynamic assessments and reassessment should be performed with offenders who are receiving correctional treatment to assess the extent to which they are exhibiting change. When positive change is not occurring as expected, correctional administrators can use the information to help assess whether their interventions are producing the effects that were intended.

Staff Style, Skill, and Training

The discussion of implementation quality inevitably leads us to more probing questions about the level of skill and the appropriateness of style used by the practitioners who deliver correctional programs to offenders. Apart from staff training and supervision, the meta-analyses have not been able to isolate practitioner-related effects on treatment outcome. Dowden and Andrews (2004) examined "staff practice" in one of their series of meta-analyses and found that the number of investigators that report on staff practice was minimal. They studied five broad staff-practice domains that can roughly be translated as style and skill (effective use of authority, appropriate modeling and reinforcement, problem-solving, effective use of community resources, the quality of interpersonal relationships). Only 15 percent of the studies reported on the various factors they attempted to code. Despite the low frequency of reporting and the number of studies for which the presence of the practices remained unknown, the authors found that when present, staff practice was positively correlated with effect size. A composite index of all of the staff practices correlated with effect size at the 0.4 level and the association was higher for subsets of programs that were classified as "appropriate."

This study was not able to assess the existence of practices at the individual program-delivery staff level. However, the results are illustrative of the potential importance of staff characteristics in achieving positive outcomes with criminal offenders. It is clear that there is a need for greater research on the characteristics of practitioners that help produce the greatest recidivism-reduction effects. We are beginning to see a renewal of interest in studies that measure practitioner style and skill. Supporting research from other branches of human intervention, these studies demonstrate what many of us have believed all along: practitioner style and skill are critical to successful outcomes—especially with offenders.

In this area, we have much to learn from the more general psychotherapy research literature that provides a rich body of studies linking therapist characteristics to successful client change. For any of us involved in working with offenders, the generalization of findings from this set of studies is not a difficult leap to make. Psychotherapy is principally concerned with helping people change their behavior. In the offender treatment arena, we are engaged in the same enterprise, but often with clients who are less interested in change.

In the early seventies, Ricks coined the term 'supershrink' to describe an "exceptional" therapist who demonstrated superior outcomes when working with high risk youth. A year later Bergin and Suinn referred to the therapist who demonstrated very dismal outcome results as the *'pseudoshrink'* (Okiishi et al., 2003). Both labels were very deliberately assigned by the respective authors to demonstrate the central role played by the individual practitioner above and beyond the actual approach used. The importance of the practitioner's behavior is now a prominent research focus (Hettema, Steele, and Miller, 2005). In fact, there is growing consensus and some research to suggest that treatment services would benefit from a research paradigm that focuses on the "how" of practice versus the content of treatment. This view highlights the importance of the approach used by the practitioners as opposed to placing an emphasis on method. That is, methods such as Cognitive Behavioral Therapy (CBT) Educational Programs, Motivational Enhancement, and so forth, may be less relevant than the way in which the practitioner interacts with the offender in delivering these interventions. In short, some argue that therapy outcome can be more closely related to therapist characteristics than to type of treatment (Lambert and Okiishi, 1997).

It is true that therapists vary in success, even when working with patients with the same disorders and using the same treatment manuals (Huppert et al., 2001). If practitioner characteristics play a deciding role in determining outcome, then it is critical that we begin to isolate and identify the most important qualities and practices contributing to successful outcomes— favorable results with offenders. Studies focusing on the impact of provider training and demographic variables have demonstrated mixed results. For example, Stein and Lambert (1995) performed a meta-analysis on the influence of therapist training and found a modest effect on outcomes associated with training level or degrees held by clinicians. This effect size was related to retaining clients and obtaining similar outcomes in shorter periods of time. Okiishi et al. (2003) found no significant differences based on demographic variables such as age, sex, level of training (for example, graduate students, pre-intern, intern and post-intern), type of training (clinical or counseling psychology), or theoretical orientation (Cognitive-Behavioral Therapy, Humanistic/ Existential Therapy, Psychodynamic Therapy). However, as with Stein and Lambert, they discovered that staff competence contributed to the reduction of symptoms in a shorter period of time.

Despite inconsistencies in how much impact the practitioner has on outcome, the general treatment-outcome literature consistently emphasizes the importance of training for providers who work with high-risk groups such as offenders. In the Landberger and Lipsey (2006) meta-analysis of cognitive-behavioral programs for offenders, the amount of training showed a positive relationship. Surprisingly, mental health background did not. The delivery of treatment by mental health personnel was identified as a significant factor within the cluster of general program characteristics in Lipsey's (1999) meta-analysis of institutionalized juvenile offenders. It may be that when delivering structured cognitive-behavioral programs, the need for practitioners with a mental health background is less essential than ensuring that providers have adequate training and supervision. This finding suggests that delivery of programs to offenders by para-professionals without extensive mental health backgrounds will not detract from the effectiveness of service. The use of staff who are not clinically trained to deliver offender training is a frequent practice.

It has been our experience that in training staff to use structured curricula, conflicting therapeutic orientations or philosophies (for example, regarding offender treatment and punishment), can create resistance and negatively impact program adherence. A similar result was reported by Siqueland et al. (2000), who assessed the impact of training on sixty-two therapists in a multi-site psychotherapy outcome study. Results suggested that experience and competence ratings prior to training were correlated with measures of change in competence during the training phase. That is, those staff most proficient at what they do, and whose style of therapy is consistent with the model being tested were more likely to demonstrate increased competency at the conclusion of training. Of relevance to this discussion was the finding that the more aligned the practitioners to a specific modality, the less likely they were willing and able to change. Hence, the available research that pertains to practitioner skill indicates that competence in delivery is critical to success. However, the literature also suggests the practitioners' disposition toward the treatment model plays an important role in their ability to acquire competence in the model. Pre-training assessments of candidates' orientations toward the treatment model may help correctional administrators and trainers do a better job of selecting practitioners who will be appropriate.

There is a mature body of research in the mental health literature that explores the following question: "What are the qualities and characteristics of the successful service provider?" When we started to look closely at this research, we were struck by the consistency in the findings. That is, providers demonstrating high levels of success with clients use a similar approach regardless of their theoretical orientation or the client's presenting problem. Allusions to these qualities already have been made in the discussion of Dowden and Andrews' staff-practice inventory.

Lambert and Barley (2002) have clustered the primary qualities of therapists into two sets of behaviors—facilitative style (empathy, warmth, congruence, positive regard, and genuineness) and the therapeutic relationship. These factors have been described as common factors in psychotherapy research, suggesting that their influence is not restricted to any one particular model of treatment delivery. Are the qualities and characteristics of effective therapists the same across different therapeutic approaches? The answer appears to be yes. Therapists' behaviors are predictive of outcome (Horvath and Luborsky, 1993; Martin, Gaske, and Davis, 2000). Moreover, predictive characteristics of therapists are consistent across therapies (for example, cognitive-behavioral, client-centered, psychodynamic, and so forth), identifiable from different perspectives (client, therapist, observer), and are applied to a variety of presenting problems (Shirk and Karver, 2003). Again, we believe this literature can be easily generalized to the enterprise of helping offenders change.

The first set of qualities described by Lambert and Barley (2002) was introduced by Carl Rogers in the late 1950s as the primary catalysts for client change and offered as the principal method of Client-Centered Therapy (Lambert and Barley, 2002). Openness, warmth, and understanding were posited as critical attitudes that the therapist must display in order for the client to move forward in gaining insight into his or her problem; it is critical for the therapist to display openness, warmth and understanding. While such qualities were at the heart of Roger's nondirective stance toward the psychotherapy client, these qualities have emerged as common factors across a variety of nondirective and directive therapies (for example, cognitive-behavioral, and so forth). Meta-analyses and reviews of literally thousands of studies across many therapeutic models have confirmed that therapists possessing facilitative styles have greater success than therapists who fail to demonstrate such skills.

The second set, which Lambert and Dean refer to as therapeutic relationship or "alliance," overlaps to some extent with the facilitative set. The therapeutic relationship focuses to a great extent on the practitioners' ability to involve the client. It has been described by Lambert and Barley (2002) as having three components: tasks, bonds, and goals. "Tasks are the behaviors and processes within the therapy session that constitute the actual work of therapy. The goals of therapy are the objectives agreed upon by both therapist and client and bonds refer to the interpersonal attachment between therapist and client" (Lambert and Barley, 2002, 358). Results from meta-analysis also have estimated that the therapeutic alliance accounts for a very significant proportion of the variance in outcomes—perhaps as high as 25 percent (Horvarth and Symonds, 1991).

Within the context of treatment for offenders, the research has clearly pointed to cognitive-behavioral approaches as the most potent methods for facilitating positive outcomes within the correctional domain. Keijsers, Schaap, and Hoogduin (2000) conducted an exhaustive review of the research literature to investigate the impact of therapist behavior on outcome specifically within the context of delivering Cognitive-Behavior Therapy. They found that both sets of therapist behaviors (facilitative style and therapeutic relationship) were associated with positive outcomes. They also described a number of client behaviors (perception of therapist's competence, motivation to change, openness, and so forth) that correlated with outcomes. Some of these client characteristics help identify responsivity issues that are very relevant to working with offenders. In addition, the client characteristics that Keijsers and his colleagues identified are dynamic elements that are amenable to change when practitioners employ the right combination of style and skill.

Marshall et al. (2003) reviewed the existing psychotherapy evidence and concluded that the behavior and personal style of the therapist was a potentially important influence on outcomes with sex offenders. Their review results prompted Marshall (2005) to begin an important empirical investigation of therapist influence with treated sex offenders in the United Kingdom. The Offenders Behaviour Programmes Unit of HM Prison Service delivers an array of treatment services to offenders including a generic cognitive-skills program based on Reasoning and Rehabilitation (Fabiano and Porporino, 2001), Controlling Anger and Learning to Manage It (Winogron, Van Dieten, and Gauzas, 1998), and Sex Offender Programming. Staff are provided with intensive training treatment manuals and are videotaped as part of the quality assurance procedures. Raters were trained to review the videotapes and to code twenty-eight therapist characteristics identified in the Marshall et al. review.

They discovered two sets of therapist features that contributed to beneficial change. The first set included the following behaviors: empathy, warmth, rewardingness, and directiveness. Marshall concluded that empathy and warmth in the first set are consistent with the facilitative behaviors described by Rogers (1957). However, rewardingness (offer verbal encouragement to clients for small steps toward a predefined goal) and directiveness (offering guidance and working collaboratively to problem solve) are behaviors that distinguish cognitive-behavioral therapists from other therapeutic orientations.

The second set also included confrontational responses described as a harsh approach to challenge clients and non-confrontational (firm but challenging) responses. A reliance on therapists who used confrontation and a harsh approach to challenge clients was negatively related to treatment outcome. These results are consistent with research across other settings and client groups. For example, Hettema, Steele, and Miller (2005); Peterson, Waldron, and Miller (1996) described a process study conducted by Peterson and colleagues which showed a relationship between demonstrations of therapist support toward the client and increased cooperation and less resistance. They conducted a sequential analysis of client and therapist behaviors during motivational enhancement therapy for problem drinking. They coded twenty-two therapeutic exchanges for thirty minutes during Motivational Enhancement Therapy sessions. The more support the therapist demonstrated toward the client, the more cooperation and less resistance. In contrast, the more confrontation employed, the more resistance and less cooperation was elicited from the client.

Schechtman (2004) reported on a recent investigation for the treatment of aggressive boys that incorporated a group psychotherapy approach administered by fifty-one therapists. Among a large number of therapists, where skills were measured using the "Helping Skills System," only two skills were significantly linked to outcome. Therapists who asked more questions showed better outcomes than therapists who asked fewer questions. The use of open questions was described by Schectman as a facilitative skill that was correlated with decreased resistance and increased cognitive and affective exploration in the young clients. The skill most negatively correlated with outcomes was "presenting challenges"—clients showed increased resistance when faced with therapists who issued many challenges. These findings are highly consistent with Motivational Interviewing (MI) techniques, to be described in greater detail below.

Decades of psychotherapy-outcome research highlight the importance of facilitative skills such as empathy, warmth, regard, and the therapeutic relationship. There is also evidence to suggest that these same qualities and behaviors are critical for correctional staff (probation officers, parole officers, treatment providers, and so forth) when working with offenders (Andrews and Bonta, 2002). In correctional climates where such qualities often do not seem quite at home, the use of facilitative skills and the therapeutic alliance may be prerequisites to achieving the behavioral change that is necessary to increase public safety.

A little known study by Andrews and Kiessling (1980) conducted in the late 1970s in Ontario, Canada, forecasted many of the findings we have described with respect to therapist style and skill. The findings of the study illustrate the results of both the meta-analyses of correctional treatment and the broader psychotherapy research literature that relates to therapist style and skill. Using audio-taped sessions, Andrews and his team coded the interactions of probation officers with their probation clients using audio-taped sessions. The central goal of the research was to test a social-learning model of intervention with offenders. A number of the probation officers were actually volunteers who had been trained to assist in providing enhanced case management services to the probation caseload. Probation officer practices were coded on a number of dimensions including relationship skills (for example, openness and understanding) as well as structuring skills (for example, providing direction, appropriate use of authority, and so forth). The relationships skills were similar to the facilitative and therapeutic relationship skills that have been described in the psychotherapy literature. In many respects, the structuring skills are parallel to the directive treatment approaches that have been associated with positive outcomes in correctional treatment (for example, skill-building, cognitive-behavioral, pro-social skill modeling, and so forth).

Results suggested that both the facilitative and structuring skills of probation officers and volunteer probation officers had recidivism-reduction impacts on the probationers who received service. Both types of skills were important to achieve optimal effects. Officers showing high levels in both facilitative and structuring areas had superior outcomes in comparison to officers who were competent in only one area. Andrews coined the optimal combination of the two skills as a "firm but fair" approach. Again, the lessons from this study seem to summarize the state of existing research on "what works" with offenders.

What about Case Management?

Most evidence favoring reductions in recidivism in correctional populations pertains to interventions that are delivered within a group context. For example, many of the brand-name cognitive programs that produced impressive results in the meta-analyses employed group settings to advance offenders through a series of curriculum components. Programs that target anger management, substance abuse, sex offending, domestic violence, and other specific offending patterns are also conducted in group settings. In some cases, such programs are supplemented with individual services (for example, counseling, release planning, and so forth). How-ever, it must be admitted that the current body of evidence on correctional treatment effectiveness is largely based on group interventions.

In our consulting work with jurisdictions that seek to implement evidence-based innovative practice that is empirically based, we encounter many agencies that have not or are unable to implement group programs for offenders. The reasons include a lack of resources to train and deliver the programs, inability to properly supervise program delivery agents, small referral volumes that make costly program implementation efforts unfeasible, and concerns related to staff turnover that will eliminate the service. In some contexts, correctional administrators are unable to identify adequate treatment resources in the community because there is a lack of services that are informed by a true understanding of the criminogenic needs and responsivity factors that are unique to offenders. For these jurisdictions, the provision of group programs target help to reach all of their high-risk offenders, but this is an ideal that cannot be achieved easily. As a result, many agencies and jurisdictions need to develop case management skills that allow them to effectively promote positive offender change and/or the skill set necessary to support the pro-social skill building work that takes place within group programs.

Overall, most of the principles of effective correctional treatment that have been confirmed by existing research apply equally well to the case management context. Yet, case management practice has been largely omitted from the research agenda. When we refer to case management, we are not simply referring to the role of the case coordinator who is responsible for maintaining the paperwork, ensuring that the correctional client complies with legal obligations, and making referrals to necessary services. We also are including a more active role in which the case manager is involved in encouraging and supporting the offender's pro-social change to reduce risk and increase public safety.

Case managers are present in almost every service context within corrections, regardless of whether it is pre-trial, custodial settings, or community supervision settings (probation and parole). In all of these settings, there is usually a relationship between the offender and the case manager, such that regular contacts are established with the case manager to review progress and ensure that the offender's behavior is consistent with the public safety role of corrections. Despite the obvious role that case managers should have in promoting pro-social change within their caseloads of offenders, there is little research that can tell us "what works" about the practices of this group of correctional practitioners who work with offenders. It seems that the responsibility for reducing risk has been primarily located within the treatment realm of corrections. While this paper certainly attests to the success of this endeavor, we argue that the importance of case managers in the risk-reduction enterprise has been understudied and not fully exploited.

Apart from the study by Andrews and Kiessling described above, the active ingredients of case management that parallel treatment effects have not been investigated. Frequently, studies of the case management function have focused on the "coordination of service role" of case managers (for example, Longshore, Turner, and Fain, 2005) to the neglect of how their relationship and facilitative skills might influence offender behavior. In studying outcomes, there has been a greater emphasis on the *frequency* of case management activity as opposed to the *quality* of case management activity. There have been several recent exceptions to this trend (for example, Harris, Gingerich, and Whittaker, 2004); yet, it is difficult to find studies of case managers that document the quality and nature of their relationships with offenders. The largeinvestment in case management to provide intensive supervision during the 1990s is an example of how the role of case managers has been relegated to monitoring and managing risk as opposed to reducing risk.

Yet, the principles of risk, need, and responsivity that have been confirmed by the existing body of correctional research seem particularly germane to the work of case managers, and this research has been in corporated into several case management models (for example, Van Dieten, Robinson, Millson, and Stringer, 2001).

However, some jurisdictions have moved away from this model and have made deliberate attempts to develop the case manager's role as an agent of change in the correctional process. In this model, case managers are actively involved in conducting assessments, case planning with the offender (for example, along the lines of the therapeutic alliance), coaching, using skill-building activities aimed at risk reduction with the offender, and reviewing and supporting the offender as he or she makes changes with the help of other treatment services. The model performs well in probation, parole, and community residential settings where offenders are being supervised by case managers who maintain regular contact with the offender. We and others have been involved in helping jurisdictions implement case management models that focus on the application of risk, need, and responsivity. The most challenging component of applying the principles to case management has been the responsivity component. Here, we are directly confronted with the issues of style and skill that have been explored above.

We have found that for many agencies and jurisdictions, the principles of risk, need, and responsivity are successfully implemented in some layers of the service system. For example, assessment of risk and the assignment of services based on the results of assessment have become a standard practice. In addition, menus of services to address criminogenic needs have been introduced to reduce risk—using treatment programs that are supported by the evidence we have reviewed above. However, the day-to-day contact between case managers and offenders fail to make use of the responsivity principle. There is hesitancy by many case managers to become involved in the more direct work of helping offenders change because this role is viewed as the preserve of social workers and counselors. The facilitative and therapeutic alliance skills that are so influential in promoting behavioral change are viewed as contradictory to the case manager's work of monitoring and supervising. This phenomenon will not be new to our readers, but it continues to remain a significant obstacle to the full implementation of the evidence-based agenda in corrections.

There is a predictable pattern of implementation that we see occurring when organizations implement "what works." In the beginning phase, which may last for several years, there is an endorsement of the model at the top of the organization and administrators begin to put training in place to implement the principles. Typically, risk assessment comes first, followed by the implementation of evidence-based programs like cognitive-behavioral therapy and other skill-based interventions. Unfortunately, implementation often remains at this level. The majority of staff who are uninvolved in the delivery working with offenders do not receive training in effective approaches.

It has been our experience that effective case management practices are embraced at a much slower rate and yet require intensive training and organizational change to achieve results. In several of the organizations we have become involved with, we see gradual but steady improvement as the model becomes absorbed at the case management level. When this happens, staff begin to see the full benefits of the application of risk, needs, and responsivity. Even though the signs of success may take time to emerge, we have not seen any organizations turn back from implementation once the model has been embraced.

Andrews and Kiessling's early study supplies additional and convincing evidence that effective case management styles can be developed, and the outcome represents a major impact on the role of the community case manager in reducing recidivism and victimization of the public. In the implementations in which we have been involved, training and ongoing support have been key mechanisms for building the organizational change necessary to move ahead.

Motivational Interviewing

One of the key developments that we have observed involves the emergence of Motivational Interviewing (Miller and Rollnick, 2002) as a key tool for use by case managers. The authors describe this therapeutic approach as "a client-centered, directive style to enhance readiness for change by helping clients explore and resolve ambivalence" (Miller and Rollnick, 2002, 218). From a number of perspectives, the approach embodies the style and skill components that have gained support from research. In many respects, Motivational Interviewing has slipped into the correctional field and gained wide support without the research base in corrections that has been associated with other methods (for example, cognitive-behavioral programs). In fact, until recently there were few tests of the effectiveness of Motivational Interviewing with correctional populations. Harper and Hardyman (2002) and Ginsburg, Mann, Rotgers, and Weeks et al. (2002) described how Motivational Interviewing might be useful in working with offender populations as an innovative and effective way to reduce recidivism. Ginsburg (2000) and Ginsburg et al. (2002) demonstrated some evidence of the efficacy of this approach with inmates randomly assigned to Motivational Interviewing or control conditions. Relative to control participants, those who received a motivational interview showed increased problem recognition of their drinking behavior.

One of the most appealing aspects of this approach is that Motivational Interviewing was designed to work with populations that are most resistant to change (for example, drug addicts, and individuals coping with health crises, and smokers). Moreover, it is not necessary to employ the Motivational Interviewing approach as a structured program, but when used as intended, it can help to ensure a more appropriate style of interacting in the day-to-day context of working with offenders. As such, it is an ideal framework for case managers to employ in the development of priority targets, motivating offenders to apply new skills, monitoring progress, and shifting the case work focus as change occurs or as new problems arise.

Recruiting and training staff to ensure that these facilitative case management skills are demonstrated can be difficult, but a number of innovative methods are emerging from the literature on Motivational Interviewing. Motivational Interviewing has been delivered both as a stand-alone intervention and as a prelude to other treatment. In the early period of its development and dissemination, several studies identified Motivational Interviewing as an effective approach to promote treatment engagement, retention, and adherence. These results were not surprising—given that Motivational Interviewing was originally designed to address resistance (Heather et al., 1996). Motivation to change is one of the key concepts in Motivational Interviewing, and the goal is to move individuals from a lack of problem recognition or willingness to change toward commitment. The Motivational Interviewing literature has produced studies showing that once individuals reach a stage of commitment to change, positive treatment outcomes are significantly enhanced. Although under-researched in corrections, there is no doubt that motivation to change is a useful construct for our field, and it has come to be seen as an important responsivity factor. Shturman, Simourd, and Rudavela (2005) conducted a meta-analysis designed to assess the relationship among motivation, treatment participation, and recidivism using a sample of thirty-five studies. They found that motivation was related to treatment readiness and retention but unrelated to future offending or substance abuse.

A number of studies of Motivational Interviewing document the connection between treatment adherence, increases in motivation, and positive treatment outcomes. Hettema, Steele, and Miller (2005) have completed the largest meta-analysis to date. They assembled seventy-two studies across a number of client-presenting problems (substance use, treatment compliance, gambling, eating disorders, and diet and exercise, and so forth) for which behavioral outcome data was available. The effect sizes for Motivational Interviewing ranged from 0.77 for short-term behavioral outcomes to 0.30 for outcome follow-up periods of one year or more. Hettema and her colleagues demonstrated significant effect sizes for Motivational Interviewing across a range of behavioral problems with the most powerful outcomes noted for substance use. Until new evidence has been developed, it is the success of Motivational Interviewing with substance abuse clients that provides the most compelling argument for the use of this technique with offenders.

The Hettema meta-analysis also provided evidence that Motivational Interviewing is particularly effective when combined with other treatments. One of the benefits of Motivational Interviewing appears to be attributable to its effects on treatment retention and adherence (Brown and Miller, 1993). Subjects were randomly assigned to an inpatient substance abuse program (control) or a condition that involved receiving Motivational Interviewing prior to treatment. Treatment practitioners were not told which subjects received Motivational Interviewing; yet, they reliably identified such patients as more motivated and having a better prognosis. Aubrey (1998) found that adolescents attended 50 percent more substance abuse sessions after receiving Motivational Interviewing at intake. Those receiving Motivational Interviewing were also twice as likely to abstain from substance use three months after program completion.

Morgan et al. (1999) recommend that in custodial settings in pre-group sessions designed to assess risk and protective factors, inmate motivation should be explored to assess offender willingness to participate. Offenders who demonstrate resistance could be provided with a brief dosage of Motivational Interviewing to enhance participation and program adherence. Stewart, Van Dieten, and Graves (1999) prepared a standardized pre-group program for the cognitive skills and anger and emotions management programs delivered by staff working for Correctional Service Canada. A two-session format was adapted from the Motivational Enhancement protocol used in the Project Match Studies. Motivational Enhancement was derived from the principles and practices of Motivational Interviewing. It provides a structured format to engage the client through feedback and goal setting. Group facilitators have verified the impact of this program to reduce resistance and enhance program compliance.

We believe the potential utility of Motivational Interviewing in a variety of case management contexts may help bring responsivity issues within closer range of the frontline workers who manage our offender caseloads. An attractive feature of the body of Motivational Interviewing techniques is that they provide a coherent framework for building the facilitative and therapeutic alliance skills that have been shown to work in helping people change.

Table 1. A Four-Stage Model for Supervision (Van Dieten, Robinson, Millson, and Stringer, 2001)

STAGE	OBJECTIVE AND ACTIVITIES
STAGE I **MAPPING**	**DISCOVERY** **PROBLEM RECOGNITION**
• Pre-Orientation • Orientation • Assessment • Case Analysis	• Review case file • Provide orientation • Administer a systematic assessment tool (for example, YASI, YLS-CMI, LSI-R, SPIN, COMPASS) • Process case and map results to develop a case plan and strategy
STAGE II **FINDING THE HOOK**	**MOTIVATION**
• Provide feedback • Prioritizing • Assessing Motivation • Focusing	• Review assessment results with client. • Work collaboratively with client to identify priority targets. • Explore readiness, importance, and confidence • Set goals, tasks, and responsibilities
STAGE III **MOVING FORWARD**	**PROVIDE TREATMENT** **OPPORTUNITIES AND OPTIONS**
• Intervention • Referrals	• Build incentives and review disincentives (barriers, obstacles, natural consequences) for change • Refer to effective intervention programs • provide advocacy and educate community agencies about the needs of offenders

Continued on next page

Table 1. A Four-Stage Model for Supervision (Van Dieten, Robinson, Millson, and Stringer, 2001) (*continued*)

STAGE IV REVIEWING AND SUPPORTING	REINFORCE CHANGE
• Monitor progress, conduct reassessments • Update case plan • Reinforce small changes	• Identify successes and obstacles to change • Modify supervision plan consistent with needs • Reward "tiny" victories • Develop maintenance strategies

Motivational Interviewing, without the need for formal clinical experience, provides case managers with skills for engaging offenders in the case-planning activities that need to be accomplished to begin working on change. Moreover, the Motivational Interviewing skill set can be extended to the ongoing activities of monitoring progress and working with the offender to adjust the case plan, as required. Over the last five years, the authors have incorporated the principles and practices of Motivational Interviewing as the primary approach and a major organizing principle for training practitioners in effective case management. Several jurisdictions, including adult and juvenile probation in New York and Illinois and juvenile probation in Washington State, are implementing the approach statewide, and a number of smaller jurisdictions also have been applying the model. The model, described as Effective Case Work, consists of four overlapping and interrelated yet distinct stages that are presented in Table 1. The model fully incorporates all of the principles of risk, need, and responsivity with Motivational Interviewing techniques providing the primary approach used to address responsivity. The stages of the model include mapping, finding the hook, moving forward, reviewing, and supporting.

In the first stage, practitioners are introduced to risk and need assessment as well as the assessment of motivation. The assessment process, which we describe as *mapping*, furnishes the results needed to apply the risk principle to appropriately channel case management resources to the highest-risk cases. The next stage, *finding the hook*, focuses on the use of Motivational Interviewing to begin engaging the correctional client in the process of changing behavior. Again, this stage attends to the issues of responsivity by individualizing the case plan—exploring the greatest potential for immediate change and gathering information about the intervention options that are most likely to mobilize change quickly. The third stage, *moving forward*, involves the introduction of interventions (often through referral sources) that make use of assessment results in a way that follows the principle of targeting criminogenic needs. The final stage, *reviewing and supporting*, focuses on the ongoing task of monitoring progress and providing the offender with the resources and skills necessary to maintain pro-social change.

By incorporating Motivational Interviewing into the Effective Case Work model, we are able to provide staff with relational skills that decrease client resistance and enhance commitment to treatment. The model is simple in presentation, using terminology that is easy to remember and appealing to practitioners who have not been classically trained in the use of clinical methods. The model is simple and flexible and does not require an extensive structured manual for delivery. The flexibility of the model allows practitioners to develop a very individualized case plan, without being trapped into typologies that sometimes fail to provide a helpful framework for facilitating offender change. Again, the model is also consistent with more formal interventions (for example, cognitive-behavioral programs) and provides a foundation for supporting the work of other practitioners who are involved in working with cases. By conceptualizing each stage of the case work process, and showing practitioners how the stages relate to the evidence base (in other words, risk, need, and responsivity principles), they have a helpful blueprint for guiding their work with offenders from intake to discharge.

A pilot study in Pierce County, Washington is currently being conducted to examine the impact of the case management model delivered by probation officers to juvenile offenders (Personal communication with T. J. Bohl, Probation Manager). By monitoring changes on their risk/needs assessment instrument, supervisors are able to determine which staff are successful in working with youth to reduce criminogenic needs that have been targeted. Although the data remains largely anecdotal at this stage of investigation, it appears that staff who demonstrate the greatest competence in using Motivational Interviewing during the case management model are more likely to demonstrate client change as measured by reductions in risk and subsequent recidivism.

The development and implementation of fully elaborated case management models that apply the principles of risk, need, and responsivity is an important step in moving the "what works" agenda from promising research findings to everyday practice. It also fully supports the continued implementation of effective or appropriate treatment modalities under conditions of high program integrity. We strongly believe that with the firm base of findings related to treatment modalities, it is time to apply these principles more deliberately at the casework level, which most offenders are exposed to while under correctional supervision. Researchers also must turn their focus to case management and evaluate the efforts to adopt evidence-based practice at that level.

Training Implications

To make fuller use of the existing knowledge base on effective correctional practices, training remains an essential tool for implementation. The authors of this paper have trained practitioners across North America and the United Kingdom in assessment, case work practice, and cognitive-behavioral and Motivational Interviewing programs. From these experiences, we have tabled the top seven ways to negate the impact of training.

SEVEN WAYS TO NEGATE THE IMPACT OF TRAINING:

1. Bring in consultants to train staff without a program-implementation strategy.
2. Don't tell staff what the training is about.
3. Send staff to training as a perk or punishment.
4. Fail to assess staff qualities and competencies prior to training.
5. Ensure that other staff in the organization are not informed about the training.
6. Never audit the program nor provide supervision to staff.
7. Ensure there is no opportunity for skill transfer by failing to inform practitioners from other agencies about the program.

Since researchers have provided us with the information necessary to develop and deliver effective programs, there is a need to demonstrate that agencies in the real world can deliver programs as effectively as those observed in research projects. In their ground-breaking book, Broad and Newstrom (1992) shed light on the training industry when they arrived at the following conclusions:

- Organizations across the United States spend billions of dollars each year training staff.
- Most of this investment is wasted because knowledge and skills gained in training are not fully applied on the job.
- To develop highly skilled staff, new methods of training that promote the transfer of learning must be adopted.

Formal workshops are still the most popular way to provide staff training. Experts agree that this method is helpful to disseminate information and to ensure some increases in proficiency. However, there is significant evidence to suggest that gains in knowledge during training sessions quickly erode without ongoing supervision (Leschied, Bernfeld, and Farrington, 2001). Miller and Mount (2001) looked at the impact of training among a sample of practitioners attending a two-day training in Motivational Interviewing. Researchers assessed fidelity to the model both pre-and post-training by requesting that participants submit audiotapes. The audiotapes were scored using the Motivational Interviewing Treatment Integrity (MITI) coding system. After training, practitioners showed small but significant increases in the practice of Motivational Interviewing. However, their skill levels were not sufficiently advanced to make any difference in how clients responded, and this phenomenon was attributed to fact that it is difficult for practitioners to put theory into practice. Miller and Mount concluded that participants need time to practice and to be provided with supervised support to realize the potential of material introduced in the workshop. By learning from this exercise, methods were developed to support the practitioner's attempts to implement new knowledge when they return to the field.

The authors have been involved in several statewide implementations to provide training in assessment, case management, motivational interviewing, and treatment. To maximize training dollars, we encourage providers to develop an implementation strategy that moves beyond formal training (Van Dieten, Robinson, Millson, and Stringer, 2001).

First, we recommend that representatives from management and line staff be involved in a planning session to increase awareness and to assess agency support. Second, implementation tasks are assigned to managers, line staff, and trainers at three stages of implementation—before, during, and following training. For example, before training, managers are responsible for providing staff with information about the training, the trainers are responsible for developing the performance outcomes and relevant curriculum, and the line staff are asked to read any preparatory material. During training, supervisors and managers are advised to participate and show their support for the learning of new models. Following training, trainers and supervisors/managers must be involved in technical support to help trainees integrate the new skills within their day-to-day practice. For supervisors, this involves additional training that helps them coach their employees and identify additional gaps in their knowledge.

Therefore, it is critical that following formal training, managers ensure that staff have the opportunity not only for practice, but also for supervised practice. Competencies will never be built within organizations if an investment is not made in staff. Managers must choose staff who have excellent relational skills and some previous training in competency-based training (CBT) or Motivational Interviewing. If no employees are certified to support the model and provide supervision, then outside resources should be enlisted to help the implementation along. A number of resources are available such as coding systems for both Motivational Interviewing and CBT programs that can be used to rate treatment adherence. There are also many professionals who provide services to monitor staff performance and provide feedback until an appropriate level of competence is reached.

Female Offenders

In this paper we have focused almost exclusively on the general literature concerned with offender change. However, impressive research reports are emerging with respect to specific offender populations. One area that we feel requires special attention is innovative work with female offenders. Women and girls are the fastest growing offender population and are also the offender subgroup that is least understood.

The "what works" literature provides a general model to guide intervention practices. However, debate continues with regard to the appropriateness of this model for specific offender groups such as women and girls. Dowden and Andrews (1999) provided the first meta-analysis of treatment effectiveness for female offenders and identified twenty-six studies with predominantly female (N = 10) or exclusively female participants (N = 16) that met the inclusion criteria. The results of the meta-analysis provided some support for the principles of Risk, Need, and Responsivity. That is, stronger treatment effects were found when programs targeted females with a more extensive criminal history, focused on appropriate criminogenic targets, and used cognitive-behavioral treatment strategies. They also found that the most powerful treatment effects occurred when the emphasis of intervention was family and peers, antisocial associates, and family process (for example, providing family members with interpersonal skills, including increased affection, communication, and problem-solving skills). These results are certainly consistent with the prediction and developmental literature, which emphasizes the importance of relationships in the lives of women and girls.

The results of this meta-analysis are viewed by many as promising, but there remains a dearth of research on female criminality and an immediate need to know more about how best to apply the principles of effective intervention with women. In fact, the application of the principles of effective intervention can have negative consequences for women when gender issues are not taken into consideration. Hardyman and Van Voorhis (2004) have recently completed two national projects designed to review classification systems for women. They discovered that most states do not use classification systems that have been validated for women and that difficulties with over-classification are not uncommon. In many instances, there is a high proportion of women who score low-risk on the instrument with a lower proportion of women at the higher- risk end. The over-classification problem results because women in the high-risk categories tend to recidivate at substantially lower rates than men at similar high-risk levels. They also found that states were better able to predict institutional adjustment and post-release behavior when they excluded criminal history risk factors or reduced their weights. In fact, dynamic risk factors were consistently better predictors of institutional adjustment than criminal history.

Staff working with women routinely report high levels of dissatisfaction with existing classification systems and risk/need assessments because they fail to address gender-specific needs, including victimization, childcare, family process, mental health conditions, and other problems. They feel the development of gender-specific risk/needs assessment is a critical first step to ensure effective case management and treatment. Current research on women's criminality suggests that men and women have some criminogenic needs that are similar. However, the level of importance and nature of association may differ. In other words, while many of the factors are the same, they appear to play a very different role and function differently for men and women (Hardyman and Van Voorhis, 2004; Bloom, Owen, and Covington, 2004; Lowenkamp and Latessa, 2002).

The developmental research provides powerful evidence that women also have unique criminogenic needs that should be reflected in assessment and treatment practices. For example, the longitudinal research has clearly established a pathway to crime (for the highest-risk boys identified as "early starters") that is marked by an array of conduct and family problems (Loeber and Farrington, 1998; Loeber and Dishion, 1983). Pathways for girls are less well understood though women with a history of violence are more likely to have experienced childhood victimization and to remain undetected by the criminal justice system until much later than boys. Despite this situation, prevention and treatment programs for children and youth with conduct problems continue to emphasize the need for skill building to develop emotional control over impulses. However, given the strong association between victimization, stressful or unhealthy relationships, and conduct problems among girls, they might benefit more from general social-skill building and a network of supportive relationships (Dodge, 2004).

It is clear that we are in the very early stages of understanding and developing effective programs for women and girls in the criminal justice system. Given the results reported in this literature review, it is critical that researchers explore not only programs that are effective but the qualities and characteristics associated with effective implementation.

Conclusions

The overarching goal of this paper was to review the current research on correctional treatment in an effort to summarize the findings from the general outcome literature. This review demonstrates convincingly that the principles of effective intervention (risk, need, and responsivity) have been confirmed in a number of important meta-analyses. Programs targeting higher-risk offenders, that provide a sufficient dosage, employ cognitive-behavioral or skill-based methods, and attend to program integrity issues are most effective. Under ideal applications, correctional treatments can realistically reduce recidivism by more than 50 percent. The effects of correctional treatments have been demonstrated for males, females, adults, and juveniles, interventions offered in custodial and community settings, and for varying offense profiles. There is no evidence that programs focusing only on criminal sanctions without treatment can have an impact on reducing recidivism. In some cases, there is evidence that such approaches may increase criminal behavior.

It cannot be overemphasized that the quality of program implementation is a significant factor in program effectiveness, sometimes doubling the impact of a treatment on recidivism. Our interpretation of the results suggests that many agencies face a significant challenge in implementing evidence-based programs. Attention to program integrity is now the key to achieving more successful program delivery. This is also the area that poses the greatest challenge to service providers and jurisdictions. We also observe an unfortunate lack of attention to the domain of case management, where we believe many of the advances in correctional treatment should be applied in a systematic way.

References

Ackerman, S. J. and M. J. Hilsenroth. 2001. A Review of Therapist Characteristics and Techniques Negatively Impacting the Therapeutic Alliance. *Psychotherapy, 38(2).*

___. 2001a. A Review of Therapist Characteristics and Techniques Positively Impacting the Therapeutic Alliance. *Clinical Psychology Review,* 23(1), 1-33.

Andrews, D. A. and J. Bonta. 2002. *The Psychology of Criminal Conduct,* 3rd ed. Cincinnati: Anderson.

Andrews, D. A., J. Bonta, and R. D. Hoge. 1990. Classification for Effective Rehabilitation: Rediscovering Psychology. *Criminal Justice and Behavior,* 17, 19-52.

Andrews, D. A. and C. Dowden, (Paper Under Review). Managing Correctional Treatment for Reduced Recidivism: A Meta-Analytic Review of Program Integrity.

Andrews, D. A. and J. J. Kiessling. 1980. Program Structure and Effective Correctional Practices: A Summary of the CaVIC Research. In R. R. Ross and P. Gendreau, eds., *Effective Correctional Treatment.* Toronto: Butterworths.

Andrews, D. A., D. D. Robinson, and M. M. Balla. 1986. Risk Principle of Case Classification and the Prevention of Residential Placements: An Outcome Evaluation of the Share the Parenting Program. *Journal of Consulting and Clinical Psychology,* 54, 203-207.

Anthony, W. A. and R. R. Carkhuff. 1977. The Functional Professional Therapeutic Agent. In A. S. Gurman and A. M. Razin, eds., *Effective Psychotherapy.* Oxford: Pergammon.

Aubrey, L. L. 1998. *Motivational Interviewing with Adolescents Presenting for Outpatient Substance Abuse Treatment.* Doctoral Dissertation, University of New Mexico (DAI-B59/03).

Beech, A. and C. E Hamilton-Giachritsis. 2005. Relationship between Therapeutic Climate and Treatment Outcome in Group-Based Sexual Offender Treatment Programs. *Sexual Abuse: A Journal of Research and Treatment,* 17 (2), 127-140.

Bien, T. H., W. R. Miller, and J. M. Boroughs. 1993. Motivational Interviewing with Alcohol Patients. *Behavioral and Cognitive Psychotherapy,* 21, 347-356.

Bloom, B., S. Convington, and B. Owen. 2004. *Gender-Responsive Strategies: Research, and Practice and Guiding Principles for Women Offenders.* Washington, DC: U.S. Department of Justice, National Institute of Corrections.

Bonta, J., S. Wallace-Capretta, and J. Rooney. 2000. A Quasi-Experimental Evaluation of an Intensive Rehabilitation Supervision Program. *Criminal Justice and Behavior,* 27, 3, 312-329.

Broad, M. L. and J. W. Newstrom. 1992. *Transfer Training.* Reading, Massachusetts: Addison-Wesley Publishing.

Brown, J. M.. and W. R. Miller. 1993. Impact of Motivational Interviewing on Participation and Outcome in Residential Alcoholism Treatment. *Psychology of Addictive Behavior,* 7, 211-218.

Calsyn, R. J. 2000. A Checklist for Critiquing Treatment Fidelity Studies. *Mental Health Services Research,* 2(2).

Castonguay, L. G., M. R. Goldfried, S. Wiser, P. J. Rauer, and A. M. Hayes. 1996. Predicting the Effect of Cognitive Therapy for Depression: A Study of Unique and Common Factors. *Journal of Consulting and Clinical Psychology,* 65, 497-504.

Cohen, M. A. 1998. The Monetary Value of Saving a High-Risk Youth. *Journal of Quantitative Criminology,* 14, 5-33.

Crane, D. R., N. D. Wood, D. D. Law, and B. Schaalje. 2004. The Relationship between Therapist Characteristics and Decreased Medical Utilization: An Exploratory Study. *Contemporary Family Therapy,* 26(2).

Creed, T. A. and P. C. Kendall. 2005. Therapist Alliance-Building Behavior within a Cognitive-Behavioral Treatment for Anxiety in Youth. *Journal of Consulting and Clinical Psychology,* 71(3).

Crits-Cristoph, P., K. Baranackie, J. S. Kurcias, A. T. Beck, K. Carroll, et al. 1991. Meta-Analysis of Therapist Effects in Psychotherapy Outcome Studies, *Psychotherapy Research,* 1(2), 81-91.

Day, A. and K. Howells. 2002. Psychological Rehabilitation of Offenders: Evidence Based Practice Comes of Age. *Australian Psychologist,* 37, 39-47.

Dodge, K. 2004. Public Policy and the "Discovery" of Girls' Aggressive Behavior. In M. Putallaz and K, Bierman, eds. *Aggression, Antisocial Behavior, and Violence among Girls: A Developmental Perspective.* New York: Guilford Press.

Douglas, A., D. Goghilland, and D. Will. 1996. A Survey of the First Five Years Work of a Child Sexual Abuse Team. *Child Abuse Review,* 5, 227-238.

Dowden, C. 1998. *A Meta-Analytic Examination of the Risk, Need and Responsivity Principles and Their Importance Within the Rehabilitation Debate.* M.A. Thesis, Carleton University.

Dowden, C. and D. A. Andrews. In press. Managing Correctional Treatment for Reduced Recidivism: A Meta-Analytic Review of Program Integrity.

Dowden, C. and D. A. Andrews. 1999. What Works for Female Offenders: A Meta-Analytic Review. *Crime and Delinquency,* 45 (4), 438-452.

___. 2000. Effective Correctional Treatment and Violent Reoffending: A Meta-Analysis. *Canadian Journal of Criminology*,42, (4) 449- 467.

___. 2003. Does Family Intervention Work for Delinquents? Results of a Meta-Analysis. *Canadian Journal of Criminology and Criminal Justice*, 45(3), 327-342.

___. 2004. The Importance of Staff Practice in Delivering Effective Correctional Treatment: A Meta-Analytic Review of Core Correctional Practice. *International Journal of Offender Therapy and Comparative Criminology*, 48(2), 203-214.

Dowden, C., D. Antonowicz, and D. A. Andrews. 2003. The Effectiveness of Relapse Prevention with Offenders: A Meta-Analysis. *International Journal of Offender Therapy and Comparative Criminology*, 47 (5), 516-23.

Fabiano, L. and F. Porporino. 2001. *Reasoning and Rehabilitation, Revised*. Ottawa, Canada: T3 Associates.

Gendreau, P. and D. A. Andrews. 2001. *Correctional Program Assessment Inventory – 2000*. Ottawa, Canada: T3 Associates.

Gendreau, P. and C. Goggin. 1996. Principles of Effective Assessment for Community Corrections. *Federal Probation*, 60 (3), 64-71.

___.1996. Principles of Effective Programming with Offenders. *Forum on Corrections Research*, 8, 38-40.

Gendreau, P., C. Goggin, F. Cullen, and D. A. Andrews. 2000. The Effects of Community Sanctions and Incarceration on Recidivism. *Forum on Correctional Research, 12 (May)*, 10–13.

Gendreau, P., C., Goggin, and P. Smith.1999. Predicting Recidivism: LSI-R vs. PCL-R. *Canadian Psychology Abstracts,* 40, 2a.

Gendreau, P., C. Goggin, and P. Smith.1999. The Forgotten Issue in Correctional Treatment: Program Implementation. *International Journal of Comparative Criminology, 43, 180-187.*

Gendreau, P. and B. Ross. 1979. Effective Correctional Treatment: Bibliotherapy for Cynics. *Crime and Delinquency*, 25, 463-489.

Ginsburg, J. 2000. *Using Motivational Interviewing to Enhance Treatment Readi-ness in Offenders with Symptoms of Alcohol Dependence*. Unpublished doctoral dissertation, Carleton University, Ottawa, Ontario, Canada.

Ginsburg, J., R. E. Mann, F. Rotgers, and J. Weekes, 2002; Motivational interviewing with Criminal Justice Populations. In, W. R. Miller and S. Rollnick, Eds. *Motivational Interviewing* New York: Guilford Press. pps. 333-346.

Gendreau, P., T. Little, and C. Goggin.1996. A Meta-Analysis of the Predictors of Adult Recidivism: What Works! *Criminology*, 34, 575-607.

Hardyman, P. and P. Van Voorhis. 2004. *Developing Gender-Specific Classification Systems for Women Offenders*. Washington, DC: National Institute of Corrections.

Harper, R. and S. Hardy. 2000. An Evalution of Motivational Interviewing as a Method of Intervention with Clients in a Probation Setting. *British Journal of Social Work*, 30, 393-400.

Harris, P. M., R. Gingerich, and T. A. Whittaker. 2004. The "Effectiveness" of Differential Supervision. *Crime and Delinquency*, 50, 235-271.

Heather, N., S. Rollnick, A. Bell, R. Richmond. 1996. Effects of Brief Counseling Among Heavy Drinkers Identified on Hospital Wards. *Drug Alcohol Review*. 15, 29-38.

Hettema, J., J. Steele, and W. R. Miller. 2005. Motivational Interviewing. *Annual Review Clinical Psychology*, 1: 91-111.

Hill, C. E. 1992. Research on Therapist Techniques in Brief Individual Therapy: Implications for Practitioners. *Scientific Forum.*

Hoge, R. D. 2001. *The Juvenile Offender: Theory, Research, and Applications.* Boston, Massachusetts: Kluwer Academic Press.

Holt, C. 2001. The Correctional Officer's Role in Mental Health Treatment of Youthful Offenders. *Issues in Mental Health Nursing*, 22 (2), 173-180.

Horvath, A. and L. Luborsky. 1993. The Role of the Therapeutic Alliance in Psychotherapy. *Journal of Consulting and Clinical Psychology*, 61, 561-573.

Horvath, A. and D. Symonds. 1991. Relation between the Working Alliance and Outcome in Psychotherapy: A Meta-Analysis. *Journal of Counseling Psychology*, 38, 139-149.

Huppert, J., L F. Bufka, D. H. Barlow, J. M. Gorman, M. K. Shear, and S. W. Woods. 2001. Therapists, Therapist Variables, and Cognitive-Behavioral Therapy Outcome in a Multicenter Trial for Panic Disorder. *Journal of Consulting and Clinical Psychology*, 69, 747-755.

Keijsers, G. P. J., C. P. D. R. Schaap, and C. A. L. Hoogduin. 2000. The Impact of Interpersonal Patient and Therapist Behavior on Outcome in Cognitive-Behavior Therapy. A Review of Empirical Studies. *Behavior Modification*, 24(2), 264-297.

Kerley, K.R. and M. L. Benson. 2000. Does Community-Oriented Policing Help Build Stronger Communities? *Police Quarterly*, 3(1), 46-49.

Lafferty, P., L. E. Beutler, and M. Crago, (1989). Differences between More and Less Effective Psychotherapists: A Study of Select Therapist Variables. *Journal of Consulting and Clinical Psychology*, 57(18), 76-80.

Lambert, M. J. and D. E. Barley. 2002. Research Summary on the Therapeutic Relationship and Psychotherapy Outcome. *Psychotherapy: Theory, Research, Practice, Training*, 38(4), 357-361.

Lambert, M. J. and J. C. Okiishi. 1997. The Effects of the Individual Psychotherapist and Implications for Future Research. *Clinical Psychology: Science and Practice*, 4, 66-75.

Landenberger, N. A. and M. W. Lipsey. 2006. The Positive Effects of Cognitive-Behavioral Programs for Offenders: A Meta-Analysis of Factors Associated with Effective Treatment. *Journal of Experimental Criminology*, 1 (4), 451-476.

Latessa, E. J. and A. Holsinger. 1998. The Importance of Evaluating Correctional Programs: Assessing Outcome and Quality. *Corrections Management Quarterly*, 2(4), 22-29.

Leschied, A.W., G. A. Bernfeld, and D. P. Farrington. 2001. *Offender Rehabilitation in Practice: Implementing and Evaluating Effective Programs.* New York: John Wiley and Sons, Ltd.

Lipsey, M. W. 1995. What Do We Learn from 400 Research Studies on the Effectiveness of Treatment with Juvenile Delinquents? In J. McGuire, ed., *What Works: Reducing Offending – Guidelines for Research and Practice.* New York: John Wiley and Sons Ltd, 63-78.
___. 1999. Can Intervention Rehabilitate Serious Delinquents? *Annals, AAPSS*, 564, 142-166.

Lipsey, M., G. L. Chapman, and N. A. Landenberger. 2001. Cognitive-Behavioral Programs for Offenders. *Annals of the American Academy of Political and Social Science*, 578 (Nov.), 144-157.

Loeber, R., and T. J. Dishion. 1983. Early Predictors of Male Delinquency: A Review. *Psychological Bulletin*, 94, 68-99.

Loeber, R. and D. Farrington. 1998. *Serious and Violent Juvenile Offenders: Risk Factors and Successful Interventions.* Thousand Oaks, California: Sage.

Longshore, D., S. Turner, and T. Fain. 2005. *Effects of Case Management on Parolee Misconduct.* The Bay Area Services Network.

Lowenkamp, C. T. and E. Latessa. 2002. Assessing Female Offenders: Prediction Versus Explanation. *Women, Girls and Criminal Justice*, 3(4), 49-64.

MacKenzie, D. L., D. B. Wilson, and S. Kider. 2001. Effects of Correctional Boot Camps on Offending. *Annals of the American Academy of Political and Social Science*, 578, (November), 126-143.

Marshall, W. L. 2005. Therapist Style in Sexual Offender Treatment: Influence in Indices of Change. *Sexual Abuse: A Journal of Research and Treatment*, 17(2).

Marshall, W. L., G. A. Serran, Y. M. Fernandez, R. Mulloy, R. E. Mann, and D. Thornton. 2003. Therapist Characteristics in the Treatment of Sexual Offenders: Tentative Data on Their Relationship with Indices of Behaviour Change. *Journal of Sexual Aggression*, 9(1), 25-30.

Martin, D. J., J. P. Garske, and M. K. Davis. 2000. Relationship of the Therapeutic Alliance with Outcome and Other Variables: A Meta-Analytic Review. *Journal of Consulting and Clinical Psychology*, 68, 438-450.

Martinson, R. 1974. What Works? Questions and Answers about Prison Reform. *Public Interest*, 10, 22-54.

McGuire, J., ed. 2002. *Offender Rehabilitation and Treatment: Effective Programmes and Policies to Reduce Re-Offending*. Chichester: John Wiley and Sons.

McGuire, J. 2002. Integrating Findings from Research Reviews. In: J. McGuire, ed. *Offender Rehabilitation and Treatment: Effective Programmes and Policies to Reduce Re-Offending*. Chichester: John Wiley and Sons.

Miller, W. R. and K. A. Mount. 2001. A Small Study of Training in Motivational Interviewing: Does One Workshop Change Clinician and Client Behavior? *Behavioural and Cognitive Psychotherapy*, 29, 457-471.

Miller, W. R. and S. Rollnick. 2002. *Motivational Interviewing: Preparing People for Change*, 2nd ed. New York: Guilford Press.

Miller, W. R., R. G. Benefield, and S. Tonigan. 1993. Enhancing Motivation in Problem Drinking: A Controlled Comparison of Two Therapist Styles. *Journal of Consulting and Clinical Psychology*, 61, 455-461.

Mitchell, K. M., J. D. Bozarth, and C. C. Krauft. 1977. A Reappraisal of the Therapeutic Effectiveness of Accurate Empathy, Nonpossessive Warmth, and Genuineness. In A. S, Gurman and A. M. Razin, eds., *Effective Psychotherapy: A Handbook of Research*. New York: Pergamon.

Morgan, R. D., C. L. Winterowd, and S. W. Ferrell. 1999. A National Survey of Group Psychotherapy Services in Correctional Facilities. *Professional Psychology: Research and Practice*, 30 (6), 600-606.

Okiishi, J., M. J. Lambert, S. L. Nielsen, and B. M. Ogles. 2003. Waiting for Supershrink: An Empirical Analysis of Therapist Effects. *Clinical Psychology and Psychotherapy*, 10(6), 361-373.

Palmer, T. 1975. Martison Revisited. *Journal of Research in Crime and Delinquency*, 12, 133-152.

Palmer, T. 1995. Programmatic and Nonprogrammatic Aspects of Successful Intervention: New Directions for Research. *Crime and Delinquency*, 41, (1) 100-131.

Patterson, G. A. and M. S. Forgatch. 1985. Therapist Behavior as a Determinant for Client Noncompliance: A Paradox for the Behavior Modifier. *Journal of Consulting and Clinical Psychology*, 53, 846-851.

Peterosino, A., C. Turpin-Petrosino, J. O. Finckenauer. 2001. Well Meaning Programs Can Have Harmful Effects! Lessons Learned from Experiments of Programs Such as Scared Straight. *Crime and Delinquency*, 46: 354-379.

Petersilia, J. 1998. A Decade of Experimenting with Intermediate Sanctions: What Have We Learned? *Federal Probation*, 62 (Dec), 3-9.

Peterson, T. R., H. B. Waldron, and W. R. Miller. 1996. A Sequential Analysis of Client and Therapist Behaviors During Motivational Enhancement Therapy for Problem Drinking, unpublished paper.

Project MATCH Research Group. 1997. Matching Alcoholism Treatments to Client Heterogeneity: Project MATCH Post Treatment Drinking Outcomes. *Journal of Studies on Alcohol*, 58, 7-29.

Project MATCH Research Group. 1998. Therapist Effects in Three Treatments for Alcohol Problems. *Psychotherapy Research*, 8, 455-474.

Rice, M. E. and G. T. Harris. 1997. The Treatment of Mentally Disordered Offenders. *Psychology, Public Policy and Law*, 3, 126-183.

Robertson, A. A., P. W Grimes, and K. E. Rogers. 2001. A Short-Run Cost-Benefit Analysis of Community-Based Interventions for Juvenile Offenders. *Crime and Delinquency*, 47(2), 265-285.

Rogers, C. R. 1957. The Necessary and Sufficient Conditions of Therapeutic Personality Change. *Journal of Consulting Psychology*, 21, 95-103.

Rollnick, S., N. Heather, N. Bell, and R. Richmond. 1994. Matching Excessive Drinkers to Brief Interventions by Readiness to Change: Brief Motivational Intervention Versus Skill-Based Counseling. Submitted for publication.

Schechtman, Z. 2004. Client Behavior and Therapist Helping Skills in Individual and Group Treatment of Aggressive Boys. *Journal of Consulting Psychology*, 51 (4).

Shirk, S. R., and M. Karver. 2003. Prediction of Treatment Outcome Form Relationship Variables in Child and Adolescent Therapy: A Meta-Analytic Review. *Journal of Consulting and Clinical Psychology*, 71, 452-464.

Shturman, M., D. Simourd, and M. Rudavela. 2005. *Motivation to Change and its Effect on Offender Treatment Outcomes: Preliminary Results of A Meta-Analysis*. A paper presented at the Canadian Psychological Association. Montreal, July 2005.

Siqueland, L., P. Crits-Christoph, J. P. Barber, S. Butler, M. Thase, L. Najavits, L. Onken. 2000. The Role of Therapist Characteristics in Training Effects in Cognitive, Supportive-Expressive, and Drug Counseling Therapies for Cocaine Dependence. *The Journal of Psychotherapy Practice and Research*, 9: 123-130.

Smith, C. and T. P. Thornberry. 1995. The Relationship Between Childhood Maltreatment and Adolescent Involvement in Delinquency. *Criminology*, 33, 451-481.

Stein, D. M. and M. J. Lambert. 1995. Graduate Training in Psychotherapy: Are Therapy Outcomes Enhanced? *Journal of Consulting and Clinical Psychology*, 63 (5), 182-196.

Stewart, L., M. Van Dieten, and G. Graves. 1999. *A Motivational Pre-Group Program for Cognitive Programs*. Ottawa: Correctional Services of Canada.

Truax, C. B. 1966. Some Implications of Behaviour Therapy for Psychotherapy, *Journal of Counseling Psychology*, 13 (2), 160-170.

Van Dieten, M., D. Robinson, B. Millson, and A. Stringer. 2001. *Effective Case Work: A Four Stage Model*. Ottawa: Orbis Partners Inc.

Van Voorhis, P. and L. Presser. 2001. *Classification of Women Offenders: A National Assessment of Current Practices*. Washington, D.C.: U.S. Department of Justice, National Institute of Corrections.

Wilson, G. T. 1998. Manual-Based Treatment and Clinical Practice. *Clinical Psychology: Science and Practice*, 5, 363-375.

Winogron, W., M. Van Dieten, and L. Gauzas. 1998. *Controlling Anger and Learning to Manage It*. Toronto: Multi-Health Systems.

REACTION ESSAY— CHALLENGES OF BRINGING EVIDENCE-BASED PRACTICES INTO THE MAINSTREAM OF COMMUNITY CORRECTIONS

8

William D. Burrell

Consultant

Lawrenceville, New Jersey

In her paper, Marilyn Van Dieten assesses the status of effective correctional treatment, also referred to as the "what works" literature and most recently, Evidence-Based Practices. Whatever the label (this author will use Evidence-Based Practices), it is clear that the field of community corrections has come to a crossroads of sorts where the primary responsibility for advancing the state of practice in offender supervision will have to shift from the academic and research community to the practitioner community. Within the practitioner community, the majority of the burden will fall on the leaders and managers of community corrections agencies.

Consensus and Challenge

The research literature on effective correctional treatment emerged in the academic community in the late 1970s[1] and continued to grow in both size and influence through the 1980s and into the 1990s. It was at this point that Don Andrews and his colleagues produced the first articles on the principles of effective correctional treatment.[2] Studies using meta-analysis techniques continued to bolster the principles and the effectiveness of well-designed and well-implemented correctional treatment. By the turn of the new millennium, it was clear that there was substantial consensus in the academic and research communities that the 'nothing works' doctrine that had predominated the sentencing and correctional policy arenas for almost three decades was indeed wrong. Well-designed and well-implemented correctional treatment programs can be effective, often significantly so, at reducing offender recidivism and increasing public safety.

Van Dieten highlights the more significant of these studies by way of demonstrating the significant and compelling consensus that exists. She then moves on to other issues that, for me, form the challenge portion of this section. An academic consensus is certainly desirable, but that alone will have little impact unless the findings are put into practice. This is the crossroad where the responsibility for Evidence-Based Practices shifts to the practitioner community and its leadership. Community corrections executives and managers will have to assume this responsibility and work hard to implement Evidence-Based Practices in probation and parole if the substantial potential of Evidence-Based Practices to reduce recidivism is ever to be realized.

Probation and Parole: In Need of Direction

It seems an extremely opportune time for probation and parole to embrace Evidence-Based Practices. For the past thirty years, the field has struggled for a meaningful identity and compelling mission. With the discrediting of rehabilitation through the "nothing works" doctrine, probation and parole lost a major component of their mission. For more than a century, achieving offender behavior change was a core component of supervision in the community. In short order, that core component was dismissed and the field struggled mightily to find direction. Attempts in the 1980s to get tough through intermediate sanctions proved futile. The massive experiment with intensive supervision programs (ISP) across the country was largely a failure.[3] In 1985, the widely noted study of felony probation by the RAND Corporation revealed high rates of recidivism for offenders under

210

traditional probation supervision, further undermining the credibility of probation.[4] Parole supervision was being abolished, restructured, restricted, and generally marginalized in this "get tough" era.[5] In contrast, Evidence-Based Practices offers hope that this formerly core element of probation and parole is indeed viable, and holds the potential to reform and revitalize community supervision of offenders. Probation and parole agencies will be able to make significant contributions to reducing recidivism and increasing public safety by embracing Evidence-Based Practices. This new approach has the potential to restore community corrections to a position creating substantial public value through its work. For a field that has been in search of a compelling core purpose and effective strategies to accomplish that purpose, Evidence-Based Practices seems like a no-brainer.

Evidence-Based Practices: Still a 'Boutique' Program

While there are some examples of good work in implementing Evidence-Based Practices in probation and parole, they remain few and far between. Practitioners are increasingly aware of Evidence-Based Practices and its value in producing better outcomes for community supervision, but this awareness is not translating into action at an acceptable rate. As a result, Evidence-Based Practices is confined to a sort of boutique status, done on a small scale in privileged agencies. These include agencies with federal help (for example, the National Institute of Corrections), those with sufficient internal resources to establish and run their own programs, or those fortunate to have external Evidence-Based Practices programs to which they can refer offenders.

Another small group of agencies have embraced and implemented Evidence-Based Practices. These agencies have visionary, committed leaders who have seen the value that Evidence-Based Practices can provide, who understand the long-term demands of organizational transformation, and who recognize the obligation that exists to use the latest, most effective strategies and techniques for offender supervision. It is these visionary leaders who are modeling the way for all probation and parole executives.

The challenge is taking Evidence-Based Practices from its present boutique status and institutionalizing it as the standard practice in community corrections. It is no longer a research issue, as the studies have been done. It is now primarily a management challenge to take Evidence-Based Practices to the next step, and the key issue in this challenge is leadership.

Elements of the Management Challenge

As this respondent has noted before, implementing Evidence-Based Practices is not an easy thing to do.[6] It is a complex model with multiple components. It involves organizational change, which is a challenging and time-consuming task. But it can be done, and the potential for improvements in performance is substantial. Also, there is a significant professional and ethical obligation to ensure that our agencies are utilizing the latest and most effective strategies and practices.

The most important component of this challenge is to translate the Evidence-Based Practices principles into tangible line practices for the average probation/parole officer. In the majority of probation and parole agencies, the probation/parole officer is through whom Evidence-Based Practices will be delivered. Most agencies do not have separate Evidence-Based Practices "programs," nor do they have access to outside agencies that offer Evidence-Based Practices programs and services.

As Van Dieten notes, many agencies cannot afford to run Evidence-Based Practices groups and they cannot force outside agencies to use Evidence-Based Practices. In the end, the probation/parole officer *is* the program and that is where Evidence-Based Practices have to be applied. When that is accomplished, Evidence-Based Practices will cease to be a 'boutique' program and will expand significantly to become the predominant correctional practice.

There are four major areas where leaders and managers need to focus their efforts to implement Evidence-Based Practices. The first is *organizational mission and philosophy*. It must be clear to all involved that the purpose of supervision is to help offenders change their behavior, to reduce recidivism, and improve public safety. There should be no doubt in anyone's mind what the organization stands for. The second area is *organizational infrastructure*. This includes policies, procedures, training, and rewards. The organizational culture should be clearly and unhesitatingly supportive of Evidence-Based Practices.

The next two areas are well explored by Van Dieten. They include the issue of *line personnel*, in terms of their qualities, characteristics, skills, and service orientation. It is critical to ensure that the right people are brought into the organization. Keeping in mind the many agencies, which have embraced a law enforcement philosophy, this selection process is critical.

Probation/parole officers must be willing and able to accept and execute the Evidence-Based Practices model of supervision, which requires a strong commitment to helping offenders change. The last area is that of *staff supervision*. First-line supervisors are critical to the success of any Evidence-Based

Practices implementation. They also must embrace and support the new approach, which poses two challenges to them as supervisors.

First, the job of first-line supervisors will change substantially, and they will have to learn and master new skills, such as coaching and mentoring officers in behavior-change techniques. Second, as the job of their officers will also change, the supervisors must fully understand the probation/parole officer's new skills and responsibilities to provide effective supervision. As Van Dieten notes, probation/parole officers will need time to practice the new skills, and they will need effective supervision, coaching, and support as they learn and ultimately master the new skills. Supervisors also play a critical quality assurance role, monitoring implementation at the case level and taking the necessary steps to ensure fidelity to the model.

Help with the Translation

Many practitioners will struggle with the job of "translating" Evidence-Based Practices into tangible practices for the line officer. It is here that Van Dieten makes her most significant contribution. In her discussion of the skills that are effective in changing offender behavior, she provides a roadmap for practicing, training, coaching, and supervising staff. She also provides powerful evidence to help resolve that age-old dilemma about the role of the probation/parole officer—is it enforcement or helping? Are we cops or counselors? Is it law enforcement or social work?

In his seminal article on the subject in 1972, Carl Klockars proposed a role definition for probation/parole officers that he called the *synthetic officer*.[7] Such an officer synthesized a new role that combined the two polar opposites, helping and enforcing, into an integrated whole. Van Dieten makes it clear that the facilitative and helping skills are essential and must be combined with the more common approaches of monitoring and supervising. The case management skills and responsibilities that often have been associated with therapists and counselors must be integrated into the work of the probation/parole officer. Supervision must incorporate the tasks of case management oriented to behavior change that have been neglected by probation and parole in recent years.

One of the core tasks of this type of case management is the development and implementation of a case plan.[8] This function has been largely ignored in probation and parole supervision in the 'get tough' era. Yet, the case plan is the vehicle for the implementation of Evidence-Based Practices. The model presented by Van Dieten in Table 1 provides an excellent roadmap to the supervision process using a case plan.

Implementing Evidence-Based Practices in community corrections will require staff at all levels to learn new skills. Many of these skills are identified and discussed by Van Dieten. While the sheer scope of this new skills set may be daunting, the good news is that none of these skills are beyond the ability of the average probation/parole officer. The skills can be learned, practiced, and mastered without extensive clinical training. Van Dieten notes that Motivational Interviewing is an excellent example of a new skill set that has been learned and effectively applied by probation/parole officers.

Core Correctional Practices

The challenge of taking Evidence-Based Practices from its boutique status into the mainstream of correctional practice will be facilitated by the implementation of a body of practices referred to as *core correctional practices* (CCP). As defined by Dowden and Andrews (2004), the components of core correctional practices provide specific guidance to correctional staff for their interactions and interventions with offenders. They "reflect the most effective and empirically validated intervention strategies for evoking positive behavior change within offenders."[9] These strategies hold great potential for transforming the work of line probation/parole officers to conform to the principles of Evidence-Based Practices.

Van Dieten's discussion of the skills and service orientations of effective correctional practitioners provides additional insight and further develops the components of core correctional practices. The toolbox of the probation/parole officer can be greatly enhanced by the addition of these new tools. With the proper training and mastery of the new tools, probation/parole officers will become significantly more effective in achieving offender behavior change, reducing recidivism, and improving public safety.

Conclusion

Van Dieten has provided an excellent summary of the state of the art of effective correctional treatment, but more importantly, she provides a helpful guide to the critical issues facing the field of community corrections. If we are to implement Evidence-Based Practices on a wide scale, which this respondent believes we must, Van Dieten has performed a great service by identifying several key challenges and providing clear and helpful solutions.

Endnotes

[1] Gendreau, Paul and Robert R. Ross. Effective Correctional Treatment: Bibliotherapy for Cynics, *Crime and Delinquency*. Vol. 25, 4. 1979, pp. 463-489. Ross, Robert and Paul Gendreau, eds., *Effective Correctional Treatment*. Toronto, Canada: Butterworths. 1980.

[2] Andrews, D. A., James Bonta, and Robert Hoge. Classification for Effective Rehabilitation: Rediscovering Psychology. *Criminal Justice and Behavior*, 17,1. 1990. pp. 19-52.

[3] Petersilia, Joan and Susan Turner. Intensive Probation and Parole, in Michael Tonry, ed. *Crime and Justice: A Review of Research*. 17. 1993. pp. 281-335.

[4] Petersilia, Joan, et al. *Granting Felons Probation*. Santa Monica, California: RAND Corporation. 1985.

[5] Rhine, Edward E. et al. *Paroling Authorities: Recent History and Current Practice*. Laurel, Maryland: American Correctional Association, 1991. pp. 20-25

[6] Burrell, William D. Why What Works Isn't Working in Community Corrections, *Community Corrections Report*, 12, 3. 2005. pp. 37-38, 45.

[7] Klockars, Carl B. A Theory of Probation Supervision, *Journal of Criminal Law, Criminology and Police Science*. 63:4, 1972. pp. 550-557.

[8] Healy, Kerry Murphy. *Case Management in Criminal Justice*. Washington, DC: National Institute of Justice. 1999.

[9] Dowden, Craig and D. A. Andrews. The Importance of Staff Practice in Delivering Effective Correctional Treatment: A Meta-Analytic Review of Core Correctional Practice. *International Journal of Offender Therapy and Comparative Criminology*. 42: 2. 2004. p. 204.

Behavorial Management Strategies in Correctional Settings*

9

Faye S. Taxman, Ph.D.
George Mason University
Manassas, Virginia

* This paper is funded by the National institute of Corrections under NIC Technical Assistance No. 07C1001. This technical assistance activity was funded by the Community Corrections/Prisons Division of the National Institute of Corrections. The Institute is a Federal agency established to provide assistance to strengthen state and local correctional agencies by creating more effective, humane, safe, and just correctional services. The contents of this document reflect the views of Faye S. Taxman, Ph.D. The contents do not necessarily reflect the official views or policies of the National Institute of Corrections. The author would like to acknowledge the insights resulting from numerous conversations with Ms. Judith Sachwald, Director of the Maryland Division of Parole and Probation. Assistance with this manuscript also was provided by Nathaniel Phillips.

Abstract

Case management is not a new idea, and many correctional agencies incorporate case management into some aspects of their core business practice. While the attention is on what aspects are delivered, little attention is given to the theoretical framework for delivering behavioral management techniques that can be embedded in case management services. This paper presents the underlying theory of behavioral management, and then discusses how it can be used in correctional settings. The paper then goes on to identify the organizational strategies that are needed to reinforce a sound behavioral-management strategy in correctional settings. Behavioral management provides the conceptual framework for correctional agencies to engage the offender in behavior change and to reinforce the change process through small, incremental accomplishments. The cornerstone to the behavioral management approach is to develop a relationship between the offender and the correctional staff, and this relationship (alliance) is needed to provide an environment where offender change is possible. The challenge to the correctional system is essentially to allow a humanistic environment where the offender can change and for correctional agencies to pursue this environment with the same diligence as offenders in the change process.

Behavioral Management Strategies in Correctional Settings

"Science is not a set of answers. Science is a series of processes and steps by which we arrive closer and closer to elusive answers."
(Norcross, 2002:14)

Community supervision agencies are in a tug of war—balancing the law enforcement and social work goals of supervision. The tendency has been to focus on law enforcement strategies as a means to protect the public. Yet, under-resourced community supervision agencies struggle to meet the needs of the public while also realizing that current strategies have not necessarily reduced recidivism, served the public good, nor even generated new resources for probation/parole agencies to continue their campaign to adequately supervise offenders in the community. A new strategy has evolved that marries the law enforcement and social worker goals, commonly referred to as a behavioral-management approach to supervision (Taxman, 2002; Taxman, Shepardson, and Byrne, 2004; Taxman, 2006). Little is available to the field on the principles underscoring this approach and the diffusion strategies to implement this innovation in the field. This paper serves to address all of these issues.

The concept of behavioral management involves a series of over-arching principles about how to work with individuals to facilitate behavioral change (in other words, to be accountable for one's own behavior). These principles involve the basic tenets of behavioral interventions that are designed to focus on actions, or behaviors. They do not focus on the attitudes or values of individuals, although it is presumed that changes in attitudes and values will come later. The behavioralist approach relies upon carefully designed strategies that serve to identify the problematic target behavior, clarify expectations, work through a problem-solving strategy on how to address targeted behaviors, and "shape" behaviors through the use of reinforcers. The target behaviors must be precise and address the small steps needed to achieve longer term goals. It is these target behaviors (steps) that are feasible within a correctional environment, particularly supervision. Behavioral management is an umbrella term that encompasses the use of specific techniques to shape law-abiding behavior. This paper outlines the behavioral management approach for community correctional agencies.

Case (*not* Behavioral) Management:
The Supporting Science

Behavioral management is not case management; yet, they have some similarities. Case management involves processes that underscore good correctional practice. The functions ascribed to case management are assessment of risk and/or needs, case planning to identify needed services/controls, linkages with other organizations to provide the services that are not available at the correctional agency, monitoring of the offender's progress, and potentially advocacy with other service organizations to obtain the needed services (Joint Commission on Accreditation of Healthcare Organizations, 1979; National Association of Social Workers, 1992). Case management programs, in practice, vary considerably based on the emphasis placed on these functions, and in many scenarios the case manager incorporates many of these functions intuitively.

As specified in the Center for Substance Abuse Treatment's *Treatment Improvement Protocol 27: Comprehensive Case Management for Substance Abuse Treatment*, They are essentially four major types of case management practices (CSAT, 1998). They are as follows:

Broker/Generalist: A generic function that tends to focus on assessment and identification of services in the community. The broker/generalist assists the offender with the link to relevant organizations and monitors access.

Strengths-Based: The emphasis is on the offenders' strengths and trying to assist the offenders in using their own assets as a resource. The goal is generally to maximize the informal social supports of offenders while providing an aggressive form of outreach. The emphasis is on providing the needed support for the offenders to have more control over their own resources as a means to address their problem behaviors.

Assertive Case Planning: Assertive case planning is a process to focus on addressing daily life problems. The emphasis is on contact with the offenders in their place of existence (for example, home, work) and working through everyday issues.

Clinical Rehabilitation: Case management and counseling are conjoined as part of the same function. These different types of case management provide a continuum of services that range from assessment to direct counseling to monitoring performance.

Is case management effective? Generally the consensus is that case management programs have limited empirical support as effective practices. This is partially due to the various broad arrays of functions and programmatic components, which are often delivered in case management programs, as well as the slight emphasis of each program.

The limited research on case management results generally shows no difference or negative results (for example, more technical violations). These findings are due to the following: (1) insufficient number of rigorous research studies that have been conducted to test the key ingredient of case management, (2) the research may be limited because the models for case management by themselves tend to be atheoretical (more on this later), and (3) the models tend to emphasize oversight where the literature has basically found that more monitoring tends to result in more observations of noncompliance. Stated simply, research does not support case management programs, as effective. The quagmire is that research does not support case management programs, but these functions must be performed. So, the question is, what should be the next steps to good correctional practice?

Moving from Case to *Behavioral* Management Models

The question of how to provide the functions ascribed to case management–assessment, case planning, treatment, matching, and monitoring—in an effective manner requires a theoretical approach for managing the case. This immediately raises the question of whether we are interested in the case or the behavior of the individual. It is obvious that it is the individual's behavior that is of concern to the legal system—that behavior which is in violation of conditions of release and predisposes an individual to be at risk for future criminal conduct (for example, antisocial values, substance abuse, criminal peers, criminal personality, and dysfunctional family).

A case management approach assumes an impact on behavior, although classic behavioral management principles are not necessarily incorporated into case management programs. A behavioral approach works on how to alter an offender's behavior (mostly the crime and substance abusing). Behavioral management centers on the concept that offenders can learn new behaviors if the offenders are conditioned or reinforced for achieving the desired behaviors. The question is how to frame this within the context of the correctional system.

Models of Accountability

As part of the adoption of deterrence-based practices in the United States, many correctional agencies espoused the mantra of accountability, or establishing standards of behaviors based on the expectations that offenders should know what society expects from them. Stated simply, the rules of conformity in society are clear about what is considered law-abiding behavior. Offenders then need to conform to these norms. Operationally, this translated into corrections agencies adopting a social control process that focused on the offender needing to "shape up," with the key assumption that offenders already know how to "shape up" and "what is expected." Over the last decade, three other models have evolved that provide a slightly different foundation for achieving accountability in correctional agencies. These models are as follows:

Restorative Justice: This three-legged theory purports that the goals should be based on restoring justice through attention to the offender, the victim, and the community. The conceptual framework for the restoration process is based on competency development, or the process of assisting the offenders to become law-abiding by building their basic skills (for example, emotional development, educational and vocational skills). Through the process of assisting the offender to become competent as a member of society, accountability is translated into restoring the harm done to the victim and community. Built into the case plan are actions to allow the offender to achieve these goals.

Risk-Need-Responsivity (RNR): An actuarial risk assessment is useful to determine the offender's risk of reoffending (and causing harm) to society. This model embraces the concept of the least-restrictive sanction based on the actuarial risk presented by the offender. Actuarial risk should determine both the number and type of accountabilities assigned to an offender. At the lower end of the spectrum, punishment should be doled out in the form of re-payment to society for harms done. Less emphasis should be on services but more on life skills and functioning.

For moderate-risk individuals, the emphasis should be on attending to the dynamic need factors (for example, substance abuse, antisocial values, negative peers and associations, dysfunctional family, low self- control, and so on) that are likely to affect the ability of an individual to be law-abiding, but the accountabilities should be minimal. The high-risk individuals are ones where competency development is needed with attention to the crim-inogenic needs or dynamic factors that affect the individual's involvement in criminal conduct. The offender is in need of the necessary skills (behavioral) that can foster changes in attitudes and values. High risk translates into more structure, more targeted behavioral objectives, and more appropriate services to facilitate a change process.

What Works? Or Evidence-Based Practices

Functions and services should only be offered that have been shown to be efficacious according to scientific literature. That is, we should only use the intervention that has been found to change offender behavior (in the desired direction) based upon scientific evidence, generally from randomized or well-designed studies. These standards are articulated by the Campbell Collabo-ration (www.campbellcollaboration.org), an international group of scientists who are committed to conducting scientific reviews of interventions (using the broadest sense of the term), although other models are available.

Under this third model, interventions should be pursued that have been found in other settings to reduce undesirable behaviors. This process dis-tributes interventions into a taxonomy of "pursue," "do not pursue," and "don't know" where the model purports that jurisdictions should consider the "pursue" and proceed caustiously with the "don't know" programs. The goal is to ascribe to the underlying tenets and operational features of the pro-gram/intervention that has been deemed to be effective.

A review of the literature on case management programs reveals little evidence to support continuation of these programs. On the other hand, the literature has identified a broad array of interventions, as shown in Table 1, that appear to reduce criminal behavior such as cognitive- behavioral ther-apy, contingency-management systems, a therapeutic community with after-care, and so on.

Table 1. Results from Meta-Analysis on Effective Correctional and Treatment Programs

Not Effective

Case Management
Intensive Supervision
Boot Camps
Alcohol and Drug Education
Non-Directive Counseling

Promising

Treatment with Testing and Sanctions
Treatment Accountability for Safer Communities
Drug Courts
Motivational Interviewing
Moral Reasoning
Emotional Skills
12 Step with Curriculum

Effective Programs

In-Prison Therapeutic Community with Aftercare
Cognitive-Behavioral Processing (Social, Interpersonal)
Behavioral Strategies
Therapeutic Communities
Contingency Management

Sources: Lipsey and Wilson, 1998; Taxman, 1999; MacKenzie, 2000; Griffith, Rowan-Szal, Roark, and Simpson, 2000; Farrington and Welsh, 2005.

Defining Behavioral-Management Strategies

These three alternative approaches to accountability have one common denominator: they focus attention on the offender's behavior. Whether it is referred to as competency development, responsivity, or effective interventions, the emphasis is on the expected behaviors or what is considered law-abiding behavior.

Each of these approaches recognizes that offenders need to be aware of their behavior, have the necessary skills to conform, and use reinforcers to assist the offender in making the transition. In the criminal justice system, it has always been assumed that the reinforcer for compliance is a negative reinforcer or the avoidance of jail or prison—a distal goal that has unpredictable probabilities of occurring. Behavioral management, as an evolving body of literature about techniques that can be used to improve behavioral outcomes, reorients attention to proximal or more immediate behaviors. The concept is that these proximal behaviors will translate into longer-term behavioral changes through a series of steps that are both reinforcing and building of new skills to alter behavior.

Defining a Research Foundation for Behavioral- Management Principles

Examining Table 1, several programs and clinical therapies have been found to be effective in changing the behavior of offenders/addicts: contingency management, cognitive processing, behavioral techniques, and therapeutic communities (with aftercare). Other promising strategies are those with some studies that have found positive outcomes, but there are insufficient rigorous studies to make that determination.

All four have common elements: (1) use of behavioral strategies, (2) use of reinforcers (for example, social or material) to shape offender behavior, (3) use of skill-building techniques with offenders, and (4) they require staff to serve in a facilitator's role. A review of the literature reveals that there are process components that are critical in effective interventions with offenders such as (1) adhering to a common philosophy about behavior change (Taxman and Bouffard, 2002), (2) using multi-dimensional programs that can address a myriad of criminogenic needs (Lowenkamp, Latessa, and Hostlinger, 2006), (3) addressing the offender's perception of the fairness of the correctional and treatment demands and the way in which they have been treated (Taxman and Messina, 2000; Taxman and Thanner, 2003/2004; Taxman, Byrne, and Pattavina, 2005), and (4) working on different skills of the offender (Lipsey and Landenberg, 2006). Effective interventions are therefore those that fit within an environment that is supportive of the overall goals of offender change and provide the framework to deliver quality services.

Landenberg and Lipsey, as shown in Table 2 on the next page, have recently completed a series of formal meta-analyses that examine program characteristics that improve offender outcomes (reduced recidivism). They have revealed the following programmatic features that are related to better outcomes (reduced recidivism): (1) cognitive-behavioral programs, particularly those that direct attention to interpersonal relationships and anger control; (2) quality assurance in the cognitive-based training programming improves outcomes including training of personnel; (3) programs directed at offenders in the community (probation or parole) where the behaviors can be tested and reinforced in a setting where offenders are directly at risk for recidivism; (4) using personnel who have a mental health background; and (5) having offenders who have more serious offending backgrounds.

Additionally, in another study, the authors found that programs that had more frequent role-play in group sessions, focused on skills, and directed efforts toward problem solving had better results than programs without these features (Lipsey and Landenberg, 2005). The emphasis on quality practices has been reinforced in other studies (Lowenkamp, Latessa, and Smith, 2006).

Lambert and Barley (2002) provide another view into the relative importance of different components of interventions that achieve better outcomes. It should be noted that their work "characterizes the research findings of a wide range of treatments, patient disorders, dependent variables representing multiple perspectives of patient change and ways of measuring patient and therapist characteristics" (Lambert and Barley, 2002, 18), and they review research on therapies that are delivered by skilled clinicians (in other words, at least a master's level clinical degree). They have basically found that extratherapeutic factors (for example, patient characteristics, severity of problem behavior, natural support systems) account for 40 percent of the change, specific therapeutic techniques (for example, cognitive-behavioral, behavioral) account for 15 percent of the outcomes, relationship between the therapist/interventionist and the client accounts for 30 percent of the outcomes, and self-improvement factors account for 15 percent of the outcomes.

Table 2. Cognitive-Based Training Meta-Analysis Results
(Landenberger and Lipsey, 2005)

Study Characteristic	Beta with Method Controls[a]
General study characteristics	
Country: United States (1) versus Canada/UK/NZ (2)	-0.03
Publication type: Report/thesis (1)	
versus journal/chapter (2)	0.13
Year of publication	-0.11
Participant Characteristics	
Juveniles (1)/Young Adults (2)	-0.03
% male	-0.07
% minority	0.16
Recidivism-risk rating	0.27**
Cognitive-Based Training Amount	
Sessions per week	0.34**
Hours per week (logged)	0.23*
Total hours of treatment (logged)	0.38**
Length in weeks (logged)	-0.03
Sessions per week times length in weeks (logged)	-0.08
Quality of Cognitive-Based Training Implementation	
Proportion of therapeutic community dropouts	0.28**
Implementation monitoring	0.20
Cognitive-Based Training for providers	0.21
Mental health background of providers	-0.07
Practice (1)/demonstration (2)/research (3) program	0.31**
Composite implementation factor	0.40**
Other program characteristic	
Treatment setting: prison (1)/community (2)	0.20
Cognitive-Based Training emphasis: with other components	
(1)/Cognitive-Based Training alone (3)	-0.30**
Specific Cognitive-Based Training Program	
Reasoning and Rehabilitation	-0.21
Moral Reconation Therapy	0.04
Aggression Replacement Therapy	0.16
Interpersonal Problem Solving Therapy	-0.09
Thinking for a Change	0.12
Substance abuse focus	0.00
Other manualized	0.02
All other	0.01
Cognitive-Based Training Treatment Elements	
Cognitive skills	0.02
Cognitive restructuring	0.27**

Study Characteristic	Beta with Method Controls[a]
Interpersonal problem solving	0.04
Social skills	0.02
Anger control	0.32**
Moral reasoning	0.11
Victim impact	-0.14
Substance abuse	0.11
Behavior modification	0.03
Relapse prevention	0.12
Individual attention (in addition to group sessions)	0.39**

Note: Beta values from random effects multiple regression.
[a]Controlling for designing problems, attrition proportion, intent-to-treat comparison, and arrest recidivism.
*$p<0.10$
**$p<0.05$

What is most relevant here is that the issue of relationship between the caregiver and the patient/offender has been factored into the equation of outcomes. The relationship includes a number of dimensions such as the personal attributes and style of the therapist, the conditions (for example, empathy, positive regard, warmth), and the direct relationship (alliance, working endeavor, etc.). The studies recognized that the environment where the services are provided and how the relationship fits within the environment are critical factors that influence outcomes.

While much of the 'what works" literature has focused on the style of therapy or program, the results from this review of the literature identify that it is both the techniques and the environment that affect outcomes. "Techniques" refers to what the intervention is—its components, strategies, processes and parts, and goals. "Environment" refers to the relationship or the conducive nature of *how* the intervention is delivered. The value of examining both of these dimensions cannot be understated in a criminal justice environment where environmental factors tend to be downplayed.

For the criminal justice system, the realization that the relationship is a critical factor in the equation demands renewed attention. Much of the prior discussion tends to focus on the coercive nature of the treatment and the need for offender accountability. When treatment is offered within a punishment-oriented structure dominated by authoritarian models, then consideration should be given to how to facilitate productive, outcome-driven relationships where the offender is part of the process. That is, coercion may provide a framework to encourage people to change, but it can also have some drawbacks by being rigid and not allowing the offender to be a true partner in the change process. And offender change is not something that can occur merely through "whipping" people into law-abiding behavior with a series of directive commands. Change is only possible if the offender agrees to the rationale for the change.

The focus on the environment for offender change has long been the interest of Rudolf Moos and others as part of a discussion of the therapeutic milieu. But, the interest in the environment has been part of evolving discussions in therapeutic communities (Melnik, 1999), therapeutic jurisprudence (Taxman and Messina, 2000), and procedural justice (Tyler, 2006). These discussions have pointed toward the concepts that show under what environmental factors improved adherence to the treatment and/or societal rules are most likely to result. For example, Tyler and others have experimentally explored the models of procedural justice, and they have found that perceptions of fairness and equity have an impact on compliance. In experiments in many arenas, it appears that even when people engage in negative behaviors and the responses of the actors of the state (an authoritarian figure) are fair and equally applied, then the offender is more likely to comply and perceive that the outcomes are just. In thera-peutic communities, the posted rules are an example of how to ensure that all patients are aware of the rules and are treated equally.

Another example is a behavioral contract that states the consequences (positive and negative) for achieving milestones. Ultimately, the environment is critical since it provides the framework for how the individual will accept the required changes and the responses by the state to the behavior of the individual.

To that end, the nature of the relationship within the confines of the criminal justice system needs more attention (Skeem and Louden, 2006; Taxman and Thanner, 2003/2004). Table 3 presents recent findings regarding principles that were elicited from the American Psychological Association's Task Force on Empirically Based Principles of Therapeutic Change that assimilated information from two separate task forces reviewing the evidence regarding treatment and therapeutic relationship factors.

Table 3. Characteristics of Effective Relationships
(Conclusions and Recommendations of the American Psychological Association's Division 29 Task Force on Empirically Supported Therapy Relationships)

Empirically Supported Relationship Qualities

- Therapeutic alliance: works with client, not against
- Goal consensus and collaboration: agree on goals for client
- Empathy: understands client
- Cohesion in group therapy: common goals, purpose

Promising Relationship Qualities

- Quality of relational interpretations: keep client on same page
- Management of counter-transference: professional should keep negative thoughts to self
- Self-disclosure: being open with client
- Repair of alliance ruptures: work out problems with client
- Feedback: keep client informed about progress
- Congruence/genuineness: be agreeable and honest with client

Source: Norcross, 2002.

The goal was to examine the science of "identify[ing] the ways in which participant, relationship, and treatment factors and qualities interacted and potentiated one another's effects, and did so without assuming the baggage of an entire model or theory of treatment" (Norcross, 2002, 5). Factors were included as principles when more than half of the studies found these constructs to be related (correlated) to improved outcomes. These relationship constructs provide a framework for considering applications within the context of criminal justice settings, and they provide more fertile ground for examining the dynamics of the offender, officer, and technique (treatment in the broadest sense). Along with procedural justice, they raise an issue about the actions of the actors of the state (for example, supervision, case managers, treatment providers)—an important ingredient from the literature review is that actors of the state must act in a fashion that facilitates a positive relationship that includes fair and equitable actions and a partnership that is deemed valuable by the offender.

Behavioral-Management Tenets as Applied to Corrections

Deriving from the available research on offender outcomes, it becomes apparent that attention should be given to the whats and hows associated with the functions of behavioral (case) management. It is not just the functions—assessment, case planning, treatment selection, referral, delivery, and compliance management, that are important, but rather the process by which the functions occur. This refers directly to the underlying environment. The contact, which is the main technique involving the offender and the officer, is the tool. The question then is: How can we move the contact from a paper-pushing exercise to an interaction that is meaningful for the offender (and the officer)? Or, how can we move away from "bean counting," or the number of contacts, to the quality of the interaction?

The behavioral-management tenets are designed to reposition the contact to be part of a process to facilitate ease of change in the offender. This change allows the "contacts" between the offender and the case manager/officer to be similar to a brief intervention, or a focused session that is designed to achieve certain behavioral objectives on the part of the offender. The behavioral-management perspective moves the officers to the position of recognizing that they have certain goals for the offender to achieve to be part of the process, and that the goals are important to the function that is performed. From these goals there becomes a picture of how to deliver the functions. The model, as previously discussed (see Taxman, Shepardson, and Byrne, 2004), has three parts that are useful to reframing contacts to be part of a change process: assessment or the definition of the targeted goals, early change to begin the change process, and sustained change to develop networks that facilitate behavioral change.

On the next page is a list of goals, processes, and operational components that can be used in this model to achieve a focus on behavioral management. The goals are critically important because they define an organizational goal that offender accountability/change must be established in an environment that clarifies expectations (how one can be successful), nurture the development of natural support systems that outlast the supervision process, and reinforce the steps that the offender is taking to be law abiding. The associated processes illustrate the steps that must be taken, integrating the operational components to achieve these goals. These processes can be translated into measurable objectives for the supervision agency as they are switching to meaningful contacts.

Goals for Behavioral-Management Orientation

- To clarify the expectations for being successful on supervision in-cluding the purpose of the sentence, the conditions of release, and the target behaviors
- To engage the offender in the accountability/change process by defining the case plan and change process
- To allow the offender to identify and work on personal goals that are consistent with a non-offending, non-using lifestyle
- To provide the necessary reinforcers to pursue a non-offending, non-using lifestyle
- To involve/develop the natural support system of the offender

Processes that Facilitate These Goals

- A correctional environment where the offender feels that he/she can be successful on supervision
- A manageable set of target behaviors that identify short-term (proximal) objectives for the offender
- A working relationship where the officer guides the offender in steps to attain success
- The ability to change the target behaviors or address circum-stances that may affect the offender's overall success
- The use of reinforcers (preferably positive) to provide immediate gratification that occurs with making strides
- The inclusion of natural support systems in the process for some offenders to guide the offender.
- Contacts that are goal oriented: engagement, reinforcement and modification of target behaviors, movement toward informal social controls

Tools or Operational Procedures that Facilitate Prior Goals and Processes

- A risk and needs tool that focuses on factors that affect involve-ment in criminal conduct, and that can be shared with the offender
- A risk and needs tool that is useful in the development of a case plan
- The identification of programs/services that are beneficial to the offenders in achieving their goals and objectives

- The case plan that is developed with the offender, with a focus on clear, target objectives
- Feedback to the offender on progress using short-term behavioral goals
- Updating of case plan based on milestones achieved

Engagement Strategies (Assessment, Case Planning, and Service Matching)

The model begins with the concept that the offender must be engaged in the process of change or accountability in order for the offender to become an active participant in the process. The processes that must occur to engage the person are as follows: (1) creating an environment where the offender can trust the supervision officer, (2) specifying the keys to being successful on supervision, (3) working on a limited number of target behaviors in which at least one is of interest to the offender, and (4) developing the natural support systems of the offender to provide the protective factors against daily stresses and influences. The engagement process begins with the assumption that ownership of the behavior requires the offender to be in an environment where the requirements are realistic and of interest to the offender. The key in the criminal justice system is to find how to accomplish this given the nature of supervision agencies and the demands of conditions that often are imposed by the judiciary, parole boards, and/or lawmakers. The organizational climate must be altered to accommodate two major constructs: procedural fairness and trust.

Operationally, there are tools that can be used to accomplish this transformation: an objective risk and needs assessment tool and a behavioral contract. The beginning of any criminal justice process should include an assessment of risk and needs of the offender. To be dynamic, this process should use an actuarial tool that has a score. The score should be explained to the offenders as part of the process of helping them understand their individual risk factors and what the risk factors indicate.

A tool that includes dynamic need factors is also important because it provides the framework for the offenders to examine the contextual factors that affect their involvement in criminal behavior—attitude, peers, family, substance use, personality, and self-control (immediate gratification). The process involved in administering the risk and needs tool should be a semi-structured interview. This allows the offender to talk about his/her life and experiences in the criminal justice system. Having a conversation is critical to establishing the rapport (relationship), allowing the offender to be part of the processing of information and the developing of a case plan. Engagement is the process of the offender feeling comfortable enough to process difficult information and to craft a plan that he/she is invested in (owns). Through this scenario, the focus should be on gathering and sharing information with the offender.

The steps are rather straightforward:

1) Gather information on the offender;
2) Help the offender identify goals that he/she would like to achieve in the next three to six months;
3) Digest the information with the offender including risk, needs, and goals;
4) Clarify expectations about success.

Together, these are the ingredients for a case plan that focuses on target behaviors.

Distinguishing this approach from the case-management function involves the alteration of the technique and of the environment to achieve the ultimate goal of engagement. The interview (and absorption of information) requires the officer to establish a tone in the meeting so a relationship can occur. That is, the officer's deportment or manner of being must be such that allows for an alliance to occur between the officer and the offender. To be effective, the alliance must revolve around goal consensus (for example, what the offender should do to be successful) and target behaviors (for example, small steps that will be taken to achieve longer-term goals). In other words, the qualitative difference is about what is done and how it is done.

The concept behind target behaviors is that the offender should have a clear perspective on what he/she is trying to achieve. The distal goals are employment, a crime-free lifestyle, a non-substance abusing home environment, and so forth. These long-term goals take a number of steps to accomplish. While we often assume that offenders know how to accomplish these goals, researchers repeatedly have found that in everyday practice, these goals are often elusive. What does it take to get a job: an application or many applications? A call for an interview, an interview. All of these are only the steps.

There is also the other part of the employment reality—finding the list of jobs to apply for, waiting for the call(s), waiting for the call(s) that do not come, finding transportation to get to the interview, and so on. In other words, it is these realities that often dissuade or discourage offenders from achieving the employment goal. Learning the steps to walk through and addressing these issues is part of the target behaviors. The focus should be on these incremental steps that allow the offender to learn how to achieve goals. Important in this process is the provision of incentives to reinforce the positive steps, since it is more than apparent that negotiating life often presents the harsh realities of rejection and wait-and-see that reinforce to the offender that he/she has a difficult road to travel. The rewards are the "adrenaline high" to help offenders continue the strides necessary to achieve their goals.

These target behaviors are part of the plan, along with the rewards and sanctions. They specify the expectations of the agency for the agent. The culmination is to have a behavioral contract or case plan that focuses on clearly targeted behavioral objectives. The plan should have the following parts:

Summarize Offender Issues. Part of the process is to help offenders come to terms with their past. Addressing the past while working through the ambivalence and the uncertainty about the change process requires helping the offenders learn about the behavioral patterns that affect their involvement in crime and substance abusing. Summarization provides for the offender a process of acquainting the offender with the people, places, and things that affect his/her behavior (for example, the demons).

Summarize Target Behaviors. No more than three target behaviors should be included in this phase of the plan—any more than three is almost impossible to achieve and likely to frustrate the offender. The goals should also be broken down into discrete steps for the offender, which allow the offender to learn more about how to work toward a rewarding goal. The steps should also involve interests of the offender.

Summarize Services (Control and Treatment). After the goals have been determined, it is then necessary to select the type of services that should be included in the plan. It is envisioned that the mix of these services probably will be changed over time as the offender achieves desirable outcomes. The three services include *formal controls,* or the limitations on the behaviors and actions of the offender (for example, face-to-face contacts with the officer, curfew, fines, electronic monitoring), *therapeutic services* (for example, treatment, educational, and vocational services), and *informal social controls* (for example, family, peers, friends), or mechanisms that can provide support to the offender.

The higher the risk to the offender, the greater the number of services that should be included in the plan—they should address more of the dynamic criminogenic needs. For example, low-risk offenders may need none of the services except for the payment of fines/fees and quarterly administrative contact with the officer (for example, mail, telephone, or kiosk). Moderate-risk offenders may need minimal therapeutic services and some limited types of formal social control or more involvement of the informal social controls. However, it is likely that this offender only has one target behavior. High-risk individuals are more likely to have more behavioral goals and require formal and therapeutic services. (Note, this does not preclude that in conversation with the offender helpful or humanitarian services should not be offered, but rather that these should not be part of any formal agreement that requires action by the state. The goal is to lessen the state interference to minimal, which then reduces the likelihood of revocation).

Summarize Rewards and Sanctions. A fair environment is one in which the expectations are clear to the offender and the agency. That is, the offender knows what to expect when he/she achieves the target behaviors and when he/she fails to do so. This process is part of creating a just playing field in which it is not up to the discretion of the officer what is the process to use; but, rather, the officer who adopts these policies and procedures levels the playing field. This process outlines the reinforcers to replace the "highs" that offenders receive from crime and substance abuse. These are the processes that provide the encouragement to continue to proceed in achieving the goals despite relapses.

Reinforcements—Compliance Management

As shown in Figure 1, monitoring is the cornerstone of the behavioral-management process. The officer needs to determine whether the offenders accomplished the behavioral goals that they agreed to. The use of objective information that the offender and officer can process together is critical in this step. The key to behavioral management is that the offender needs to be reinforced for taking steps in a timely fashion and using both positive and negative responses appropriately. No response by the officer informs the offender that his/her efforts are not sufficient; the officer's silence removes any immediate gratification that the offender can receive. A response is necessary to reinforce the goal, and to help the offender obtain the needed reinforcers to be loyal to the behavioral contract/case plan. The interaction should be to help the offender achieve an adrenaline rush, similar to the one for obtaining risky behaviors. This "rush" is the reinforcer that the offender needs to keep committed to the target goals.

Figure 1. Behavioral-Management Process

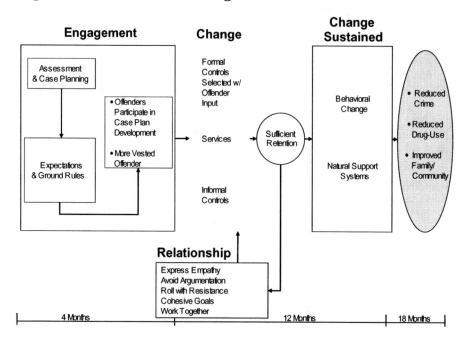

The best place to seek guidance on the process for reinforcers is the deterrence and contingency-management literature. Essentially, both have two features—swift and certain—which have been empirically supported. Severity is not one of the effective factors, and, in fact, severity does not shape behavior. This means that the reinforcers need to be timely and certain so that the offender is aware of what to expect. Swiftness means that there is a need to provide reinforcers as the behavior occurs, not weeks or months later. Certainty means that the schedule or protocol for the reinforcers should be well-known (in other words, shared with the offender) and in the best of scenarios, negotiated with the offender. That is, it is critical that the consequences for failing to achieve the targeted behaviors are clear and concise to the offender (and to the criminal justice system, which should apply them fairly).

A behavioral contract should be monitored at least weekly (or on some other schedule that meets the goals of supervision). To be effective, the offender needs to understand what the reinforcers are and when they are to be applied. The contract or case plan needs to spell out the reinforcers in a way that the offender can understand the target behaviors and the steps that will be taken to reinforce the attainment of goals.

The contingency-management system has a number of examples of a variety of reinforcement techniques that can be used to include community-reinforcement vouchers, fishbowl (a bowl which has names in it where the agency can randomly select a winner), and rewards. The "rewards" that are provided in response to goal attainment are focused on activities that the offender desires—social rewards (for example, "'Atta boys"; letters to family/spouse/criminal justice system on progress; access to limited activities such as gym passes, recreation programs) and material rewards (for example, financial rewards, vouchers that can be traded in for goods).

Similarly, a punishment structure must be in place for dealing with the offender's failure to comply with behaviors. It involves the same principles of swiftness and certainty. The offender needs to know (particularly for those steps that involve long-term change such as drug use) what the consequences of continued drug use are and whether these are the same as the consequences for a new arrest, failure to make a treatment session, or other common factors. Using the reinforcement principle, offenders cannot be "shaped" if they do not feel the consequences, and the tendency to stack up failures only contributes to the offenders' perception that the system is "out to get them." The failure of the officer to acknowledge that the offender did not comply with the contract results in the offender believing that he/she has "gotten over" on the officer, until the hammer hits and the offender feels that the officer does not give him/her a chance. That is, the lack of response by the officer creates an environment in which offenders can blame the system instead of themselves.

Part of the reinforcement structure is to acknowledge when an offender has reached key milestones, and then to redefine the contract to allow the offender to continue to progress. Usually this is referred to as *the reassessment process*, but under a behavioral-management framework, it is a practice that can occur at each contact. The attention is to the tasks and target behaviors instead of distal goals. By attending to these incremental target behaviors, the offender can focus on short-term target behaviors. This makes the reassessment process dynamic, where each contact provides the forum for providing feedback to the offender.

An untapped resource in the reinforcers is the natural support systems of offenders. Social controls are most frequently provided in the natural setting (for example, house, employment, hanging out) by non-governmental organizations such as the family, peers, associates, employers, guardians, or other support mechanisms. The role of these natural supports in behavioral decisions has not been highlighted in the criminal justice literature—it has mainly been a sideline that assumes that offenders can resume contact with their social support networks. The goal of supervision overall should be to assist the offender in developing, repairing, and maintaining these natural (prosocial) support systems.

Translating the Concept to Practice

Change is difficult, whether it occurs at the individual or organizational level. Case management can become behavioral management with small changes in the environment. The similarities between the concepts of case and behavioral management are important; they help to ensure that adoption and implementation are more likely to occur under situations where the innovations are small incremental changes to the existing practice (Rogers, 1995). The conditions under which diffusion is likely to lead to adopting and sustaining of the practice are the following: (1) the changes are modest, (2) the organization tries some of the processes, (3) the tools are in place to make the adoption practical, and (4) the purpose is consistent with the organizational goals.

Additionally, Rogers (1995) mentions five aspects of innovations that can affect the speed at which they are accepted. These include (1) its relative advantage, or how much better the innovation is than the old idea; (2) compatibility, or how well the innovation meshes with social norms; (3) complexity, or how easy the innovation is to understand; (4) "trial-ability," or how easy it is to test the innovation; and (5) observability, or how visible the results are. The behavioral-management strategy builds upon how corrections should be practiced but addresses some of the conceptual practices that are necessary to change the climate of the organizations.

The environmental change in many criminal justice/correctional agencies is probably the most challenging part of the process in moving toward a behavioral-management strategy. The critical environmental shifts that must be recognized (and planned, and thoughtfully designed) include:

- Reducing the discretion of individual officers
- Enhancing the offender's role in the assessment
- Using case planning and monitoring processes
- Developing office policies that support and enhance the role of the offender as a partner in the change process.

These are critical environmental shifts that must be recognized, planned, and thoughtfully designed. Environment refers to the norms of the operating office. They include what the expected priorities are for the agency and for the staff, how offenders are handled, and how to integrate the treatment and other resources into the supervision environment. Climate influences the likelihood that new programs and services will thrive and flourish versus becoming short-lived entities. As noted during the flurry of intermediate-sanction reforms of the 1990s, the climate determines whether the existing services will "starve off" or sink new ideas to allow existing practice to prevail. The issues affected in climate change involve a series of strategies.

Participatory Management and Decision Making

Depending on the style of the organization, the creation and innovation or adoption of new ideas can be either a top down (management driven) or bottom up (grassroots) approach. While either can successfully generate ideas, implementation of the ideas is more often affected by the manner in which the ideas are introduced to and processed by the organization, and then generated into a design or plan.

The key element needed for change to occur is that the creation of a plan must be translated to each individual working unit to fit within the culture of that working unit and to be adapted to the resources, staffing, and unique characteristics of each unit. Team processes that include vertical slices of the organization are important in the design, development, and implementation process. These slices must include the middle managers who often are the backbone of any new innovation and are also the group who ultimately can determine its success or failure.

The goal of participatory management is to have the team translate the concepts into a workable plan and design for the unit. To do this, the team must walk through four major issues:

1) How should cases (offenders) be processed in this office, or what is the business process that underscores the movement of an offender from intake to discharge?
2) How should the assessment tools be used, both in terms of informing the offender about criminal drivers and for the purpose of developing behavioral contracts?
3) What type of offender-related behaviors should result in incentives and in sanctions?
4) What type of relationship should exist between offenders and staff to achieve the goals of the organization?

Answers to these questions can then help with the transformation of the office to one that uses a behavioral-management model.

Vision Cohesion. Part of the efforts should be devoted to developing cohesion on the vision of the organization and on the goals of managing offender behavior. Cohesion means that management and staff are in agreement with the vision and goals. Cohesion occurs from both a participatory-management focus on goal cohesion and through bilateral discussions with management as to the direction of the organization and its primary goals. Cohesion serves to reduce the notion that the change is temporary and emphasizes that the change is directed to the main goals of the organization.

Translation. Participatory management and teamwork together are designed to translate the model into operational practice. As suggested above, answers to key questions need to be given to align the model to the unit. Alignment is critical because it requires the team to translate the ideas and concepts into operational procedures that are workable within the organizational setting. It also forces the organization to determine and tailor the components to the specific organization and staff resources. This translation must involve definitions of key concepts, work processes, decision points, and checks and balances. The translation is a key to one of the main concepts of diffusion—trial-ability. The innovation cannot be tried until it is structured in such a manner as to make it fit within the organization.

Tools: the Guts of the Translation. Often, the operational concepts should involve the creation, adoption, or modification of tools that affect the workflow. The behavioral-management model has a number of concepts that require associated tools or procedures which the organization must be responsible for in order for the model to be implemented with a certain degree of structure to ensure that the model is being adhered to. These tools include:

1) A risk and needs assessment tool that translates the domains that are pertinent for the case plan or behavioral contract
2) Feedback to the offender of the results of the assessment process
3) A behavioral contract to outline the expectancies including the menu of rewards and sanctions that are viable for the field
4) A reassessment process or criteria for judging the offender's achievement of target behaviors
5) A process to assess the quality of the interaction or relationship between the offender and the staff

The organization should have in place tools that replace existing agency paperwork or protocols to reinforce the innovation.

Staff and Management Skills. The model, which addresses the "hows" of managing offender behavior, requires an assessment of the skill sets of the staff and organization. At a minimum, the new model requires the adoption of four basic skills: (1) communication, (2) relationship or rapport building in an interview setting, (3) ability to engage in contingency-management sessions, and (4) ability to deal with ambivalence and resistance (both offenders and staff). Each component focuses on certain skills that address the underlying components. A review of the training available in most jurisdictions has revealed that these components typically are not provided in the pre-service or in-service training at most correctional agencies. An agency adopting this model will need to learn to bring new training for these skills in to their organization.

Benchmarks and Performance Management. Just like participatory management, the key step in the implementation of the innovations is to have a series of benchmarks that define implementation. The benchmarks should be in terms of measurable-programmatic objectives that can be used to determine whether the agency is making progress in the transformation. Each step in the model should have benchmarks that guide implementation and provide feedback to the unit and the staff on the progress made. While there may be a tendency to identify a laundry list of benchmarks, the following is a list of measurement benchmarks that can be used to determine progress:

- Percentage of assessments that use a standardized risk and needs assessment tool (use of assessment tool)

- Percentage of behavioral contracts that include the criminogenic needs identified in the risk and needs assessment tools (relevant behavioral contracts)

- Percentage of progress on target behaviors that are provided incentives as documented in the case notes, and the average number of days from the behavior to the incentives (use of positive reinforcers)

- Percentage of progress on target behaviors that provide sanctions, and the average number of days from the behavior to the sanction (use of negative reinforcers)

- Percentage of offenders who report for their required meetings (rapport building)

- Percentage of offenders who have a violation warrant, and the average number of days from the behavior to the warrant (outcome)

- Percentage of offenders who are arrested for a new crime while under supervision, and the average number of days from the intake to the arrest (outcome)

While other measures are pertinent and useful, this list provides a starting point to understand the progress in implementing the initiative. As the initiative develops, new benchmarks may be decided upon to assist the staff in assessing their progress in implementation. In this case, more is not better since the goal is not to overload the staff but to establish priorities for the organization in the implementation process.

Conclusion

Behavioral management provides a breath of fresh air into the antiquated and often underconceived concept of "contacts" that defines the business of case management or supervision. The behavioral-management principles are relevant because they are compatible with the flow of work in the correctional system. But, the behavioral-management approach focuses the efforts of the supervision officer or case manager on being a facilitator of offender change. The authority of the supervision officer or case manager can be used as an incentive in that this individual is in a position to assist the offenders in making difficult choices about the direction of their lives. The behavioral-management approach positions the officer/case manager to guide, problem-solve, and reinforce the offender in a pro-social direction. The hardest part of the behavioral-management approach is that it requires attention to the core principles of relationship (rapport) between the offender and staff—without building this component, the other components (for example, engagement, prosocial behaviors) are unlikely to occur.

In fact, behavioral management is more about the socio-political environment of the change process. Techniques are important—risk assessment, use of rewards and sanctions as reinforcers, type of therapy, and behavioral contracts—but they are only as important as the ability for the offender to be a human being (with our many imperfections) in the process of change. And for a criminal justice agency both the humanitarian and the shaping processes are challenges based on the past three decades of "get tough" policies. Therein lies the real challenge.

References

Center for Substance Abuse Treatment (CSAT). 1998. *Treatment Improvement Protocol 27: Comprehensive Case Management for Substance Abuse Treatment.* Rockville, Maryland: Department of Health and Human Services.

Farrington, D. and B. Weldon. 2005. Randomized Experiments in Criminology: What Have We Learned in the Last Two Decades? *Journal of Experimental Criminology,* 1:1-29.

Griffith, J. D., G. A. Rowan-Szal, R. R. Roark, and D. D Simpson. 2000. Contingency Management in Outpatient Methadone Treatment: A Meta-Analysis. *Drug Alcohol Dependency,* 58(1/2): 55-66.

Joint Commission on Accreditation of Healthcare Organizations. 1979. *Principles of Accreditation of Community Mental Health Service Programs.* Oakbrook Terrace, Illinois: Joint Commission on Accreditation of Hospitals.

___. 1995. *Accreditation Manual for Mental Health, Chemical Dependency, and Mental Retardation/Developmental Disabilities Services. Vol. 1, Standards.* Oakbrook Terrace, Illinois: Joint Commission on Accreditation of Healthcare Organizations.

Lambert, M. J. and D. E Barley. 2002. "Research Summary on the Therapeutic Relationship and Psychotherapy Outcomes." In J. Norcross, ed., *Psychotherapy Relationships That Work.* New York: Oxford University Press. Pgs 17-36.

Landenberger, N. A. and M. W. Lipsey. 2005. The Positive Effects of Cognitive-Behavioral Programs for Offenders: A Meta-Analysis of Factors Associated with Effective Treatment. *Journal of Experimental Criminology,* 1(4): 451-476.

Lipsey, M. W. and N. A. Landenberger, 2006. Cognitive Behavioral Interventions. In B. C. Welsh and D. P. Farrington, eds., *Preventing Crime: What Works for Children, Offenders, Victims, and Places?* Great Britain: Springer, pgs 57-71.

Lipsey, M. W. and D. Wilson. 1998. Effective Intervention for Serious Juvenile Offenders: A Synthesis of Research. In R. Loeber and D. P. Farrington, eds., *Serious and Violent Juvenile Offenders: Risk Factors and Successful Interventions.* Thousand Oaks, California: Sage.

Lowenkamp, C. T. and E. J. Latessa. 2005. Increasing the Effectiveness of Correctional Programming through the Risk Principle: Identifying Offenders for Residential Placement. *Criminology and Public Policy,* 4(2), 263-289.

Lowenkamp, C. T., E. J., Latessa, and A. M. Holsinger. 2006. The Risk Principle In Action: What Have We Learned From 13,676 Offenders and 97 Correctional Programs? *Crime and Delinquency*, 52(1), 77-93.

Lowenkamp, C. T., E. J. Latessa, and P. Smith. 2006. Does Correctional Program Quality Really Matter? The Impact of Adhering to the Principles of Effective Intervention. *Criminology and Public Policy*, 5(3):575-594.

MacKenzie, D. L. 2000. Evidence-Based Corrections: Identifying What Works. *Crime and Delinquency*. 46 (4): 457-461.

Melnik, G. M. 1999. Clarifying the Nature of Therapeutic Community Treatment: The Survey of Essential Elements Questionnaire (SEEQ). *Journal of Substance Abuse Treatment*, 16(4): 307-313.

National Association of Social Workers. 1992. Case Management's Cost, Benefits Eyed. *National Association of Social Workers News*. Washington, DC: NASW Press.

Norcross, J. 2002. *Psychotherapy Relationships That Work: Therapist Contribution and Responsiveness to Patients*. New York: Oxford University Press.

Rogers, E. M. 1995. *Diffusion of Innovations*, 5th ed. New York: The Free Press.

Skeem, J. and J. E. Louden. 2006. Toward Evidence-Based Practice for Probationers and Parolees Mandated to Mental Health Treatment. *Psychiatric Services*, Mar, 57(3): 333-42.

Taxman, F. S. 1999. Unraveling "What Works" for Offenders in Substance Abuse Treatment Services. *National Drug Court Institute Review II*, (2): 93-134.

Taxman, F. S and J. Bouffard. 2002. Assessing Therapeutic Integrity in Modified Therapeutic Communities for Drug-Involved Offenders. *Prison Journal*, 82(2): 189-212.

Taxman, F. S. and N. Messina. 2002. Civil Commitment and Mandatory Treatment, in C.G. Leukefeld, F. Tims, and D. Farabee, eds., *Clinical and Policy Responses to Drug Offenders*. Lexington, Kentucky: Center on Drug and Alcohol Research, pgs. 283-300.

Taxman, F. S., E. Shepardson, and J. M. Byrne. 2004. *Tools of the Trade: A Guide to Implementing Science into Practice*. Washington, D.C.: National Institute of Corrections, Maryland Division of Parole and Probation, and Maryland Governor's Office of Crime Control and Prevention, http://www.nicic.org/Library/020095

Tyler, T. R. 2004. Enhancing Police Legitimacy. *The Annals of the American Academy of Political and Social Science*, 593: 84-99.

___. 2006. Legitimacy and Legitimation. *Annual Review of Psychology*, 57, 375-400.

REACTION ESSAY— GUIDING PRINCIPLES FOR IMPLEMENTING CASE MANAGEMENT *

10

Marilyn Van Dieten, Ph.D.

Orbis Partners, Inc.
Toronto, Ontario, Canada

* This paper was funded by the National institute of Corrections under NIC Technical Assistance No. 07C1001. This technical assistance activity was funded by the Community Corrections/Prisons Division of the National Institute of Corrections. The Institute is a federal agency established to provide assistance to strengthen state and local correctional agencies by creating more effective, humane, safe, and just correctional services.

This report was prepared through a cooperative agreement, at the request of the International Community Corrections Association, through the coordination of the National Institute of Corrections. The contents of this document reflect the views of Marilyn Van Dieten, Ph.D. The contents do not necessarily reflect the official views or policies of the National Institute of Corrections.

Abstract

Agencies and staff working with offenders routinely perform functions that fall under the rubric of traditional case management. Assessment, case planning, referral, and brokerage are ongoing daily activities that often are viewed as a set of discrete or unrelated tasks. Rarely are these functions performed in concert with theory, and far too often, the potential impact of these activities remains unrealized.

In her paper, *Behavioral Management Strategies in Correctional Settings*, Dr. Faye Taxman (2008) presents an alternative approach to case management using behavioral theory to anchor the goals, processes, and functions into an integrated model. The goal of this paper will be to summarize key components of the Taxman model that are endorsed by the evidence-based practice literature. In addition, we will merge research from the fields of mental health and corrections to propose a set of guiding principles to assist with the implementation of case management practices.

Introduction

Case management as a practice has a long and controversial history in the field of corrections. Although used for decades, the debate continues with respect to if and when case management is viable and effective. Emerging in the early 1970s, the first case-management models were designed to address the closing of mental-health hospitals. The primary goal of the "case manager" was to assist clients to identify needs and then access medical, psychiatric, psychological, and social services dispersed throughout the community. Since this time, we have witnessed various iterations of the original model. It can be argued that some form of case management, whether formal or informal, is used in almost every human service agency.

The range of differences in models and approaches that are subsumed under the umbrella of case management has created an ongoing challenge for researchers hoping to explore its relative impact. According to Marshall (1996), there has been a tendency in the literature to lump these models together and to view case management as a single-replicable approach. As a result, more promising practices are viewed under the same lens as those reporting negative outcomes. This has contributed to the erroneous belief that case management has a negligible impact and that it is largely ineffective.

This paper will serve as a companion piece to Dr. Taxman's chapter (in this volume) *Behavioral Management Strategies in Correctional Settings*. The first segment of this paper offers a critical examination of the case-management literature to help identify the key elements, functions, and practices that have been found to contribute to favorable outcomes in mental health settings. We then will look more closely at the correctional literature and the model proposed by Taxman to highlight the case-management components that are necessary for effective work with offenders. In the third and final segment of this paper, we propose some guiding principles to assist with the implementation of effective case-management practices in correctional settings.

What Can We Learn From Mental Health Research?

The field of mental health has devoted considerable attention to the development and evaluation of case-management approaches with the severely and persistently mentally ill (see, for example, the comprehensive list of resources and research abstracts available through the National Resource Center on Homelessness and Mental Illness, www.nrchmi. samhsa.gov). Though a number of authors have reported negative or neutral outcomes (Holloway and Carson, 2001; Marshall, Lockwood, Green et al., 1998), some evidence suggests that when approaches are separated to reflect differences in ideology, practice, and function, the differential impact of case management is more readily apparent.

For the purpose of this paper, we will distinguish between standard case management, Assertive Community Treatment, and intensive or clinical case management. Marshall (1998) describes "standard" case management as a low-intensity approach in which case managers offer a largely office-based service, brokering interventions from other agencies. Each case manager has a caseload of thirty or more clients who they see infrequently and the primary emphasis is on managing the case versus the reduction of symptoms, behavioral change, and improved life satisfaction.

By contrast, Assertive Community Treatment (ACT) is a form of case management that is distinguished from a standard approach by several important features. First, rather than a case manager coordinating services, an Assertive Community Treatment multidisciplinary team provides services directly to an individual that are tailored to meet his/her specific needs. An Assertive Community Treatment team typically includes members from a variety of fields including psychiatry, nursing, psychology, and social work with increasing involvement of substance abuse and vocational rehabilitation specialists. Based on their various areas of expertise, the team members collaborate to deliver integrated services of the recipient's choice, monitor progress toward goals, and adjust services over time to meet the recipient's changing needs. The staff-to-recipient ratio is small (one clinician for every ten recipients) and services are provided twenty-four hours a day, seven days a week for as long as they are needed.

The third approach, commonly referred to as intensive-case management, incorporates a range of functions and services that are more intense than standard approaches and resemble the Assertive Community Treatment model in some respects. Schaedle, McGrew, Bond, and Epstein (2002) compared experts' views on the critical ingredients of Assertive Community Treatment and intensive case management and found that these approaches resemble each other but that Assertive Community Treatment is more clearly articulated and refined.

As indicated previously, researchers have established that these approaches vary with respect to impact. Marshall, Lockwood, Green et al. (1998) analyzed eleven controlled studies of standard case management and reported largely negative findings. In their review of standard case management models, Holloway and Carson (2001) verified these results and once again described largely negative effects. To date, only one isolated study has demonstrated positive results, and this may be attributed to the fact that the number of contacts with the case manager was significantly higher than practiced in most standard settings.

In contrast to the less than satisfying outcomes reported for standard case management approaches, more than twenty-five controlled outcome studies have demonstrated the effectiveness of Assertive Community Treatment, and it is now recognized as an evidence-based practice (Drake, Mueser, Torrey et al., 2000). Marshall and Lockwood et al., (1998) conducted the first meta-analysis of Assertive Community Treatment and found that clients in these programs benefited on a wide-range of performance outcomes. In their meta-analysis of mental-health case management, Ziguras and Stewart (2000) compared outcomes for Assertive Community Treatment and intensive (clinical) case management. Of the forty-four studies reviewed, thirty-five compared Assertive Community Treatment or clinical case management with usual treatment and nine directly compared Assertive Community Treatment with intensive (clinical) case management. Both types of case management were more effective than mental health services without case management in three domains: lowering the cost of care; reducing family burden; and achieving overall family satisfaction with services. The authors concluded that Assertive Community Treatment and intensive (clinical) case management improved the effectiveness of mental health services, with Assertive Community Treatment demonstrating a greater impact on reducing hospitalization.

Existing research supports the use of intensive and Assertive Community Treatment case-management models in mental health settings. However, these approaches were designed specifically to address the needs of the severely mentally ill. To determine the usefulness and value of modifying and adapting elements of these approaches within correctional settings, it is important to identify the specific and common factors that contribute to positive outcomes.

Unfortunately, with the exception of Assertive Community Treatment, few of the case-management programs reported in the literature have clearly articulated models. As a result, the following discussion is limited to an exploration of Assertive Community Treatment.

Assertive Community Treatment has evolved considerably since its first inception in the 1970s and is currently used across North America, Europe, and Australia. The primary outcomes of Assertive Community Treatment have been to provide decentralized, local, community-based mental health care and subsequently decrease the use of inpatient services, enhance the quality of life of severely mentally ill patients, and address substance abuse problems. Despite commonalities in outcomes and targets, variations in Assertive Community Treatment programs with respect to scope, eligibility, caseload, and size contribute to difficulties in clarifying the elements critical to ensure positive outcomes. Mueser, Bond, Drake, and Resnick (1998) conducted an extensive review of the Assertive Community Treatment literature but could not find evidence linking specific program elements to outcomes.

In 2004, the Lewin Group was contracted by the Substance Abuse and Mental Health Services Administration (SAMSHA) and the Health Care Financing Administration (HCFA) to identify critical factors of the Assertive Community Treatment model that contribute to and/or represent barriers to successful outcomes. Like Mueser et al. (1998), they conducted an exhaustive review of the existing research and were unable to explain why Assertive Community Treatment is successful. They decided that a more promising method to identify the critical factors was to review and compare four fidelity models that have been constructed to assess adherence to Assertive Community Treatment. Several studies have found that higher fidelity to the Assertive Community Treatment model is linked to positive outcomes (McGrew and Bond, 1995; McHugo, Drake, Teague et al., 1999; Latimer, 1999). By looking across these studies, the Lewin group was able to identify factors considered critical by the literature and expert consensus.

Preliminary results suggested that several elements are frequently associated with positive outcomes. These elements and their operational definitions are presented in Table 1.

The Lewin Group concluded that the most consistently reported critical factors include ensuring continuity of service delivery; targeting clients with severe and persistent mental illness (those who need it most); relying on a team approach with high levels of contact and low caseload size; and assessing individual needs and matching needs to comprehensive services. Finally, they emphasized the importance of staff skills to engage and motivate the client.

Table 1. Critical Components of Assertive Community Treatment

Critical Components	Operational Definitions
1. Admission criteria	Explicit admission criteria are used to ensure that a defined population receives Assertive Community Treatment services. Treatment and support services are individualized
2. Time limits	Services are provided until consumer treatment goals are met; intensity varies according to needs
3. Provide a comprehensive range of services	Assessment Case management Treatment planning Crisis intervention (24-hour crisis lines) Individual supportive therapy Medication prescription and monitoring Substance abuse services Work-related services Support for activities of daily living (ADL) Social, interpersonal relationship, and leisure skills training Education, support, and consultation to consumer's families and other supports Vocational supports Coordination of hospital admissions and discharges Other support services
4. Small case load	Retain a relatively small caseload size with the staff to consumer ratio ranging from 1:10-1:20 depending on the needs of the program
5. Team approach	Qualified and well trained personnel who work together to coordinate and provide services while ensuring continuity of care
6. Setting	Interventions are carried out at the locations where problems/issues occur and support is needed (in vivo) rather than in hospitals or clinics
7. Engagement methods	The team actively engages individuals in treatment using motivational strategies and monitors their progress while respecting the recipient's right to choice and privacy

The Efficacy of Case Management in Corrections

The mental health field has devoted considerable effort toward the refinement and evaluation of case-management practices. Holt (2000) has argued that the critical components and functions identified for mental health models can be used as a starting point for corrections as long as approaches are altered to address differences in agenda and outcome. Despite available information, corrections has directed less attention toward the identification of critical elements and the establishment of working models.

Several groups have introduced standard and more intensive-case-management models with substance abusing offenders. Results suggest that the impacts of these approaches vary dramatically with less-than satisfactory outcomes. This has contributed to heightened skepticism in the field of corrections regarding the value of existing approaches (Longshore, Turner, and Fain, 2005; Taxman, 2008).

Our review of the outcome literature yielded only a handful of well-designed outcome studies. Rhodes and Gross (1995) evaluated two case-management programs for drug-involved offenders on pretrial and probation status. Offenders were assigned to one of three conditions: (1) service referrals, (2) service referrals plus one session of counseling, or (3) service referrals with weekly contacts from a case manager for a period of six months. Offenders in the latter group who received weekly contacts were less likely to have engaged in further crime or to use illegal drugs; however, the results were significant for only one of the two programs that participated in the study.

Martin, Inciardi, Scaripitti, and Nielsen (1997) explored the impact of case management on parolees with substance-abuse problems transitioning from prison to the community. Parolees were randomly assigned to standard parole or a modified "assertive-case management" model. Results suggested that parolees receiving case management were more likely to receive drug treatment, stay in treatment longer, were less likely to be rearrested or to report drug use at an eighteen-month follow-up. Unfortunately, the effects on treatment duration and drug use were not always statistically significant.

In a study conducted by Longshore, Turner, and Fain (2005) the impact of case management was explored using a quasi-experimental design. Substance-using parolees were assigned to a case manager in the community and provided with a needs assessment, placement in drug abuse treatment, and other social services. Results at the end of a six-month follow-up period suggested that there were no differences between the control and the experimental group. However, a moderate impact on drug use and recidivism emerged when case management was delivered in greater dosages (defined as more frequent phone and office contact).

No doubt there are difficulties in assessing the efficacy of existing case-management approaches and determining the critical factors for correctional populations. Relatively few controlled-outcome studies have been conducted, and there are numerous inconsistencies among them with respect to the target population, dosage, caseload size, functions performed, staff training, experience.

A more promising avenue of inquiry has emerged from a qualitative study conducted by Partridge (2004). Partridge completed a national review of case-management models delivered across probation departments in the United Kingdom. Using a survey format, information was elicited from thirty-one of fifty-four departments. This permitted the researcher to systematically classify case-management practices into three main models: specialist, generalist, and hybrid.

The *specialist* model most closely resembles the standard-case model presented earlier in this paper. Essentially, assessment and service provision are separated and case managers play the role of referral agent versus service provider. The advantage of this approach is that staff can become extremely competent in specific functions such as assessment. In contrast, the *generalist* model most closely resembles the clinical-case management or Assertive Community Treatment models in that efforts are made to develop a personal relationship with the offender, and there is an emphasis on the continuity-in-service provision.

By assessing links between the models and performance outcomes, Partridge concluded that each model had benefits for different stakehold-ers—senior management, practitioners, and offenders. Specialist models were greatly valued by senior management because service delivery could be more readily coordinated and targeted. Alternatively, generic models appeared to enhance staff motivation because they allowed staff to work with mixed caseloads and permitted them to follow the offender and thus witness the impact of their work. Offenders also preferred the generic models as they provided a "more coherent supervision experience" (Partridge, 2004, 4). Partridge concluded that regardless of the model used, several core-case-management principles were more likely to enhance the outcome. Not surprisingly, these principles resonate with the findings from the mental health literature discussed earlier.

First, there is a clear role for assessment to determine: who should receive services, the intensity of intervention, the needs of the offender, and the establishment of an individualized case plan. Second, continuity of contact with the same case manager and/or team is essential to building rapport and enhancing motivation. The transition of an offender from one caseload to another can be managed by providing an introductory meeting between parties. Third, the greater the level of task separation and referral to disparate programs and activities, the more the offender reported confusion. This was particularly true when contact with the case manager was limited. An increase in face-to-face contact resulted in a greater sense that identified needs were being addressed. Finally, openness, flexibility, and support demonstrated by staff were key motivating factors for offenders.

Available empirical evidence provides only limited support for the standard-case-management practices typically adopted in the field of corrections. The Partridge study (2004) suggests that a more promising body of research to guide the development of an effective approach is the "what works" and evidence-based practices literature (Andrews and Bonta, 2002). The goals, processes, and operational procedures proposed by Taxman (2006) as well as a four-stage case-management approach developed by Van Dieten, Robinson, Millson, and Stringer (2002) were influenced directly by this body of research.

Taxman (2008) demonstrates how adherence to the principles of risk (use a standardized assessment to identify who requires intervention and how much); need (specify criminogenic needs or the appropriate targets of intervention); responsivity (rely on treatment modalities such as behavioral strategies to facilitate change); and program integrity (provide staff with training and ongoing supervision to monitor program fidelity) are important activities linked to reductions in recidivism and should guide case management practices. A summary of these key functions and activities recommended by Van Dieten et al. (2002) are presented in Table 2 on the next page.

In addition to the "what" of effective-case-management practice, Taxman (2008) also devotes considerable attention to the "how" and emph-asizes the importance of the relationship between the practitioner and the offender. Andrews and Bonta (2002) and colleagues reported an example of the importance of style, which categorized the approach used by probation officers to establish two broad categories of skills. The first set included structuring skills (for example, contingency management, effective reinforcement, disapproval) and the second empathy, or relationship skills.

Table 2. Summary of the Key Functions and Activities Required to Achieve Favorable Outcomes

Assessment	Engage, listen, and elicit challenges and strengths	• Establish risk to community and set supervision standards • Identify criminogenic needs • Identify protective factors or strengths
Enhance motivation	Provide feedback, set agenda, and complete case plan in collaboration with the offender	• Determine priority need areas • Establish commitment to work on need areas
Effective treatment and intervention	Provide information or access to comprehensive services; build formal and informal supports	• Criminogenic needs are reduced • Strengths are increased/enhanced • Formal and informal supports are established and maintained
Monitor and support	Constantly review progress and update the case plan; work proactively to prevent recurrence of criminal or antisocial behavior	• Satisfactory reintegration into the community • Completion of supervision order • Reduced recidivism and future criminal justice involvement

Though additional research is needed to verify the importance of these skills, some evidence suggests that both are necessary to increase compliance with the court order and support other favorable outcomes linked to recidivism. The style and approach used by the correctional practitioner was also a significant finding in the Partridge (2004) study. As indicated previously, staff perceived as more flexible, available, and able to demonstrate interest in the offender were rated as more effective and better able to contribute to a successful probation experience.

A renewed interest in the "how" of case management and supervision has become increasingly evident in the field of probation. For example, in the last decade, probation departments have expressed interest in practices designed to engage and motivate offenders. The popularity of Motivational Interviewing (Miller and Rollnick, 2002) is one example of this shift from a risk-management focus (where the function of supervision is to monitor the court order) to a more deliberate interest in risk-reduction strategies.

Moving Toward an Integrated Case-Management Approach

The "what works" literature provides a wealth of information to assist in the development of effective models and approaches (Taxman, 2008; Van Dieten, Robinson, Millson, and Stringer, 2002, 2006). We know what tasks and functions should be performed to ensure positive outcomes. At the same time, a renewed interest in the importance of "how" also has led to advancements in our understanding of the style and approach that should be used to both engage and motivate offenders. Finally, lessons learned from the field of mental health as Assertive Community Treatment and other models that have evolved, provide us with a method to operationalize the process of case management and to evaluate program adherence.

In this segment, we would like to integrate lessons learned from research and field practice into a set of guiding principles for case management. We believe that these principles will help to ensure the effective implementation and evaluation of case-management models within correctional settings.

Principle #1: Case management is a process that requires continuity in the delivery of services.

Perhaps the most consistent finding across the mental health and corrections research is the importance of continuity in the delivery of case-management services. Case management should be a dynamic, seamless process that commences at the time of sentencing and continues beyond discharge from prison and/or community supervision until the offender has stabilized in the community.

Looking back at the Assertive Community Treatment literature summarized by the Lewin group and the case-management processes described by Partridge (2004), strong evidence suggests that the case-management process is enhanced when a team approach is formally prescribed and used. The best results appear to occur when a multidisciplinary team works with the individual throughout her or his involvement in the criminal justice system. The notion of team, although well-established in the mental health field, has not gained popular acceptance across correctional settings in North America. The primary obstacles associated with the establishment of a team approach include the lack of resources and time to coordinate efforts (for example, team meetings), unwillingness by various professional groups to share information, and the belief that functions and responsibilities of team members vary sufficiently to warrant separate consideration.

The team experience employed in England and Wales called for small groups, typically made up of one or two probation officers, one or two probation service officers (treatment specialists or clinical specialists) and a case administrator. These teams worked effectively when the roles and responsibilities of team members were clearly defined, when regular meetings were established, when team members worked out of the same office or in the same area, when caseload sizes remained manageable, and when information relevant to risk and need was easy to access and share (Partridge, 2004).

Working as a team has many advantages for staff members and the offender, including—not the least of which is shared responsibility for cases, ongoing review and updating of the case plan, and ultimately continuity in the type and method of services delivered. Consumer satisfaction reports from mental health clients, their families, and those reported by offenders in the Partridge survey suggest that continuity of care reduces confusion, helps to build trust and rapport, increases willingness to engage in treatment services, and enhances motivation.

In settings where the team approach is not feasible, continuity can be achieved by ensuring that staff who join in to work with offenders at different stages of the transition process have access to information concerned with risk and criminogenic need, identified targets and services received, as well as the offender's response to and progress in addressing targeted need areas. In addition to information sharing, the sense of continuity can be achieved by ensuring that new staff are introduced to the offender before the case is turned over to another specialist or case manager. Three-way meetings are extremely powerful not only in providing a sense of cohesion for the offender but also ensuring that the priority-need areas continue to be the focus of intervention.

Principle #2: The development of an individualized case plan should be based on results from a standardized risk assessment and provide the team/case manager with a map to identify the targets of intervention and to monitor reductions in recidivism.

As indicated previously, many departments and agencies working with offenders implement some of the functions of traditional case management. For example, risk assessment has become standard practice across North America and currently is used to make decisions with respect to classification and supervision. Advances in assessment over the last two decades also permit the simultaneous assessment of criminogenic needs and protective factors, and this information can assist practitioners in making decisions on treatment and other services necessary to reduce risk for re-offending. It is not unusual for departments to complete a standardized assessment to determine risk for re-offending, supervision level, and contact standards. Unfortunately, this information is less likely to be used to determine criminogenic targets and to assist in the development of an individualized case plan. Once the supervision or custody level is established, results are placed into a file or database, and the court order is used to determine treatment placement.

The underutilization of risk/need assessment to guide case planning is just one of the unfortunate misuses of the tools and resources that have emerged from the literature on evidence-based practices. Another common practice is to require offenders to participate in treatment programs without attention to the risk level (which should determine intensity and dosage), the criminogenic need(s) of the offender (which should determine program type), or level of motivation. The latter should determine readiness to participate and any obstacles that might prevent an offender from fully benefiting from a program. A number of cognitive-behavioral programs based on social-learning theory continue to demonstrate positive outcomes with offenders who are at greatest risk and who need such interventions (Landenberger and Lipsey, 2006). However, these programs were designed to address specific needs and entry criteria should be established before offenders are referred to them.

A final strategy that is often misused is the actual case/supervision/ service plan. As indicated by Taxman (2008), the plan should be written as a behavioral contract that the offender has committed to work toward. Many agencies and departments require staff to set goals and to document progress in achieving them. Unfortunately, this exercise very easily becomes a paperwork exercise with little value. In fact, goal setting is futile and meaningless in any one of the following situations: (1) the goal is written in the absence of the offender, (2) the offender does not value the goal, (3) the offender does not commit to the goal, or (4) the goal is too large, written in vague language, unattainable, and/or unrealistic.

Assessment, service plans, and referral to treatment are important tasks linked to a risk-reduction strategy, but these activities should not be performed as separate and discrete functions. Rather, practitioners should use the assessment results to make decisions about the needs of offenders, the types of referrals and services that are necessary to reduce risk, and to assist them to monitor the direct impact of these interventions on outcome (in other words, observable decreases in dynamic criminogenic targets). Case managers, who provide feedback to the offender after administering the assessment, may use this information to increase awareness and establish the priority targets for change. The case plan then becomes a meaningful document that is easily reviewed and updated while serving as an official record for sharing information and monitoring progress.

Principle #3: Case management is a process designed to work collaboratively with the offender to address mutually agreed upon outcomes.

Taxman (2008) devotes considerable attention to the "how" of intervention and the relationship between the practitioner and the offender. Research clearly suggests that when treatment and intervention strategies are delivered respectfully and empathetically, such activities are likely to have an impact on offender behavior. This goal only can be achieved within an organizational culture that values a person-centered approach and that provides staff with training and resources that support this ideology. Unfortunately, in many settings, the need to hold offenders accountable has been translated into the language and practice of control and punishment, and this continues despite the fact that these practices effectively transfer responsibility for change from the offender to the staff member. We need to provide staff with the skills to intentionally and effectively manage offender behavior within the boundaries of sound professional practice.

Motivational Interviewing provides an excellent framework within which the core skills of case management, supervision, and treatment (empathy, skillful responding to resistance, collaboration, recognition of and support for client strengths, eliciting of clients' goals and values to motivate change) can be systematically taught. Developing an expertise in Motivational Interviewing makes any practitioner, regardless of orientation, a more skillful and intentional practitioner.

Principle #4: Case management should provide a range of options and opportunities to address multiple and complex needs of high-risk offenders.

As indicated above, researchers have identified a number of promising programs that contribute to positive outcomes with offenders (Landenberger and Lipsey, 2006). Unfortunately, this development has led to the mistaken belief that entry into a group program is sufficient to address the complex and multiple criminogenic needs of high-risk offenders. The notion that one program can serve as a panacea for offender change is misguided for several reasons. First, research suggests that high-risk offenders require more intensive intervention and access to a wider range of services. The provision of a cognitive program may facilitate decision-making, problem-solving, and goal setting skills that help the offender address the stresses of daily living across criminogenic targets, but these skills are likely to erode if aftercare services are not provided and/or if the offender has not had sufficient practice to apply these skills in high-risk situations.

A second reason why focusing on "a" program as the primary determinant of outcome is that we begin to romanticize its impact and miss other potential sources that are linked to offender change. The Pathfinder project implemented throughout England and Wales' probation service provides some reason to exhibit caution when outcome is driven solely by offender participation in a cognitive-behavioral program. Raynor (2004) suggests that by focusing on one dimension of offender change, other significant contributors to effectiveness such as case management, sentencing patterns, and staff skills may be overlooked.

In fact, several studies suggest that treatment effects such as entering, staying, and demonstrating short-term effects are enhanced when effective case management practices are implemented in conjunction with treatment (Lewin, 2004; Martin and Inciardi, 1997). There is also a growing body of research recognizing the importance of staff skills, and the approaches they use, as significant factors that contribute to outcome (Dowden and Andrews, 2004; Taxman, 2008).

The recent meta-analyses conducted by Lipsey (2006) as well as the studies conducted in Washington State by the Institute for Public Policy (see for example, Barnoski, 2004) demonstrate that how a program is implemented and the level of adherence to the model are absolutely critical to program success. Finally, Raynor (2004) suggested that what worked best in the Pathways study was the combination of facilitating access to resources to address criminogenic needs while simultaneously addressing attitudes and motivation. His observation is supported by Hettema, Steele, and Miller (2005), who reported evidence that Motivational Interviewing may be most effective when combined with other treatments.

One of the guiding practices of the Assertive Community Treatment model is the availability of a range and variety of services. When working with a high-risk offender, it is not unusual to require family counseling, mental health services, assistance with vocational, financial, medical and housing needs, and substance abuse treatment. This will require links to and relationships with service providers throughout the community. Ultimately, a cognitive program may be helpful but not entirely sufficient.

Principle #5: Case management is a process that should focus on building social capital.

One of the critical elements of Assertive Community Treatment and intensive-case-management approaches that contribute to positive outcomes is the deliberate effort made to assist clients to build social capital. Social capital refers to connections among individuals and social networks and the resulting reciprocity in purpose and respect that emerges from healthy social interactions. In his interviews with offenders, Maruna (2002) concluded that a critical factor for men and women who were able to eventually desist from a long history of criminal justice involvement was access to formal and informal supports. The need to provide aftercare is not a new concept for the field of corrections. For example, the reentry literature paints a bleak picture with respect to extraordinarily high return rates of men and women transitioning from prison.

Often, the supports and resources made available to offenders while involved with the criminal justice system are removed once court-ordered obligations have been met. This can contribute to destabilization and a recurrence of problematic and/or criminal behavior. To circumvent the impact of this reality, case-management models should work deliberately not only to enhance personal strategies for change but to assist offenders to mobilize healthy and reciprocal social supports.

Summary

It is our belief that existing research and field experience provide sufficient information to support the development and implementation of an effective case-management approach. Existing models such as the Behavioral Management Strategies proposed by Taxman (2008) require evaluation to identify critical components and to facilitate replication. To enhance the implementation of this model, we believe that case management must be perceived as a process with functions and tasks delivered continuously throughout involvement in the criminal justice system and beyond. We also believe that the "how" of effective case management is critical. A collaborative approach, continuity in contact, and the ability of staff to motivate and engage offenders are critical elements of success. Offenders must be provided with an array of service options and opportunities to address multiple criminogenic needs and to mobilize existing strengths. Finally, deliberate attention must be paid to assist the offender to build social capital. This will help to ensure that supportive and positive relationships are available to offenders beyond their initial involvement with the criminal justice system.

References

Andrews, D. A. and J. Bonta. 2003. *The Psychology of Criminal Conduct, 3rd* ed. Cincinnati: Anderson.

Barnoski, R. 2004. Outcome Evaluation of Washington State's Research-Based Programs for Juvenile Offenders. Olympia, Washington: Washington State Institute for Public Policy, Document ID: (04-01-1201).

Brown, J. M. and W. R. Miller. 1993. Impact of Motivational Interviewing on Participation and Outcome in Residential Alcoholism Treatment. *Psychology of Addictive Behavior*, 7, 211-218.

Bond, G. R., R. E. Drake, K. T. Mueser, et al. 2001. Assertive Community Treatment for People with Severe Mental Illness: Critical Ingredients and Impact on Patients. *Disease Management and Health Outcomes*, 9: 141-159.

Dowden, C. and D. Andrews. 2004. The Importance of Staff-Practice in Delivering Effective Correctional Treatment: A Meta-Analysis. *International Journal of Offender Therapy and Comparative Criminology*, 48: 203-214.

Drake, R. E., K. T. Mueser, W. C. Torrey, et al. 2000. Evidence-Based Treatment of Schizophrenia. *Current Psychiatry Reports*, 2: 393-397.

Hettema, J., J. Steele, and W. R. Miller. 2005. Motivational Interviewing. *Annual Review of Clinical Psychology.* 1: 91-111.

Holloway, F. and J. Carson. 2001. Case Management: An Update. *International Journal of Social Psychiatry*, (47)3: 21-31.

Holt, P. 2000. *Case Management: Context for Supervision.* Lanham, Maryland: University Press.

Lambert, M. J. and D. E. Barley. 2002. Research Summary on the Therapeutic Relationship and Psychotherapy Outcomes. In J. Norcross, ed, *Psychotherapy Relationships That Work.* New York City: Oxford University Press, pgs 17-36.

Landenberger, N. A. and M. W. Lipsey. 2006. The Positive Effects of Cognitive Behavioral Programs for Offenders: A Meta-Analysis of Factors Associated with Effective Treatment. *Journal of Experimental Criminology.* 1 (4), 451-476.

Latimer E. A. 1999. Economic Impacts of Assertive Community Treatment: A Review of the Literature. *Canadian Journal of Psychiatry*, 44, June, 443-454.

Lewin Group. 2004. *Assertive Community Treatment Literature Review.* Health Care and Financing (HCFA) and Substance Abuse and Mental Health Services Administration (SAMHSA). Washington, DC.

Longshore, D., S. Turner, T. Fain. 2005. Effects of Case Management on Parolee Misconduct. *Criminal Justice and Behavior*, (32) 2, 205-222.

Marshall, M. 1996. Case Management: A Dubious Practice. *British Medical Journal.* Vol. 312, March: 523-524.

Marshall M. and A. Lockwood. 1998. Assertive Community Treatment for People with Severe Mental Disorders. *Cochrane Database of Systematic Reviews* 1998, Issue 2. Art. No.: CD001089. DOI: 10.1002/14651858.CD001089.

Marshall, M, A. Gray, A. Lockwood, and R. Green. 1998. Case Management for People with Severe Mental Disorders. *Cochrane Database of Systematic Reviews*, Issue 2. Art. No.: CD000050. DOI: 10.1002/14651858.CD000050.

Martin, S. S. and J. A. Inciardi. 1993. A Case Management Treatment Program for Drug-Involved Prison Releases. *The Prison Journal*, 73, 319-331.

___. 1997. Case Management Outcomes for Drug-Involved Offenders. *The Prison Journal*, 77 168-183.

Martin, S. S., J. A. Inciardi, F. R.Scaripitti, and A. C. Nielsen. 1997. Case Management for Drug Involved Parolees: It Proved to be a Tough ACT to Follow. In F. M. Tims, J. A. Inciardi, B. V. Fletcher, and A. M. Horton Jr., eds. *The Effectiveness of Innovative Approaches in the Treatment of Drug Abuse.* pp. 115-133. Westport, CT: Greenwood.

Maruna, S. 2002. *Making Good: How Ex-Convicts Reform and Rebuild Their Lives.* Washington, D.C.: American Psychological Association Books.

McGrew, J. H. and G. R. Bond. 1995. Critical Ingredients of Assertive Community Treatment: Judgments of the Experts. *Journal of Mental Health Administration*, 22(2), 113-125.

McGrew, J. H., G. R. Bond, L. Dietzen, and M. Sayers. 1994. Measuring the Fidelity of Implementation of a Mental Health Program Model. *Journal of Consulting and Clinical Psychology*, 62:670-678.

McHugo, G. J., R. E. Drake, G. B. Teague, et al. 1999. Fidelity to Assertive Community Treatment and Client Outcomes in the New Hampshire Dual Disorders Study. *Psychiatric Services*, 50: 818-824.

Miller, W. and S. Rollnick. 2002 *Motivational Interviewing: Preparing People for Change*, 2nd Ed. New York: The Guilford Press.

Mueser K. T., G. R. Bond, R. E. Drake and S. G. Resnick. 1998. Models of Community Care for Severe Mental Illness: A Review of Research on Case Management. *Schizophrenia Bulletin*, Vol. 24, No. 1.

Mueser, K., W. Torrey, D. Lynde, P. Singer, R. Drake. 2003. Implementing Evidence-Based Practices for People with Severe Mental Illness. *Behavior Modification*, 27(3): 387-411.

National Resource Center for Homelessness and Mental Health. 2004. Case Management and Assertive Community Treatment: Resources and Abstracts. http://www.nrchmi.samhsa.gov/Resource.aspx?id=19690

Partridge, S. 2004. Examining Case Management Models for Community Sentences. *Home Office Online Report 17/04.* United Kingdom, http://www.homeoffice.gov.uk/rds/pdfs04/rdsolr1704.pdf

Raynor, P. 2004. The Probation Service: 'Pathfinders' Finding the Path and Losing the Way? *Criminal Justice*, 4 (3): 309-325.

Rhodes, W. and M. Gross. 1995. *Case Management Reduces Drug Use and Criminality among Drug-Involved Arrestees: An Experimental Study of an HIV Prevention Intervention.* (Available from Abt Associates Inc., 55 Wheeler Street, Cambridge, MA 02138).

Schaedle, R., J. H. McGrew, G. R. Bond, and I. Epstein, I. 2002. A Comparison of Experts' Perspectives on Assertive Community Treatment and Intensive Case Management. *Psychiatric Services*, 53(2), 207-210.

Stein, M. D. and A. B Santos. *Assertive Community Treatment of Persons with Severe Mental Illness.* New York: W. W. Norton and Company, Inc.

Taxman, F. 2009. Behavioral Management Strategies in Correctional Settings. In *What Works: Research Into Practice: Bridging the Gap,* Edward Rhine and Donald Evans, eds. American Correctional Association and International Community Corrections Association. Alexandria, Virginia.

Van Dieten, M., D. Robinson, B. Millson, A. Stringer. 2002. *A Four-Stage Model for Effective Case Management.* Ottawa: Orbis Partners.

____. 2006. Women Offender Case Management Model. *National Institute of Corrections.* Washington, DC.

Ziguras, S. and G. Stuart. 2000. A Meta-Analysis of the Effectiveness of Mental Health Case Management over 20 Years. *Psychiatric Services*, 51(11), 1410-1415.

SECTION 4:

FAMILIES AND COMMUNITIES: NATURAL SUPPORT SYSTEMS FOR OFFENDERS

FAMILIES, COMMUNITY, AND INCARCERATION

11

Donald Braman, J.D., Ph.D.

Associate Professor
George Washington University School of Law
Washington, DC

Introduction

Incarceration, something few families faced fifty years ago, is now an integral part of family life in urban America. Nearly every long-time resident of the District of Columbia can name friends or family members who have been or are presently incarcerated, and many have themselves spent time in jail or prison. Our nation's capital city, a place of residence and work for many national policymakers who draft the federal criminal codes and sentencing guidelines that directly affect poor urban communities, is also a prime example of the recent dramatic expansion of the criminal-justice system nationwide.

In many neighborhoods, more than three-quarters of young men can expect to be incarcerated at some point in their lives. A few decades ago, these would have been staggering statistics in any city, but today, compared with other cities, the District is just average. At a cost of more than $40 billion a year, the United States now holds one out of every four of the world's prisoners. But the numbers themselves can be numbing. To gain a truer sense of the costs of mass incarceration, we need to see it through the eyes of people who live with it every day.

In this paper, I want to do three things. First and foremost, I want to suggest some of the broad social effects of our current approach to criminal justice by describing the experiences of one of the thirty families who participated in a three-year ethnographic study of incarceration and family life in the District of Columbia (Braman, 2002, 2004, 2004a). Second, I want to briefly describe the significant opportunity that I believe exists for reform today—perhaps the best opportunity we have had in the last twenty-five years. And third, I want to suggest how we, as advocates for disadvantaged families and communities who work in the area of corrections, can make the most of this opportunity.

One Family's Perspective

Londa and her three children live in a small row house that is part of a Section-Eight housing project in central Washington, DC. Inside her home, surrounded by the debris of family life—toys, a few empty kid-size boxes of juice, dishes on the table from a lunch just finished, bottles and baby blankets strewn over the couch. She is apologetic for the mess. "But," she tells me, "I've got three kids, a broken leg, and a husband who's locked up." She has been struggling against her husband's crack addiction and struggling to keep her family together for fifteen years. Gesturing out the window, she says, "I don't want to end up like everyone else. I guess I'm halfway there. But my kids need a father. I look around here and none of these kids have fathers. It's a mess what's happened."

Londa sees her relationship with Derrick as the culmination of her long struggle with his drug addiction and incarceration, a struggle that has left her feeling utterly drained. Derrick has years ahead of him in prison, and both of them are unsure of what kind of father he'll be able to be for his children. While all families are unique, Londa and Derrick's story illustrates many of the concerns of other families I interviewed, providing a fair account of the broad array of complex problems that families of prisoners face.

Derrick and Londa's story, neither one of flagrant injustice nor triumph against the odds, shows a family facing addiction, the criminal justice system's response to it, and the mixture of hardship and relief that incarceration brings to many families of drug offenders. Stories like theirs are almost entirely absent from current debates over incarceration rates and accountability. Indeed, the historical lack of the familial and community perspective of those most affected by incarceration can help to explain the willingness of states to accept mass incarceration as a default response to social disorder.

Once we begin attending to the accounts of people directly affected by criminal sanctions, however, we can begin to understand how our policies have exacerbated the very social problems they were intended to remedy. By holding offenders unaccountable to their families and communities, incarceration—at least as it is currently practiced—frustrates the fundamental norms that form the basis of the social order itself.

Derrick has been in and out of prison and addiction for more than a decade. Like most of the inmates added to our criminal justice system in recent years, Derrick is a nonviolent offender (Mauer, 1999, 34). Like most offenders who use drugs, he has neither been sentenced to nor received anything approaching serious treatment. As a result, like most prisoners, he is also a repeat offender (Bureau of Justice Statistics, 2002). Perhaps most significantly, he, like most inmates, is also a father and, like most incarcerated fathers, both lived with his children prior to incarceration and remains in contact with them now (Mumola, 2000).

In many ways, Derrick and Londa had a lot going for them. From early on, Derrick made reliable money performing manual labor: laying carpet, working construction—any job that he could get to help them along. Unlike many young men in the neighborhood where he grew up, he knew that he could earn a living if he worked at it, and he made it through his teens without any serious trouble. Londa, for her part, was a good student and, after high school, able to get work as a secretary. It wasn't long before Londa was pregnant. Derrick was twenty-two, and Londa twenty-one.

Around the same time that Londa became pregnant, though, Derrick's drug use, once limited to the occasional party, became more serious. By the time their daughter was born in 1987, Londa could see changes in Derrick as he started covering for his growing addiction. Anyone who has experienced addiction in the family will know the litany of problems that Londa encountered: mood swings, lying, erratic behavior, late-night disappearances, pleading for money, and eventually stealing.

As Londa realized how serious things had become, she tried to hold Derrick accountable as a parent, something she felt that she deserved and their daughter needed: "You get yourself together [and you can see her] but I don't think she should get less from you and more from me. . . . The best you can do is to come over here like that? No. I'm sorry, she deserves more than that." Shortly after she cut him off from seeing their daughter, Derrick was arrested and sentenced to eighteen months on a possession charge.

Although Derrick did not enter drug treatment while he was incarcerated, he managed to stay off of drugs and felt as if he had recovered from his addiction. Londa was surprised to see that Derrick once again seemed like the person she'd fallen in love with: "the old Derrick was back," and he was insisting that he had reformed his ways, writing long letters of regret, talking about his religious reform in prison, and suggesting that they get married.

Derrick's family also pleaded with Londa to give Derrick another chance. Concerned about Derrick's morale, they were worried that his isolation from Londa and his daughter would push him back into his drug use.

> I think when I got married I was thinking, too, that I really, really wanted this person that I knew. Not necessarily he had to be the same as that person or act the same way. I didn't want that person where the demons had taken over. You know? I just wanted my Derrick back.

Many of the women I speak with, including Londa, already feel that way themselves—particularly if they have children or consider themselves a family. As one woman said of her child's incarcerated father, "We're family. You don't . . . you can't just say 'bye-bye.' Either you're family or you're not, and if you are then you do what's right."

When Derrick was released, Londa did marry him and Derrick did work hard to provide for his family. Indeed, many family members said that he worked harder after his release than he had prior to his arrest. As his sister Brenda told me:

> Derrick is a workaholic when he's not on drugs. And he told me why he does it: to keep his mind off drugs. He wants to stay busy, because that's what he needs when he's first out. And like he told me, he also . . . he's scared of society. He says, "It's scary out here," because he don't want to go back to jail.

Unfortunately, Derrick's recovery lasted a little less than a year. Then, he was back on drugs and back in jail, a cycle that he would repeat several times. He would attend NA meetings for a while, work hard, pay the bills, and then one day he would run into some "friends" and it was all over—another binge and another set of broken promises. The difficulty faced by Londa increased as, over the next five years, their daughter was joined by two sons.

Addiction and Incarceration

Most of the offenders in this study, like most of the prisoners added to our prisons over the last twenty years, were incarcerated on drug-related offenses.

The families I spoke with described a cycle that drug offenders who don't receive treatment often repeated. The addicted family member would be incarcerated on some minor charge (usually possession or larceny), given a year or so in prison without drug treatment, and then released on parole. As was the case with Derrick and Londa, the parole board would contact the family to make sure that the offender had a place to live and a supportive environment. Families, knowing full well that their relative received little or no drug treatment, are then in a bind. If the family does not agree to take him in, he will simply spend more time in jail or prison without treatment. If they do agree, they do so knowing that he is likely to relapse and re-offend. Unsurprisingly, most families—urged on by the pleadings of the incarcerated family member—are ever hopeful that they will be able help him through recovery. They agree to have him released to their care. Thus, the cycle of good intentions and promises, followed by relapse, deeper addiction, and then reincarceration goes on.

Families in this study described the cycle as ending in one of two ways. That which they feared most was death, and many drug offenders do die—victims of a drug overdose, an illness secondary to their addiction, or violence. Over the three years of this study, in fact, three of the fifty offenders who participated died drug-related deaths. But a fair number survive, and their cycle of abuse and incarceration ends another way: they commit a more serious offense or wear out the patience of a judge, garnering a lengthy sentence, and if they do not die in prison, they get released late in life (Robertson, 1997).

While it is too early to say for sure, the latter appears to be what is likely to happen in Derrick's case. After receiving several sentences for which he served less than two years each, Derrick found himself in front of an unsympathetic judge who simply saw no reason why this time would be any different. And so, what might have garnered a suspended sentence or parole for a first-time offense got him eight-to-twelve years.

There are, of course, far more desirable but also far less common ways of breaking the cycle. A very small proportion of offenders will be sentenced to mandatory drug treatment while incarcerated, followed by mandatory transitional treatment in a halfway house and then mandatory outpatient treatment. As a number of national studies have now demonstrated, this approach is highly effective when the quality of the treatment is high and the duration reasonably long (Gaes, Flanagan, Motiuk, and Stewart, 1999; National Center on Addiction and Substance Abuse, 1998). Despite the widely held belief that treatment must be voluntary to be successful, this same

research has demonstrated that mandatory treatment is as successful as voluntary (Travis, 1999).

The issue is not a trivial one. More than 40 percent of the District's offenders test positive for illegal drugs, and more than 70 percent report current or recent drug use (Drug Strategies, 1999). While mandatory treatment would thus seem to be an attractive sentencing option for judges and offenders alike, the chances of such a sentence being handed down and treatment being provided are slim. Even those judges who support treatment confront the practical reality that treatment—both in the correctional setting and in the community—is frustratingly scarce. As Faye Taxman, a University of Maryland professor who studies the District observed:

> [P]robably half of the sentences for probation have drug treatment required, but probably only 10 percent get any type of services, and I use the word "services" lightly. The system has been structured to provide the minimum. We provide something less than the minimum and say we are providing services. (Slevin, 1998, A01)

Indeed, while it is estimated that 65,000 District residents need drug treatment, well over 80 percent cannot be placed because of lack of treatment facilities (Slevin, 1998). The lack of available drug treatment also creates unintended incentives for inmates to avoid admitting to a drug problem and submitting to drug treatment as part of their sentencing. Because inmates can wait months—or even years—to gain entry into a drug treatment program that is a requirement of their release, many try to avoid sentencing that includes treatment even if they believe it would help them. They would rather just do "straight time" and be released than sit on a waiting list for a nonexistent slot in a drug program (Slevin, 1998). As one inmate told me, "Then, at least, you know. This other way, you maybe get out, you maybe don't. And then even if you do get out, you have to deal with all the nonsense with your parole officer." This, of course, increases the likelihood that they will be returned to their family and community without treatment and will relapse into drug use.

Derrick will likely spend at least another eight years in Maryland and DC facilities, and it could be as much as twenty. While he is not happy to be separated from his family, he acknowledges that there are some benefits to his being incarcerated in Maryland where there are drug treatment and job training programs available. He told me that he saw his incarceration as taking a burden off of his family, and it is hard not to agree that his current incarceration is, on the whole, better for his family than his behavior when he was out and using drugs.

But Derrick's sister Brenda views his predicament with less equanimity than he does, and her lament was one I heard from many family members of drug offenders. The cycle of release, relapse, and reincarceration is one that she thinks could and should have been avoided:

> It's hard when people don't have the income or know how to find people that you can talk to, to know how to get into them [a drug treatment program], because a lot of people don't want to listen to smaller people like us. . . . Big people got people, big people, helping them, pulling them out of situations. And when people, little people, get like that, that's a different story. For them, they get thrown away in jail and locked up, while people that's in high places, they'll take them somewhere privately to a program, and then they get clean. Then they're around positive people and live in positive areas. But they don't do the same thing for people that's small people. . . . That's what I believe. That's what I see. I mean, why they don't see that?

Clearly, the efforts of police, judges, correctional officers, wardens, departmental administrators, members of congress, and citizens—all of whom have produced our current correctional system—are not conspiring against poor families and communities. And yet, one can see why, from the perspective of families dealing with the criminal justice system, it seems like the product of a willfully ignorant if not malicious effort rather than a beneficent one.

Material Consequences

The cycle of incarceration followed by relapse and re-incarceration can have a devastating effect on families. Perhaps the most obvious effects of current criminal practices are material. Reviewing Londa's income and expenses, it becomes clear that her financial problems are directly related to the loss of Derrick's income and the additional costs that accompany his incarceration.

She lives on a fixed income of $463 a month from AFDC. After $100 for rent and another $300 for groceries (which works out to less than $3 of food per day, per person), there is not enough to pay for electricity, the phone, and transportation. She is far from lazy, but with two children and one infant, she doesn't have the resources to care for them herself. "Oh, I can't stand to ask anybody to help me with anything. So, I really hate asking my mother now, but I can't walk, I can't get around. So, it's just really, really hard right now."

Londa's mother helps care for the children, buys groceries, and even pays Londa's rent when things are tight. But her assistance is limited to what she herself can afford, and that is not much. Already, Londa feels she has asked far too much far too often from her mother. "I know that she doesn't have a lot, too, so that's something I have to think about." Derrick's sisters also try to help when they can, but they have families of their own and are struggling just to get by. Derrick's sister, Brenda, describes her surprise at how "it just all adds up." "The phone bills—the phone bill is something else!"

One of the more unpleasant surprises to many families is the high cost of phone calls from prison (Duggan, 2000). Inmates can only call collect, and additional charges for monitoring and recording by the prison phone company add up quickly. Indeed, many families have their phones disconnected within two months of an incarceration.

While Londa is fortunate to have family who are willing to help her in Derrick's absence, her family does not have much to help her with. By spreading the costs of raising Derrick's children and maintaining ties with him, Londa and Derrick's families have enabled Londa to keep and care for her children. While this is undoubtedly desirable, the cost has simply been spread to other low income households with few resources, lessening the impact on any one person, but creating a steady drain on the extended family.

Londa, for example, can no longer afford her own car—an issue that became quite serious when her mother's car broke down and, largely as a result of helping Londa, her mother was unable to afford the repair costs. Derrick's sister Brenda has also struggled with the sacrifices that she makes to keep her brother in touch with his family.

> I'm gonna be there regardless of what. And his wife, well she's having it rough, her and her kids, because, she don't have anything, which I don't have anything either, but a lot of times I [still help out]. My kids don't like it, because I try to give to [Derrick's family], because, you know . . . I . . . I feel for them and for him in that jail. [And] when school comes it's like, do my kids, do they get new shoes or does he get to talk to his kids. And, you know, I just think he needs to talk to them.

Families can be tremendous resources, but they are not limitless funds of wealth and generosity. The costs of Derrick's repeated incarcerations have been dear both emotionally and materially.

While most accounts relating poverty and crime generally describe poverty as driving criminal activity and thus involvement in the criminal justice system, stories like Londa's provide evidence that the relationship runs both ways and is arguably cyclical. Many inner-city families not only experience incarceration because they are poor, they are also poor because the experience incarceration. In light of their experiences, standard correlations such as those shown below take on a very different meaning:

Figure 1.   Figure 2.

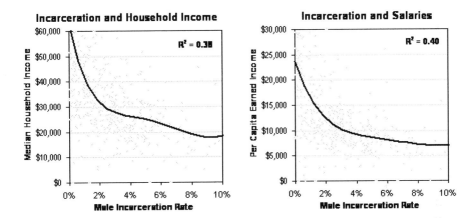

Data from the D.C. Department of Corrections and the U.S. Census.

One way—the traditional way—of interpreting these data is captured in William Julius Wilson's book, *When Work Disappears:* "As many studies have revealed, the decline in legitimate employment opportunities among inner-city residents has increased incentives to sell drugs" (Wilson, 21). Poverty leads to crime, which then leads to incarceration.

But the experiences of these families tell us that the reverse is also true: incarceration can significantly lower the income and increase the expenses of prisoners' families. The cumulative impact on familial wealth across generations can be substantial. By depleting the savings of offenders' families, incarceration inhibits capital accumulation and reduces the ability of parents to pass on wealth to their children and grandchildren through inheritance and gifts. Indeed, incarceration's draining of the resources of extended family members in this study helps explain why there has been so little capital accumulation and inheritance among inner-city families in general and minority families in particular.

This becomes apparent when we see Derrick's family struggling to save enough to buy his children school supplies, let alone provide for their inheritance. The disproportionate incarceration of men like Derrick helps to explain why black and Latino families are less able to save money and why each successive generation inherits less wealth than their white counterparts. Criminal sanctions—at least in their current form—act like a hidden tax, one that is visited disproportionately on poor and minority families, and while its costs are most directly felt by the adults closest to the incarcerated family member, the full effect is eventually felt by the next generation as well.

Viewed in this light, the racial disparities in arrests, sentencing, and parole described by Donziger (1996), Kennedy (1997), Currie (1998), Cole (2000), Mauer (1999), and Tonry (2001) take on a broader significance. For example, census data show that blacks typically possess only one-third the assets of whites with similar incomes (Lynch, 1998; Blau and Graham, 1990; Oliver and Shapiro, 1995). While this pattern is generally attributed to lower savings and inheritance (Smith, 1995; Avery and Rendall, 1997; Menchik and Jianakoplos, 1997), this explanation begs the question of why savings and inheritance are lower—something that the concentration of incarceration in minority communities and its effect on capital accumulation help to explain.

Finally, it is worth noting that familial costs also can decrease investments in what is often called "human capital," (Becker, 1981; England and Folbre, 1997) as moving to a better school district, purchasing an up-to-date computer, and attending college all become less affordable. Educational attainment is one of the best predictors we have for avoiding the criminal justice system, but the benefits of investing in (and the costs of neglecting) human capital extend well beyond crime rates. As the stock of resources that a family possesses diminishes, and as members are prevented from caring for one another, more than money and objects are lost. Indeed, the material losses these families face, serious though they are, may in the end be the least significant concern.

Pulling Families Apart

In addition to material concerns are those respecting the integrity of the family itself, and it is here that incarceration's impact is perhaps most troubling. The difficulties involved in trying to visit Derrick, the expense of his calls, the wear and tear of untreated addiction are all things that Londa feels are pulling her and Derrick apart. In this way, the enforced imbalance of their relationship is coloring her perception of him and what he is capable of. While she still loves him dearly, Londa feels like fifteen years of struggling to hold her family together has taken its toll on her emotionally. Even though he may get treatment this time around, she is unsure of whether she can hold out hope for another eight years.

If Londa's patience is wearing thin, that of her own extended family is worn out. In this sense, it is not simply self-reliance that makes Londa reluctant to ask for help from her family: "My mother can't even hear me talk about him. She'll be like 'What? Are you crazy?'" His aunt tells Londa point blank that, "He needs to stay where he is."

> She's just really, really bitter about it. And, I didn't know this until I spoke with her awhile back. And, I didn't know she felt like that. But she was really, really headstrong about him. "He needs to stay where he is and he better never come see me again." It's hard. Like he tells me a lot, he tries to make amends with people, and, he can't.... And it's because, most people don't understand addicts. They just know that they are addicts and they don't want to have nothing to do with them.

Londa has largely stopped talking to her extended family about Derrick and tries not to ask for help except from Derrick's sisters—a point that begins to indicate how the economic impacts of incarceration are often bound up with its effects on family dynamics. For Londa, the material, emotional, and moral concerns are related in ways that she feels are straining her ties with both her own and her husband's family.

Londa's concerns also often turn to her three children—Sharon who just turned eleven, Cooper who is two, and DJ who is one. As hard as the cycle of addiction and incarceration has been for Londa, she feels it has been far harder for her daughter, who still has trouble understanding why her father could be loving and responsible one month but manipulative and reckless the next. "Trying to explain to a kid why her father left with her radio and why he's not allowed in the house at the moment, that's just not something a kid can really understand." The fact that Derrick, when sober, was a good father made the times that he wasn't all the harder. Londa described their relationship as a close one that has slowly deteriorated. But Londa does not think that her daughter ever forgot what it was like when Derrick was sober. "She really misses that, because when she was little they were really, really close."

In addition to missing her father and coping with her own ambivalence toward him, though, Sharon has also had to manage the information about her father in her encounters with friends and teachers. Londa believes that

Derrick's incarceration has led her daughter, already a quiet girl, to become increasingly private and withdrawn.

> Everybody is dealing with their fathers and school and their mothers. They come see them in [school plays] and stuff. . . . You could see the hurt. I mean it's not more or less she's gonna come out say it. She's gonna keep everything in 'til she can decide "Okay, who do I want to talk to?" . . . But I could see it. She has girl-friends and stuff, but they don't know.

Londa is particularly concerned with how Derrick's incarceration is affecting Sharon's performance at school.

> My daughter is a brain. You know. [She's gotten] As ever since she made kindergarten. She's never gotten a C. Never. [When she was in fifth grade, Derrick] went to jail and everything just . . . in the fifth grade year I receive her report card and they said she had to repeat a grade, I cried, I . . . I hurt. It bothers me now. It still bothers me. You just think, you know, there is nothing that you can do. What can you do?

While Derrick's sons are still quite young, his incarceration also raises troubling questions about their development. Indeed, one of the best predictors of male involvement in the criminal justice system is, of course, the incarceration of a parent.

Londa looks back on the times that she had nothing and was not sure how she would feed her kids, often sending them to stay with relatives while she went to look for work. She feels like she has been torn between wanting to be a supportive wife and being a good mother to her children, often feeling like she failed at the latter.

> I feel like I let my kids down. I feel like I really *really* let them down. And [this last time] I was out of work. I didn't have no money. I felt like I was just getting exactly what I deserved and, you know. Even all the good I did, it didn't outweigh the bad or something. I just felt like I was just getting everything that I was supposed to get. I was bitter. I didn't want to talk to nobody.

Londa's experience of depression and isolation was one that many women I spoke with described as they tried to find some way to be a good mother and a good partner without adequate resources to do either.

The last time I interviewed Derrick in person, he knew he was losing Londa. He was struggling to figure out how to cut his time down or be relocated near DC so that he could avoid losing touch with his family altogether.

> My problem now is this. I got to choose between the treatment route, the education route, and the job route. Now on the treatment route, I'll get nothing [in the way of money]. Doing school, maybe just enough to cover cosmetics, but that's it. I go the job route, and I can send home some money and, see, that helps out Londa and keeps the family intact. The point is, though, that they ain't coming to see me here and ain't taking my calls 'cause they can't afford the collect. But if I take the job, I don't get the drug treatment. So I'm trying to focus on the family, but I'm also kinda trying to get out of here. But it's also, too, I want to get back with them.

For Derrick, the choice was nearly impossible. Without working, he would be effectively cut off from his family for years and, in all likelihood, lose them. Working gives him access to money which helps him to play the role of a father, even if he is not there in person, by sending home money.

> I try to do that, you know. So if I keep up the job, I can send back money, keep Londa a little more happy, keep the kids knowing me. But then I just go in circles. The judge said I have to do the treatment here before I go for parole. . . . I mean, I look at it and it would have been so easy to be a father out there. Maybe not easy, but it's like it's impossible here.

These issues weigh heavily on Londa, as she considers how much her commitment to Derrick has cost her. Perhaps the greatest loss that Londa has suffered is not material at all; it is the loss of her faith in the family itself. Looking back on her relationship with Derrick, she describes what many young women in her situation dream of:

> I always thought that, "Okay, we want to raise our kids together." There's not too many [families], there's not any that I can think of at this time that's not a single parent family. I never wanted that for my kids. I wanted them to have something that I didn't have. So you try to give them this and you try to give them that. But to me it is more important to have both your parents there. And I've always thought, you know, "Okay, that will happen." I always thought that would happen.

What is striking in Londa's account and the accounts of other mothers I spoke with is the degree to which that dream, against all odds, remains alive—even if only as a dream. While she still holds out some faint hope that Derrick might be released early to a treatment program, she is exhausted from years of trying to work it out with Derrick. After this last incarceration, Londa reluctantly began considering filing for divorce.

The meaning of family to Londa remains powerful, but given her long struggle with Derrick's addiction and her desire to achieve middle-class status for herself and her children, that meaning came with a heavy price. Before asking whether, in hindsight, she was wise to bear the costs of that commitment, we might ask what the costs (both public and private) would be were she and others in poor inner-city families to decide that their commitments are too heavy to bear and withdraw their support, concern, and care from one another.

Most of the women and men I met had marital ambitions but low expectations of achieving them—a finding consistent with a number of previous studies (Tucker, 2000; Manning and Smock, 1995; Brien and Lillard, 1999). And many wives of prisoners, like Londa, said that they would have left their partners had they not been married to them—a finding in keeping with the only longitudinal statistical study to date of incarceration's effect on family formation using individual-level data (Western and McLanahan, 2000).

Figure 3. Incarceration and Father Absence

Source: DC Department of Corrections and U.S. Census.

But as is apparent in Londa's story, incarceration lowers the likelihood that women like her will view marriage as a tenable option. The data show that this effect is especially strong in pre-marital relationships, even where children are present (Western and McLanahan, 2000); but as Londa's case illustrates, the meaning of marriage can change for those who have taken their vows as well.

Data on incarceration and household composition present a similar story. In neighborhoods where the male incarceration rate exceeds 2 percent, fathers are absent from more than half of the families. Among the District families living in the areas with the highest incarceration rates, fewer than one in four has a father present. These data are borne out in a strikingly simple graph of the correlation between incarceration and father absence.

Figure 4. Incarceration, Father Absence, and Median Household Income

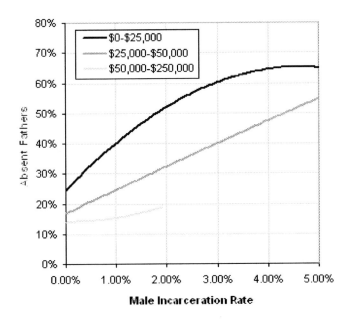

Source: DC Department of Corrections and U.S. Census.

While it might be argued that it is not incarceration but differences in income or education that affect family structure, controlling for these other variables in a regression analysis shows that incarceration has a statistically significant and independent relationship with family structure. Indeed, in the analyses I conducted, male incarceration is second only to educational levels in correlating with father absence, and incarceration accounts for nearly twice the variance that community-gender ratios do.

An examination of the relationship between incarceration and father absence in different income groups, shown as three fitted polynomial lines in Figure 4, illustrates the extent to which income may mediate the impact of incarceration on family organization.

For all three income groups, where incarceration rates are at their lowest, father absence occurs in fewer than 25 percent of households with children. As the incarceration rate increases among lower-income families, however, father absence increases at a far greater rate than it does among middle-income families, among whom father absence increases at a greater rate than among upper-income families. (Note that no upper-income census block group has an incarceration rate of more than 2 percent.) So, as the incarceration rate increases to 2 percent, the percentage of families with absent fathers in upper-income neighborhoods climbs about 5 percent; in middle-income neighborhoods, it climbs about 15 percent; and in lower-income neighborhoods, it climbs more than 25 percent.

The commonsense implication of this is that families like Londa's are not only exposed to incarceration more often, but they are far more likely to be broken by it. This is not because they don't want a family or lack family values. It is simply that their money, time, and emotional energy are already stretched too thin to bear the additional burdens that incarceration brings.

This, then, is the tragic dilemma that families like Londa's find themselves in: They can shoulder the burdens that accompany the incarceration of their loved one, suffering significant material hardship and emotional strain, or—an even less appealing option for many—they can withdraw from their social commitments, sacrificing the norms of trust and mutual responsibility that give meaning to their lives. Londa's story begins to indicate how the burden of incarceration is spread through intimate relationships, and thus brings us a good deal closer to understanding why measures of social capital have fallen so precipitously in low-income urban neighborhoods in recent decades.

Loss of Community

One of the great puzzles of recent studies of urban life has been the attenuation of extended open-ended networks of exchange over the last three decades, particularly in poor and minority urban communities (Roschelle, 1997). Regular and significant social exchange was widely documented among the urban poor in the 1960s and 1970s, but with far less regularity during the 1980s and 1990s. One recent national study found that, by the late 1990s, these networks of friends and family were far less extensive among low-income, urban, and minority families than had previously been observed.

Attending to the manner in which incarceration disrupts the economic and moral functioning of these networks can help to explain this decline. The first consequences that families of prisoners feel are often material, immediate, and substantial. The small measure of capital that they may have accrued over a lifetime of hard work quickly can be transformed into debt. During the last twenty years, many women—particularly low-income and minority women— have found out the hard way just how much their love and care for a son, brother, or husband can cost them.

But a second set of consequences—ones that cannot be fully captured in economic terms—come into play in the longer term. While incarceration forces offenders to answer to the state, it also forces them to abrogate their familial and community responsibilities. As families feel the slow grind of unreturned assistance and care, social consequences can ripple out from the initial material failings. These consequences can be described in terms of cooperation and defection from basic social responsibilities at the community level.

As numerous studies have demonstrated over a wide variety of settings, humans are more likely to cooperate if they see others cooperating, and more likely to defect from socially responsible behavior if they see others defecting. So when persons commit a criminal act, they not only create the typical harms that are associated with crime, they also impose a cost that is associated with the erosion of the norm of pro-social cooperation, a cost that is diffused throughout the community as an increase in the probability that others in the community will follow suit.

Consider, for example, Derek's case. His drug use and thieving directly drive down the rate of socially responsible behavior in his community, making others less trusting and perhaps even more likely to behave irresponsibly themselves. But his incarceration, which attempts to curb these harms by imposing a cost on Derek, actually reinforces them by creating other forms of irresponsibility. His continued failure to be a responsible father, spouse, brother, and son while incarcerated signals defection from familial obligations—a signal that reaches not only members of his family, but others in his community; his failure to compensate his victims or the community at large for the harm he has caused signals defection from basic social obligations; and his failure to reform himself, to work, to pay taxes, or to vote, signals a further defection from his obligations to his family, community, and society at large. His detention may deter irresponsible behavior in some ways, but to the extent that it forces these other irresponsible behaviors, it also promotes the very social problems that feed crime in his community, particularly from an intergenerational perspective.

Bear in mind, too, that in Londa's neighborhood, incarceration and the defection from responsible behavior that it entails do not just influence the norm among young men—statistically speaking, they are the norm. Nearly every house on her block has a family member who has been or is behind bars. In the year during which Derek was arrested, there were sixty-four arrests for drug possession and distribution within a two-block radius of her residence. More than 120 men living within the same two-block radius were admitted to the DC correctional system during that time, about one-quarter of them on drug possession or distribution charges. Many others, like Londa's husband Derek, were incarcerated on other charges related to drug addiction. It is not hard to see how that level of addiction and criminality can establish a new norm within Londa's community, one that is likely to shape future generations.

Humans, extensive research suggests, predictably adapt their behavior to what they perceive to be the "going rate"—that is, to what appears to them to be ordinary behavior in the relevant reference group. In communities where most fathers spend time in prison or jail, and where doing so means not being present for one's spouse, not providing for one's children, not working, not paying taxes, not voting, not paying one's debts, and not compensating one's victims—the going rate for responsible behavior is discernibly lowered. Multiply Derek's defections by the millions of men who spend time in prison or jail each year, and one begins to grasp how incarceration can alter basic norms related to family, community, and citizenship in many already-disadvantaged neighborhoods.

By tampering in such a forceful way with the ability of so many individuals to engage in basic moral behavior, we risk doing far more than inflicting an overly harsh punishment. Mass incarceration is pulling away the basic building blocks of social life itself. When individuals are pressed hard to withdraw their care and concern from one another, the effect is more than the impoverishment of individuals; as over-incarceration increases the costs of caring relationships, the losses become moral, and in time, it is our culture itself that becomes impoverished.

It is fair to say that by employing incarceration—the bluntest of policy instruments—as the primary response to social disorder, policymakers have significantly missed the mark. The very laws intended to punish selfish behavior and further common social interests, in practice, have strained and eroded the personal relationships vital to family and community life. Crime cannot go unpunished. But by draining the resources of families and communities, by frustrating the norm of reciprocity that inheres in family and community life, and by stigmatizing poor and minority families, our current regime of criminal sanctions has created a set of second-order problems that furthers social detachment.

A Problem and an Opportunity

It is commonly assumed that the rise of incarceration reflects a peculiarly punitive attitude among Americans. I once thought so myself, but now believe otherwise. Having spent a fair portion of the last three years poring over public opinion data and traveling around the country interviewing ordinary citizens about their attitudes toward the criminal justice system, the one thing that is certain—almost no one is happy with the status quo. Indeed, when asked to rank their satisfaction with the various parts of the criminal justice system, Americans put prisons at the bottom of the list.

Rather than more incarceration, most Americans favor a thoughtful and socially constructive response to crime. By a margin of nearly two to one, Americans favor fighting crime through reforms that feature spending money on "social and economic problems" more than spending money on "police, prisons, and judges."

The question is whether the state can meet the public's preferred response to crime, help push offenders back into a cooperative, pro-social stance, and thus strengthen the norm of cooperation and responsibility-taking in their families and communities. If the state can do this, a natural outcome will be increased participation in the social networks essential to healthy family and community life. Recall that in Londa's neighborhood, this would not be an effect at the margins; it would alter the behavior of a substantial majority of the young men.

The answer, as those involved in community corrections know, is a resounding yes. The state can meet the public's preferred response to crime, help push offenders back into a cooperative, pro-social stance and thus strengthen the norm of cooperation and responsibility-taking in their families and communities. The best programs are not institutional responses that attempt to replace failing social networks with the heavy hand of incarceration, but thoughtful preventative programs that make the most of the social networks already in place in families and communities.

By reassuring individuals in a community that the state will push offenders back into responsible behavior rather than remove them from it, pro-social interventions can help increase the likelihood that others in the community also will behave responsibly—which, in turn, makes it more likely that individuals will enter into and remain in the pro-social relationships that sustain and are sustained by that behavior.

But while this may make perfect sense to those involved in community corrections, it is not always apparent to those who make policy. To remedy that, here are three suggestions to correctional reformers about the way we talk.

First, and perhaps most controversially, we should replace talk about rehabilitation with talk about offender accountability. Progressives have long been wedded to rehabilitation talk, but it suffers from two serious defects. Perhaps the most obvious defect is that, for many Americans and policy-makers, rehabilitation has become code for expensive and ineffective programs that look a lot like perks or rewards for criminal offenders at the taxpayers' expense. This, of course, strikes them as morally questionable. Even if one could convince them that the outcome is beneficial, they would have to face down their moral opposition to rewarding criminal behavior with valuable social services. In this regard, interventions that are structured around and can be described as facilitating greater offender accountability are less likely to be mistaken as soft on crime than those that are described in terms of rehabilitation.

Another reason for talking about accountability instead of rehabilitation is that it pushes the discussion away from the offender as a solitary individual and toward a conversation about responsible behavior within important social relationships. It allows for a conversation that asks precisely how and to whom the offender will be held accountable. Whenever someone asks me if I support increases in spending on rehabilitation, I respond by saying that, for both moral and practical reasons, I think about interventions that are geared toward increased offender accountability. I then talk about how reintegrating offenders into social networks and pushing them into responsible behaviors that benefit others is central to this goal.

This brings me to my second suggestion: rather than talking about offenders as individuals, we should talk about them as members of families and communities. I have often been surprised by the number of people who, while seeing their immediate world in terms of home, family, and community, shift their framework of understanding to one of radical individualism when discussing criminal justice. Conceptually stripping offenders of all their social relations seriously mars their understanding of what appropriate sanctions should look like. The isolated offender is a useful political fiction, but a fiction that has come to so thoroughly dominate our analysis of what our criminal law should and can do that we are blind to its limitations.

Sitting in the office of a conservative congressman on Capitol Hill, for example, I recounted an abbreviated version of Londa and Derek's story to a congressional aide. Her response was surprising: "Why did she stay with that loser for so long? What these women need is to get out of these bad relationships." At the time, the aide's response seemed to contradict traditionally conservative "family values." Here was a low-income African-American woman living in the one of the most drug-ridden neighborhoods in our Capital city making significant sacrifices to keep her family intact against all odds—and a white, politically conservative member of the middle class was wondering why she bothered. That the congressman the aide worked for had publicly decried the casual attitude toward divorce encouraged by our culture had led me to think that the aide would be a sympathetic advocate for this family.

Having since spoken with many policymakers (both liberal and conservative), however, I would be far less surprised today than I was then. It was not that the aide did not value family; rather, it is that Derek's status as an offender prevented the aide from seeing Derek as part of a family, much less one that would judge it immoral to abandon a family member. "For better, for worse, in sickness and in health," are the traditional vows of marriage, and many of the wives of prisoners that I spoke with recited them to me when I asked why they chose to stay with their husbands. The stereotype of the offender is that of an individual isolated from all social relations. The aide's suggestion stemmed from a misunderstanding of the strength and meaning of family for the rest of Derek's relatives. Had it been her own brother or husband addicted to drugs and in prison, I suspect that she would have reacted differently. Framing correctional responses in terms of responsibility within social networks can help move us away from inaccurate stereotypes and toward more useful discussions about interventions that truly further offender accountability.

My third piece of unsolicited advice is directed at progressives: Do not be afraid of conservatives. If you talk in terms of accountability and strengthening the mechanics of accountability in families and communities, you will have a common language that will make your conversations far more productive. In fact, having traveled around the country to talk to ordinary people about crime and punishment, I would argue that the reluctance of conservatives to embrace more pro-social responses to crime has more to do with the way progressive reformers talk than with any fundamental disagreement over what sanctions should look like.

Of course, the work of crafting a message is secondary to having a message to convey, and that is what the field of community corrections is about. In conveying the stories of people like Londa and Derrick that we come to know through our work, I believe we should find ourselves not disappointed for falling so far short of what we, as a society, ought to be doing, but rather inspired by the knowledge that we have, probably for the first time in the history of crime and punishment, begun the hard work of truly understanding how corrections can help build—or at least avoid destroying—healthy families and communities. Much of it is common sense, but given the rarity of that commodity, it is also nice to have empirical research on our side.

We should be encouraged, too, by an increased willingness of legislators in many states, both liberal and conservative, to take a fresh look at their sentencing laws and correctional programs. Mass incarceration, they are coming to see, is far too costly to be sustained in the long run and works against the values they want to see the law promote.

This renewed interest in sentencing reform is apparent in the substantial interest state legislators, judges, and administrators have shown, for example, in the Vera Institute's State Sentencing and Corrections Program, which brings these parties together to discuss and share ideas about the substantive needs and political realities that often make sentencing and corrections reform difficult to achieve. A number of programs (including the Family Justice Program) are also talking across state borders to help each other better understand what is working and what could use improvement. What is encouraging here is state officials' increased interest in what community corrections professionals have to offer them in terms of cost savings and public safety—an interest that has brought them into a broader dialog about healthy families and communities.

Interest in sentencing reform is also apparent in what has been perhaps the largest expansion of community corrections in the last thirty years: the move by several states toward mandatory community-based drug treatment as a first alternative to incarceration for drug offenders. Consider, for example, the trend in popular referenda on sanctions for drug offenders. In 1996, Arizona voters passed the Drug Medicalization, Prevention, and Control Act of 1996, mandating court-supervised drug treatment and education programs instead of incarceration. Four years later, California voters enacted the Substance Abuse and Crime Prevention Act of 2000. Through each of these programs, first-time drug offenders can avoid prison and a felony conviction if they plead guilty and complete an approved treatment program. A detailed evaluation of the California Act shows that it has saved Californians millions of dollars and has substantially reduced recidivism-related costs for most offenders. The research suggests a number of ways to improve existing programs, and similar acts have begun to appear on the ballots in other states.

While we should be chastened by the immense cost that our criminal justice system has needlessly imposed on disadvantaged families and communities, it seems the time is ripe for change. It should be inspiring to know that, if we work hard enough and smart enough, Londa's daughter, and the millions of children growing in families and communities like hers, can have a far brighter future.

Conclusion: Rethinking Accountability

People like Londa do not often appear in accounts of the criminal justice system, but they have much to teach us. Their accounts begin to indicate how much many family members are willing to sacrifice to achieve their dreams of family life. It is, in a way, heartening that many family members are willing to bear high costs in order to show their dedication to one another. But families are not limitless trusts of generosity, and if the costs become great enough, the meaning of family itself can change or be lost.

In policy discussions, family and community life in our inner cities are described more often as a contradiction in terms rather than a realistic policy goal. Indeed, many commentators reason that if substantial family and community ties existed in our inner cities, our inner cities would not have the kind of social problems that are now endemic there. But in doing so, they miss the corrosive effect that our criminal justice system is having on those ties, and thus the contribution that one of our foremost public institutions is making to social disorder in disadvantaged communities.

Unfortunately, the pervasive stereotype of an urban "underclass"—one that is uninterested in and unable to forge a coherent family or community life—has had significant practical effects. Policymakers, seeing no families or communities to protect in crime-stricken areas, have come to view residents of minority, urban, and low-income neighborhoods as somehow outside of and untouched by the social norms of society at large. The result has been a set of policies that, out of ignorance, have essentially given up on family and community life in the ghetto and attempt instead to maintain public order by using punitive sanctions.

Criminal policies are often justified with assertions of moral accountability. If the law is the embodiment of our collective will and sanctions the enforcement of our collective norms, then it is important to think carefully about how and to whom we are holding offenders accountable. Incarceration, the preferred punishment in American criminal law, does more than punish and deter. As the stories of prisoner's families make clear, incarceration also transforms the material and moral lives of many of the families it touches, often enforcing a lack of accountability in ways that are both meaningful and destructive. The current practice of mass incarceration thus does far more than inflict an overly harsh punishment. By prohibiting so many from engaging in basic moral behavior, it is cutting away at the basic building blocks of social life itself. As over incarceration increases the costs of caring relationships, the loss becomes a social and a moral one.

But, along with this problem we also have a substantial opportunity. Perhaps it is, as the Reverend Martin Luther King once said, "dark enough to see the stars." States are desperately looking for ways to safely reduce their prison populations. We have a more detailed and thorough understanding of how sanctions affect family and community life than we have ever had. And, we are beginning to see adoption of programs that are, at the very least, good first steps toward a rational and moral response to the social problem of crime.

References

Avery, R. B. and M. S. Rendall. 1997. *The Contribution of Inheritances to Black-White Wealth Disparities in the United States*, BLCC Working Paper #97-08.

Becker, G. S. 1981. *A Treatise on the Family*. Cambridge, Massachusetts and London, England: Harvard University Press.

Blau, F. D. and J. W. Graham. 1990. Black-White Differences in Wealth and Asset Composition. *Quarterly Journal of Economics*, 105:321-339.

___. D. 2002. Families and Incarceration. In M. Mauer and M. Chesney-Lind, eds. *Invisible Punishment*. New York: The New Press.

___. D. 2004. From One Generation to the Next. In J. Travis and M. Wald, eds. *Prisoners Once Removed*. New York: Urban Institute Press.

Braman, D. 2004a. *Doing Time on the Outside: Incarceration and Family Life in Urban America*. Ann Arbor, Michigan: University of Michigan Press.

Brien, M. J. and L. A. Lillard. 1999. Interrelated Family-Building Behaviors: Cohabitation, Marriage and Non-Marital Conception, *Demography.* 36:535.

Bureau of Justice Statistics. 2002. *Special Report, Recidivism of Prisoners Released in 1994*. Washington, DC: Author.

Cole, D. 2000. No Equal Justice. New York: The New Press.

Currie, E. 1988. *Crime and Punishment in America*. New York: Henry Holt and Company.

Donziger, S. 1996. *The Real War on Crime: The Report of the National Criminal Justice Commission*. New York, NY: HarperCollins Publishers, Inc.

Drug Strategies. 1999. *Facing Facts: Drugs and the Future of Washington*, D.C. Available at www.drugstrategies.org/acrobat/WashingtonDC99.pdf

Duggan, P. 2000. Captive Audience Rates High; Families Must Pay Dearly When Inmates Call Collect. *Washington Post*, January 23, p. A03.

England, P. and F. Folbre. 1997. *Reconceptualizing Human Capital*. Paper presented at the annual meetings of the American Sociological Association, Toronto, Canada, August.

Gaes, G. G., T. J. Flanagan, L. L. Motiuk, and L. Stewart. 1999. Adult Correctional Treatment. In M. Tonry and Joan Petersilia, eds. *Prisons, Criminal Justice: A Review of Research*. Chicago: University of Chicago Press.

Kennedy, R. 1997. *Race, Crime, and the Law*. New York: Vantage Books.

Lynch, M. 1988. Piece of the Pie. *Reason*. July.

Manning, W. D. and P. J. Smock. 1995. Why Marry? Race Relations and Transition to Marriage among Cohabitors. *Demography*, 95:509.

Mauer, M. 1999. *Race to Incarcerate*. New York: The New Press.

Menchik, P. L. and N. Jianakoplos. 1997. Black-White Wealth Inequality: Is Inheritance the Reason? *Economic Inquiry*. 35:428-442.

Miller, J. G. 1996. *Search and Destroy: African-American Males and the Criminal Justice System*. New York: Cambridge University Press.

Mumola, C. J. 2000. *Incarcerated Parents and Their Children*. Washington, DC: Bureau of Justice Statistics.

National Center on Addiction and Substance Abuse. 1988. *Behind Bars: Substance Abuse and America's Prison Population*. Available at www.casacolumbia.org/Absolutenm/articlefiles/5745.pdf

Oliver, M. and T. Shapiro.1995. *Black Wealth/White Wealth*. New York: Routledge.

Paris, J. W. 1998. *We've Seen This Coming: Resident Activists Shaping Neighborhood Redevelopment in Washington, D.C.* Available at www.anthrosource. net/doi/pdf/10.1525/tran.2001.10.1.28

Roschelle, Anne R. 1997. *No More Kin: Exploring Race, Class and Gender in Family Networks*. Thousand Oaks, Calfornia: Sage.

Roberston, T. 1997. How to Pay for Elderly Prisoners? *Minneapolis Star Tribune*, January 20, p. 1B.

Slevin, P. 1998. In D.C., Many Addicts and Few Services; Lack of Treatment Programs Keeps Substance Abusers in Jail or in Trouble. *Washington Post*, August 25, p. A01.

Smith, J. P. 1995. Racial and Ethnic Differences in Wealth in the Health and Retirement Study. *Journal of Human Resources*, 30:S158-83.

Tonry, M. 2001. *Malign Neglect.* New York: Oxford University Press.

Travis, J. 1999. *Addressing Drug Abuse in the Justice Context: The Promise and the Challenge, Remarks before the National Assembly on Drugs, Alcohol Abuse, and the Criminal Offender.* Available at http://www.ojp.usdoj.gov/nij/speeches/drug abuse.htm

Tucker, M. B. 2000. Marital Values and Expectations in Context: Results from a 21-City Survey. In Linda J. Waite, ed. *The Ties That Bind.* New York: Aldine de Gruyter.

Western, B. and S. McLanahan. 2000. Fathers Behind Bars: The Impact of Incarceration on Family Formation. In G. L. Fox and M. L. Benson, eds. *Families, Crime and Criminal Justice.* New York: JAI/Elsevier.

REACTION ESSAY— TURNING OUR ATTENTION TO FAMILIES: A NATURAL RESOURCE FOR IMPROVING REENTRY OUTCOMES

12

Carol Shapiro
Executive Director
Family Justice, Inc.
New York, New York

Introduction

In his revelatory book *Doing Time on the Outside*, Donald Braman illuminates the devastating impact of incarceration on families in the United States. He uses powerful data bolstered by the voices and experiences of those most affected by the country's overreliance on imprisonment. As it stands, the U.S. criminal justice system exacerbates conditions of poverty and perpetuates cycles of involvement across generations. In this chapter, this author will respond to Braman's textual portrait with her vision of what this system could look like in ten years if we shift our unit of analysis from the individual to that of the family.

We must prioritize the health and safety of poor families and the communities to which they belong, to transform our use of incarceration and to change our approach to the return home from jail and prison. Even though the issue of reentry from American prisons and jails is gaining momentum, a recent lengthy article in *The New York Times Magazine* (December 24, 2006) had only two fleeting references to family, an omission that is disturbingly familiar. By contrast, as *Doing Time on the Outside* demonstrates, we know more than ever about the destructive influence of crime and victimization on families and communities. We also know what our strengths are and how to put them to work.

Governmental entities—including community corrections officers—and nongovernmental organizations have the power to help reduce rates of crime and victimization and positively affect the millions of people entangled in the criminal justice system by shifting their lens away from the individuals who commit crimes and focusing on each person's social network, including the family. Families are intuitive and natural, are often available twenty-four hours a day, and already exist. Who knows *you* best? Chances are that your answer is the same as most people's. Members of our family, as we define *family*, know us better than any service provider—or anyone else—possibly could. And unlike any programs or services, families are free. Family members also belong to the same culture, which is rarely true of the agencies that affect their lives.

To foster healthy families, safe communities, and positive outcomes, we must reject a perspective that pathologizes individuals and accentuates their deficits and evolve to a strength- and place-based focus on families and social networks. We must consider innovative solutions to the challenges faced by poor people involved in the criminal justice system to ensure that the action we take does not aggravate or propagate existing problems, but inspires widespread beneficial change.

Involvement in the U.S. Criminal Justice System

Incarceration and involvement with the criminal justice system have become a way of life for an increasing number of poor families in the United States. One in four people incarcerated in the entire world is locked up in U.S. jails and prisons (Braman, 2004). Nationwide, more than six million people are under some form of correctional supervision—on parole or probation, in jail or prison (Barreras, Drucker, and Rosenthal, 2005). Almost three million American children have one or both parents incarcerated (Bureau of Justice Assistance, 2000). This is unconscionable. As *Doing Time on the Outside* testifies, imprisoning huge numbers of people has profound tangible and intangible costs.

The criminal justice system is straining to cope with the sheer volume of incarcerated individuals as well as the $67 billion annual price tag for operating jails and prisons (Hughes, 2003). Involvement in this system takes a tremendous toll on poor families. As Braman (2004) painfully and insightfully observes, "There is considerable evidence that the last twenty years of mass in-carceration has been pulling apart the most vulnerable families in our society."

Every year, nearly 650,000 people are released from U.S. prisons (Serious and Violent Offender Reentry Initiative website, May 13, 2004), and more than seven million are released from jails (Hammett, 2000)—which has enormous repercussions for millions of families. The stigma associated with incarcera-tion damages social capital and extends beyond the individual to the family and community, affecting interpersonal relationships, employment, and the integrity of neighborhoods (Clear et al., 2001). Every year, many of these peo-ple return to the system due to drug use and addiction, though it is extremely rare to hear anyone talk about the toll this cycle takes on families.

Those individuals who remain at home face numerous daunting obsta-cles. For example, half of all prison and jail inmates were diagnosed with men-tal health conditions (Bureau of Justice Assistance, Sept. 6, 2006), which significantly affects the people in their lives whether the individual is incar-cerated or at home. The person's illness can seriously affect loved ones, and additionally, such conditions are often generational, which means that more than one family member may be confronting mental illness, whether diagnosed or undiagnosed. Seventy-four percent of state prisoners and 76 percent of local jail inmates with mental health problems also struggled with substance dependence or abuse in the year before their admission (Bureau of Justice Administration, Oct. 11, 2006), conditions that have dire conse-quences for the individuals' children and other family members.

Furthermore, like David of *Doing Time on the Outside,* many people combat not only the stigma and hardship of involvement in the criminal justice system, but also an HIV-positive status. The Department of Justice recently reported that in a 2004 survey, the highest rates of HIV infection in state prisons were among those ages forty-five and older and among people ages thirty-five-to-forty-four in federal prisons (*Bureau of Justice Statistics Bul-letin,* November 2006). This has a profound impact on seniors and deeply affects the HIV-positive individuals' children, grandchildren, and other loved ones. A 2005 study of La Bodega de la Familia—Family Justice's first direct service learning center and a community support program on New York's Lower East Side—demonstrated the prevalence of criminal justice involvement, HIV/AIDS, and substance abuse co-occuring among families.

Of the 62 families (with a total of 592 individuals), 82 percent had at least one other member besides the index case with a history of substance abuse, 62 percent had two or more, and 40 percent had three or more; 72 percent had one other member with a history of criminal justice involvement, 45 percent had two or more, 24

> *percent had three or more. At least one member had HIV/AIDS in*
> *49 percent of the families, 16 percent had two or more, 10 percent*
> *had three or more. Of the 105 family members who reported a his-*
> *tory of criminal justice involvement, 88 percent had a history of*
> *substance use.* (Barreras, Drucker, and Rosenthal, 2005)

If you are poor and the health care system you are accustomed to is punitive, it does not inspire confidence to get the care you need. This, in turn, affects the health outcomes of children whose parents have learned to distrust
medical providers and the systems that deliver care. If we really care about
the success of people reentering our communities, and the health and safety
of their families, we will ensure the availability of quality health care—including mental health services and substance abuse treatment—from providers
who are compassionate and not coercive.

In addition to these health issues, families welcoming a member home
from jail or prison share the frustration of seeing a loved one experience difficulties finding employment and securing housing. Those who rejoin families
living in public housing may not be able to return to their former residences
on penalty of eviction. If we really care about the success, health, and safety
of these families, we will provide educational programs, job training or placement, medical support services, and access to secure housing that takes family relationships into account. In ten years, imagine a system that—instead
of building costly, so-called "supportive" housing for individuals where they
are cut off from their loved ones—gives families money so they can support
themselves and stay together. This would also help poorer communities
thrive.

Many of the almost three million children deprived of a parent due to
incarceration suffer from trauma, anxiety, guilt, shame, and fear (Women's
Prison Association and Home, 2004). They may manifest sadness, withdrawal, low self-esteem, aggressive behavior, truancy, a decline in school performance, and use of drugs or alcohol (Lawhorn, 1992). As Braman's depiction
of David's daughter dramatically illustrates, such families often struggle to make
ends meet while parents are unable to contribute financial support. Braman
writes:

> *Children . . . made fatherless by incarceration are not only more likely*
> *to be abused, to live in poverty, and to burden their extended family*
> *but also more likely to be involved in the criminal justice system them-*
> *selves, contributing to a cycle of abuse and neglect across generations.*
> (Braman, 2004)

Poverty, criminal justice involvement, and other concurrent issues not only constitute seemingly insurmountable obstacles for individuals, but are destructive to whole families.

Comprehending the scope of devastation exacted by criminal justice involvement—and envisioning a means for change—demands a perspective much broader than a focus on a single victim or offender. The effects of conviction, incarceration, probation, and parole radiate out, debilitating families and neighborhoods across generations.

A 2006 study on opportunity in the United States, edited by Isabel Sawhill and Sara McLanahan, concluded that it takes an average of five generations to overcome the inhibiting effects of family poverty. It is not just David who is adversely affected by criminal justice involvement, but also his mother, his wife, his daughter, his son, and his grandson who bear the burdens.

The Natural Strengths of Families

Even strong ties among family members can be tremendously strained when people are trying to support a loved one who is involved in the criminal justice system and is struggling with chronic illness, mental illness, substance abuse, unemployment, insecure housing, and/or poverty. However, recognizing the powerful potential of the strength and support that families naturally provide can revolutionize our approach to these families.

Families are part of social networks. A strong network of support can improve well-being and reduce crime (Wolff and Draine, 2004). Networks help determine one's social capital. As Nancy Wolff and Jeffrey Draine explain:

> *Each individual has a unique stock of social capital comprised of a network of personal connections that can be called upon for assistance in times of need. What benefits individuals can draw from their stock of social capital depends in part on the strength of their ties to other people and in part on the wealth potential of those with whom they are connected* (Draine and Wolff, 2004).

Family members know each other best and are experts about their own experiences. Research indicates that family support can positively influence juveniles under criminal justice supervision (Quinn and Van Dyke, 2004) as well as adults reentering communities (Niven and Stewart, 2005). Additionally, studies have found that "intimate partner and family relationships [are] significantly related to the intermediate reentry outcomes of employment and staying off drugs" (Visher et al., 2004).

Developing Existing Workforces

Due to the insidious expansion of the criminal justice industry, the field has a vast and swollen workforce, which includes providers of mandated drug treatment and mental health interventions, and teachers of parenting classes, to name a few. That said, existing workforces are a significant untapped resource. Professionals at every level have the experience and expertise to help promote the health and safety of poor families and the communities to which they are connected.

The strengths of professionals already engaged in criminal justice also can be tapped to empower the workforce. Our criminal justice system suffers from a "flavor du jour" mentality instead of encouraging participation in the workplace to help set goals and develop long-term strategies. Line staff and mid-level managers in the corrections field are typically disenfranchised. It is rare that we draw on their valuable insight and experience to find meaningful solutions for the environment they know best. We can elicit the strengths of professionals at every level, just as we encourage them to draw out the strengths of clients and their families. However, until we treat staff differently in a widespread, systematic way, they will not be empowered to recognize families as resources for support and insight.

One effective approach is to form diagonal workgroups, which bring together a cross-section of people with a wide range of expertise, perspectives, responsibilities, and characteristics (Family Justice, 2005). Broad representation ensures that issues come to light, are addressed, and are effectively incorporated into planning and implementation. The role of a diagonal working group is threefold: to develop and enhance strategies to achieve an established institutional and/or community goal; to serve as a laboratory for exploring the challenges to and opportunities for effecting organizational change; and to demonstrate the value of engaging experts and validate the experience of individuals who will have the responsibility for implementing new approaches and systems.

Existing workforces can implement a wealth of strength-based, family-focused strategies to achieve greater family well-being. For example, imagine a prison or jail that does not charge families triple or quadruple rates for collect phone calls to a loved one. In a system truly committed to assisting families and maintaining healthy relationships, we could provide inmates and their families with phone cards to help them stay connected instead of charging exorbitant amounts for collect calls. We could facilitate more frequent visitation by extending hours, providing transportation to distant institutions, hosting special events for families, and making the process of entering correctional institutions more welcoming and less humiliating.

Many facilities already have programs in place to foster literacy, parenting, and job-training skills, and to address substance abuse. Any intervention of this type presents the opportunity to create connections between providers and families, broadly defined. These programs can serve a dual purpose: Reading and writing exercises can become opportunities for reaching out to friends and family and for analyzing and exploring relationships. Making literacy programs practical and personal has obvious benefits and should come at relatively little cost where such programs exist. Phone cards and improved visitation conditions will require additional expenditures, but the amount of money saved through more effective prevention and intervention will surely cover these costs.

Innovators around the country are taking steps toward a focus on family and community. In Michigan, the Department of Corrections offers free video-teleconferencing to inmates and families. In Ohio, the Department of Rehabilitation and Corrections instituted a program that reunites incarcerated fathers and children at three prisons. Inmates, parenting partners, and children are offered programming including educational and experiential activities that allow loved ones to spend time together. Transportation to the institution is provided at least twice a month.

Partner organizations in the community assist families in identifying and accessing resources. After release, family-focused programming continues at the partner organization. If we really care about family well-being, we will take steps to strengthen existing relationships—to bring families together rather than pull them apart. We can do this by using family-focused, strength-based methods and tools to empower families and elicit their strengths, and by training supervision officers and non-governmental organization staff to use these practices.

Case managers and other professionals who work with families involved in the criminal justice system are increasingly using mapping techniques—similar to the ones police use in law-enforcement efforts—to explore crucial relationships. Eric Cadora and his colleagues at the Justice Mapping Center in Brooklyn, New York, have created maps of twelve U.S. cities that identify neighborhoods whose residents have been incarcerated in a given year (*The New Yorker*, January 8, 2007). With this tool, they have calculated the costs of incarceration, block by block, which has significant ramifications for how we plan and deliver services to families.

In *Doing Time on the Outside*, Braman uses genograms to map the relationships among the people he interviews. With proper training, practitioners in the criminal justice field can adopt mapping tools in order to tap the strengths of formal and informal family relationships, understand problems and complexities, and improve outcomes. For example, the Oklahoma Department of Corrections has adopted Family Justice's Bodega Model®, a strength-based, family-focused method of case management (Jones and Shapiro, American Probation and

Parole Association *Perspectives*, Winter 2007). Officers are routinely taught to think about the family and not just the individual. Ultimately, if family members get the attention and services they need, their outcomes can improve, even if the person most directly involved with the criminal justice system returns to prison, relapses, or has other serious ongoing problems.

Shifting the Lens: Blended Funding

Imagine our criminal justice system ten years in the future, when we recognize and capitalize upon the influence and the expertise of families, community-based organizations, and government. Currently, individual families are consuming an exorbitant amount of resources—at an immense cost. Too often, these resources are pitted against each other, increasing—not decreasing—both expenditures and tensions. Our work at La Bodega has shown that it is not unusual for a family to be involved in parole, probation, child welfare, public housing, and SSI. Yet, too often, each of these agencies has a limited, almost myopic focus on the individual connected to that service sector and views the person as merely a parolee, probationer, child, lease holder, or head of household. Imagine a system that coordinates efforts among all of these agencies in order to assist the family as a cohesive unit. This system would combine or blend funding from multiple sources not only to create cost efficiencies, but to promote outcomes that uniformly support family well-being.

Family as the Unit of Analysis

In addition to changing policy and practice, a commitment to halting cycles of poverty and criminal justice involvement by focusing on the strengths of families and communities will transform the way research is conducted in the field. We will see more studies that use the family as the unit of analysis to inform us about the broader impact of sentencing policies, incarceration, parole, and probation. Applied research will lead to the creation of better tools for studying relationships among multiple people and institutions—and studying individuals in the context and the reality of their lives.

Researching with a new lens will allow us to more accurately evaluate the successes and the weaknesses of our policies and practices. It is this type of research and evaluation that leads to constant learning and improvement. We must take risks, but we must also work from a strong foundation of informed policy and evidence-based practice.

Conclusion

If we truly want to promote health, safety, and well-being, we must not passively let the effect of criminal justice involvement take its course across generations; we must act decisively. We must capitalize upon the natural strengths and resources of families, communities, governments, and nongovernmental organizations. We must continue to innovate by learning from all of the experts—governmental and nongovernmental workforces, families, and the neighborhoods they are connected to. We know that it pays to draw on families' strengths, and we don't have the luxury of time; we must put these plans into action to give families a fair chance now and to help future generations break the cycle of continued incarceration, addiction, illness, crime, victimization, and poverty.

Imagine that in ten years, families are always part of this discussion and part of the solution. It costs nothing to draw on the strengths of families. Yet, the price of ignoring our most valuable resource is astronomical.

Bibliography and References

Barreras, Ricardo E., Ernest M., Drucker, David Rosenthal. 2005. The Concentration of Substance Use, Criminal Justice Involvement, and HIV/AIDS in the Families of Drug Offenders. *Journal of Urban Health: Bulletin of New York Academy of Medicine,* (82)1:162-170.

Braman, Donald. 2004. *Doing Time on the Outside.* Ann Arbor: University of Michigan Press.

Bureau of Justice Statistics. 2000. Incarcerated Parents and Their Children. Washington, DC: U.S. Department of Justice. http://www.ojp.usdoj.gov/bjs/pub/pdf/ iptc.pdf

___. 2006. Drug Use and Dependence, State and Federal Prisoners, 2004. U.S. Department of Justice: Washington DC. October 11. http://www.ojp.usdoj.gov/bjs/pub/pdf/dudsfp04.pdf

___. 2006. Mental Health Problems of Prison and Jail Inmates. U.S. Department of Justice: Washington D.C. September 6. www.ojp.usdoj.gov/bjs/abstract/mhppji.htm

Clear, Todd R., Dina R. Rose, Judith A. Ryder. 2001. Incarceration and the Community: The Problem of Removing and Returning Offenders. *Crime and Delinquency,* (47)3:335-351.

Family Justice Inc. 2005. Forming a Diagonal Workgroup. Author: New York, June.

Hammett, Theodore. 2000. *Health Related Issues in Prisoner Reentry to the Community.* Urban Institute's Reentry Roundtable: Washington, DC, October.

Hughes, Kristen A. 2006. Justice Expenditure and Employment in the United States, 2003. Bureau of Justice Statistics Bulletin. U.S. Department of Justice: Washington D.C. April.

Jones, Justin, and Carol Shapiro. 2007. The Oklahoma Family Justice Project: Improving Community Supervision Outcomes One Family at a Time. *Perspectives.* Winter.

Lawhorn, Sharron. 1992. Children of Incarcerated Parents; A Report to the Legislature Pursuant to ACR 38, Resolution Chapter 89, Statutes of 1991, Filante. New York Assembly Office of Research, May.

MacIntyre, Lauren. 2007. Criminal Justice Rap Map. *The New Yorker.* January 8.

Marciniak, Edward. 2002. Standing Room Only: What to do about Prison Overcrowding. *Commonweal.* January 25.
Maruschak, Laura M. 2006. HIV in Prisons, 2004. Bureau of Justice Statistics Bulletin, U.S. Department of Justice: Washington, DC. November.

Niven, Stephen, Duncan Stewart. 2005. Resettlement Outcomes on Release from Prison in 2003. Research, Development and Statistics Directorate of the Home Office.

Quinn, William H. and David J. Van Dyke. 2004. A Multiple Family Group Intervention for First-Time Juvenile Offenders: Comparisons with Probation and Dropouts on Recidivism. *Journal of Community Psychology,* 32, No. 2.

Serious and Violent Offender Reentry Initiative website, U.S. Department of Justice: Washington D.C. Retrieved May 13, 2004. www.ojp.esdoj.gov/reentry/ learn.html

Suellentrop, Chris. 2006. The Right Has a Jailhouse Conversion: How Conservatives Came to Embrace Prison Reform. *The New York Times Magazine.* December 24.

Sullivan, Eileen et al. 2002. *Families as a Resource in Recovery from Drug Abuse: An Evaluation of La Bodega de la Familia.* Vera Institute of Justice: New York.

Visher, Christy et al. 2004. *Returning Home: Understanding the Challenges of Prisoner Reentry.* Urban Institute: Chicago.

Wolf Harlow, Caroline. 2003. "Education and Correctional Populations." Bureau of Justice Statistics Special Report: Washington DC. www.ojp.usdoj.gov/bjs/pub/pdf/ ecp.pdf

Wolff, Nancy and Jeffrey Draine. 2004. Dynamics of Social Capital of Prisoners and Community Reentry: Ties That Bind. *Journal of Correctional Health Care.*

The Women's Prison Association & Home, Inc. 2004. *Family to Family: Partnerships between Corrections and Child Welfare,* Part Two, A Project of the Annie E. Casey Foundation.

SECTION 5:

CIVIC ENGAGEMENT, THE COMMUNITY, AND REENTRY

Doing Good to Make Good: Evaluating a Civic-Engagement Model of Reentry

13

Gordon Bazemore, Ph.D.
Florida Atlantic University, Port St. Lucie, Florida

Rachel Boba, Ph.D.
Florida Atlantic University, Port St. Lucie, Florida

Introduction

In general, offender-reentry strategies have failed to consider the community either as a support, or as an obstacle, to reintegration. We present a theoretical model and an evaluation protocol for a "civic-engagement" reentry focused on both the offender and the community transformation. Grounded in restorative-justice principles of decision making and the reciprocal obligation to repair the harm of crime, this model features strategically designed community service as a primary intervention aimed at reducing community barriers to the development of positive identities for formerly incarcerated persons; altering the community's image of such persons; and mobilizing and/or building community capacity to provide informal support and assistance.

Formerly incarcerated persons face two general types of barriers to successful reentry. The first type—legal status barriers—impose restrictions that deny or limit access to a variety of roles that bind most citizens to conventional society. For example, returning felons face restrictions on voting rights, difficulties in obtaining occupational licensing, loss of parental rights, prohibition from holding elective office or serving on juries, as well as other forms of formal and informal social stigma that limit access to employment opportunities (Uggen and Manza, 2002).

Because personal and civic identity are largely determined by the relative strength of ties to various social institutions (for example, those linked to work and family), such bans greatly diminish the reintegrative capacity of persons formerly under correctional supervision.[1] The second type of barriers include access to family assistance, education, housing, and a range of support services including treatment for drug abuse and other problems. When addressing concerns beyond basic surveillance, reentry and parole policy and practice have focused primarily on these latter individual treatment and service needs.

Rarely addressed are *community-level* barriers, such as lack of willingness and/or capacity to reintegrate offenders and the negative public and self-image linked to formerly incarcerated persons. While some reentry discourse has addressed important human-capital issues of employment and education (Travis and Petersilia, 2001), with few exceptions (Clear, Rose, and Ryder, 2001), the field generally has failed to consider the role of community social capital (Putnam, 2000) in offender reintegration. Moreover, although communities, not programs, are the "destination" of the reentry journey, the reentry literature remains devoid of broader policy visions that include a specific role for the community.

As depicted in Figure 1, the basic reentry equation is straightforward. The extent to which returning offenders can be expected to successfully reintegrate depends on *both* the formerly incarcerated person's ability to resist recidivism *and* the community's capacity and receptivity.

Figure 1. Participation and Service Impact

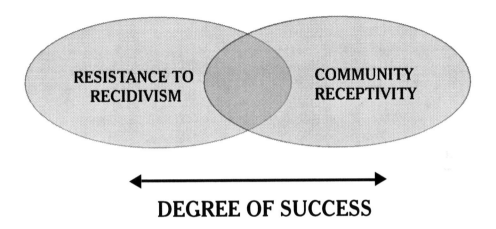

Thus, the influence of the community is fundamental and can be seen as both an *independent variable*—that effects the capacity of offenders and their supporters to be successful in reintegration—and a *dependent variable* to be acted upon in the intervention context. The community may be criminogenic in its impact, but also must be a potential resource, and if given necessary support, can exert positive, pro-social influence. For example, at the macro-level, communities are important targets of capacity-building activities that increase skills and resources that help offenders reintegrate. At the micro-level, the community may engage the offenders in experiences that restore trust and demonstrate utility to the community that can transform the offenders' public identity. Finally, at the middle range, offenders and their advocates look to the community to supply social support and guardianship.

The scarcity of implementation of community-focused interventions is *not* due to an absence of criminological theory and research. Indeed, the irony is that despite a rich and practically relevant community-oriented tradition of scholarship in criminology, reentry protocols have been characterized by a "disconnect" between research/theory and community-oriented intervention. In recent years, however, an emerging model of reentry has sought to engage community obstacles at the micro-level by attempting to change the image and role of the offender from liability to asset, and at a more macro-level, to build awareness and community capacity for reintegration. This *civic-engagement model* (Bazemore and Stinchcomb, 2004a; Uggen, Manza, and Thompson, 2006) is focused on the following goals:

- Weakening community barriers to the development of pro-social identities for persons who have been under correctional supervision
- Altering the community's image of such persons
- Mobilizing and/or building community capacity to provide informal
  support and assistance
- Policies based on a *civic-engagement* model emphasize three primary practices: restorative justice decision making and reparation,
  civic community service, and voting enfranchisement and democratic participation (Bazemore and Stinchcomb, 2004a)[2]

The focus of this paper is on the role of "civic service" in rebuilding and
strengthening ties between the offender and the community through a practical intervention aimed at addressing human and infrastructure needs.
Restorative justice is especially important as a non-adversarial decision-making process designed to maximize participation of the victim, the offender, and
the community in determining how to repair the harm of crime through
restorative-group-conferencing practice (Bazemore and Umbreit, 2001; Bazemore and Schiff, 2004; Van Ness and Strong, 1997), and it can also guide
implementation of community service to ensure the integrity of program
intervention.[3]

Most importantly, the civic-engagement model is grounded in core criminological and social science literature—broadly described here as identity
transformation, life course, and social disorganization/social capital
research. Although they have not been systematically applied to reentry policy and practice, this research literature addresses micro, middle-range, and
community levels of analysis and provides a logical basis for linking variables associated with each of the three practice dimensions of the civic-
engagement model to successful reentry.[4]

The specific components of this theoretical and empirical grounding are
discussed in detail elsewhere (Bazemore and Stinchcomb, 2004a, 2004b),
and, therefore, are outlined only briefly in this manuscript.[5] Our purpose
herein is to propose a theory-based evaluation protocol (Chen, 1990; Weiss,
1997) that can do the following:

- Provide standards and process measures for assessing the strength and integrity of civic-engagement-reentry intervention
- Propose intermediate outcomes (or "intervening variables") that provide clear linkages to long-term outcomes (for example, reintegration)
- Identify and refine "theories of intervention" (Weiss, 1997) underlying the civic-engagement model that can also *guide and shape practice.*

Literature Review

While perhaps unfamiliar to many in the criminal justice field, the concept of *civic engagement* is not new in the political science and sociological literature, or in specific areas of study in a variety of disciplines (Barber, 1992; Putnam, 2000). Although much of this literature focuses on young people, the socialization process, and youth development (Bazemore and Terry, 1997; Sherrod, Flanagan, and Kassimir, 2006), concepts of civic engagement can apply to all demographic categories.

This literature review provides a brief historical overview of the normative basis of service in American society and briefly summarizes empirical support for community service and related interventions for reentry. It is followed by the specific theoretical components of a civic-engagement model of community service and corresponding components of a formative-evaluation protocol. The evaluation protocol is aimed at helping practitioners and researchers assess the strength and "integrity" of the intervention to determine whether it was a strong model of civic engagement, or something entirely different, which accounted for the impact of the program.

The Defensible Basis of Community Service: Underlying Values and Research Findings

" . . . by dint of working for one's fellow citizens, the habit and taste for serving them is at length acquired." Alexis de Tocqueville

The Value Base of Community Service

Community service can be defended on both normative and empirical grounds. Some argue simply that community service is the right thing to do.[6] In addition, empirical and theoretical support for community service is grounded in the American tradition of mutual support and assistance (Barber, 1992; Bellah, Madsen, Sullivan, Swidler, and Tipton et al., 1991; Coles, 1993; Dewey, 1958).

For example, in 1835, de Tocqueville observed that Americans —while individualistic at least by European standards—saw intrinsic value in helping others.

A century later, Harvard philosopher William James, in a difficult period in American history, urged his fellow citizens to take up the call of national service. Echoing this theme, in 1933, President Franklin Delano Roosevelt issued his own call for action to ease the suffering of thousands of unemployed young men and reclaim the country's forests and wilderness lands by announcing the formation of the Civilian Conservation Corps (Salmond, 1967), a program now regarded as the original model for various youth conservation corps programs.

The civic-service tradition and the natural call to service that some believe is part of the American psyche is also clearly grounded in the civil rights movement; Native American movements; settlement houses; labor unions; various faith traditions; African-American traditions; and various mutual aid or "self-help" societies. More recently, social scientists concerned with the decline of "social capital" (Coleman, 1988; Putnam, 2000) note that the disbursement of work, mobility, time pressure, family disruption, and suburbanization have led Americans away from networks of collective support and relationships built on mutual trust and cooperation, and have also weakened this service tradition.[7]

Community Service and Offenders

Yet, those who have committed crimes, especially those known to have done so by virtue of conviction and sentencing to correctional supervision, are thought by some to be very different from the general population of citizens. Among these supposed differences would certainly be a lack of empathy and a lack of awareness of others' needs that would underlie a desire to help their communities and fellow community members.

However, the tradition of voluntary service by persons incarcerated and formerly incarcerated seems to turn this stereotype on its head. Service projects are conceived and carried out on a daily basis in the prisons of this country by incarcerated persons and in communities by those formerly incarcerated (Maruna, LeBel, and Lanier, 2003). Perhaps most impressive are the recent examples of inmates who raised money to support 9/11 relief efforts. For example, in New York State, incarcerated persons raised $75,000 from donations from fellow prisoners earning thirty-five cents per day (Ellis, 2003).[8]

The Empirical Basis for Civic Service as a Reentry Practice

Although the empirical evidence of the impact of community service on re-offending and other outcomes is substantial, the number of evaluations in the thirty or more years of use of community service is relatively small compared to other correctional interventions. The larger body of relevant research includes direct evaluations of community service, follow-up studies of inmates who complete service, research on related interventions (for example, work experience), research on service with non-offender or mixed populations, and surveys and longitudinal studies with normative populations (see Bazemore, Karp, and Schiff, 2003).

An example of longitudinal studies of the impact of service on normative populations, for example, is Uggen and Janikula's (1999) cohort study of the impact of a community-service experience for high school students on adult outcomes. In this prospective national survey of a thousand adolescents, the authors document a strong negative relationship between involvement in voluntary, uncompensated service to the community in adolescence and crime in early adulthood. Although service has a cumulative impact over time (in other words, the more service involvement, the less likely is involvement in crime), its impact in young adulthood appears most important in shaping one's *public identity* through civic engagement.

An example of evaluation research on mixed offender and nonoffender populations with service and related interventions is the Youth Corps program (the precursor to AmeriCorps) evaluated by Abt Associates in the late 1990s. For participants with offense records, the study revealed significant reductions in re-offending and gains in job placement and retention for all participants (Jastrzab, Blomquist, Maskder, and Orr et al., 1997). This evaluation is important because the program's structure is similar to that being implemented in programs being developed to pilot the "Civic-Justice-Corps" model of civic service proposed herein (see endnote 5). The brief literature review presented below, however, is focused on evaluations of community-service programs with offenders as an alternative to other sanctions (for a more detailed discussion of the broader service research on related interventions and populations, see Bazemore and Karp, 2004).

Direct Evidence: Offender Populations

Although community service is thought to have varied effects on participants under criminal-justice supervision (Bazemore and Maloney, 1994), most studies have focused on recidivism. Overall, it is most important to note that no studies report negative findings (for example, increased re-offending), and most indicate positive outcomes of the impact of community service on offender or nonoffender populations (for detailed summaries, see Bazemore and Karp, 2004).

Studies comparing community-service participation with alternative sentences document some reduction in recidivism or, at worst, no increase in recidivism. Pease (1982), for example, reports that early studies in Great Britain were inconclusive regarding reductions in re-offending while McDonald's (1986) comprehensive evaluation of New York City's Vera Institute program found no significant reduction in recidivism when community-service orders were compared to short jail sentences. Part of this lack of difference in recidivism, however, was offset to some degree by the finding of a significant reduction in the use of jail sentences for relatively chronic felony property offenders, a reduction that did not increase the re-offense rate beyond the usual post-jail recidivism rate.

In a more recent study of the Vera Institute service-project participants, Caputo (1999) reported that the program had maintained the rate of recidivism reported by McDonald in the earlier 1980s study (about 25 percent). In addition, this rate was achieved despite the fact that the more recent findings were based on a population of higher-risk participants (with an average of ten prior offenses and a higher proportion of offenders with prior felonies— 9 percent). Finally, the finding that the program is maintaining relatively high completion rates (74 percent), despite serving a more high-risk population, has positive implications for future concerns with public safety. It is also consistent with other studies, which report a strong negative correlation between completion of reparative sanctions (for example, restitution and community service) and re-offending (Schneider and Schneider, 1984).

Another important study of recidivism for community-service participants under correctional supervision was based on an Israeli field experiment using service as an alternative to short-term sentences (Nirel, Landau, Sebba, and Sagiv, 1997). In this randomized trial, researchers documented significantly lower rates of recidivism for the experimental group whose members completed community service as an alternative to serving the last six months of their prison sentence. In a similar Swiss study in which about half of a group of convicted offenders who would have received short-term prison sentences of up to fourteen days were randomly assigned to an experimental group that participated in community service, researchers found higher rates of re-arrest for the incarcerated group (Killias and Aebi, 2000). Another study which examined recidivism rates for parolees randomly assigned to community service and those assigned to a control group found that the recidivism rate for the community-service group was only 29 percent in comparison to 50 percent for the parole group (Jengeleski and Richwine, 1987).

Although not strictly an evaluation study, Maruna's (2001) research on incarcerated inmates in the United Kingdom linked willing participation in community service both inside correctional facilities and post-release to reductions in re-offending. Moreover, his study is relevant to our subsequent theoretical discussion of change in self-image and public identity as a result of completion of service as a primary factor in successful reentry (see Maruna, 2001; Toch, 2002; McAdams and de St. Aubin, 1998).

Large-scale aggregate studies of the impact of service also show promising results. Butts and Snyder's (1991) study of two large populations of Utah juvenile offenders referred during a five-year time period to diversion and probation programs, respectively, showed significant differences of 8 and 10 percent reduction in reoffending for youth who completed community service as part of either probation or diversion dispositions compared to other probation and other diversion youth who did not do so.

One of the most important and most large-scale recent studies of the impact of community service for felony offenders released from prison is Wilkinson's (1998) research on incarcerated men and women released from Ohio prisons during the last three months of 1994. Comparing groups of individuals who had not performed community service (N=4,102) with a smaller group that had completed service in the year prior to release (N=384), Wilkinson reported significant differences in recidivism in favor of the community-service participants. While not an experimental study, these differences persisted when a variety of variables related to recidivism—including prior incarcerations, commitment offense, race, educational attainment, and so on— were controlled statistically.

In summary, the research literature on community service with correctional populations is generally positive, especially regarding the impact community service had on recidivism. However, much remains to be learned about how the *quality and type* of service may be related to re-offending and other outcomes, and how community members perceive service participants. For example, it is likely that explicitly punitive forms of service have *not* been evaluated and might be expected—given consistent findings from aversive programs using other interventions (for example, Finkenhauer and Gavin, 1999)—to have a *negative* impact on a variety of outcomes.

Most importantly, strategically designed, comprehensive, principle and theory-based service interventions have not been evaluated either. Although there is some evidence that service "works" in terms of its influence on several outcomes, we know relatively little about the theory behind the apparently positive impact of service, and there have been no studies of carefully designed, restorative community service, or service aimed at achieving higher-level objectives. With the exception of a few studies that also make use of qualitative data (for example, Maruna, 2001; Uggen et al., 2006), we know relatively little about how correctional participants view service—that is, what the service experience means to offenders.

Service on Its "Highest Plane": A General Practice Model

The emphasis on community service as the core practice in the civic-engagement model of reentry may catch some criminal justice practitioners and researchers by surprise. Many exposed to what passes for community service in the typical probation department or jail work-release options would have difficulty imagining service as a potentially strong and highly effective intervention with offenders reentering their communities. Even more disturbing in recent years have been examples of punitive community service whose proponents argue that service should be a retributive tool, focused on degradation and humiliation (Kahan, 1999) not unlike chain gangs of another era (Amnesty International, 1996).[9]

Yet, as suggested previously, there are other traditions of community service both within and outside the realm of correctional supervision. The concept of service on its "highest plane" (Bazemore and Maloney, 1994; Maloney, 1998) clearly acknowledges a fundamental distinction between routine service intended as punishment, a routine sanction, or a weak rehabilitative tool, and what can be viewed as a potentially transformative activity designed with the highest possible expectations for the participant and the community.

A general practice model that illustrates this "higher plane" of service is needed to develop propositions related to service impact. We suggest that a general civic-engagement model of service has four essential practice dimensions:

- The level and nature of participant and community stakeholder involvement in decision making
- The vision and role of the participant envisioned by promoters and organizers of service projects
- The nature, purpose, and expected impact of the service on the community
- The impact of the service on the offender

Stakeholder Involvement in Decision Making

The theoretical logic of the first assumption is that, in general, the level and diversity of participation of those affected by crime in decision making about the response to crime increases the overall effectiveness of outcomes. This premise is not new and is indeed central to both procedural (Tyler, 1999) and restorative (Van Ness and Strong, 1997) justice models. Such participation is also a tenet of democratic decision-making (Barber, 1992; Braithwaite, 2002). Although offenders and victims seldom receive the exact outcomes they hope for in the criminal justice process, they are more satisfied with the outcome when they view the process as fair, have a voice in the decision, and receive information about their case. In general, citizens denied information and opportunities for meaningful participation may become apathetic, or even suspicious, distrustful, cynical, and finally oppositional (Barber, 1992; Tyler, 1999).

A summary proposition about this first premise is depicted graphically in Figure 2. This model suggests that, all other things being equal, the extent of stakeholder involvement in service project *selection, design, and the activity itself* (*see* horizontal axis) is a primary factor in increasing the collective benefit or impact of the activity (*see* the vertical axis). The figure also suggests that as the nature of participation changes qualitatively from providing input to actual participation, the impact is increased. For example, court-ordered service with no input from the offender or the community about the nature and location of the service effort represents the lowest level of participation, while it is possible at the highest levels to maximize participation in choices about service location and focus and to allow for participation of all stakeholders in the service activity itself.

Figure 2. Participation and Service Impact

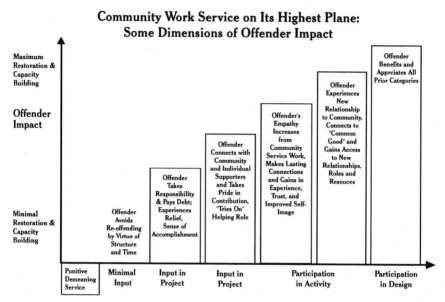

**Community Work Service on Its Highest Plane:
Some Dimensions of Offender Impact**

Offender Involvement

Participant and Citizen Role in Service

Second, the role of the offender as a participant envisioned by organizers of civic service and the community may be viewed in a variety of ways. Too often, in modern societies, community members—and especially more marginalized individuals such as offenders—are viewed essentially as passive "objects" waiting to be told what to do and where to go, to be ordered to do something, to be processed, and so forth.

A somewhat more positive view of the citizen is as a *recipient* of services. Yet, the individual in this role also too often is viewed as a passive "client" in need of assistance (McKnight, 1995) rather than as an acting, thinking citizen with something to offer.

Substantially better is the view of the participant/citizen as "contributor," as a resource with something to offer his/her fellow citizens, and someone needed by the community as a whole. The highest level is a vision of the citizen as an active "steward" of the community and of its human and other resources. This role is inclusive of the role of contributor, as it involves a higher level of community leadership in support of civic involvement (see Barber, 1992).

The Nature, Purpose, and Expected Impact of Service Intervention

Third, the nature and intended impact of the service intervention is also presumed to be critical to achieving specific kinds of outcomes. Punitive, demeaning service, or service intended only as a means of structuring time, we suggest, does not justify the effort required in civic-service design.[10] Other service projects may be geared to accomplish one or more of several, perhaps *equally* desirable goals: holding the offender accountable to the community to repair harm caused by the offense; providing a direct, visible community benefit (for example, building a park; planting a community garden); providing individual assistance to community members in need (for example, the elderly, young people who need tutoring, victims of domestic violence who need shelter and childcare assistance); and literally, "building community."

Service projects that illustrate the community-building objective include those that provide opportunities for creating new relationships and levels of understanding (in other words, between racial and ethnic groups), developing collective skills in conflict resolution, and in monitoring and supporting youth at risk. As the vertical bars in Figure 3 (on the next page) suggest, we also propose that there is a theoretical hierarchy of community service projects wherein the best projects are multidimensional interventions that accomplish a wide range of objectives. The tallest bar on the far right of the Figure 3 graph would, therefore, be an example of a project or set of projects that met comprehensive needs and accomplished goals that could be said to *simultaneously*: (1) build and strengthen community capacity; (2) provide direct assistance to individual community members in need (for example, the elderly, homeless persons, youth at risk); (3) provide a general benefit to the community as a whole; and (4) allow an offender to demonstrate accountability or make amends by repairing harm to the community.

Figure 3. Service Objectives

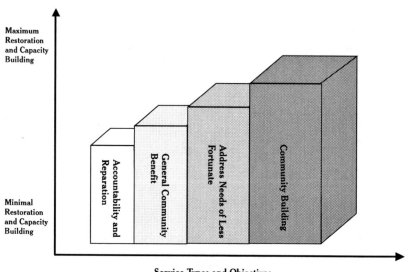

Service Types and Objectives

This hierarchy therefore implies differences in the *nature and level of planning and execution* rather than any necessary value-based ranking of priorities between, for example say, providing a general community benefit versus projects that meet the needs of the elderly. Because communities are likely to differ in their most pressing needs and, therefore, should have maximum input into project selection, the ultimate benefit of a given project is an *empirical* question of impact. Evaluation aimed at gauging offender, community, and victim impact would therefore subsequently help to increase understanding of which types of service, and what kinds of specific projects are most effective, as well as most appropriate, in a given community context.

Offender Experience and Impact

While civic service can be designed to maximize positive impact on community, offender, and victim (Bazemore and Stinchcomb, 2004), Figure 4 depicts the relationship between the *offender's* experience and the potential service impact (Bazemore et al., 2003). As previously suggested, in each type of service, there is an implied movement toward greater responsibility at each level, and as suggested on the vertical axis, greater opportunity for impact. However, because there is no empirical evidence that one type of service focus (for example, direct service to individuals in need versus community beautification projects) has greater impact on re-offending than another type, an experimental civic- engagement program would provide an opportunity to examine the validity of theoretical propositions related to both.

Figure 4. Participation Role and Impact

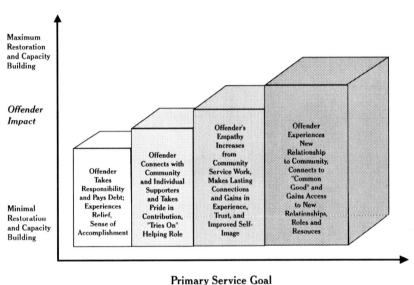

Primary Service Goal

The focus on offender impact in Figure 4 is in part a function of involvement, the view of the offender as a participant in the service activity (as in Figure 3),[11] and the nature of the service focus. The first bar would suggest an outcome for the offender that may provide a sense of relief or accomplishment for having "made amends" for the harm caused to the victim and the community as a result of the offense. The second bar suggests, in addition, a connection with the community at a macro level by participation in a project that has broad, general-community impact and may allow for the offender to be seen in a different "helping" role in the community. The third bar could provide the same kind of offender impact but also suggests an outcome linked to the provision of direct service to less fortunate members of the community. The final bar suggests an added effect in the form of a macro-impact on quality of life and social capital that may provide the ultimate community connection for the offender and, as suggested previously, also may include outcomes related to service at other levels of analysis.

Summary

To make service relevant and effective as a core feature of a reentry strategy capable of changing both community and offender capacity, it is necessary to envision and operationalize service on a "higher plane." Such a vision and plan would include a clear conceptualization of and protocol for community and offender involvement in planning and executing service projects, a new vision of the role of the participant as active contributor or "steward," and a new understanding of the purpose and anticipated impact of service.

In the following sections, we focus in a more specific and explicitly theoretical way on the nature and potential impact of the community service activity itself. We discuss the relevance of several intervention theories and the role of community service aimed at having an impact on reentry and offender reintegration at three levels of analysis. Our goal is to provide a theoretical basis and a direction for research by developing measures of both immediate and intermediate impact as well as process.

Civic Service and the Need for Intervention Theory

> "The extent to which immediate and intermediate goals can be divorced from ultimate goals as valid in themselves poses a difficult question. Certainly there is a tremendous amount of activity, perhaps the largest portion of all public service work, devoted to the successful attainment of immediate and intermediate goals, which appear to have only a very *indirect bearing on ultimate goals.*" (Suchman, 1967, 55; emphasis ours)

As the quote suggests, the idea of connecting immediate and intermediate goals via use of logic models (Weiss, 1977) with long-term outcomes is nothing new. While most evaluators are aware of the need to make such connections and attempt to conduct "theory-driven" evaluation (Chen, 1990), these linkages are often not articulated as part of formative evaluation designs. What we propose here is even less typical; that is, using theory and research to *shape* and assess a variety of intervention designs to achieve specific immediate and intermediate outcomes.

While our summary of research findings suggests that service can have beneficial impacts on offenders (as well as service recipients and communities), in this section we focus on why this is so, based on theory-driven research in criminology. More importantly, we consider why these programs merit further demonstration accompanied by rigorous formative evaluation, followed by theory-testing impact evaluation (Chen, 1990; Weiss, 1997). For example, such demonstrations could provide further evidence of the *conditions* under which an approach is likely to work, how and why it works, and what problems need to be overcome to ensure success.

A policy or program of any kind can be viewed as a hypothesis about the future. Intervention theory helps us to define the variations in practice priorities in a way that allows for clear replication, development of outcome measures, and continuous testing. Such definitions help us to "know best practice when we *see it*" so that we can on an ongoing basis gauge the integrity of the intervention (Weiss, 1997). We cannot know what service means to participants and community stakeholders until we have a standard for determining *intermediate* results (for example, bonding to prosocial community members), and their relationship with an ultimate outcome (for example, desistance from crime). We therefore must articulate the theory, or theories, of intervention that guide practice to make sure that what is believed to be "positive community service work" is implemented in a manner consistent with core principles of civic engagement.

As noted earlier, service has been linked to a number of theoretical frameworks in criminology and other social sciences. Uggen and Janikula (1999), for example, explain the potential impact of service using several theoretical traditions in criminology that emphasize informal social control. In their view, control theory (Hirschi, 1969), differential association, social learning, and various versions of what they label "reintegrative" theories (for example, Braithwaite, 1989, 2002) can provide support for meaningful community service in promoting successful reentry.

In the remaining sections of this manuscript, we focus on the nature and quality of the community service activity itself by considering three general theoretical approaches that are consistent with the objectives of weakening barriers to pro-social identity, mobilizing support and informal control, and community building. These perspectives—which address micro-social psychological, middle-range, and community levels of analysis respectively—are described herein as: *identity transformation; life course criminology/social control, and social capital/collective efficacy.*

We will look at the perspective in three ways:

1. The intended impact of service at the most micro, interactionist level of interpersonal-identity transformation as a result of family, mentor or support person, support group, and peer influences
2. The mid-range level of analysis focused on informal social support
3. The macro-level of social control at the extended family, parochial group, and neighborhood levels

The Interactional Level: Identity Transformation

Identity-transformation research is concerned with accounting for how individuals change the way they view themselves in relationship to others and how they shape the way others view them. Grounded in symbolic-interactionist perspectives (Erikson, 1964; Matsueda and Heimer, 1997; Schwartz and Stryker, 1970), in the reentry context, these social-psychological theories explain how specific interventions may be designed to change the *public* image of those who have harmed individuals and communities while also changing their own *self*-image. The civic-engagement model, of course, is concerned with the role of service in both. The three primary, practically relevant theoretical dimensions at this level include: repairing harm, developing a new public identity/image, and changing one's *personal* self-image.

Repairing Harm and Public Identity: Making Amends

The focus on repairing harm in restorative practice typically has been concerned with encouraging the offender to make amends for the harm caused by his/her actions, and seeking to rebuild damaged relationships between offender, victim, and communities (Bazemore and Schiff, 2004). We focus on the dimension of amends in this section and consider relationship building in the discussion of informal social control and social support at the mid-range level of analysis.

Theoretical Assumptions

Crime creates an imbalance and an inequity in relationships. Reciprocity therefore requires an effort on the part of the offender to make up for what he/she has done. Theories of social exchange (Gouldner, 1960; Molm and Cook, 1995) assume that the failure to make amends results in a sense of imbalance and a lack of reciprocity on the part of the offender. The repairing-harm dimension implies a primary goal of community service as providing for offender accountability and reparation to those impacted by the crime. Repairing the harm done by making things right is therefore a necessary first step in meeting the material and emotional needs of victims and communities.

Community service also may be of great importance in changing the image of the offender in the eyes of both. That is, civic service may be a primary vehicle for replenishing the offender's negative "trust account" balance (Maloney, 2006) if it allows for a change in his/her *public* image while restoring the sense of reciprocity and balance, and hopefully also vindicating individual and community victims effected by the harmful behavior.

Service Practice and Intervention Integrity

The service practice associated with repairing harm or making amends is focused primarily on fixing what has been broken or damaged by the offense. In addition to offenders directly addressing the needs of their victim, service oriented repair could also be indirect, for example, crime-repair crews who repair damage inflicted on other victims of crime. The integrity of reparative service can be ensured by linking it directly or symbolically to the individuals or communities most affected by the offender's action, and giving these individuals and communities direct input into determination of the service. We assume, consistent with the emphasis on participation of stakeholders discussed in the previous section, that a restorative-group conference or similar inclusive decision-making process would be used, and use of such a process, therefore, is assumed in the discussion of outcomes which follow below and in each subsequent component of this section of the manuscript.

Research Questions and Indicators

The relative intensity of focus on the amends dimension and restorative outcomes in civic service can be gauged by the extent to which the service accomplished the intervening *intermediate* outcome of accountability and reparation to the communities most impacted by the offender's action.

Specifically, one may ask if (1) the offender gained an understanding of responsibility for the harm caused; (2) the offender completed the service project; and (3) the other effected parties (for example, the victim and the community) recognized that the offender completed the service project and value the service as a way of making things right.

To document the strength and integrity of intervention, researchers will need to measure the extent to which the decision-making process used to determine the service obligation (1) clearly presented the purpose of the offender's obligation as repairing the harm caused by the offender's action; (2) gave conference participants the opportunity to hear about the harm from the victim, the offender, and other effected parties (for example, neighbors); and (3) allowed the offender to accept responsibility for the crime in the conference.

Finally, to gauge the extent to which participants in a civic service decision-making process (for example, a restorative-group conference) are likely to achieve the intermediate goals of making amends to the community (and/or the direct victims) in the form of reparation as service, researchers would need to address the extent to which this process led to the following immediate outcomes: meaningful and direct input into the service choice and reparative agreement by victims, offenders, and other community stakeholders; ensured that the service obligation, either directly or symbolically, was matched to the harm done by the offender(s); allowed or encouraged participants to play a specific role in working with and supporting the offender in carrying out and monitoring the reparative agreement (for example, participate with the offender in service projects).

Changing Self-Image

Whereas restorative community service focused on repairing harm has been typically concerned with a change in the offender's *public* image, another focus of service is more about changing the offender's view of *self*. Not all formerly incarcerated persons respond positively to the idea of "earning their redemption" through making amends. Yet, they may nonetheless see service as important in its own right, and may even make service a personal mission. In one type of service, the offender makes a cognitive choice to redefine his/her personal identity around the role of helping others, particularly younger generations (Maruna, 2001). In a slightly different situation, the offender directly experiences the feeling of helping others in a new role as service provider, mentor, parent, or teacher—and thereby changes both his public and private image.

Theoretical Assumptions

According to Erickson's theory of "generativity," changing one's self-image is a process through which offenders make a personal commitment to help others (Erickson, 1967). This transformation may occur through a cognitive "restorying" process (Maruna, 2001; Zehr, 2001) in which an offender emotionally creates a new definition of self or "life script" (Matseuda and Heimer, 1997). However, as illustrated by the following quote from an incarcerated person in Maruna's study (which found strong, positive correlations between post-prison re-offending and participation in community service in a sample of long-term inmates), community service appears to go hand-in-hand with this process. Although such service may not involve direct interaction with the recipients of the service, the offenders are given knowledge of the general group being helped. As one inmate described his experience:

"Since I've been here, I've made three big playhouses, like eight-foot wide . . . the first one we made, we donated it to the children's home. We took so much out of the community . . . now we're putting it back."

As suggested by this statement from an inmate making blankets for a shelter for abused children: "I'm doing it for kids I'll never see and they'll never see me. But that makes me feel so good that I'm doing something here that's not about me. You know that's not selfish" (quoted in Uggen and Manza, 2003).

We suspect that the transformation in self-image is most likely to occur in an experiential, rather than purely cognitive context, in which the change in self-image becomes concretely anchored in the process of "practicing" new prosocial behavior. Our theoretical assumption is that the *activity* of service for the less fortunate or young people is what accounts for the change in self-image.

As Cleveland reentry practitioner Reverend Charles See puts it, "It is easier to act one's way into better thinking than to think one's way into better acting" (quoted in Bazemore and Schiff, 2004). This belief is consistent with the "helper principle" in psychology and social work (Kolb, 1984; Reissman, 1965; Toch, 2002), as well as with "strengths-based" and youth development models (Saleebey, 2002; Bazemore and Terry, 1997), which tend to support this experiential view of identity change. The transformation brought about by the change in role—from someone who *harms* others, to someone who *helps* others—also may be enhanced by the opportunity for face-to-face assistance to the disadvantaged. It also may occur when community and victims have input into the nature of service and, ideally, given opportunities to participate in the project alongside offenders.

Moreover, by working with others to help those in need, offenders may make improvements in their own interpersonal skills, make new connections, and gain empathy. In other words, helping others may become a way of ensuring one's own transformation and identity as a person who "makes good" by *doing good* (Maruna, 2001).

Service Practice and Intervention Integrity

Service aimed at addressing self-image change should help offenders begin to think of themselves as persons with a new life goal and a new identity. According to this model, such service often would directly address the individual needs of disadvantaged groups or those less able (for example, young people, the elderly). The more experiential perspective would emphasize a change in the offender's *role* from client of service to provider, and the service itself would build a sense of accomplishment and self-worth. Whether or not a direct contact is made with those being helped, working together with other helpers also may help to reinforce the connection and the new role. For some, service may create opportunities for sustained direct contact with pro-social community members.

The general premise that it is better to give help than receive it (Pearl and Riessman, 1965; see Maruna et al., 2003) is strategically applied to reentry practice by ensuring that service is aimed at changing the community perception of the offender from liability to asset and at responding to the needs of the less fortunate, as well as to crime victims and victimized communities. Examples of such service activities include collective activities such as: firewood delivery and assistance to the elderly; mentoring and tutoring youth and disabled populations; food bank assistance; transportation assistance for youth or the elderly; and service to individual victims (for example, offender crime repair crews) or groups of victims (for example, service provided to domestic abuse shelters).

Research Questions and Sample Indicators

To gauge the extent to which community service participants view themselves as persons who are needed by others, especially future generations, researchers would need to measure whether participants develop "a [broader] concern for and commitment to promoting the next generation, manifested through parenting, teaching, mentoring, and generating benefits for others" (McAdams and de St. Aubin, 1998, cited in Maruna, 2001, 99). More specifically, they would need to gauge the extent to which participants are likely to achieve the intermediate objective of changing their self-image to one of a helper who is needed by others.

To determine whether participants achieve the goals of providing effective service that changes the offender's self-image, researchers would need to address the extent to which the service experience did the following things:

- Placed participants in situations where their impact on disadvantaged groups was direct and visible
- Made the connection between the service and the participant's cognitive and emotional experiences through time devoted to reflection, processing, and discussion of the service experience
- Was viewed by participants as rewarding
- Provided for modeling of helping behavior by including community members in the *process* of carrying out and monitoring the service work

To document the strength and integrity of intervention to achieve these objectives, researchers would need to measure the extent to which the decision-making process did the following things:

- Offered victims, offenders, and other community stakeholders meaningful and direct input and an opportunity to take ownership of and play roles in developing the service agreement
- Allowed participants to identify and empathize with disadvantaged populations, especially in the offender's community
- Included representatives of such groups in the decision-making process

Middle Range Impact: Informal Social Control, Social Support, and Reintegration through the Life Course

At the mid-range level of analysis, *life course criminology* is concerned with how offenders develop pro-social ties to family, work, other formal and informal groups, and individuals. Grounded in research that suggests that patterns of offending are not—as some criminologists (Gottfredson and Hirschi, 1990) suggest—fixed at an early age, life course researchers argue that informal social controls and support provided by pro-social groups keep most offenders connected in some way to conventional society. In doing so, they allow for movement from attachment to criminal peers and participation in illegal activity to a commitment to conventional activities at different points of the life-course (for example, Piquero, Brame, Mazerolle, and Haapanen, 2002). Resistance to crime, and successful reentry is, therefore, largely a function of the relative strengths of these connections to informal social controls that create a "bond" to pro-social groups and institutions.[12]

There are two primary dimensions of potential service impact at this mid-range level of analysis. First, service may initiate and/or enhance informal connections that provide social *support* and guardianship. Second, service may enhance the *human capital* (Becker, 1964) of formerly incarcerated persons. While human capital theorists promote a kind of *instrumental* attachment based on the value to employers and communities of members with skills that contribute to the workforce, social support theorists (Cullen, 1994) would emphasize the less formal, *affective* components of these relationships. For example, familial, extended family, and mentorship connections are based less on skills and assets and the need for reliable labor than on emotional connections.

Linking these concepts to the neighborhood level, Hunter (1985) distinguishes two types of informal social control. Families and friends exercise "private controls" that tend to be more affective in nature and are based on emotional ties. Parochial controls, on the other hand, are those that emanate from neighbors, peers, community organizations, and faith-community groups, and are generally more instrumental in nature. It is also possible for private controls to function partly through instrumental means (for example, where ties to parents and relatives are based on involvement in a family business), and parochial controls may take on an affective quality (for example, when neighbors or employers develop personal friendships with employees). Research that addresses the "resiliency" of young people growing up in the most high-risk neighborhoods who manage to avoid or transition out of high-risk behavior (for example, crime, drug abuse) generally finds that they do so through positive informal affective relationships with prosocial adults (Rutter, 1996; Werner and Smith, 1992).[13]

Restorative justice practice and the experience with community service suggest that both private and parochial controls can exert influence through a relationship-building process that may emerge through working together with pro-social community members, and through mentoring activities—as well as more intimate connections to family and intimate friendships (Bazemore and Schiff, 2004; Uggen and Manzaet et al., 2002). Indeed, it has been argued that positive relationships associated with social support are a prerequisite for informal social control (Cullen, 1994).

Theoretical Assumptions

The goal of service focused on relationship building is based first on the restorative justice assumption that crime causes harm not only to individuals and communities but also to relationships (Van Ness and Strong, 1997; Zehr, 1990). Moreover, a fundamental premise in social support theory (Cullen, 1994) is that offenders in ongoing relationships of informal support, who have access to roles that create a legitimate identity and build new connections that commit them to conforming behavior, will be less likely to re-offend (Bazemore, 2001; Maruna, 2001). An underlying concern of social support theory—to revitalize informal family and community support—is, in fact, in part a response to the conceptual limits of both treatment and punishment responses. Indeed, neither response seems capable of moving beyond the focus on professionals as the sole providers of offender-focused intervention. As Maruna (2001, 28) observes, "even the most extreme partisans" of either the 'medical model story' or the 'deterrence story' "do not suggest that either state rehabilitation or punishment can account for most ex-offenders desisting in any consistent way."

Service to address relationship building is aimed in part at building prosocial, affective connections that resemble social support relationships in the resiliency literature (Rutter, 1985; Werner, 1986; Werner and Smith, 1992). Such relationships would focus on what has been referred to as the "individual social capital" that develops from both prosocial adult friendships and youth-peer relationships formed in a common situation of adversity (McCarthy, Hagan, and Martin, 2002). Civic service may then provide for bonding to others for companionship, mutual assistance, and even protection against harm. Relationships with older prosocial adults in the service experience may in addition also provide the opportunity for advocacy and guardianship in support of efforts to avoid criminogenic influences.

Service may be structured specifically to connect the offender to prosocial groups and individuals. Work on community projects that involve a wide range of persons under correctional supervision and community volunteers in meaningful service may be a means of strengthening existing positive relationships or creating new connections.

Community-service intervention should be strengths-based (Saleebey, 2002) and relationship-focused, rather than risk-based and control focused or need-based and treatment-focused. To assess the extent to which participants in a civic engagement community service effort achieve the *intermediate* goals of building relationships of support, assistance, and guardianship, researchers would need to address the extent to which the service experience has achieved the following social support theory-based outcomes: bringing together formerly incarcerated persons with one or more prosocial adults in planning, implementing, and following up for the service experience; and established sustainable, supportive, ongoing relationships with organizations regularly involved in civic community building and development.

To gauge the extent to which participants are likely to achieve these *immediate* goals of relationship building, researchers would need to address whether the conference/decision-making process included participants who may be willing to suggest specific service projects and/or work with offenders on these projects, and whether the service experience includes offenders from different backgrounds and prosocial community mentors working together.

To achieve this immediate objective, researchers will need to measure the extent to which the restorative decision-making *process* (1) included participants who are, or may become, emotionally important in the lives of the offender and are willing and able to provide affective social support; (2) encouraged and built upon supportive comments about the offender; and (3) assigned participants a specific role to work with and support the offender and others in carrying out and monitoring the community service agreement.

From a human capital perspective, *demonstrating* competency, reliability, and trustworthiness are critical to community willingness to accept and help to reintegrate returning offenders. As Maloney (2006) expresses it—the offender's "reputation deficit"—might also be characterized as the equivalent of low human capital as indicated by: limited or non-existent references, a restricted range of job skills, child support and family obligations, or restitution and court-ordered community service requirements. Meaningful civic service may offer an opportunity to build a portfolio rich in volunteerism and meaningful service, a new reputation for the offender as a contributor, new personal references, demonstrable work skills, a means to complete restitution/community service obligations, and/or a reliable support network.

Theoretical Assumptions

Such rebuilding of the "trust account" based on skill development does not diminish the importance of making amends through service and other efforts toward personal and public identity transformation. A human capital model, however, would go beyond such reparative and individual change efforts to demonstrate reciprocity and rebuild community trust by viewing the service experience primarily as an opportunity for the offender to practice and demonstrate marketable competencies.[14]

The strengths-based aspects of service mentioned above are most associated with the human capital dimension of service, and thus have implications for ensuring that the service experience allows formerly incarcerated persons the opportunity to demonstrate skills and reliability. Strategically, envisioning even minor service roles as stepping stones to more responsible roles would be vital considerations for those who wish to use service as a means of increasing the human capital of formerly incarcerated persons.

Human Capital

Examples of service to meet these human-capital objectives would include: conservation, beautification, and public works projects; planting and maintaining community gardens; building homes or shelters, or other activities that connect offenders to potential employers and civic and service groups. Ideally, the offender would have an opportunity for a public demonstration of skills and competencies that present an image of a community asset. In summary, we reinforce the need for prosocial, affective support relationships, as well as more instrumental and experiential opportunities for a formerly incarcerated parent to demonstrate skills in a visible way in responsible roles in work, family, and community that may then lead to other connections, new roles, and ultimately stable and coherent identities (Schwartz and Stryker, 1970, 15).

Research Questions and Sample Indicators

Regarding human capital, to assess the extent to which service projects provide opportunities for establishing a track record of employment readiness, researchers must determine whether the experience increased skills and job opportunities. One also may ask whether the experience provided visible opportunities to:

- Practice and demonstrate competencies to multiple audiences
- Establish a "track record" as a reliable employee
- Increase marketable skills

The *intermediate* objective would be to ensure that such service is completed in a context that is visible rather than isolated in "offender-only" work crews, and is viewed as valuable to individuals and communities. It should allow the participant to also demonstrate reliability and ultimately help to change the image of the person under correctional supervision from being a liability to becoming an asset.

To achieve these goals, the *intermediate* objective of the service experience should be to: involve participants and community members (especially business persons and other potential employers) in planning and executing projects; celebrate and reward accomplishments and provide, whenever possible, for community recognition; involve multiple tasks and maximize opportunities to demonstrate a variety of skills. Service practitioners should reinforce the experience with classroom learning—also building in time for reflection about the value of the work, skills, and competencies participants are developing in the service activity. To achieve this immediate objective, researchers will need to measure the extent to which the restorative decision-making process:

- Has included participants who bring special resources to the agenda or are willing and able to provide instrumental social support
- Are encouraged to make and build upon supportive comments about the offender
- Are assigned a specific role to work with and support the offender and others in carrying out and monitoring the community service agreement

Macro-Level Impact: Service to Build Community and a Theory of Social Capital and Collective Efficacy

Community building ... is more an orientation than a technique, more a mission than a program, more an outlook than an activity. It catalyzes a process of change grounded in local life and priorities and addresses the developmental needs of individuals, families and organizations within the neighborhood. A community's own strengths are seen as central. (Lisbeth Schorr, 1997, 361-362)

In Hollow Water, ex-offenders are not shunned forever, but seen as important resources for getting under the skin of other of- fenders and disturbing the webs of lies that have sustained them. Better than anyone, they understand the patterns, the pressures and the ways to hide. As they tell their personal stories in the circle, they talk about the lies that once protected them and how it felt to face the truth about the pain they caused. (Rupert Ross, 1996)

It is a rare occurrence in modern life when someone seems to be treating formerly incarcerated persons as if they were resources to their communi- ties. Even assuming that such treatment could be common in the relatively limited sense of Ross' important insight that such persons might at least be helpful to *other offenders*, expecting them to participate in and enrich com- munity life seems almost outrageous on its face.

Thus, when Shrifa Wilson, former Mayor of East Palo Alto, California—a densely populated urban community which in the late 1990s and early years of this century claimed the highest number of felons returning from prison to reside there than any other California city—came to the conclusion that the population of formerly incarcerated persons in her city were a key compo- nent (possibly half) of her constituency, she was most likely out of step with other California mayors. When she began to think and talk about these persons as "resources" and to recruit several of them to advise her on issues of community and workforce development, many of her colleagues must have expressed concerns about her mental health, as well as her future as a politician.

In viewing all citizens of East Palo Alto as part of the stock of human and *social capital* (Putnam, 2000), however, Wilson exemplified an understand- ing that formerly incarcerated persons are certain to impact their commu- nities and be impacted by them. In viewing them as resources—expecting them to contribute to the community, and providing opportunities for them to "do good"—Mayor Wilson built on a fundamental insight that communities are often built by what may appear to be unhealthy, less than stable, and cer- tainly imperfect people (McKnight, 1995). Her insight was that these new individuals were assets essential to developing a sense of community strength, efficacy, and ownership of problems such as crime, high unem- ployment, drug abuse, and illiteracy. They were also part of the social capi- tal necessary to provide for collective efficacy (Sampson et al., 1997) in the provision of informal social control and social support at the macro level.

Service and Community Building

The primary findings in the growing body of research on community "collective efficacy" indicate that crime is lower to the extent that neighborhood adults and community groups feel empowered to intervene in response to troublesome behavior by neighborhood members, particularly youth (Braithwaite, 1989; Sampson, Raudenbush, and Earls, 1997). Informal social control is strengthened when community members intervene in each other's lives. Beyond informal social control and guardianship, it is important to take account of the role community plays in providing "social support" (Cullen, 1994) as well as the assistance provided for youth and families who are impacted by crime. The collective provision of informal social support is particularly powerful, especially when this is exercised through "natural helpers"—that is, community members known to provide direct support for those in need or to help connect these individuals with services and support (Annie E. Casey Foundation, 2001).

At this macro level, a civic-engagement model is concerned with neighborhood and related community level (for example, schools, housing projects) service and outcomes. While service projects are expected to physically and socially rebuild community infrastructure, such projects may also be viewed as having the potential to mobilize and build the social capital needed for supportive relationships and networks of relationships to ensure trust, collaboration, and more effective reintegration of offenders into neighborhoods.

Such social capital is viewed by many as a prerequisite for the collective efficacy needed to encourage community members to take action in exercising informal social control and social support (Cullen, 1994; Sampson et al., 1997). Civic community service implemented to build community would be grounded in the capacity of citizens to mobilize to improve community life, and in doing so increase their own level of competency as citizens. The theoretical propositions and principles for practice below summarize the assumptions behind, and guidelines for, such service.

Theoretical Assumptions

What is different about this macro, social-ecological level of analysis is a vision of improving local capacity to take care of community members and community problems as well as for developing a better quality of life. What also may be new is service that may invite or spark *community dialog* about shared norms and values, about mutual responsibility for socialization of young people and social control, and about the value of persons—who have the experience of both harming the community through participation in crime and *being harmed* by the criminal justice system—in helping others to avoid this pattern of becoming victimizer and victim.

In addition, the goal of building new relationships and networks of trust and support may often be led (as in the East Palo Alto example) by community coalitions. These coalitions include persons once viewed as part of the problem (and by many as without hope), but now seen as a necessary part of a solution to promote peacemaking and a better quality of justice and community life.

Some communities, particularly those in urban ghettos, have been severely effected by crime. They also have been negatively impacted by the disproportionate incarceration of their residents. Ironically, although incarceration policies of the past two decades have been based on the commonsense notion that increased incarceration results in decreases in a community's crime rates, Rose and Clear (1998) argue, and a growing body of research (for example, Fagan et al., 2004) now suggests, that increases in incarceration actually undermine the stability of families and community institutions and ultimately *increase crime rates*. Alternatively, if released offenders are consistently involved in community building, community organization and social control may be enhanced.

To the extent that volunteer work produces a public good, it benefits participants and nonparticipants alike (Coleman, 1990). The crime-reductive potential of volunteer work is therefore even greater in the *aggregate* than in the sum of the individual effects [on participants] (Uggen and Janikula, 1999, 356; emphasis ours).

As suggested above, the theoretical basis for these assumptions about the community-level impact of strategically designed community service is grounded in the emerging literature on social capital (Putnam, 2000), collective efficacy (Sampson et al., 1997), and the theory of civic engagement itself (Bazemore and Schiff, 2004). Theoretical propositions relative to civic service—and the community mobilization processes that lead up to it—are concerned with a broad collective impact that creates "added value" beyond the obvious direct, practical benefits of the service itself. First, this *added value* is represented in the new relationships, and *networks* of relationships created by the civic service effort—essentially social capital (Putnam, 2000). Second, the new skills developed at the community level for mobilizing to rebuild neighborhoods and meet human needs—and to reintegrate offenders—essentially provide the basis for collective efficacy as seen in networks that provide for informal social control and social support. Third, the service projects themselves should create a sense of ownership forged in the decision-making process that allows for input and participation in the service itself.

Service Practice and Intervention Integrity

Service initiatives seem most likely to enhance collective efficacy when they encourage community members and groups to participate along with ex-offenders (Bazemore and Maloney, 1994; Bazemore and Stinchcomb, 2004a). In doing so, these communities may increase their own skills in promoting prosocial behavior and reinforcing behavioral norms while also lending support to returning formerly incarcerated persons. While ex-offenders no doubt will need assistance from the communities they return to, through the experience of providing service *to* their communities, they, in turn, may demonstrate their leadership skills and serve as positive examples to young people.

Community service to *build community* would be grounded then in a clear vision about the capacity of all citizens to mobilize to improve community life, and in doing so subsequently increase their own level of competency as citizens. Service projects most likely to build and enhance new networks of relationships as social capital, improve collective efficacy, and promote the sense of ownership that is the essence of civic engagement might include: Habitat for Humanity; school improvement projects; park construction and repair; and elderly assistance and engagement programs. Other services might include assisting with public fundraisers and voter registration drives and peacemaking and racial tolerance initiatives.

As the East Palo Alto experience suggests, the more returning offenders—as well as crime victims and neighborhood volunteers—are involved as *leaders* in these initiatives, the wider and deeper the expected impact according to the theories of social capital, collective efficacy, and civic engagement.

Research Questions and Sample Indicators

Community service activity that seeks to build community will be based on a vision of collective learning and skill building for the future that promotes community ownership and leadership in resolving problems and developing solutions. To gauge the extent to which participants are likely to achieve these *intermediate* goals, researchers would need to examine whether the service experience includes: a variety of community members who may work well as co-participants with offenders in a service project for which these community members share a common enthusiasm; and whether the service is strategically designed to impact social capital, collective efficacy, and a sense of community ownership over problems and their solutions.

338

The decision-making process to design such community-building service would need to achieve the following *immediate* objectives: identify collective benefits for the community; discuss collective skills to be developed from such service; engage community civic and business leadership and maximize participation of "out" groups as well as "in" groups; focus on social justice while not neglecting the needs of individuals and families harmed by crime and the need for collaboration and partnerships; clearly articulate goals, including strengthening or building new relationships or networks (as social capital), and collective capacity for informal social control, social support, conflict resolution, and socialization of community members; and build in time for reflection about accomplishments that reinforce collective resolve, discussion of civic and social justice implications of the service work, and development of more effective advocacy strategies.

Summary and Conclusion

In summary, we have argued for a new civic-engagement model of prisoner reentry that seeks to engage both the community and the offender side of the reintegration equation. Centered on the idea of changing the image of the formerly incarcerated person in the eyes of the community, enhancing the self-image and skill sets of these persons, and building community capacity for support and guardianship, this model moves beyond individually focused surveillance and services. Accompanied by a theory and principle-based evaluation protocol grounded in restorative justice and criminological theory at individual, mid-range, and community levels, the model is aimed at maximizing the integrity of implementation in a variety of contexts.

Discussion: Obstacles and Opportunities

No one should be deluded regarding the level of difficulty in reintegrating formerly incarcerated persons. Thus, despite its appeal, the civic-engagement model must overcome several barriers. As discussed in the introduction, formal and informal obstacles imposed by restrictions on family, employment, voting, and other rights and benefits of citizenship limit the possibilities for smooth reintegration. Similarly, rules of post-prison supervision (for example, parole) whose violation has now become the leading cause of return to prison in many states present a significant challenge (Travis, 2006). Such restrictions and rules are but one example of an extended regime of punishment that appears to know no limits.

Unfortunately, the current, nearly complete legitimization of punishment for its own sake that became popular in the 1980s with the "just deserts" model—ironically promoted as a means of restricting excessive punishment primarily through use of sentencing guidelines (for example, von Hirsch, 1976, 2006)—now unfortunately equates uniformity with justice and replaces careful consideration of the circumstances of crimes with the application of guidelines. Indeed, the new culture of retribution appears to equate punishment with justice itself.

The popularity of retribution, without much apparent concern for strict limits on the scope of punishment, now appears to justify a wide array of open-ended, extended restrictions on the rights of citizenship. Most notably, the continuing disenfranchisement of persons charged with felonies is the most vivid illustration that such restrictions are fundamentally about continuous retribution rather than public safety, or any other utilitarian aim. In this climate, even the civic community service model, therefore, may be vulnerable to being perceived as, if not actually used as a means to require service as extended punishment rather than a voluntary means of giving back and building connections and citizenship skills of formerly incarcerated persons, as well as community capacity for reintegration. While these now systemic abuses of the "purist" retributive model nullify its claims to rational limits on punishment, a new metric is needed for gauging the quantity and quality of "justice" that takes into consideration goals other than equality of punishment.

Conclusion

What are these justice goals? Restorative justice is a model that rejects punishment for its own sake and promotes instead a focus on offender obligations to victim and community to repair the harm caused by his/her offense as a means of accountability to victims and the community. It provides a clear alternative to what has become an obsession with punishment.

While also compatible with the need to ensure public safety—and consistent even with deterrence and incapacitation goals for serious and violent offenders as well as with rehabilitation objectives (Braithwaite, 2002; Bazemore and Schiff, 2004)—restorative justice is primarily concerned with doing justice by repairing harm rather than causing additional harm (Van Ness and Strong, 1997). Given this framework, a civic-engagement model of community service provides an explicit means of engaging the community while also building and restoring capacity by allowing offenders to reestablish trust and build a new image through service while taking responsibility for their actions.

While a retributive model might assume that "doing one's time" is an indication that justice has been done and that the offender has done what is necessary to be reaccepted into the community, "doing time" in no way demonstrates the capacity for *doing good*. The civic-engagement model offers offenders, on a voluntary basis, the opportunity to change their image in the eyes of the community, to reinforce change in their own identity, and to demonstrate value and competence as productive citizens, while through the service activity, also meeting important community and individual needs and building a reputation as people who deserve trust.

An evaluation model, such as the one proposed here, is necessary to ensure first that service is not employed as a means of extended punishment, but rather is tied to outcomes that gauge connection to pro-social community groups and individuals and builds community capacity to provide informal support and assistance.

Endnotes

[1] Confronting many of these barriers requires legislative action that, at least in the current political climate, does not appear to be forthcoming. However, several advocates are beginning to make in-roads at least at the level of raising public awareness of issues such as felon disenfranchisement (Allen, 2004; Uggen and Manza, 2002), and as a result, there is greater awareness that no crime control or other public benefits accrue from what must be viewed as a purely retributive strategy of banishment from voting booths for those who have already been punished (Bazemore and Stinchcomb, 2004a). For a discussion of additional barriers imposed by technical violation of parole supervision rules—now the leading cause of return to prison—see Travis' (2006) examination of what he refers to as "back-end sentencing."

[2] This paper focuses primarily on the first dimension, civic-community service, with some attention given to restorative-justice decision making. For discussions of how voting and democratic participation might increase the likelihood of offender desistance and reintegration, *see* Bazemore and Stinchcomb, 2004a; Flanagan and Faison, 2001; and Uggen and Manza, 2002.

[3] Restorative justice provides the *justice* component of what has also been referred to as a "civic-justice" model. Victim involvement also is viewed as an essential aspect of the program by a number of practitioners. For a discussion of this component, *see* Bazemore and Stinchcomb (2003b) and Community Justice Institute Partnership (2003). While some view restorative-justice conferencing models as the *only* restorative practice, other restorative-justice writers conceptualize a broad range of potentially restorative practices—including community service itself and victim service—when these are grounded in restorative-justice principles and seek to achieve outcomes that repair the harm of crime (Bazemore and Walgrave, 1999).

[4] The civic-engagement model is broadly informed by recent research that suggests that the expansion of incarceration policies in recent decades actually may have *increased* crime in those neighborhoods that experienced the highest rates of incarceration (Fagan, West, and Holland, 2004; Rose and Clear, 1998), and is also consistent with recent policy reforms aimed at reinvestment of correctional system funds in local community initiatives.

[5] The civic-engagement model was developed with initial funding from a planning grant awarded to the Community Justice Institute at Florida Atlantic University. The planning period among other things provided for input from three stakeholder groups with interest in the model: formerly incarcerated persons currently working in reentry and/or parole reform; community-based reentry practitioners and volunteers, including faith-based community groups; and corrections administrators and other system professionals. Although civic engagement as a reentry model is in its infancy, several pilot initiatives are underway in various communities around the country to develop *civic justice corps* as a holistic reentry strategy. Three demonstration sites were funded in 2004-2005, and up to six additional sites will be supported through the Department of Labor working in conjunction with the National Association of Service and Conservation Corps. Demonstration programs are currently underway in North Charleston, South Carolina; Portland and Central Oregon; and Washington D.C. (the latter program is focused on juvenile offenders currently housed in secure facilities in the District of Columbia). The complete program model includes a range of educational, vocational, substance abuse resistance, and other interventions.

[6] The tradition of community service also has experienced a more formal and ongoing revitalization in the decade of the 1990s. The great rise in popularity of a range of organized service efforts including AmeriCorps, Habitat for Humanity, Youth as Resources, City Year, and a range of local and more short-term initiatives such as conservation corps, service learning programs, and similar programs appear to have tapped into a reservoir of desire among U.S. citizens to assist those in need and to strengthen their communities (Barber, 1992; Bellah et al., 1991). The call to service seems to be supported by groups and individuals representing a variety of political persuasions, perhaps most clearly united in this support under a resurgence of communitarianism (Etzioni, 1996). Ultimately, such modern service programs also build strongly on the philosophical positions of William James, John Dewey, and others who also have popularized a commitment to experiential learning as a primary theory of education (Freire, 1973; 1996; Kolb, 1984), which suggests that it is through involvement in serving others, and in the struggle for social justice, that human beings maximize their learning about themselves, democracy, and the world.

[7] Although the decline in social capital noted by Putnam (2000) and others has no doubt limited its naturalistic occurrences, willingness of Americans to reach out to others in need still can be witnessed clearly in times of natural disaster—most recently in the local and national outpouring of support for the victims of 9/11. It also is apparent that some communities never completely lost their sense of connectedness and mutual responsibility for others that is also associated with safe, low-crime communities (Sampson et al., 1997).

[8] Such efforts illustrate a common desire to help others within a population whose own personal and family needs would overwhelm most average Americans.

[9] Most disturbing in recent years have been examples of punitive community service whose proponents argue that service should be a retributive tool focused on degradation and humiliation (Kahan, 1999) and resemble chain gangs of another era (Amnesty International, 1996). Speaking more positively of the *potential* power of community service

with a different intent, Tonry (1996) notes that even the most well-intended community service is "the most underused and misused intermediate sanction" (p. 121), and that it is likely that its growth and application has been both unsystematic and incoherent.

[10] Indeed, community service may have incapacitation value (for example, offenders who work hard during the day will not be involved in day-time burglary, for example, and may be too tired for nighttime criminal activity), and has indeed been used in this way, often in the context of providing an alternative punishment that could substitute for jail time (see McDonald, 1986). This is however a very limited application—and except for the rather mindless completion of service "hours" and explicitly humiliating service—is the least compelling reason for investing in service work.

[11] Similar graphs also can be developed that depict an expanded role for the community and crime victim in project selection, participation, and design for theorized maximum impact on these stakeholders.

[12] Some have also argued that the negative impact of formal, criminal justice controls also weaken informal social controls (Di Li, 1999; Paternoster, 1989; Rose and Clear, 1998).

[13] Regarding service on an ongoing basis as a predictor of pro-social behavior as adults, Bernard (2002) summarizes several studies that demonstrate that opportunities for high-risk youth to contribute in the home and community (including even caring for younger children or assisting with care of the elderly) have positive impacts on pro-social behavior in later life. Research and theory on adult felons who transition in and out of pro-social roles and criminal involvement suggest the importance of both formal institutional controls of work and education, as well as the affective controls of families (Piquero et al., 2002).

[14] Indeed, the U.S. Department of Labor co-sponsorship of several of the previously mentioned Civic Justice Corps projects has been a result of staff beliefs that the civic-justice-service experience is part of a job training and re-socialization experience for returning formerly incarcerated persons that builds or rebuilds job skills.

References and Suggested Readings

Allen, J. 2004. Introduction to the Symposium on Race, Crime, and Voting: Social, Political, and Philosophical Perspectives on Felony Disenfranchisement in America. *Columbia Human Rights Law Review*, 36: 1-15.

Amnesty International. 1996. Florida Reintroduces Chain Gangs. Amnesty International. www.amnesty.org.ru/library/index/ENGAMR510021996?open&of=ENG360

Annie E. Casey Foundation. 2001. *Walking our Talk in the Neighborhood: Partnerships Between Professionals and Natural Helpers*. Baltimore, Maryland: Author.

Barber, B. 1992. *An Aristocracy of Everyone: The Politics of Education and the Future of America*. Oxford, United Kingdom: Oxford University Press.

Bazemore, G. 2001. Young People, Trouble, and Crime: Restorative Justice as a Normative Theory of Informal Social Control and Social Support. *Youth and Society*, 33 (2):199-226.

Bazemore, G and D. Karp. 2004. A Civic Justice Corps: Community Service as a Means of Reintegration. *Justice Policy Journal*, 1(3): 1-35.
Bazemore, G., D. Karp, and M. Schiff. 2003. Social Capital and Restorative Justice: Theory Building for Community Building in the Informal Response to Youth Crime. Draft Monograph, Community Justice Institute, Florida Atlantic University, Fort Lauderdale, Florida.

Bazemore, G. and D. Maloney. 1994. Rehabilitating Community Service: Toward Restorative Service in a Balanced Justice System. *Federal Probation*, 58:24-35.

Bazemore, G. and M. Schiff. 2004. *Juvenile Justice Reform and Restorative Justice: Building Theory and Policy from Practice*. Cullompton, Devon, United Kingdom: Willan Publishing.

Bazemore, G., and J. Stinchcomb. 2004a. Civic Engagement and Reintegration: Toward a Community-Focused Theory and Practice. *Columbia Human Rights Law Review*, 36: 241-286.

___. 2004b. Involving Community through Service and Restorative Justice: Theory and Practice for a Civic-Engagement model of Reentry. *Federal Probation*, 68 (2): 14-24.

Bazemore, G. and C. Terry. 1997. Developing Delinquent Youth: A Reintegrative Model for Rehabilitation and a New Role for the Juvenile Justice System. *Child Welfare*, 74(5): 665-716.

Bazemore, G. and M. Umbreit. 2001. A Comparison of Four Restorative Conferencing Models. *Juvenile Justice Bulletin*. Washington DC: Office of Juvenile Justice and Delinquency Prevention, Office of Justice Programs, U.S. Department of Justice.

Bazemore, G. and L. Walgrave. 1999. "Restorative Juvenile Justice: In Search of Fundamentals and an Outline for Systemic Reform," In G. Bazemore and L. Walgrave, eds., *Restorative Juvenile Justice: Repairing the Harm of Youth Crime*. Monsey, New York: Criminal Justice Press.

Becker, G. 1964. *Human Capital.* New York: National Bureau of Economic Research Press.

Bellah, R. N., R. Madsen, W. Sullivan, A. Swidler, and M. Tipton. 1985. *Habits of the Heart: Individualism and Commitment in American Life.* Berkeley, California: University of California Press.

___. 1991. *The Good Society*. Berkeley, California: University of California Press.

Bernard, B. 2002. "Turnaround People and Places: Moving from Risk to Reliance," in D. Saleebey, ed. *The Strengths-Based Perspective in Social Work Practice,* 3rd ed. London: Allyn and Bacon.

Braithwaite, J. 1989. *Crime, Shame, and Reintegration*. Cambridge, England: Cambridge University Press.

___. 2002. *Restorative Justice and Responsive Regulation*. New York: Oxford University Press.

Butts, J. and H. Snyder. 1991. *Restitution and Juvenile Recidivism*. Monograph. Pittsburgh, Pennsylvania: National Center for Juvenile Justice.

Caputo, G. A. 1999. Why Not Community Service? *Criminal Justice Policy Review*, 10(4):503-519.

Chen, H. 1990. *Theory Driven Evaluation*. Thousand Oaks, California: Sage.

Clear, T., D. Rose, and J. Ryder. 2001. Incarceration and the Community: The Problem of Removing and Returning Offenders. *Crime and Delinquency*, 47 (3):335-351.

Coleman, J. 1990. *Foundations of Social Theory*. Cambridge, Massachusetts: Harvard University Press.

___. 1988. Social Capital in the Creation of Human Capital. *American Journal of Sociology*, 94 (Supplement):S95-S120.

Coles, R. 1993. *The Call of Service*. New York: Houghton-Mifflin.

Community Justice Institute Partnership. 2003. *The Civic Justice Corps: Service in the Interest of Others*. Planning Monograph, Florida Atlantic University.

Cullen, F. T. 1994. Social Support as an Organizing Concept for Criminology: Presidential Address to the Academy of Criminal Justice Sciences. *Justice Quarterly*, 11:527-559.

De Li, S. 1999. Legal Sanctions and Youths' Status Achievement: A Longitudinal Study. *Justice Quarterly*, 16 (2):377-401.

Dewey, J. 1957. *Reconstruction in Philosophy*. New York: Beacon Press.

Erikson, K. 1964. Notes on the Sociology of Deviance. In H. S. Becker, ed., *The Other Side*. New York: The Free Press. pp. 9-22.

Etzioni, A. 1996. The Responsive Community: A Communitarian Perspective. *American Sociological Review*, 61(1): 1-12.

Fagan, J., V. West, and J. Holland. 2004. Neighborhood, Crime, and Incarceration in New York City. *Columbia Human Rights Law Review*, 36: 71-108.

Finkenhauer, J. and P. Gavin. 1999. *Scared Straight: The Panacea Phenomenon Revisisted*. Prospect Heights, Illinois: Waveland Press.

Flanagan, C. A. and N. Faison. 2001. Youth Civic Development: Implications of Research for Social Policy and Programs. *Social Policy Report*, XV (1). Ann Arbor, Michigan: Society for Research in Child Development.

Gottfredson, M. and T. Hirschi. 1990. *A General Theory of Crime.* Stanford, California: Stanford University Press.

Gouldner, A. 1960. The Norm of Reciprocity: A Preliminary Statement. *American Sociological Review*, 25:161-178.

Hirschi, T. 1969. *Causes of Delinquency.* Berkeley, California: University of California Press.

Hunter, A. J. 1985. Private, Parochial and Public Social Orders: The Problem of Crime and Incivility in Urban Communities. In G. D. Suttles and M. N. Zald, eds., *The Challenge of Social Control: Citizenship and Institution Building in Modern Society.* Norwood, New Jersey: Aldex Publishing.

Jastrzab, J., J. Blomquist, J. Maskder, and L. Orr. 1997. *Youth Corps: Promising Strategies for Young People and Their Communities.* Cambridge, Massachusetts: ABT Associates.

Jengeleski, J. L. and D. J. Richwine. 1987. *Community Service Centers in Pennsylvania: An Assessment of Post Release Outcomes.* Shippensburg, Pennsylvania: Shippensburg University.

Kahan, D. M. 1999. Punishment Incommensurability. *Buffalo Criminal Law Review*, 1:691-708.

Killias, M. and M. Aebi. 2000. Does Community Service Rehabilitate Better Than Short-Term Imprisonment?: Results of A Controlled Experiment. *Howard Journal of Criminal Justice*, 39(1):40-57.

Kolb, D. 1984. *Experiential Learning.* Englewood Cliffs, New Jersey: Prentice Hall.

Maloney, D. 1998. The Challenge of Restorative Community Justice. Address at the Annual Meeting of the Juvenile Justice Coalition, Washington DC.

___. 2006. Civic Service and the Challenge of Stewardship: A New Approach to Reentry. Paper presented at the First Annual Conference of the International Association for Reentry, Columbus, Ohio.

Maruna, S. 2001. *Making Good: How Ex-Convicts Reform and Rebuild Their Lives.* Washington, DC: American Psychological Association.

Maruna, S., T. P. LeBel, and C. S. Lanier. 2003. Generativity Behind Bars: Some "Redemptive Truth About Prison Society." Draft Paper.

Matsueda, R., and K. Heimer. 1997. A Symbolic Interactionist Theory of Role-Transitions, Role-Commitments, and Delinquency. In T. Thornberry, ed., *Developmental Theories of Crime and Delinquency.* New Brunswick: Transaction Publishers. pp.163-213.

McAdams, D. P. and E. de St. Aubin.1998. Introduction. In D. P. McAdams and E. de St.Aubin, eds., *Generativity and Adult Development: How and Why We Care for the Next Generation.* Washington, DC: American Psychological Association.

McCarthy, B., J. Hagan, M. J. Martin. 2002. In and Out Of Harm's Way: Violent Victimization and the Social Capital of Fictive Street Families. *Criminology,* 40 (4):831-866.

McDonald, D. C. 1986. *Punishment Without Walls: Community Service Sentences in New York City.* New Brunswick, New Jersey: Rutgers University Press.

McKnight, J. 1995. *The Careless Society: Community and its Counterfeits.* New York, NY: Basic Books.

Molm, L. and K. Cook.1995. Social Exchange and Exchange Networks. In K. Cook, G. Fine, and J. House, eds., *Sociological Perspectives on Social Psychology.* Boston: Allyn and Bacon.

Nirel, R., S. F. Landau, L. Sebba, and B. Sagiv. 1997. The Effectiveness of Service Work: An Analysis of Recidivism. *Journal of Quantitative Criminology,* 13:73 ff.

Paternoster, R. 1989. The Labeling Perspective and Delinquency: An Elaboration of the Theory and an Assessment of the Evidence. *Justice Quarterly,* 6: 359-394.

Pearl A. and F. Riessman. 1965. *New Careers for the Poor: The Professional in Human Service.* New York: The Free Press.

Piquero, A., R. Brame, P. Mazerolle, and R. Haapanen. 2002. Crime in Emerging Adulthood. *Criminology,* 40 (1):137-169.

Putnam, R. D. 2000. *Bowling Alone: The Collapse and Revival of the American Community.* New York: Simon and Schuster.

Reissman, F. 1965. The "Helper Therapy" Principle. *Social Work,* 10:27-32

Rose, D. and T. Clear. 1998. Incarceration, Social Capital and Crime: Implications for Social Disorganization Theory. *Criminology,* 36 (3):471-479.

Ross, R. 1996. *Returning to the Teachings: Exploring Aboriginal Justice.* London: Penguin Books.

Rutter, M. 1985. Resilience in the Face of Adversity: Protective Factors and Resistance to Psychiatric Disorder. *British Journal of Psychiatry,* 147:598-611.

___. 1996. Transitions and Turning Points in Developmental Psychopathology: As Applied to the Age Span Between Childhood and Mid-Adulthood. *Journal of Behavioral Development*, 19:603-636.

___. 2002. Introduction: Power in the People. In D. Saleebey, ed., *The Strengths Perspective in Social Work Practice*, 3rd ed., London: Allyn and Bacon.

Salmond, J. A. 1967. *The Civilian Conservation Corps*, 1933-1942: A New Deal Case. Durham, North Carolina: Duke University Press.

Sampson, R., S. Raudenbush, and F. Earls. 1997. Neighborhoods and Violent Crime: A Multi-Level Study of Collective Efficacy. *Science Magazine*, 277(4):918-924.

Schneider, A. and P. Schneider. 1984. *The Effectiveness of Restitution as a Sole Sanction and as a Condition of Probation: Results from an Experiment in Oklahoma County*. Eugene, Oregon: Institute for Policy Analysis.

Schorr, L. B. 1997. *Common Purpose: Strengthening Families and Neighborhoods to Rebuild America*. New York: Anchor Books.

Schwartz, M., and S. Stryker. 1970. *Deviance, Selves and Others*. Washington DC: American Sociological Association.

Sherrod, L. R., C. A. Flanagan, and R. Kassimir. 2006. *Youth Activism: An International Encyclopedia*. Westport, Connecticut: Greenwood Press.

Suchman, E. 1967. *Evaluation Research: Principles and Practice in Public Service and Social Action Programs*. New York: Russell Sage.

de Tocqueville, A. 1956. *Democracy in America*. New York: Mentor. (Original work published in 1835).

Toch, H. 2002. Altruistic Activity as Correctional Treatment. *International Journal of Offender Therapy and Comparative Criminology*, 44:270-278.

Tonry, M. 1996. *Sentencing Matters*. New York: Oxford University Press.

Travis, J. 2006. Back-End Sentencing and Parole Reform. Paper presented at the Stanford Law School Symposium on Back-End Sentencing and Parole Reform, Criminal Justice Center, Stanford Law School, Palo Alto, California.

Travis, J. and J. Petersilia. 2001. Reentry Reconsidered: A New Look at an Old Question. *Crime and Delinquency*, 47(3): 291-313.

Uggen, C. and J. Janikula. 1999. Volunteerism and Arrest in the Transition to Adulthood. *Social Forces*, 78:331-362.

Uggen, C. and J. Manza. 2002. Democratic Contraction? The Political Consequences of Felon Disenfranchisement in the United States." *American Sociological Review*, 67:777-803.

___. 2003. "Lost Voices: The Civic and Political Views of Disfranchised Felons." In Mary Pattillo, David Weiman, and Bruce Western, eds., *The Impact of Incarceration on Families and Communities*. New York: Russell Sage Foundation.

Uggen, C., J. Manza, and M. Thompson. 2006. Democracy and Criminal Justice In Cross-National Perspective From Crime Control To Due Process. *The Annals of the American Academy of Political and Social Science*.

Van Ness, D. and K. H. Strong. 1997. *Restoring Justice*. Cincinnati, Ohio: Anderson.

Von Hirsch, A. 1976. *Doing Justice*. New York: Hill and Wang.

Weiss, C. 1997. How Can Theory-Based Evaluation Make Greater Headway? *Evaluation Review*, 21(4):501-524.

Werner, E. 1986. Resilient Offspring of Alcoholics: A Longitudinal Study from Birth to 18. *Journal of Studies on Alcoholics*, 47: 34-40.

Werner, E. E., and R. S. Smith. 1992. *Overcoming the Odds*. Ithaca, New York: Cornell University Press.

Wilkinson, R. 1998. The Impact of Community Service Work on Adult State Prisoners Using a Restorative Justice Framework. Dissertation. University of Cincinnati.

Zehr, H. 1990. *Changing Lenses: A New Focus for Crime and Justice*. Scottsdale, Pennsylvania: Herald Press.

Reaction Essay— Making Restorative Justice the Norm

14

Phyllis Lawrence, J.D.

Restorative Justice Consultant

Alexandria, Virginia

"A great human revolution in just a single person will help achieve a change in the destiny of a nation and, further, will cause a change in the destiny of all humankind."

This statement by Daisaku Ikeda, a renowned Buddhist leader and philosopher, epitomizes the spirit each one of us (whether victim, offender, community member, or professional in the justice system) needs to have to fully realize the potential of our personal impact in every sphere of our lives. Implicit in this is the principle of interconnectedness. Without the reality of the dependency of one on another and of all of us on each other, the potential impact would not be nearly as tremendous. Given that underlying reality, this notion, that by taking responsibility for transforming *my* life I can help create a society based on compassion, dignity, and respect, is very empowering.

In the aftermath of crime and trauma, we *speak* about the need of those who have been harmed by crime to gain, or re-gain as the case may be, this sense of empowerment and sense of control over their lives. But do we—as a society and as professionals involved in dealing with crime and its aftermath—create the environment for victims to experience this empowerment?

Of those who create the harm, the public demands to see a positive change of attitudes and behaviors, regardless of the methodology used. Yet, it is likely that much of the general public is not thinking about the similar need of those who have committed harm to experience a sense of empowerment. Over the years, most justice system professionals were not thinking in those terms either. But, that is changing. Certainly, the work of Dr. Gordon Bazemore (and many other researchers and practitioners) reflects the understanding that without recognizing, supporting, and enhancing the positive attributes, strengths, and assets of both the individuals who have done harm and the oft-called "criminogenic" communities, we are imposing unrealistic expectations for positive change.

Thus, the essential questions are virtually the same: Do we consistently recognize the need and the value of empowerment as a key source of the changes society demands of offenders? And, are we creating the environment for those who have offended to experience this empowerment?

Dr. Bazemore's paper recognizes the principle of interconnectedness when he speaks of the importance of addressing both human and infrastructural needs to achieving successful reintegration of formerly incarcerated persons, and the value of civic service in creating bridges. For the offender, opportunities for civic engagement forge connections with positive influences in the community, whether with one person or many. Research has shown that having a connection with one positive adult role model is key to reducing a juvenile's likelihood of offending.

This particular work by Professor Bazemore looks within the broad framework of restorative justice to examine civic engagement and community service with their specific restorative outcomes. This author focuses on the importance of experiencing this connection for both victims and offenders by contrasting the likelihood of that outcome within the traditional criminal justice processes compared with the outcome when participating in restorative approaches.

This author's comments are based on her observations over the past thirty years of the experiences of both victims and offenders in the traditional adversarial system and, during the last twelve years, their experiences with restorative justice practices. Although she is familiar with only some of the many current innovations, such as problem-solving courts and community-based prosecutor's and defender's offices, the vast majority of victims and accused individuals experience the traditional system.

Her descriptions of the criminal justice process are from the point of view of offenders, and, most particularly, of victims—how they *experience* the structure, regardless of the lawyers' explanations of why it needs "to be that way." She is not necessarily describing how workers within the system have to operate within that structure. Through her work for the National Organization for Victim Assistance (NOVA) and her continued connection to the field, she personally knows many professionals "in the system" who deal very sensitively with victims. She especially wants to honor the many victim advocates who make tremendous efforts to support victims despite insufficient funding, time, and resources.

Howard Zehr, one of the foremost pioneers of the restorative justice response, very simply describes the contrast: The judicial idea of justice is encapsulated in three questions: What laws have been broken? Who did it? What do they deserve? Restorative justice starts with three different questions: Who's been hurt? What are their needs? Whose obligations are they? (Bolton, January 12, 2006)

From a restorative justice perspective, victims should have the opportunity (and some would say, even the obligation), to define the ways in which they were harmed and to identify what kinds of actions could be taken by the offender, the community, and the government to repair the harm, to "make things right" as much as possible. Experts in trauma and healing have made it clear for some years now that a major piece of the recovery process for victims of crime or other trauma is "telling the story" and receiving validation that the story is heard and accepted as their truth. The simple act of listening to victims and accepting their truth without judgment or questioning goes a long way toward supporting victims' sense of regaining control over their own bodies, environment, and life—their sense of self—that is, their feelings of empowerment.

Victims also frequently feel some sense of separateness or isolation from the "normal" world of friends, family, and community. It may come from the feelings of shame and humiliation that unfortunately accompany many types of victimization. In some cases, there is an actual physical separation, such as that forced by a hospitalization or move. In any case, the emotional isolation—the loss of connection—is another aspect of the disempowerment victims may experience from the "tear in the fabric of community," as some define crime.

Human beings in the normal course of affairs need information to be able to make sense of our experiences and to take action. That need is even stronger when "the ground has been shaken," when stability and normalcy have been snatched away. The victim rights movement has long advocated for victims to, at the minimum, have the right to be notified, present, and heard. All jurisdictions in the United States have granted these rights, although major gaps exist in implementation.

Being notified of court and other processes is obviously one critical piece of information. Whether subpoenaed or choosing to be present, victims need information about these processes and their roles. Victims' voices should be heard during the course of these processes, not only because they too have a stake in the outcomes, but also as a means of empowerment for them. In theory, prosecutors should be seeking input from victims and offering that to the court.

Victims have the right to be heard in their own words. In most cases, this happens only at sentencing through a Victim Impact Statement. In some jurisdictions, they are not allowed to actually speak, but may submit their written statement prior to sentencing. Typically, victims are not supposed to speak (or write) about what kind of sentence they feel should be meted out by the judge.

However, crime victims often, and quite legitimately, express regret that even when their legal rights have been fully implemented, their permitted role in determining what justice is and what outcomes will help them is minimal. Many prosecutors who do ask victims, "What do you want?" present options only in terms of punishment measured in units of time in custody and/or in dollars for restitution, and perhaps conditions relating to safety. Victims are rarely given opportunities to give their input about civic service options or to propose creative solutions to repairing the harm.

For all the rhetoric about offender accountability, in the traditional adversarial process, that generally is defined only as punishment. This often has nothing to do with whether the offender is truly accountable. When victims have a chance to think about what accountability means to them, it becomes more of a question of what justice would look like. True accountability in the minds of most victims means at least that:

- The person actually hears all the ways in which his or her actions affected the victim, the victim's family and others, and the community at large
- The victim's experiences are validated
- The offender acknowledges and accepts full responsibility for his or her role
- The offender takes on the obligation to take action to make things right, preferably in the manner that meets the victim's needs, to the greatest extent feasible

- The offender completes the obligation
- The offender understands what attitudes and behaviors led to him or her causing harm, is willing to accept help, and works on changing those attitudes and actions

Victims often define this true accountability by the offender in very simple terms: "She 'gets it' and she feels bad. Her apology was 'for real.' She did what she promised; now, we both can wipe the slate clean."

Conceivably, all of the above could happen in the courtroom, *if* the opportunity existed for the defendant to find out about the impact and needs of the individuals and the community some time substantially before sentencing. How could a person validate the actual experience of the harm he or she caused, to say nothing of trying to repair it, without knowing what that unique experience was and what repair would look like to that specific victim and to that specific community? If one purpose of the traditional victim-impact statement is to make the offender listen to and understand the harm, it may be unrealistic to expect the offender to be capable of that in the midst of his or her own anxiety about the judge's sentence. If we want offenders to have made amends, how could they do that without knowing how "amends" are defined in specific, measurable, and achievable terms and having the time to fulfill them?

One piece of true accountability is providing the truth. As part of the healing process, victims need to make sense of the violation, of the awful thing that happened to them. For that, they may need answers, which only could come from the person who did the harm. Sometimes these questions would not be fitting in a victim-impact statement, and, in any case, only could be asked in a rhetorical manner within that statement—there is no requirement for any response. And, some questions and many answers may be too personal or uncomfortable to be dealt with in a courtroom full of strangers, and with no guidance and protection, and no opportunity for follow-up.

The following questions typically plague victims: "Why me?" "Who in the heck are you to do this to me?" "Have you done something like this before?" "Will you do it again to me or someone else?" and "No? How can you prove that to me?" Questions exist regardless of the degree of seriousness, violence, or trauma, although those factors may affect the importance of the answers.

Many victims who this author has spoken with, ever since her first days at NOVA in 1995, have stated that incarceration of a low-risk offender for any lengthy sentence actually costs the victims and the community as well. They lose the opportunity to:

- Receive financial restitution in a more timely fashion from a person who could be working on the outside, and society loses a tax-paying contributor to the economy
- Tell their own story safely, fully, and directly to the one who harmed them, obtain answers to their questions, and receive some form of serious acknowledgement of the harm by the one who caused it
- Gain some insight into the efforts of the offender to make full actual or symbolic reparation
- Witness and ensure that the local government and the general public meet their responsibilities for public safety by monitoring the offender's behavior and compliance with the terms of probation and of any agreements to repair the harm
- Possibly develop or reconstruct a healthy relationship with the offender

Surprisingly, many victims of even relatively serious crimes, often with some degree of physical harm—unless they fear for their own safety or the safety of others—feel justice is served under these conditions more effectively than if the offender is locked up for extensive periods of time. Seeing or being aware of all these conditions being met greatly alleviates victims' fears of future harm as well.

These survivors rank these opportunities as more, even *much more* important to them than punishment. Interestingly, it is apparent that if we embark on the road of addressing the needs of victims and the community, before long we *will* arrive at the road we need to take to enable offenders to take responsibility, make repair, and reintegrate successfully. This route is well-traveled because one way in which victims make sense of what they went through is to care about making sure "this does not happen to anyone else."

Now, we turn to the experience of the person who is accused of the crime. The offender may lament: "I don't understand what's going on here. Nobody, not even my lawyer, will take the time to explain. And no one lets me tell my whole story, my way. Why won't anybody just listen to me?"

This need to tell their story is beneficial to law enforcement. Police are taught that many wrongdoers, on some level, are aching to tell their story, even if it means admitting they broke a law. Thus, the often effective use of this interrogation technique: "Go ahead—get it off your chest; you'll feel better."

However, as a means of control, law enforcement and corrections officials may deprive or reduce the opportunities for offenders to connect with those they care about through cell assignments, limits on visitation, and other communication restrictions. These tactics may increase the institution's ability to control "the population," but at the same time, are likely to increase the individual's sense of isolation, loss of control, and dehumanization.

Thus, people who are accused of committing harm and those who suffered harm often share similar experiences and complaints with the traditional system: frustration, increased isolation, insufficient resources and support to move in a positive direction, very little knowledge of or power over the process, and often lengthy delays.

However, in the not-so-distant past—and still in close-knit communities—people who were harmed by wrongdoing, even if it met the requirements of a crime, did not always automatically call in the police. Victims, the offenders, and their loved ones often were more concerned about the breach of individual or community relationships than the breach of the law.

Community leaders were more likely involved, and parties relied upon the existing networks of relationships to collectively determine responsibility for the harm and what needed to be done to make things right. Police were able to trust in the strength of those networks—that "interconnectivity"—to provide oversight and possibly support to ensure compliance. Strong matrices of connections provide both the impetus to work things out and support for rebuilding relationships. Of course, this version of community justice did not always produce healthy or fair results, to say the least. Now, in our very diverse and mobile American society, those networks are not as strong, may not be as inclusive, and are certainly less conspicuous.

When you roam the chambers of justice, the halls of legislatures, the rows of jail cells, and even the movie theaters and the web—the divisive sense of "It's them versus us" can be overwhelming. Our unfortunate human tendency to be very attached to our differences leads us to assumptions about who belongs to the "other" camp, further destroying our awareness of our fundamental interconnection.

But what is the reality? When I ask adult audiences, "How many of you have been the victim of any kind of crime?" usually at least 75 percent of the hands go up. I then flip the question: "How many of you—well, to protect privacy—you, or someone you are personally connected to, have been incarcerated?" I usually see close to the same percentage of hands go up. Regardless of class or status (and partly due to our rate of incarceration), most adults do care about—or are connected to—someone who is or has been on the other side of the law. Of course, in many families, there are both victims and offenders. Many individuals have been victimized and have victimized others. Recall Walt Kelly's beloved cartoon creation Pogo, who said, "'We have met the enemy and he is us." In truth, victim or offender: "They is us." How can we not appreciate that interconnectedness?

Broadly speaking, restorative approaches, and not just those that involve face-to-face meetings, create opportunities to experience connections with others. At the heart of restorative justice is the power of story-telling. This allows the truth to come out when someone feels it is safe to tell. When you tell your story about how you were victimized and what you have gone through since that time, it is often captivating, even to the people who did the harm. People can declare your accusations false, people can challenge your opinions and assumptions, but they cannot deny your experience, your feeling, however painful it may be to hear. However, often your truth will spark a memory of that same experience, that same feeling, in the person who hurt you, and thus, a spark of empathy is lit.

Telling someone "eyeball to eyeball," "This is how you hurt me. You can't change that, you can't fix it, but I will feel that you made it up to me as best you could if you do (this)," is an exercise in taking back your power.

In the safe place that it is the responsibility of the facilitator to create, truths may be shared. The offenders' story of wrongdoing emerges in answering the following questions: what led up to the crime, what did they actually do, how did they feel right after and when they got caught, and did the offenders realize who they hurt and how, and how do the offenders feel toward the victims now. The people the offender hurt may have wanted to lecture them, but often that urge gives way to questions, curiosity, and a need to understand the offender's "truth."

It may strike a cord of familiarity in one of the people you hurt— "Geez, he's making me remember some of the things I've done and gotten away with . . . " and suddenly, another spark of empathy, of human connection, is lit. The other person you hurt may think, "How different our lives have been! If I had gotten the hand he was dealt, I might not have believed I had other choices either. He's willing to tell me his truth—that must be tough to do . . . hmmm." Thus, another spark of recognizing and appreciating the humanity of the "other" jumps across the space of the circle. Your truth, your story, and your feelings cannot be denied either.

Listening with respect, trying to be open enough to feel what they felt, letting your reactions to their story show, sincerely offering an apology, truthfully answering questions, and trying to agree with what they want you to do or being honest about what you reasonably cannot do and then offering a workable alternative is an exercise in building your own sense of self-worth and sense of accomplishment in "doing the right thing."

Such victim-offender encounters, or conferences, are most powerful and satisfying when each of the participants, including supporters or anyone else who will be present, have the opportunity to prepare with the facilitators some days in advance of the joint meeting. Each person can think through the risks and the benefits of participating and come to a conclusion about volunteering to participate. Some additional time may be spent with offenders to help them understand victim trauma and think about all the possible ways the direct victims and other participants, including their supporters, may have been affected by their actions.

When that kind of work has been done prior to the joint meeting, the many "ifs" enumerated earlier which are so unlikely to collectively happen in a courtroom-sentencing hearing are the fairly regular ingredients of restorative dialogs. The restorative dialog feels like true accountability. This is demonstrated by the words and actions of the offenders, and by the sense of empowerment, satisfaction, and connection experienced by both the victims, the offenders, and the other participants. Some of us have come to refer to restorative conferencing as "a sacred space"—and it truly is an honor to have a part in it.

Whether victims meet face-to-face with the people who harmed them or communicate through an intermediary, a process that allows informal and natural interaction and a much greater degree of decision-making has proven to help victims experience a reduction in their fear and typical trauma reactions.

Restorative dialogs regularly result in agreements that the offender will perform a certain number of hours of community civic service. As with any outcome created by a meeting of the minds of the parties, the likelihood of actual performance is better than when the outcome is imposed by another. Most well-run restorative conferencing programs consistently report an extremely high rate of compliance, often more than 95 percent. Research has shown that even when parties convey their feelings through an intermediary, such as by letter or video, or "shuttle diplomacy" efforts by the facilitator, there is a great deal of satisfaction and very high rates of completion with terms of agreements.

Often times, courts impose a sentence that includes "hours of community service." But they fail to recognize the potential of community service as a means of victim and community recovery and as a pathway for successful reintegration of offenders.

Those goals, however, could be met even if the victim and the offender are not able to meet in person.

What are the criteria for "restorative community service"?

1. The victims and/or individuals representing the victim or the community should self-identify the financial, physical, and possibly emotional needs resulting from this crime.

2. These same individuals or groups propose the form of reparation that they believe will at least symbolically meet those needs or be related to the type of harm.

   The victims could suggest service that they would receive directly, such as the person mowing their lawn for some number of weeks after having trashed the lawn, or in lieu of paying for a broken window, as time and energy may be all the offender can afford.

   When an institution is the victim—for example, a drunk driver smashes into a nonprofit agency, a school, a church, or the police station—representatives of that institution could suggest direct service (as well as financial compensation) to the organization itself or for service connected to the type of harm, such as volunteering at Mothers Against Drunk Driving.

3. The victim and/or community representative could propose that offenders volunteer for a certain number of hours at a nonprofit or government agency of their choice.

4. The offender or a staff person could seek out civic service that will allow the offender to gain new skills or enhance existing ones. Competency development is one of the goals of restorative justice. So, ideally, the offender will build skills. In fact, all participants in a restorative process are learning new skills in communication, anger management, and conflict resolution.

Proposal to Make Restorative Justice the Norm, and the Adversarial Process the "Alternative"

Here is this author's proposal for a major systemic change to promote restorative outcomes with adversarial and punitive outcomes as the alternative. This brief description is a starting point for discussion of many more details than space will allow and probably many more issues than those considered here.

A new agency should be established to do outreach and provide services, referrals, and programs to both victims and offenders. This would not necessarily be in the same physical facility, but would use the same staff for outreach and referral activities, described below. Restorative justice values would be at the core of the mission with restorative approaches standard operating procedure.

Implementation of this in many jurisdictions may take major shifts in public opinion and political support, but it is possible. One example of a similar effort is in Genesee County, New York, which instituted a "one-stop-shop" agency that works in collaboration with others to respond to crime restoratively. Instead of building a new jail in 1981 to alleviate overcrowding, "Genesee Justice" has saved the taxpayers more than $4.1 million in jail costs, and a new jail has never been built. (For more impressive information, see http://www.co.genesee.ny.us/dpt/communityservices/progress .html).

The "them versus us" factor that is often pervasive within current services on both sides will be reduced substantially by the use of a team/case management system, which no jurisdiction has yet employed. Teams would operate as "honest brokers," working with all parties, including community volunteers and supporters of both victims and offenders and seeking balanced and holistic solutions and outcomes.

In this proposed model, confidentiality protection would be guaranteed by statute, so that clients could speak freely to team members (with appropriate exceptions regarding child abuse and future threats). Confidentiality is imperative and would include interactions with the other parties. A major goal is to offer victims and offenders opportunities for the earliest and most restorative resolution possible, but that means when they are ready.

The team's work would begin with outreach to victims. When a crime occurs, members of an outreach team would contact the victim—immediately in cases of violence or crisis (such as a missing child or a house burning down)—and provide emotional support, connect them, and help with the transition to professional and community-based services and support groups, be the liaison to the police, help the victim understand law enforcement procedures, their victim rights and victim compensation, and other assistance, as needed. In essence, ideally the team would provide the services that the best victim/witness offices do currently, but they no longer would be part of the law enforcement or prosecution agencies.

Whether or not someone is charged with the crime, the team support and services for the victim would continue. Whether there ever is an identified offender, restorative processes would be offered, such as a circle of support, which is a safe place for someone to experience the benefits of telling the story and receiving validation and ongoing emotional and practical support from other community members. Opportunities for participation in victim awareness classes and victim impact panels, or volunteering as a victim advocate, speaker, or restorative conference facilitator also would be made available over time, as appropriate.

Once someone is charged, or earlier if the police refer the case, the team would make contact, explain their role, and provide information about the criminal justice system. They would advise the victims to retain an attorney of their choice, or would provide one for consultation, as soon as possible. The team would explain that if the offender agrees that he or she is responsible for the harm that the victim has already described to the team, and that through a restorative conference or via a shuttle process they come to an agreement about what he or she will do to repair the harm, and then fulfills those terms, that will have an effect on the outcome of the criminal case. The case may be delayed for a reasonable amount of time for the restorative process to occur and repair terms to be met and then dismissed, or the judge may adopt the repair agreement into the sentence, with or without additional terms.

Both victims and offenders may choose not to participate in any restorative process, including communicating through the facilitator at this time, and still would be able to receive other services from the agency. If the offender denies responsibility or wants to wait to see what might happen in court, the traditional process will continue. Victims also could choose to send a representative to tell their story, hear from the offender and then, or at a later time, discuss repair options. If the offender is willing to cooperate, if it is an appropriate case for pre-trial resolution, and if the victim does not want to be involved in any way, surrogate victims (volunteer victims of similar crimes) or community members could conference with the offender and supporters.

Research shows that we could expect to see the natural byproducts of using restorative approaches. This could include reduced court caseloads, fewer people being incarcerated, fewer needing as intensive supervision, and reduction in the social and financial costs of crime and recidivism for victims and the community. However, the hope for these savings should never come before attending to the needs of the clients. The combination of the restorative principles of "do no harm" and "maintain respect and dignity for all parties" translates to never requiring victims to participate in justice processes—whether restorative or adversarial—and allowing defendants to choose between restorative and adversarial processes.

Therefore, it generally would be assumed that the planners of the agency policies would include something like a "classification system" to provide guidance to staff and the courts about what types of cases could be resolved without judicial approval and what types would require judicial approval and permit judges to also sentence defendants to confinement or probation, or add other conditions, such as referrals to programming.

Presumably, the more serious and violent offenses would have to be addressed by the court. But exactly because of the greater negative impact on victims, the more important it is that they have the opportunity for input. It may be that most victims of severe violence or homicide survivors would not be at all interested in or emotionally prepared to meet with the person accused within the time period a criminal case is ready for trial. But some may be, or at least may want to tell their story to the defendant without the limitations placed on victim-impact statements, for example, by video or letter, and they should have that opportunity. Victims of unknown or unwilling offenders find healing in participating in other restorative processes, such meeting with a surrogate offender (someone already convicted of the same crime, and who has taken responsibility) or speaking to offenders in victim awareness classes; team members should be able to offer those opportunities under the appropriate circumstances.

People charged with very serious offenses, facing severe penalties, may well be more concerned with "getting out of it," than focusing on their responsibility. But many defendants may want the opportunity to thoroughly discuss what happened and even to understand the impact on others—for months, all this is pent up inside them because their lawyers have said not to talk about it, even to them. Wouldn't it be helpful if someone would work with them in a confidential setting, even before the trial, to work through all this and possibly move them toward accountability?

Police, defense counsel, prosecutors, probation officers, judges, and magistrates could jointly or individually call in teams or refer cases to a team. Thus, from the time a suspect is identified all the way through sentencing, the potential for dialog, or at least a shuttle process, could be explored. Successful conferences—those that reach an agreement—could be part of the sentence or probation conditions.

Further, the team would "check in" with offenders after sentencing to discuss restorative interventions whether the person is on probation, incarcerated, or near release. The latter is an excellent time. Many victims of serious crimes may never have wanted to communicate in any way with the person who caused such harm, but once they are notified of pending release, they would like to get a sense of "where this guy's at now," before he is back in their community.

Restorative processes already fit into our current system. Many programs offer these—where the judge, the lawyers, victim, and offender all agree. It may be as diversion, or using a suspended imposition of sentence, or as part of sentencing. Generally, though, these are used only occasionally. If we consider all the cases which get pled out, especially the millions of cases that end with probation or jail sentences, yet without any input from the victim, the potential is huge for community restorative processes that are inclusive and empowering to be the norm. The adversarial process and the resources of professionals could be more thoroughly devoted to the cases—that is, the people, both victim and offender—who need the most attention.

Thousands of victims, their loved ones, and community members report that, in the safe haven of the restorative conference setting, seeing the offender in person and hearing that person's own words (rather than the lawyer's), changed their perceptions of the individual and increased their sense of safety. Perhaps, ironically, many offenders also fear that victims might physically retaliate, and assume that at the least, the victim and their supporters will yell and scream at them in anger. Offenders often comment on their surprise at the lack of antagonism, and even expressions of care and feeling of connectedness they experience from the other conference participants. Again, storytelling leads to connection, which produces understanding, cooperation and commitment—a change in the heart and spirit of each person.

Conversely, in the unfamiliar and formal court environment, which is controlled by professionals, victims hear the defendant, who has been pleading "not guilty" for months, suddenly say "Yes, I did it and I'm sorry," and hear the defendant's family speak about their "good boy." Many victims' reaction: "What a sob story," or "She got off too easy." This author asked a classroom of police officers, "How many victims do you think come out of juvenile court satisfied?" The response: none.

Thus, this author's question—How can we let this go on? To the readers of this paper, here are some questions for you to ponder.

- **Why not work on accountability, competency development, and repair during the days and months before sentencing, if at all possible?**
- **Why not meet the needs of the victims, the community, the offenders and their families as well, with practical and proven-effective practices as early as possible?**
- **Why not adjust the timing and flow of cases to meet their needs?**
- **Why not allow more defendants to remain under supervision in the community and leave incarceration to those who are threats to our safety?**
- **Why not focus on our connectedness rather than promoting isolation and allow for the possibilities of accountability, repair, and healing before presuming punishment is required?**

Bibliography

Bolton, Andrew Interview. January 12, 2006. Retrieved from http://www.cofchrist.org/peaceaward/zeh-intvw2006.asp

Genesee County, NY. retrieved from http://www.co.genesee.ny.us/dpt/communityservices/progress.html

Epilog

Epilog: In Pursuit of Effective Community Corrections

Donald G. Evans

Canadian Training Institute, President
Toronto, Ontario, Canada

Introduction

In this closing chapter, I will be addressing the work of the International Community Corrections Association (ICCA) and its efforts to promote "what works" in correctional programming. In the first section, I will briefly examine what ICCA has achieved in promoting effectiveness in community corrections, and secondly, I will discuss what needs to be done in the future. This backward- and forward-looking effort will highlight the advances, limitations, and the critical need for more research. It also will stress the importance of the academic-practitioner interface that this volume illustrates. The history of ICCA'S "what works" journey is also a history of not only the research conferences but the subsequent training partnership that was developed with the National Institute of Corrections, U.S. Department of Justice, and a joint publishing venture with the American Correctional Association.

Looking through the Rearview Mirror

History

I begin with a brief retelling of the history of ICCA. The association has its origins in the early 1960s when it was formed to provide a support network and offer training to those working in the then-emerging halfway house movement that was known as the International Halfway House Association (IHHA). Over the years, as the field of community corrections grew and the populations being served became more diverse, the organization broadened its membership and was renamed the International Association of Residential and Community Alternatives. This name change reflected the development of a number of innovative approaches to managing offenders in the community. It was the period of rapid growth in the use of intermediate sanctions and other measures geared to the supervision of offenders in community settings but not necessarily in residential environments. During this period, the first research conference on "what works" was convened. As the field of community corrections continued to undergo change and become more complex, it was necessary once again to entertain a change of name that more adequately reflected the membership base and the services offered by the members. Thus, the International Community Corrections Association became the organization's name, which more accurately reflected the changes in the correctional environment.

ICCA is a private, nonprofit membership service organization representing the continuum of community corrections programs. It strives to provide information, training, and other services to enhance the quality of services and supervision for offenders and to promote effective management practices. ICCA is committed to promoting and enhancing community corrections as a vital component of the criminal justice system.

ICCA maintains close ties with other similar organizations and has affiliation agreements with the American Correctional Association (since 1975) and full voting status with the United Nations Alliance of Non-Governmental Organizations in Criminal Justice (since 1982). More recently, it has entered into affiliation agreements with the American Probation and Parole Association, the International Corrections and Prison Association, and the National Association of Probation Executives. It also maintains liaison relations with various levels of government, including the Federal Bureau of Prisons in the United States and the Correctional Service of Canada.

Membership is open to all agencies operating programs and services to community corrections clients. This includes nonprofit and for-profit agencies in both adult and juvenile justice arenas. There is also an individual membership

370

category. It has held conferences in Denmark, England, Bermuda, Canada, and the United States.

This brief description of the history, mission, and membership of ICCA should give you a general idea of the evolution of the association. I would like to turn now to what it has done and is doing to further effective community correctional practice.

The Research Conferences

Concerned about the state of correctional programming, ICCA embarked on an ambitious effort to bring to the attention of its membership and through its journal and publications to others working in corrections, the results of research that indicated what was working in correctional programming. The first conference was held in Philadelphia, Pennsylvania in 1993. The conference featured a review of the literature on what works and examined the growing demand by practitioners and policymakers for evidence of effective practices.

This conference resulted in the publication by Sage Publications of the proceedings, edited by Alan T. Harland, *Choosing Correctional Options That Work: Defining the Demand and Evaluating the Supply* (1996). The success of this conference led ICCA to plan future research conferences, and it has continued to hold these conferences annually. The proceedings continue to be published as a result of a partnership with the American Correctional Association. To date, this publishing venture has produced seven volumes, and this one is the eighth.

The conferences were based on a growing body of research literature that points to the critical elements in understanding what works and what does not work in reducing re-offending. Briefly, this literature suggests that there are principles of effective intervention and that these principles can be summarized as follows:

- Intensive services that are behavioral in nature.
- Intensive services occupy 40-70 percent of the offender's time while in a program and are of three to nine months in duration.
- Behavioral strategies are essential to effective service delivery. Examples are token economies (reinforcement system for motivating offenders to perform prosocial behaviors), modeling (offenders observe another person demonstrating a behavior which they can benefit from), and cognitive-behavioral (attempt to change offenders' cognitions, attitudes, values, and expectations, which maintain their antisocial behavior).

- Behavioral programs that target the criminogenic needs of high-risk offenders.
- Responsivity, that is, matching the treatment approach with the learning style and personality of the offender, matching the characteristics of the offender with those of the therapist, and matching the skills of the therapist with the type of program offered.
- Program contingencies/behavioral strategies enforced in a firm but fair manner.
- Therapists relate to offenders in interpersonally sensitive and constructive ways and are trained and supervised appropriately.
- Program structure and activities disrupt the delinquency network by placing offenders in situations (people and places) where prosocial activities predominate.
- Relapse prevention in the community is part of the program.
- High level of advocacy and brokerage with community services that are offering appropriate programs.

This research literature also suggests what does not work! Examples are programs that target low-risk offenders, punishing smarter strategies, programs that involve intense group interactions but fail to gain control over the contingencies, nondirective client-centered counseling, and various "medical model" interventions.

Because of the need for trained staff and the need to create awareness of this body of research, ICCA expanded beyond just providing conferences and publications, (both in book form and in its quarterly journal) to the provision of training seminars. In a joint project with the National Institute of Corrections, U.S. Department of Justice, we have been conducting a series of regional conferences on the theme of "Public Protection through Offender Risk Reduction." Between 1998 and 2004, there have been more than half a dozen two-day seminars in various cities in United States and Canada. These seminars sought to disseminate to administrators and practitioners the results of the research literature on what works and to promote the development of programs that will be effective in reducing re-offending. The result of these seminars and the conferences has been a demand for more training and for skill building activities that will help with the implementation of programs that are research-based. Publications related to effective practice and the implementation of "what works" have appeared in the *Journal of Community Corrections* (ICCA), *Perspectives* (APPA), and *Corrections Today* (ACA).

Value of Professional Associations to Effective Practice

Why have I spent so much time discussing this focus of ICCA on "what works"? It is because I believe it is a good example of the value of professional associations to the development of effective community correctional practice. Government agencies sometimes run into problems of sharing, getting involved in larger networks and being able to debate and participate in dialog in environments where a number of perspectives and ideas are represented. This volume illustrates the point of dialog between academics and practitioners. The ability of professional associations to transcend the narrow confines of any given department or agency is a value that members of these associations enjoy.

What are the key values of professional associations? The following outlines my perspective on the key role associations can play in promoting effective practice.

For sometime now, we have become used to the fact that we are living in the information age, but we have not necessarily been able to accommodate or adapt to the impact that this influx of information brings. Generally, we get lost in the excitement of innovation and program development and fail to acknowledge that what leads innovation is information. I believe that the growth and development of professional associations is one adaptation to the information age. Associations are becoming "communities of memory" for many professions as well as a source for keeping current in what is happening in professional practice. ICCA is one of these professional associations that provide information on current practices in the field of community corrections through its conferences, publications, and training seminars.

Associations such as ICCA and ACA provide practitioners with ready access to an information network through their memberships. Contacts made at meetings of the associations can be used to stay in touch and to exchange information from various jurisdictions and disciplines; it allows us to exchange addresses and, with Internet access, to travel the information highway with like-minded professionals. Associations provide a cross-fertilization process that enables those working in corrections to get out of their individual self-interests and learn what is happening elsewhere.

Not so long ago, the notion of a borderless world was used to describe events transpiring in the corporate world and suggested the need to find new ways of getting beyond the boundaries—or borders—of our current organizations to find more effective and efficient ways of doing business. The walls between us continue to be more of a hindrance a than help, and we need to work at transcending them. Those in the correctional profession can no longer afford to be isolated from each other. In the borderless world of the future, we must recognize that no one person, organization, or association can hold back the free flow of knowledge that informs and educates all correctional professionals. We need to be in touch with other like-minded associations and groups to generate multiple approaches and solutions to meet the challenges of reducing re-offending and securing justice in our communities.

Just as successful companies and corporations look for ways to collaborate and form strategic alliances to remain competitive in a global marketplace, so have professional associations sought to collaborate with affiliates, other international and national organizations, and government agencies in the fostering of best practices in corrections.

Finally, I would like to end by discussing another major value of professional associations in correctional work. This value is the growing advocacy role that some associations are beginning to play. ICCA holds a one-day event in Washington, DC, each year to meet with legislators and their staff to provide educational materials and research reports that describe effective practices in corrections. Other associations are doing similar activities—or are providing their members with legislative briefings on what is happening or likely to happen in terms of new legislation. The ability of an association to offer a collective voice where individual voices would not be able to speak out is indeed a value-added component of a professional association. Whether speaking on behalf of the profession to the media, legislators, or the public, this is a role I can only see becoming increasingly important in the future.

For those of us who have an affinity for the development of and the utility of "learning organizations," the professional association is an important adjunct to the search for and implementation of effective penal practices.

Looking Ahead, Keeping Our Eye on the Road

The efforts by researchers and practitioners to advance effective programming in the community continue, but the returns on reduction of recidivism seem slow in coming. The task is not over. Conferences, projects, training events—all geared to promoting "what works"—should not assume that what they are doing is no longer necessary. Just because the "what works" or "evidence-based" vocabulary appears to be on every correctional tongue and in every policy presented does not mean there is widespread implementation and adequate resources available. The task is definitely not over.

The task is not over in three critical areas: responding to the critics, improving implementation, and advocating for more research and an enlarged contest for what works.

Responding to Critics

It would be a mistake to assume that the debate about what works is over. The approach taken by "what works" advocates still meets with opposition both in academic circles and among practitioners. Currently, the critical comments come from three sources. There are those who still wish to maintain the now-tiresome debate on rehabilitation versus punishment. Sometimes those in this camp choose a particular rationale for punishment as the reason for opposition. For example, there is still strong support for a deterrence approach to the managing of offenders (Farabee, 2003).

A second group of critics comes from those who support a rehabilitative approach to offenders but disagree with various elements in the "what works" approach. The battleground here seems to be the assessment process and the designations of risk and need, especially the notion of criminogenic need (Mair, 2004). Some of these criticisms are dealt with by Andrews in this volume and in other writings (Andrews, Bonta, and Wormith, 2006).

The third set of commentators tend to be more accepting of the goal of the "what works" agenda but are concerned with what they see as shortcomings in the theory or limitations in the evidence (Maruna and Immarigeon, 2004; Ward and Maruna, 2007).

It is still important to familiarize ourselves with these critics and to engage them in constructive dialog with the intention of improving and enhancing our efforts to assist offenders to become law-abiding citizens and thus contribute to safer communities. The stance we should take is "What can we learn from our critics that will improve our service delivery systems and produce an effective community correctional service?"

McGuire (2005) reminds us that the traffic in ideas is not a one-way street. He also notes that practice can be a major guide to research. This reminder should encourage us to become research practitioners and to assist in the production of knowledge about what works in community corrections. So, as the title of this volume attests, continuing the commitment is indeed a necessity.

Improving Implementation

If there is one area where current research seems to agree, it is in regard to the matter and manner of implementation. This volume contains ideas for improving how programs are implemented, especially regarding effective case work and in facing specific challenges in implementing evidence-based practice. One of the major problems is the speed with which implementation has outpaced the research. Racing to implement evidence-based approaches without careful planning, preparation of staff, and organization is likely to lead to less effective outcomes. McGuire (2005) notes that implementation problems usually affect the success of programs due to three factors:

- Rapid expansion of programs
- Ineffective targeting of programs
- Higher than expected attrition rates

In a recent article, Dr. Andrews makes eight key points regarding adherence to risk-need-responsivity principles in implementation. He is especially concerned with quality control and wishes to see quality made a matter of policy. The eight points are as follows:

- Employ structured and validated risk/need assessment instruments
- Never assign low-risk cases to intensive services
- Reserve intensive treatment for moderate and higher risk cases
- Always target a predominance of relevant criminogenic needs
- Always employ cognitive-behavioral and social learning interpersonal influence strategies
- Managers and supervisors must attend to the relationship and structuring skills of service delivery staff
- Clinical supervision entails regular, ongoing, high-level modeling and reinforcement of relationship and structuring skills.
- Make monitoring, feedback, and corrective action routine, as a matter of policy (Andrews, 2006).

I would add the following note regarding the need for administrators introducing evidence-based programs to begin with pilot projects, thus preparing the organization for large-scale change. Plan for and expect a counter-movement in the organization. Leaders will also have to deal with the real problem of when to disengage the old work for the new; otherwise, the burden on the staff is too great and hinders their ability to attend to the new tasks. Research on implementation is greatly needed and is an area that ICCA should address in future research conferences.

Moving Beyond Risk

On the road ahead, there are obstacles, and one of these obstacles may be the myopia that can develop around the idea of risk and risk management. Rather than constantly expanding the categories of risk, I would like to see future conferences look at the issue of offender re-offending in a larger context. Can we rehabilitate notions of community development, for example, the role of poverty and crime, and what can be done in our schools to prevent them from becoming fortresses? If this seems like a drift from the Risk-Need Responsivity (RNR) principles, I would argue that it is an extension of the concepts of need and responsivity.

I would like to see more dialog between the RNR theorists and the restorative justice advocates and, while we are at it, an opening up of discussions with theorists studying desistance from crime. The road ahead is full of promise and potential as long as we take a principled path in searching for ways to make our communities safer. One such effort is undertaken by Tony Ward and Shadd Maruna in a thoughtful discussion of rehabilitation theory. Their examination of the strengths and weaknesses of the RNR model and the Good Lives model helps us move beyond risk (Ward and Maruna, 2007). We need more efforts of this sort if we are to advance in finding effective ways to deal with the very complex problems created by crime and disorder in our communities.

Conclusion

ICCA and similar associations need to continue their commitment to pursue effective community approaches to correcting offending behavior. The past decade and a half has seen an expansion in the knowledge base, but there are still gaps and questions yet to answer. The pursuit continues, and it will be important, as we travel the road ahead, to also look occasionally in the rearview mirror. History in corrections is not irrelevant to future developments. In future volumes, I hope to see a developing dialog between researchers and practitioners as we collectively pursue effectiveness in community corrections.

References

Andrews, D. A. 2006 Enhancing Adherence to Risk-Need-Responsivity: Making Quality a Matter of Policy. *Criminology and Public Policy.* 5 (3): 595-602.

Andrews, D. A, James Bonta, and J. Stephen Wormith. 2006. The Recent Past and Near Future of Risk and/or Need Assessment. *Crime & Delinquency.* 52 (1): 7-27.

Farabee, David. 2003. *Rethinking Rehabilitation: Why Can't We Reform Our Criminals?* Washington, D.C.: The AEI Press.

Mair, George. 2004. *What Matters in Probation.* Cullompton, Devon: Willan Publishing.

Maruna, S. and R. Immarigeon. 2004. *After Crime and Punishment: Pathways to Offender Reintegration.* Cullompton, Devon: Willan Publishing.

McQuire, James. 2005. Is Research Working? Revisiting the Research and Effective Practice Agenda. In J. Winstone and P. Pakes, eds., *Community Justice: Issues for Probation and Criminal Justice.* Cullompton, Devon: Willan Publishing.

Ward, Tony and Shadd Maruna. 2007. *Rehabilitation: Beyond the Risk Paradigm.* London and New York: Routledge.

ABOUT THE AUTHORS

D. A. (Don) Andrews

D. A. Andrews is Professor Emeritus in the Department of Psychology and the Institute of Criminology and Criminal Justice at Carleton University, Ottawa, Ontario. He is also Distinguished Research Professor in Psychology. His research interests include a variety of assessment, intervention, evaluation, and theoretical issues in juvenile and criminal justice, corrections, and other human service agencies. He is also interested in the social psychology of criminological knowledge. He is co-developer of risk/need assessment instruments in wide-scale use with young offenders and adult offenders. *The Psychology of Criminal Conduct*, co-authored with James Bonta, was nominated for the Hindelang Award of the American Society of Criminology. His research and theoretical contributions to correctional policy and practice were recognized by the American Probation and Parole Association through the University of Cincinnati award in 1997. In addition, he received the Margaret Mead award for contributions to social justice and humanitarian advancement from the International Community Corrections Association. The Correctional Service Canada has named an annual lecture series in his honor, and he received the Career Contributions award from the Criminal Justice division of the Canadian Psychological Association. In 2004, he received the Distinguished Senior Scholar Award from DCS of the American Society of Criminology. The Don Andrews Scholarship in Criminology and Criminal Justice was announced at Carleton University in June 2006.

Gordon Bazemore

Gordon Bazemore is currently Professor of Criminology and Criminal Justice and Director of the Community Justice Institute at Florida Atlantic University. His research has focused on juvenile justice and youth policy, restorative justice, crime victims, corrections, and community policing. Dr. Bazemore's recent publications appear in *Justice Quarterly*, *Crime and Delinquency*; the *Annals of the American Academy of Political and Social Sciences*; and the *American Behavioral Scientist*. He is the author of *Juvenile Justice Reform and Restorative Justice: Building Theory and Policy from Practice* (with Mara Schiff), (Willan Publishing), and he has completed two edited books, *Restorative Juvenile Justice: Repairing the Harm of Youth Crime* (co-edited with Lode Walgrave), (Criminal Justice Press), and *Restorative and Community Justice: Cultivating Common Ground for Victims, Communities and Offenders* (co-edited with Mara Schiff), (Anderson Publishing). Dr. Bazemore has directed research projects funded by the National Institute of Justice, Office for Victims of Crime, the Robert Wood Johnson Foundation, and other public and private agencies. He is currently principal investigator of the Balanced and Restorative Justice Project funded by the Office of Juvenile Justice and Delinquency Prevention. He was the recipient of Florida Atlantic University's Researcher of the Year Award in both 1995 and 1999.

Rachel Boba

Dr. Rachel Boba is an assistant professor of criminology and criminal justice at Florida Atlantic University. She teaches methods of research, criminal justice systems, crime prevention, problem solving, and analysis in policing and conducts research in the areas of problem solving, accountability, problem analysis, and crime analysis. Previously, Dr. Boba was director of the Police Foundation's Crime Mapping Laboratory, where she directed federally funded grants in the areas of crime analysis and crime mapping, problem analysis, and school safety. She has worked as a crime analyst at the Tempe, Arizona, Police Department, where she conducted a wide variety of crime analysis. Most recently, Dr. Boba has written the Sage Publication, *Crime Analysis and Crime Mapping*, one of the first books for undergraduate and graduate students in crime analysis. Dr. Boba holds a master's and doctorate degree in sociology from Arizona State University.

Donald Braman

Donald Braman teaches criminal law and evidence at George Washington Law School in the District of Columbia. He studied law and anthropology at Yale University.

William D. Burrell

William D. Burrell is an independent consultant specializing in community corrections, evidence-based practices, performance measurement, leadership development, public management, and organizational change. From 2003 to 2007, he was a faculty member in the Department of Criminal Justice at Temple University in Philadelphia. Prior to joining the Temple faculty, Bill served for nineteen years as chief of adult probation services for the New Jersey State Court System. He was responsible for oversight and monitoring of probation services in the twenty-one local probation divisions and for providing support services such as research, training, program development, and technical assistance to probation administrators and staff.

Bill is chairman of the Editorial Committee for *Perspectives*, the journal of the American Probation and Parole Association (APPA). He also serves as a member of APPA's Board of Directors. Bill currently serves as a member of the editorial board of *Community Corrections Report* and writes a bimonthly column on management issues. He has consulted, developed, and delivered training on performance measurement management for probation agencies at the federal, state, and county levels.

Donald G. Evans

Donald G. Evans is President of the Canadian Training Institute, Toronto, Canada, and a past president of the American Probation and Parole Association and the International Community Corrections Association. Currently, he is chair of the American Correctional Association's International Affairs Committee.

Charley Flint

Professor Charley Flint received her B.S. degree from North Carolina A&T State University and her M.A. and Ph.D. degrees from Rutgers University. She teaches criminology; sociology of corrections; senior seminar in criminal justice; internship in criminal justice; gender, crime, and society; and serves as criminal justice coordinator at William Paterson University in Wayne, New Jersey. Her publications include: a book review of *White Nation: Fantasies of White Supremacy in a Multiracial Society* in the *Journal of International Migration and Integration* (2004); *Women and Reentry*, The New Jersey Institute for Social Justice, (2004); co-editor of *Transforming the Curriculum: Teaching Resources from The New Jersey Project* (Teachers College Press, 1995); "Black Women in Higher Education: Forging Ties With Other Women of Color," *The Black Scholar: Journal of Black Studies and Research*, Fall 1995, 25(4); and "A Psychometric Analysis of Aggression and Conflict-Resolution Behavior in Black Adolescent Males" (with Sherle Boone), *Journal of Social Behavior and Personality* 16 (1988), 215-226. She has presented numerous papers and lectures at various colleges and universities, professional meetings, conferences and other venues. She has been interviewed on CBS, NBC, FOX, and BET, as well as in local, national and international newspapers on issues related to race/ethnicity, criminal justice, and gender. Her current research interests are interracial families, women (especially mothers) in corrections, and assessing community-based corrections as an alternative to incarceration. She serves as research consultant to the Juvenile Drug Team of the Superior Court of Passaic County, Family Division.

Professor Flint is President of the Board of Trustees of the New Jersey Association on Corrections, President of the Board of Directors of the YWCA of Eastern Union County, member of the Board of directors of the New Jersey Chapter of the American Correctional Association, and on a number of other social, professional, and community boards. She is vice president of the New Jersey Association of Criminal Justice Educators, a member of the Eastern Sociological Society, American Sociological Association, American Correctional Association, The International Community Correctional Association, and the Association of Black Women in Higher Education.

Norman G. Hoffmann, Ph.D.

Dr. Hoffmann, a clinical psychologist, has evaluated behavioral health programs and developed assessment instruments for screening, diagnosing, and treatment planning. His work formed the basis for the first ASAM patient placement criteria, provided clinical evidence for the distinct nature of dependence versus abuse, and served as the basis for more than 150 publications. He provides consultation services for state and federal agencies, corporations, and public organizations throughout the United States and Europe, and he is a frequent presenter at national and international conferences. Dr. Hoffmann is President of Evince Clinical Assessments and formerly Associate Professor of Community Health at Brown University.

Phyllis Lawrence

Phyllis Turner Lawrence's perspective on improving how we could better "do justice" derives from her earlier sixteen years of law practice and from the last fourteen years in which she has been trained in, practiced, and trained others nationally and locally on victim advocacy, restorative justice principles and practices, and criminal justice reform. She currently offers both victim-sensitive training and technical assistance to professionals and community members on these issues and works as a sentencing advocate in individual criminal cases, ranging from misdemeanors to capital murder charges.

Over the years, Ms. Turner Lawrence worked as a project coordinator for the National Organization for Victim Assistance (NOVA), Ralph Nader's Center for the Study of Responsive Law, the American Civil Liberties Union Capital Punishment Project, and the Prince William County, Virginia, Restorative Justice Project, as an attorney in solo practice, and for California Rural Legal Assistance. She was awarded both her law degree and her B.A. in social welfare from the University of California at Berkeley and is a graduate of various training for trainers, including the National Institute of Correction's Balanced and Restorative Justice Project, the Alternatives to Violence Project, NOVA's Community Crisis Response Team, and the National MultiCultural Institute. She hopes this paper, describing a still-developing construct, will inspire discourse. She welcomes your reactions and suggestions and can be reached at phyllislaw@comcast.net.

Edward E. Rhine

Edward E. Rhine, Ph.D., is Deputy Director, Office of Policy and Offender Reentry, Ohio Department of Rehabilitation and Correction. In this capacity, he also serves as the Director of the Ohio Institute on Correctional Best Practices. Dr. Rhine's career has included leadership and management positions in both juvenile and adult corrections. He was formerly the Chairperson of the Release Authority and Deputy Director of Parole, Courts and Community Services for the Ohio Department of Youth Services. Prior to that, he served as the Director of Field Operations for the Georgia Board of Pardons and Paroles. Dr. Rhine has written and edited numerous publications addressing the history and practice of paroling authorities, the impact of due process on prison discipline, leadership, and change issues in probation and parole, offender reentry, and "best practices" in corrections. He served as the Community Corrections Features Editor for *Corrections Management Quarterly*, and is currently on the Editorial Committee for the American Probation and Parole publication, *Perspectives*. He served as the chief editor for such recent publications as *Transforming Probation through Leadership: The 'Broken Windows' Model*, and *Best Practices: Excellence in Corrections*. He is President-Elect of the International Association of Reentry. He is also a member of the Probation Reinvention Council, the American Probation and Parole Association, and the American Society of Criminology. Finally, he is a member of and has served as chair of the Exemplary Practices Coordinating Council of the American Correctional Association. He is the recipient of the 2004 E. J. Henderson Award bestowed by the International Community Corrections Association, and the 2005 Bennett J. Cooper Award bestowed by the Ohio Community Corrections Organization. Dr. Rhine received his doctorate in sociology from Rutgers University in 1981.

David Robinson, Ph.D.

Dr. David Robinson has more than twenty years of experience conducting research and developing tools for assessment and case management in community corrections and custodial settings. He graduated in 1990 with a doctorate in psychology from Carleton University. Dr. Robinson served as a senior research manager in the Research Branch of Correctional Service Canada, where he managed research projects in adult corrections and parole for nine years. The studies he directed included validation of assessment tools, program evaluation of "What Works" initiatives, and a number of surveys of both staff and offenders.

During his early years in the field, Dr. Robinson was involved in the development and validation of the Level of Supervision Inventory (LSI) and the Youth Level of Service Inventory (YLS-CM1). He also worked on the design and validation of a number of assessment instruments in family therapy, substance abuse, employment counseling, youth services, and domestic violence. He has managed a number of program evaluations in adult corrections and delinquency prevention. Dr. Robinson is widely published on offender assessment and treatment in criminal justice services. His research has included studying the response of criminal justice workers to organizational change and attitudes about working with offenders. In addition to many program evaluation efforts, his recent work includes the introduction of the YASI (Youth Assessment and Screening Instrument) in New York, Illinois, Michigan, Mississippi, Vermont, Virginia, Scotland,

and other jurisdictions. He was the lead developer on SPIn (Service Planning Instrument), a risk and strengths assessment and case planning model for adult offenders. Recently, he was a co-developer of a gender-responsive assessment for women offenders (SPIn-W).

Gerald D. Shulman, M.A., M.A.C., FACATA

Gerald Shulman is a clinical psychologist, Master Addiction Counselor, Fellow of the American College of Addiction Treatment Administrators and certified by the American Academy of Psychologists Treating Addiction. He has authored more than eighty published articles and assessment instruments. He has clinically or administratively supervised or managed the delivery of care to alcoholics and drug addicts for forty-five years. He provides training and consulting in behavioral health with an emphasis on the implementation and use of the ASAM PPC-2R, of which he is an author. This instrument provides a quality treatment protocol for use in managed care for those working with reduced resources. He is re-engineering treatment to provide an evidence-based assessment that is outcome-driven for older adults with substance use and mental health disorders. He was a workgroup facilitator for CSAT's TIP #26, Substance Abuse Among Older Adults and has designed and supervised a treatment program for older adults with substance use disorders.

Carol Shapiro

Carol Shapiro is the founder and executive director of Family Justice, Inc. She is a nationally known innovator in the field of criminal justice. Over the past thirty years, she has devised numerous approaches to improving public safety and family well-being in the fields of drug abuse, mental health, housing, and law enforcement. As the founder and executive director of Family Justice, a national family-focused justice reform agency, Carol serves as an advisor to many governmental and citizen-sector initiatives. Additionally, she provides technical assistance and consulting services on policy, planning, and implementation of social justice reform initiatives to federal, state, and local governments, not-for-profit organizations, and the media. In 2001, Carol was recognized as a social entrepreneur by being named an Ashoka Innovator for the Public Fellow, one of the first ten so honored in the United States. She is also the recipient of the 2006 Maud Booth Correctional Services Award from Volunteers of America in recognition of her leadership and vision in the field of corrections and Family Justice's successes in addressing reentry. In 2002, Family Justice's neighborhood family support center, La Bodega de la Familia, in partnership with the New York State Division of Parole, was named a winner of Harvard University's Kennedy School of Government Innovations in American Government Award.

David Simourd, Ph.D., C.Psych.

Dr. Simourd received his Ph.D. in psychology from Carleton University in Ottawa, Canada in 1992. For nine years he was employed as a psychologist with Correctional Service of Canada in the medium-security Collins Bay Institution in Kingston, Ontario. He also served as chief psychologist for five years. From 2001 to 2003, he was the clinical director of a thirty-bed mental health facility for forensic patients in Kingston Ontario. Since 2003, Dr. Simourd divides his time between operating a private practice in psychology dedicated primarily to forensic correctional matters and operating a correctional research and consulting company. Dr. Simourd has maintained an active program of research and evaluation on the assessment and treatment of offenders. He has published several articles and conducted numerous training workshops in these areas and has consulted to several justice-related agencies throughout North America, Asia, and the Caribbean. He is the book review editor for the journal *Criminal Justice and Behavior* and holds an adjunct research professor appointment in the Department of Psychology at Carleton University. He can be reached at: dave@acesink.com.

Faye Taxman, Ph.D.

Dr. Taxman is a professor in the Administration of Justice Program at George Mason University and affiliated with the Institute for Drug and Alcohol Studies at Virginia Commonwealth University. Dr. Taxman is the principal investigator for the Coordinating Center for the NIDA funded Criminal Justice National Drug Treatment Studies (CJ-DATS) (www.cjdats.org) where she directs a national survey of practices in correctional settings and is involved in several experimental studies. One such study explores the use of contingency management and incentive systems for drug-involved offenders. She is also the principal investigator on two studies devoted to understanding adoption of science-based practices in criminal justice and juvenile justice systems: a clinical trial to demonstrate the efficacy of a criminal thinking curriculum on the outcomes of substance-abusing offenders and a clinical trial to understand the technology-transfer practice that results in juvenile justice workers' use of assessment tools in acquiring services for juvenile offenders. She is the senior author of *Tools of the Trade: A Guide to Incorporating Science into Practice*, a publication of the

National Institute of Corrections, which provides a guidebook to implementation of science-based concepts into practice. She is on the editorial boards of *the Journal of Experimental Criminology* and the *Journal of Offender Rehabilitation*. She has published articles in the *Journal of Quantitative Criminology*, the *Journal of Research in Crime and Delinquency*, the *Journal of Substance Abuse Treatment, Journal of Drug Issues*, and *Evaluation and Program Planning*. She received the University of Cincinnatti award from the American Probation and Parole Association in 2002 for her contributions to the field.

Marilyn Van Dieten, Ph.D.

Marilyn Van Dieten is a registered clinical psychologist with more than twenty-five years' experience in the implementing, training, and developing of programs for offenders. She received her doctorate in clinical psychology from the University of Ottawa in 1989 and has devoted the last twenty years to the development and implementation of programs for youth and adults in the criminal justice system. Dr. Van Dieten received the Brian Riley Award in 2006 from the International Community Corrections Agency and was the recipient of the Maud Booth Award in 2003 from the Volunteers of America for her contributions to the field.

Dr. Van Dieten's professional experience includes direct provision of treatment and clinical services, supervision of staff, and design of service operations for high-risk populations. As the Director of Family and Youth Services for the John Howard Society, she was responsible for the development, implementation, and evaluation of domestic violence programs including programs for offenders and the victims of violence. Subsequent to this position, she served as the Director of Training and Research for Volunteers of America Delaware Valley. Her responsibilities included the redesign of services to offenders and homeless persons and the integration of evidence-based practices in assessment, programs, trainings, and management information.

As a consultant, Dr. Van Dieten has designed training for a number of assessment and case management approaches. Early in her career, Dr. Van Dieten co-authored a number of nationally recognized offender programs including *CALM* (Anger Management), *Counter Point* (cognitive skills programming for addressing antisocial attitudes) and recently, *Community Transitions* (maintenance strategies for substance abuse).

Over the last ten years, Dr. Van Dieten has devoted her attention to the development of innovative strategies and approaches for women and girls in the criminal justice system. She is the author of *Moving On,* (a program for women offenders) and recently co-authored a Women's Programme for acquisitive females in the United Kingdom, *Girls Moving On* which was created for youth between 12-21. It was completed in 2006 and is currently being piloted in Illinois and Los Angeles. Finally, Dr. Van Dieten is working with the National Institute of Corrections to design and evaluate a gender-responsive case management model for women.

Nancy Wolff, Ph.D.

Nancy Wolff, Ph.D., is a professor of public policy in the E. J. Bloustein School of Planning and Public Policy at Rutgers University and the director of the Center for Mental Health Services and Criminal Justice Research in the Institute for Health, Health Care Policy and Aging Research. Her research focuses on issues related to measuring the societal costs of interventions for persons with mental illness, designing cost-effectiveness analyses, exploring the effect of insurance design on access to care, and modeling and analyzing intersystem dynamics. Her intersystem research focuses on the interactions between the criminal justice and mental health systems and the public policies that influence those interactions. In addition, she has studied the quality of life inside prison, the victimization of inmates, and reentry programs.

INDEX

Note: A t after a page indicates a table. An f plus a number indicates a footnote.

A

AA see Alcoholics Anonymous (AA)
ACA see American Correctional
 Association (ACA)
Accountability of offender, 225
Accreditation
 of correctional treatment, 181-82
 of health care, 133
ACT see Assertive Community Treatment
 (ACT) model
Addiction treatment,
for mental health issues, 87
 in prisons, 130-31
Adolescents, 64
 assessments in, 63-64
 co-occurring problems in, 63-68
 females, see Female adolescents
 males, see Male adolescents
 mental health screening tools for, 88
 Motivational Interviewing with, 195
 screening instruments, 87
 substance abuse brief screening test,
 CRAFFT for, 87
Adolescents at high risk, see also
 Substance-dependent adolescents
 affective and anxiety diagnosis of, 67
 behavioral health conditions of, 70
 community service and reduction in
  re-offending, 323
 conduct disorder, 68
 co-occurring conditions of, 65-66
 contrast with clinical population, 67-71
 and depression—major, 67
 education and learning
  difficulties in, 66, 71
 ethnic composition of, 66
 female and male offenders, see Female
  adolescents; female juvenile
  delinquents; Gender issues;
  Male adolescents at high risk
 hallucinations of, 67
 learning problems of, 66
 maltreatment of, 70
 medication issues of, 66-67
 mental health assessments of, xi-xii, 88

and Motivational Interviewing, 195, 197
 multiple mental health conditions
  prevalent in, xi-xii, 71
 service needs of, 70-71
 sexual abuse and criminal
  activities of, 91
 substance abuse and dependence
  among., 67, 68, 69, see also
  Substance-dependent
  adolescents victimization of, 71
 youth awaiting treatment, 70
Adult correctional populations
 ethnic differences of, 75
 gender comparisons in, 74-75
 mental health issues in, xi, 71-72
 substance use issues in, xi, 72-74
Adversarial and restorative justice system
 contrasted, 361
African-Americans
 male cocaine dependence in, 75
 traditions and American call to
  service, 320
Agencies, see also Organizations
 assessment of, 33-41
 coordination of family issues by, 309
 Risk, Need, and Responsivity
  knowledge and technology
  assessments needed, 46
Alcohol dependence, see also Adolescents
  at high risk; Substance abuse;
  Substance dependence;
  Substance-dependent adolescents
 in British prisons, 76
 of females, 74
 and Native-American male
  dependence, 75
 versus alcohol abusers, 74
Alcohol screen
 UNCOPE, 78
Alcoholics Anonymous (AA)
 in correctional setting, 131
American Correctional Association (ACA)
 Corrections Today, 381
 Partnership with ICCA, xvii, 377, 378
American Probation and Parole
 Association, 378
American Psychological Association
 Characteristics of Effective

Relationships, 233t
Task Force on Empirically Based
Principles of Therapeutic Change,
232-33
American Psychiatric Association, 128
AmeriCorps, 351f6
Andrews, Dr. Don, x-xi, 214, 387-88
Andrews et al's meta-analysis,
169, 171-72
Andrews and Bonta, 53
Andrews, Bonta, Hoge, 4, 53-54
Andrews, Bonta, Wormith, 4, 7t-8t
Andrews and Kiessling study, 189, 193
Andrews, Zinger, et al, 4
impact on practice in corrections,
53, 58
Anger management, 89-90, 175
and inmate drinking, 90
in prisons, 131
Antisocial attitudes as criminal risk factor,
13t, 30t, 55
Antisocial companions as criminal risk
factor, 13t, 55
Antisocial girls versus boys, 90-91
Antisocial personality disorder
in British prison, 76
in conduct disorder of adolescent
males, 76
pattern of, 55
screen for, 87
Anxiety disorders
in girls, 90
screening for, 78
Arizona and Drug Medicalization,
Prevention, and Control Act
of 1966, 296
Assessment, see Mapping
Assessment generation of predictive
criterion validity estimates, 19-22
Assessment instruments for use on
offenders
Andrews' update, x-xi, 3-52
first generation (subjective) to second
generation (actuarial) gap, x, 4
generations compared, 19-22
ICCA conference topic, x
second to third generation
(criminogenic needs), x, 4
third generation with criminogenic
need assessment, x, 4
fourth generation with Risk, Need,
Responsivity, x-xi, 4
treatment planning and delivery

predictive validities of, xi, 56
prompts for Risk, Need, and
Responsivity, 46
Assessment of programs, 33-41
effect size by CPAI score, 34-36
mean effect size and CPAI treatment
scores, 36-41
Assessment training, 199-201,
see also Mapping
Assertive Community Treatment Model
(ACT), 135
Atlantic City, New Jersey
ICCA conference, x
Attention-Deficit Hyperactivity Disorder
(ADHD), 86-87
Attrition rates and implementation problem
with What Works, 384

B
Bachrach, Leona, 106
Barriers to reentry, 317
Bazemore, Dr. Gordon, xvi, 360, 388
and civic engagement approach, xvi
and civic service, xvi
on restorative justice, xvi, see also
Restorative justice
Behavioral contract's fairness
component, 232
Behavioral health disorders, see also
entries beginning with Mental health;
and Substance abuse
in corrections, 99
in female adolescents, 90
and mental illness in prisons
and jails report, 100
and substance use history, 100
treatment cost effectiveness of, 80
Behavioral health systems
criminal justice coordination
with, xii, 98
Behavioral health treatment for criminal
deviance
community based, 98
coordination between systems, 98
as cure for criminality, 107
to enhance public safety, 98
to reduce criminal deviance, 98
Behavioral history and criminal
risk factors, 55
Behavioral management, see also Case
management
approach to supervision, xiv
and community supervision, xiii-xiv

defining strategies of, 228-33
difference from case management,
    223, 224
part of case management, 222
principles of, 223
relationship between offender and
    correctional staff, 222
research foundation for principles,
    228-33
tenets applied to corrections, 234-242
Behavioral objectives, 234
developing natural support system
    for offender, 236
and engagement strategies, 236-39
and goals for behavioral-
    management orientation, 235
and procedural fairness, 236
as process that facilitates
    behavioral-management goals, 235
tools of process, 235-36
transformed by behavioral
    management, 234-242
and trust, 236
Behaviors and Experiences Inventory, 86-87
documents ADHD, 86
documents reading disorders, 86
documents victimization, 86
for law enforcement, xiv
uses social work goals, xiv
Big four criminal risk factors, 55
Boba, Dr. Rachel, xvi, 388-89
civic engagement approach, xvi
civic service, xvi
Boot camps
counseling component adds
    positive effect, 169
MacKenzie, Wilson, and Kider's
    meta-analysis of, 169
lacks recidivism reduction, 169
without treatment ineffective, 167
Borderline personality disorder in British
    prison, 76-77
Boys' pathways to crime, 203
Brad H v. City of New York, 130
Braman, Dr. Donald, xv, 389
British prisons, see also United Kingdom
alcohol dependence in, 76
and alternative sentencing to
    community service, 322
borderline personality disorder in,
    76-77
cocaine dependence in, 76
heroin dependence in, 76

marijuana dependence in, 76
mental health disorders in, 76-77
Offenders Behaviour Programmes Unit
    of HM Prison Service, 187
post traumatic stress disorder in, 76
substance abuse problems in, 76
Broad and Newstrom's training book,
    199-200
Broken windows, 114
Brooklyn, New York Court for mentally ill, 122
Burrell, William, xiii-xiv, 389-90
probation and parole using
    evidence-based practices, xiii

C
CAAPE, see Comprehensive Addiction and
    Psychological Evaluation (CAAPE)
CAFAS, see Child and Adolescent Functional
    Assessment Scale (CAFAS)
CAGE, 62
California
Substance Abuse and Crime
    Prevention Act of 2000, 296
Campbell Collaboration's intervention
    reviews, 226
Canada, 181, see also Correctional
    Service of Canada
correctional treatment accreditation
    process, 181-82
Capital accumulation halted by
    incarceration, 282
Case management, xiv, 190-93
advocacy to obtain needed
    services, 223
and assessment instrument, 236-37
and assessment of risk and needs,
    xiv, 223
uses assertive case planning, 224
and behavioral contract, 236
and behavioral management
    principles, xiv
and broker/generalist, 224
part of case planning, xiv, 223
and clinical rehabilitation, 224
and community involvement, xiv
and compliance management, xiv
definition of, 223
impact of incarceration on, 304-05
instruments prompts for Risk, Need,
    and Responsivity, 46
ISP and IPS, 124
for mental health, xiv
of mentally ill jail leavers, 135

models, see also Case management
models
monitoring of offender's
progress, 223
move to behavioral-management
models, 225
and research on effectiveness of, 224
service delivery, xiv
strategies, x
strengths-based, 224
and types of practices of, 224
versus ACT model, 135
Case management models, 198-99
based on Risk, Need, Responsivity,
192-93
for juvenile offenders, 198
Case management training, 199-201,
see also Staff training
Effective Case Work model,
196-97t, 197-98
Motivational Interviewing, 197
Case manager
as agent of change, 191-92, 193
case-management styles can be
developed, 193
role, 190, 191-92
uses Motivational Interviewing, 193
Case plan, xiv, 218
Case work,
Motivational Interviewing, xiii
training in, 199-201
Caucasian males and stimulant
dependence, 75
Central eight criminal risk factors, 55
Certified programs, see Accreditation
C.F. v. Terhune, 130
Child and Adolescent Functional
Assessment Scale (CAFAS), 88
Childcare in classification of female
offenders, 202
Childhood abuse, see also Abuse;
Childhood sexual abuse; Emotional
abuse; Mental abuse; Physical
abuse; Sexual abuse Incarcerated
girls suffered, 91-92
Childhood sexual abuse, see Abuse,
Maltreatment, Physical abuse,
Sexual abuse
drug dependence in women, 92
psychiatric disorders in adult
women, 92
Children diverted from criminal justice, 160
Choosing Correctional Options that Work:

Defining the Demand and Evaluating
the Supply, 379
Chronic conditions
adolescents need life-long
management, 80
life-long management needed, 80
women, 80
City Year, 351f6
Civic engagement models
forge positive connections, 360
sites for pilot projects, 35005lf5
Civic Engagement Model of Reentry
evaluation protocol, 318-19
goals of, 317-18
literature review, 319
value basis of, 319
Civic-Justice-Corps model, 321
Civic service as reentry practice, 321,
see also Community service
Civil rights movement and American
call to service, 320
Civilian Conservation Corps, 320
Classification systems
for biological and criminal
disorder, 140
for female offenders, 202
Clear, Todd, 109
women, 80
Client-centered therapy, 186
Clinical services
adolescents with co-occurring
problems as norm, 79
reduce criminal recidivism, 79
substantial need in correctional
populations, 79
Cocaine
and African-American male
dependence, 75
and British prison dependence on, 76
Coercion and change, 231-32
Cognitive-behavioral approaches and
therapist's behavior, 187
Cognitive-behavioral interventions, 5t
anger control, 175
cognitive restructuring, 175
community programs, 175
component of successful
recidivism reduction, 203
counseling combined with, 175
effective programs, 169, 171

Landenberger and Lipsey meta-
analysis, 173-76

manuals, 177
and recidivism, 170
training for staff, 199-201
Cognitive-behavioral therapists, 188
Cognitive Behavioral Therapy (CBT), 184
Cognitive perspective on crime, 11t-12t
Cognitive restructuring, 175
Cognitive social-learning theory, 5t
Cohen, 169
cost-benefit analysis on criminal
sanctions for sex offenders, 169
Collect phone-call rates, 307
Community alternatives, 378
Community-based prosecutor's and
defender's office, 361
Community collective efficacy, 344
Community corrections, see also
probation and parole
agencies' offender supervision
practices advance state of
practice, 213
evidence-based practice, xiii
expansion in, 296
mandatory drug-treatment in
community-based facilities, 296
professionals and legislators
increased interest in, 295
programs in Ohio, 37
Community dialog, 345
Community-level barriers to reentry, 316
lack of willingness to reintegrate
offenders, 316
negative image, 316
Community programs, 175
Community service
American tradition of, 319
beneficial impact on offenders, 331
to build community, 346-47
centers for, 141
core practice in civic engagement
model, 324
examples of projects, 346-47
hierarchy of community service
projects, 327-28
and human capital development,
338, 346
impact on recidivism—no negative
findings, 322
identity transformation, 332
offender experience and impact,
320, 328-30
Community service (continued)
primary intervention to reduce

community barriers for formerly
incarcerated, 316
protocol for offender involvement, 330
not retributive tool, 324
research questions, 347
service projects for community
building, 327-28
stakeholder involvement in decision
making, 325-30
strengths based, 340
as transformative activity, 324-25
using theory and research to shape
intervention designs, 330
versus jail, 322-23
for victim-offender recovery, 368
Community social capital, 316
as resource for offender's skills
and resources, 317
as source for experiences to restore
offender's trust and public
identity, 317
supply social support and
guardianship, 317
Community supervision agencies
balance between law enforcement
and social work goals, 222
Community transition from jail, 135
Competency-based training,
coding systems for, 201
Comprehensive Addiction and Psychological
Evaluation (CAAPE)
and frequency of problems in
British prisons, 76
Community alternatives to incarceration
increased with use of LS/CMI, 8t
Community-based services, 5t
Risk, Need, Responsivity principles, 5t
Community policing, 115
Community standards
customary and reasonable "price"
for crime, 120
response to deviance, 114-15
Community supervision, see also Probation
and parole; Probation; Parole
special conditions, 124
Conduct disorder, 68
by boys, 90
boys with substance abuse issues, 91
screen, 87
Conference of Chief Justices, 121
Conference of State Court
Administrators, 121
Confrontational approach negatively

related to treatment outcome, 188
Consensus Project Report, 134
Contagion, 128
Contingencies and punishing smarter, 380
Contingency-management systems
  interventions reduce criminal
    behavior, 227
Contracting
  medical claims, 133
  prison mental health services, 132-33
  utilization management, 133
Co-occurring conditions
  in adolescent populations, 63-68, 79
  in British prison study, 76-77
  in high-risk adult populations, 79
  routine assessments for, 62
Core correctional practices (CCP), 218
Correctional budgets and publicity about
    mentally ill violence, 138-39
Correctional health care, 128-29
  accreditation of, 133
  coordination with mental health
    system, 160
  Estelle v. Gamble, 128
  funding, 128-29, 160
  Ruiz v. Estelle, 128
Correctional health care coordination,
    133-39
  barriers to, 136-39
  recommendations, 139-141
  and risk aversion, 138-39
Correctional knowledge, advances in, 54-55
Correctional Medical Services (CHS),
    132, 133
Correctional population, see Adult
  correctional population
Correctional Program Assessment
  Inventory (CPAI)
  assess adherence to effective
    interventions, 181
  correlation with effect size figure, 40
  enhanced risk, need, responsivity
    adherence, 6, 9, 57
  reliability, 33
  scorable content, 9t
  score, 35, 36
  score of self-esteem programs, 37
  supports Risk, Need, and
    Responsivity, 45
Correctional programming,
  ICCA conference topic, x
  quality of implementation, 171
Correctional risk/need assessment

instruments outperform forensic
  mental health assessments, 46
Correctional Service of Canada, 378
  Motivational Enhancement Protocol
    with Project Match, 195
Correctional staff, see also Staff
  diagonal workgroups, 306-07
  empowerment of, 306-07
  knowledge of mental illness
    lacking, 160
Correctional supervision rate, 302
Correctional treatment, see also
  Evidence-Based Practices;
  What Works
  behavioral management and
    community supervision, xiii-xiv
  case management, xiii, see also
    Case management
  ICCA conference topic, x
  quality of implementation, xiii
  supervision, xiii
Correctional treatment accreditation
    process, 181-82
  in Canada, 181
  in United Kingdom, 181
Corrections
  mental health treatment in, 160
  as part of criminal justice system,
    122-23
Cost-benefit analysis, 167-68, 169
Counseling
  combined with cognitive-behavioral
    interventions, 175
  component of boot camps, 169
Courts
  coordination with mental health
    system, 134
  as part of criminal justice system,
    118-22
  specialized, 121, 122, 136, 138
CPAI see Correctional Program
  Assessment Inventory (CPAI)
CRAFFT, 87
Crime, 157
  and negative correlations with
    community service, 321
  victims' empowerment, 360
Criminal behavior
  and the central eight, personal
    emotional distress and
    lower class origins from eight
    meta-analyses, 14t
  and mental disorder relationship, 105

and substance use, 86
Criminal deviance and biological
  disorders, 97
Criminal justice and behavioral health
  systems,
  cost and confusion between, xii
Criminal justice and mental health
  coordination, see Mental health
  services coordination with
  criminal justice
Criminal justice system
  alternatives to, 292
  blacks and Latinos in, 283
  cost of each subsystem, 109
  disarray of, 112
  dissatisfaction with, 292
  funding for, 109-11
  impact on inner cities, 297
  mental health system
    interrelationship, 98
  mental and substance abuse illness
    in, 99-101
  and mental health system
    interrelationship, 98
  and money for social and economic
    problems rather than prisons, 292
  and people with mental illness, x,
    109-25
  police, court, corrections, 109-12
  preventative programs, 293
  prisons viewed least favorably, 292
  process, 112-125, 157
Criminal justice system coordination
  legal liability, 138
  and mental health system
    interrelationship, 98
  process, 112-125, 157
  professional norms, 138
  trial courts, 134
Criminal liability of seriously
  mentally ill, 160
Criminal risk factors, 55
Criminal sanctions
  criminal sanctions not related
    to recidivism, 172

  hidden tax on black and Latino
    families, 282-83
  minus treatment yield harmful
    results, 203
  not effective in recidivism
    reduction, 171, 172
  tax on poor and minority families, xv

Criminality is common risk factor, 54
Criminalization of mentally ill, 156

Criminogenic and noncriminogenic
  needs' mean effect size, 18, 27,
Criminogenic need; reduce to lower
  offending, 4
Criminogenic Programming and Treatment
  Effect, 38
Criminologists on social learning/cognitive
  view of crime, 11-12
Crisis intervention versus police, 114-15
Criticisms of Risk, Need, and Responsivity, 4
Custody without treatment ineffective, 167

D
De Tocqueville on American community
  service, 319
Decarceration, 156
  of persons with behavioral health
    problems, 98
Depression
  of abused women, 92
  and antidepressants, 62
  in British prisons, 76
  bipolar depression, 62
  and cognitive-behavioral therapies, 62
  of girls with substance abuse
    issues, 91
  PADDI, 76
  result of abuse, 91
  unipolar, 62
Diagnostic evaluations versus quick
  screening, 78, 79
Diagnostic tools versus screening tools, 62
Diminished capacity, 128, 160
Diminished responsibility, 156,160
Disordered behavior of persons with
  mental illness, 156-57
  and mental health treatment, 105-108
District of Columbia
  families of incarcerated, xv
  juvenile offenders' project, 351f5
District of Columbia (DC) correctional
  system, 291
  drug treatment programs in, 279
Diversion
  cost effectiveness of programs, 134-35
  direct supervision in programs, 135
  of mentally ill—standards for
    lacking, 159
  policies, 121
  at sentencing, 121

to treatment criteria, 140
intense supervision and
    reincarceration, 135
and net widening, 135-36
Doing Time on the Outside, 301
Domestic violence
    counseling in prisons, 131
    and social health, 7t
Dowden and Andrews (1999), xiv, 170
    female offenders, 170
    Risk, Need, and Responsivity, 170
Dowden and Andrews (2003), 170
    family interventions reduced juvenile
        recidivism, 170
    meta-analysis of female offenders, 201
Dowden, Antonowicz, and Andrews, 170
Driving under the influence, 74
Dropouts have poorer outcomes, 175
Drug classification, 86
Drug courts
    and employment, 136
    net widening of, 136
Drug dependence
    and childhood sexual abuse of
        women, 92
    and UNCOPE screen, 78
Drug treatment in correctional setting
    Alcoholics Anonymous, 131
    detox, 131
    education, 131
    estimate of need for, 131
    Narcotics Anonymous, 131
    rather than incarceration
        programs, 296
    therapeutic communities, 131
    trial court coordination of, 134
    wait for, 279
Drug use
    and parole revocation, 124
    as result of abuse, 91
    trial court coordination of, 134
DSM-IV-TR Diagnostic Criteria for
    Substance Abuse, 69, 85, 86
DSM-IV-TR Diagnostic Criteria for
    Substance Dependence, 84, 86
Dynamic validity, 26

E

East Palo Alto, California, 343-44, 347
Economic opportunity lacking, 157-58,
    see also Poverty
Education, see also Staff training
    attainment is best predictor for

avoiding criminal justice
    system, 283
attainment in justice and clinical
    adolescent populations, 90
learning difficulties of adolescents in
    juvenile justice population, 71
prevention programs, 93
programs for judges and
    prosecutors on mental illness and
alternatives to criminal
    processing, 141
as risk/need factor, 13t
services in prison for adolescents
    and adults, 90
Effect
    cognitive-behavioral, 172
    skill building, 172
Effect size
    correlations by Nesovic figure, 35
    and CPAI correlation figure, 40
Effective case work model, 196-198
Effective correctional and treatment
    programs, see also Risk, Need,
        Responsivity; What Works
    advocacy and brokerage with
        community services offering
        appropriate programs, 380
    behavioral strategies enforced in firm
        and fair way, 380
    cognitive-behavioral processing, 227
    delinquency network disrupted by
        offenders placed where prosocial
        activities dominate, 380
    effective human service in justice
        principles, 5t
    empirical understanding of, 16-19
    intensive behavioral services, 379
    intensive services occupy
        offenders' time, 379
Emotional abuse, 7t, 70, see also
    Maltreatment; Physical abuse;
    Sexual abuse
Employment-opportunities
    decline leads to crime, 282
    limited for formerly incarcerated, 316
Empowerment for victims and
    victimizers, 360
Environment
    definition of, 231
    of therapeutic community, 232
Estelle v. Gamble, 128
Ethnic comparisons on substance abuse, 75
Evans, Donald G., 390

Evidence-based practices
    boutique program, 215-16
    implementation of programs for, 176-83
    line officers implement, 216
    a management challenge, 216-17
    mission of organization, 216
    organizational challenges of, 216-17
    in probation and parole, 214-15
    and promise of, 215
Evidence-based program
    administrators, 385
Ex-offenders, see Formerly
    incarcerated face barriers

F

Fairness and equity perceptions impact
    on compliance, 232
Faith traditions and American call to
    service, 320
Families, x, xi
    and cost of incarceration, 296
    and communities support systems
        for offenders, xv-xvi
    definition of, 302
    of female offenders, 202
    health and safety of, 302
    natural strengths of, 305-06
    as resource for prisoners, 281
    and poverty as cause of
        incarceration, 281
    as risk/need factor, 13t
    as unit of analysis, 309-10
Family interventions reduced
    juvenile recidivism
    Dowden and Andrews
        meta-analysis, 170
    Higher risk juveniles targeted, 170 Family
Justice Program, 295
Family of offender faces isolation
    and depression, 285
Family process in classification of
    female offenders, 202
Father absence in inner city
    neighborhoods, 287-288
Fear of punishment as minor '
    criminal risk factor, 55
Federal Bureau of Prisons, 378
Felon disenfranchisement, 350f1
Felony probation in RAND study, 215
Female adolescents, see also Adolescents
        at high risk; Female juvenile
        delinquents
    and childhood abuse, 91

conduct problems of, 203
co-occurring disorders in, 68
and exposure to violence, 91
high behavioral-health problems in, 90
maltreatment of, 70
pathways to crime, 203
prevention strategy for those
    at risk, 93
self-abusive behavior, 91
social skill building for, 203
substance abuse treatment needs, 71
Female juvenile delinquents, see also
    Adolescents at high risk,
        Female adolescents;
    family problems is underlying
        cause of delinquency, 91
    *Report on Women in Criminal
        Justice*, 91
    running away from sexual abuse, 91
    strategy for those at risk, 93-94
Female offenders, 201-03;
    see also Female juvenile delinquents
    classification systems for, 202
    contrasted with male offenders,
        74-75, 290
    criminogenic needs of, 202-03
    Dowden and Andrews meta-analysis
        (1999), 170
    and family involvement, 202
    overclassification of, 202
    reducing recidivism rate of, 93
    *Report on Women in Criminal
        Justice*, 91
    substance abuse dependence, xii, 74-75
    treatment needs of, 75, 80
    treatment recommendations on
        need and responsivity, 31t, 32t
    What Works, 201
Females, see also Female adolescents,
        Female juvenile delinquents;
    Female offenders
    prevention from becoming part of
        the system, 93
    reducing recidivism rate of, 93
Feminist challenges, 41-44, 46
Feminist and Critical Criminological
        Criticisms of Risk, Need,
            and Responsivity, 41-44
Figures
    Comparison of Recidivism
        Rates on Effect Size, 15
    Correlations with Effect Size: M-A by
        Nesovic, 35

CPAI Correlation with Effect Size, 40
CRAFFT, 87
Critical Points of Intervention and
    Related Referral Options, 113
Description of the Criminal Justice
    System, 110
The DSM-IV-TR Diagnostic Criteria for
    Substance Abuse, 85
The DSM-IV-TR Diagnostic Criteria for
    Substance Dependence, 84
Gendreau, Little, and Goggin
    (Criminology, 1996), 26
Incarceration and Father Absence, 287
Incarceration, Father Absence, Median
    Household Income, 288
Incarceration and household income,
    282
Incarceration and salaries, 282
LSI and Recidivism by
    Offender Age, Gender, and
    Socio-Economic Status, 43
LSI (4) x Age (2) x Gender (2) x
    Reliance on Welfare (2) in
    Relation to Recidivism, 43
Mean Effect Size by Adherence to
    Principles, 17
Mean Effect Size by Adherence to Risk,
    Need, and Responsivity, 17
Mean Effect Field by CPAI Score, 35
Mean Effect Size and CPAI Tx Score Eta
    by Setting and Offender Type, 35
Mean Effect Size and CPAI Tx Score Eta
by Quality of Primary Studies, 36
Figures (continued)
    Mean Effect Size and CPAI Tx Score Eta
    by Type of Program (Targets), 35
Mean Effect Size by Criminogenic
    Noncriminogenic Needs, 18
Mean Effect Size by Specific Needs
    Targeted: Criminogenic Needs, 27
Mean Effect Size by Specific Needs
    Targeted: Noncriminogenic
    Needs, 27
Mean Number of New Offenses by
    Service, 28
Participation and Service Impact, 317
Recent Study of Community
    Correctional Programs in Ohio, 37
Relationship Between
    Proportion of Criminogenic
    Programming and Treatment
    Effect, 38
Relationship Between Role Playing and
    Treatment Effect, 39
Relationship Between Significant
    Factors and Treatment Effect for
    Halfway Houses, 40
Relationship Between Treatment
    Model and Treatment Effect, 38
Relationship Between Treatment and
    Supervision, 39
Reliability of CPAI, 33
Risk, Need, and Responsivity
    Adherence and Effect Size by
    Gender, 43
Self-Esteem Programs: Mean Effect Size
    by CPAI Score, 37
Third Generation and Fourth
    Generation Increase in r
    Square, 27
The UNCOPE Screen, 78
Financial issues and social well being,
    7t, see also Poverty
Finding the hook and motivation, 196t,
    197-98
Flint, Dr. Charley, xii
Forensic Mental Health Construction
    Sample for VRAG,
    major and minor risk/need factors 24t
Forensic mental health estimates, 22-26
    outperformed by correctional
    risk/need assessment instruments, 46
"Forgotten Issue in Correctional Treatment:
    Program Implementation," 177
Formerly incarcerated face barriers, 316
Fourth generation assessment instruments,
    7t-8t, see also Level of Services/Case
    Management Inventory
    benefits of, 46
    enhance adherence with Risk, Need,
    Responsivity, 6
    Gendreau, Goggin, Smith, 177
    identify need areas, 46
    identify responsivity issues, 46
    identify risk level, 46
    level of service/case management
    inventory (LS/CMI) examples,
    7t-8t
    structure service from planning
    through closure, 46

G
Gender issues
    in comparisons of substance
    abusers, 74-75
    and female mental health problems, 90

and LSI and offender recidivism, 43
and responsivity research, 46
Risk, Need, and Responsivity
adherence, 43
Gender-specific needs in classification
systems, 202
Gender-specific programs and recidivism
reduction strategy for incarcerated
females, 93
Gendreau, Paul, 166
Gendreau, Goggin, and Smith,
"Forgotten Issue in Correctional
Treatment: Program
Implementation," 177
Gendreau, Little, and Goggin
(Criminology, 1996) figure, 26
General Personality and Social
Learning/Cognition underpins Risk,
Need, Responsivity, 54
Violence Risk Appraisal Guide, 56
Genesee County, New York, 369
restorative process rather than
new jail, 369
Girls, see Female adolescents; Female
juvenile delinquents
Good Lives Model, 44-45, 385
Great Britain
alternative sentencing to community
service, 322

Group interventions and recidivism
reductions, 190

H
Habitat for Humanity, 346, 351f6
Halfway houses and significant factors
and treatment effect for, 40
Handgun violence and trial court
coordination of, 134
Hardyman and Van Voorhis,
classification systems for female
offenders, 202
Harland, Alan, 379
Harm-creators empowerment, 360
Harmful use defined, 86
Health issues, 132-33, see also entries
beginning with Mental health;
Substance abuse
of poor families, 304
prison's funding of services for, 128-29
and social health, 7t
Heroin dependence in British prisons, 76
Hettema, Steele, and Miller meta-analysis

Motivational Interviewing, 195-96
High school diploma, see also Education
absence and relapse, 90
High-risk behavior avoidance and positive
informal affective relationships, 338
High-risk offenders, 175, 380
behavioral strategies essential to
service delivery, 379
cognitive-behavioral methods for, 203
and program integrity issues, 203
and relapse prevention occurs in
community, 380
responsivity necessary with therapist
and programs, 380
sufficient dosage for, 203
therapists relate to in interpersonally
sensitive and constructive
way, 380
HIV-positive status of inmates, 303
Hoffmann, Dr. Norman, xi, 391
Housing access to by reentry inmates, 304
Human capital development and
community service work, 338, 341, 346
Human need and psychological
definitions of, 46
Human service principles in justice
context, 5t

I
ICCA see International Community
Corrections Association
Identity transformation, 332-37
Ikeda, Daisaku, 359
Illinois
adult and juvenile probation use
Motivational Interviewing, 118
Impaired driving, 7t
Impulse control, 89
and inmate drinking, 90
Incarcerated males
abrogate familial and community
responsibilities, 290-91
income and father incarceration, 289
Incarceration
and community costs, 290-92
emotional costs on families, 283-89
family income and, 289
and family structure, 289-92
hardship of on mentally ill, 126
impact on families, 301
increasing use of, 123
increases crime rates, 345
lowers income and increases expenses

of family, 282
rate of, 302, 303
and therapeutic jurisprudence, 127
transforms material and moral lives,
297-04
and voluntary service, 320
Income and father's incarceration, 289,
see also Poverty
Information systems establish shared
systems for mental health and
criminal justice, 141
Inner city areas and crime, 108-09
Informal social controls
bond to pro-social groups and
institutions, 338
community members intervene in each
other's lives, 343
crime causes harm to individuals,
relationships, and communities,
339
informal positive relationships'
value, 339
Inmate, see Offender
Intake treatment planning and Risk, Need,
Responsivity, xi
Intensive probation supervision (IPS), 124
Intensive supervision parole (ISP), 124
Intensive supervision programs, 214-15
Assertive Community Treatment
Model (ACT), 135
and reincarceration, 135
Intellectual judgment and inmate
drinking, 90
Intermediate sanctions, 214-15
International Association of Residential
and Community Alternatives, 378
International Classification of Disease,
psychoactive drug classification, 86
International Community Corrections
Association (ICCA)
advocacy role of, 382
and American Correctional
Association partnership, xvii,
377, 378, 379
and American Probation and Parole
Association, 378
and Correctional Service of
Canada, 378
and Federal Bureau of Prisons, 378
history of, 378-79
implementation research area for new
ICCA work, 385
and International Corrections and

Prison Association, 378
and International Halfway House
Association, 378
Journal of Community Corrections, 381
membership of, 379
name changes of, 378
and National Association of Probation
Executives, 378
National Institute of Corrections
partnership, 377, 380
research conferences, 379-381
training seminars, 380
United Nations Alliance of Non
Governmental Organizations in
Criminal Justice, 378
and what works promotion, ix, 377
International Corrections and
Prison Association, 378
International Halfway House
Association (IHHA), 378
Interventions for better outcomes in
therapy, 229-30
environment where services are
provided, 231
relationship between caregiver
and offender, 231
Interventions that reduce criminal behavior
cognitive-behavioral therapy, see
Cognitive-behavioral
interventions
contingency-management systems, 227
non-effective programs, 227
promising programs, 227
therapeutic community
with aftercare, 227
Iowa and prisoner health care funding, 129
Israel and community service as
alternative to jail, 322

J
Jails
different than prisons, 142f2
health care costs, 129
mental health treatment, see
Jails' mental health treatment
numbers of and function, 123
services in, 143f17
substance abuse treatment in, 143f14
Jails' mental health treatment
accreditation of, 133
case management in, 131
counseling or therapy in, 131
estimate of need for, 131

funding for, 129
group therapy in, 131
mental health treatment in, 131
psychiatric evaluation, 131
psychotropic medication, 131
reentry assistance, 131
screening at intake, 131
twenty-four hour care, 131
Jails and prisons as toxic environments, 126
James, William, 320
Job-training skills, 307
Judges
with discretion to incarcerate, 158
influenced by legal culture of
community, 158
sentencing style of, 120
training for, 159
Judicial sanctions without treatment
ineffective, 167
Jury service of formerly incarcerated
restricted, 316
Just deserts model, 348
Juvenile delinquency effective programs
to curb
case management model with, 198
connection with one positive adult
role model, 360
counseling, 173
family support for, 306
longer programs, 173
low dropout, 173
meta-analysis of Lipsey, 172-73
researcher involvement, 173
skill-building of juveniles in, 173
Juvenile Justice Delinquency
Prevention Act
gender-specific programs
mandated, 93
Juvenile justice population,
see also Adolescents at high risk
Juvenile recidivism
Lipsey's meta-analysis, 169
Dowden and Andrews
meta-analysis, 170

K
Klockars, Carl, 217

L
La Bodega de la Familia,
HIV/AIDS and substance abuse
co-occurrence, 304
Labor unions and American call to

service, 320
Lamb, Richard, 106
Landenberger and Lipsey
meta-analysis of cognitive-behavioral
interventions, 173-76
Latessa and Lowenkamp, 37
Law enforcement and correctional
supervision component, xiv
Lawrence, Phyllis, xvi-xvii
restorative justice, xvii
Learning problems, see also Education
assessment for, 63
in justice and clinical adolescent
populations, 90
Leisure pursuits as criminal risk
factors, 13t, 55
Level of Service/Case Management
Inventory (LS/CMI), 4, 6, 7t-8t
comparison with other fourth
generation systems, 8tf
and recidivism by offender age, gender,
and socio-economic status
figure, 43
risk/needs assessments' clinical
value, 4
youth version, 8t
Life course criminology, 337-38
Life skills in prisons, 131
Line officer
case management skills, 218
facilitative and helping skills, 217-18
monitoring and supervising, 218
Line personnel, xiii
Line supervisors, 217
Lipsey meta-analysis 169, 171-72
juvenile delinquents prospered under
cognitive-behavioral
programs, 169, 172-73
Lipsey, Chapman, and Landenberger, 170
cognitive-behavioral treatment and
recidivism, 170
Literacy programs, see also Education
and reaching out to families and
friends, 307
Lockups, 123
Lowenkamp, Chris, 37-40
Lower social class is minor criminal risk
factor, 55
LS/CMI see Level of Service/Case
Management Inventory (LS/CMI)

M
MacKenzie, Wilson, and Kider,
    meta-analytic analysis of boot
        camps, 169
Maine
    Juvenile justice data, 64
Male adolescents at high risk
    co-occurring disorders in, 68
    maltreatment of, 70
    substance abuse treatment needs, 71
Maltreatment, 65, see also Abuse; Emotional
    abuse; Physical abuse;
        Sexual abuse and affective
        and anxiety disorders, 70
    defined, 70
    history of for adolescents, 70
Manic episodes
    in British prison, 76
    PADDI in adolescent population, 76
Manuals, 177-78
    use and recidivism reduction, 171
Mapping, see also Assessment instruments
    for use on offenders
    channel to highest-risk cases,
        196t, 197
    and costs of incarceration, 308
Mapping Center, Brooklyn, New York, 308
Marijuana dependence, 73
    in British prisons, 76
Martinson, Robert, 166
Mass incarceration
    costs of, 295
    impact on families, xv-xvi, see Families
Massachusetts Youth Screening
    Instrument-Version 2
    self-report for mental health
        problems, 88
Match mode and strategies with strengths
    of offenders, 5t
Mc Guire
    *What Works: Reducing Reoffending
    Guidelines from Research and
    Practice, 173*
MCM-III, see Millon Clinical Multiaxial
    Inventory-III (MCM-III)
Mean Predictive Criterion Validity Estimates
(r) from Meta-Analytic Studies by
    Generation: Based on Andrews,
    Bonta, and Wormith, 20t
Media coverage and violent mentally
    ill, 138-39
Medication cost for mental illness, 132
Mental disorders and criminal deviance, 156

Mental health
    addiction treatment no cure for
        criminal behavior, 87
    of adult populations, xi, 303
    assessment of, 63
    in classification of female
        offenders, 202
    and commitment statute in
        Washington state, 138
    court in Washington State, 138;
        see also Courts
    criminological research aids, 136
    and criminal justice system, see
        Mental health services
        coordination with criminal justice
        delivery system and contractors,
        132-33
    disorder, see Mental health disorder
    in funding of state correctional
        facilities, 130
    of juvenile populations, xi-xiii, 67-71
    management and publicity, 138-39
    medication cost for, 132
    of offenders, 303
    risk aversion, 138-39
    screening, see Mental health screening
        and diagnostic tolls; Screening
        instruments
    standards for care for, 128
    trial court coordination of, 134
Mental health disorder
    adolescents need ongoing treatment
        as adults, 71
    assessment instruments, 56
    in British prison population, 76-77
    case management aspect, xiv, see also
        Case management;
    case management models court-
        supervised drug treatment, 296
    by gender, 90-91
    not meeting diagnostic criteria for,
        89-90
    screen, see Mental health screening
        and diagnostic tools; Screening
        Instruments
Mental health screening and diagnostic
    tools, xi, 78, 79, 89; see also
        Screening instruments
    risk estimate, xi
    screening tools for adolescents, 88
    VRAG, 19-22
Mental health services coordination with
    criminal justice, 98, 134; see also

Mental health treatment in
    correctional setting
classification system for
    biological and criminal
    disorder, 140
develop diversion to treatment
    criteria, 140
education programs for judges and
    prosecutors on mental illness
    and alternatives to criminal
    processing, 141
establish community service
    centers, 141
ICCA conference topic, x
individual agency responsibility, 139
integrate funding and services, 141
interdisciplinary training on
    coordination, 140
performance measures of coordination
    at all levels of system, 140
police contact with, 101
privatization, 139, 140
probation and parole officers
    reward for social integration, 140
provide incentives for
    coordination, 140
recommendations, 140-41
risk aversion, 138-39
shared information systems, 141
trans-institutionalizing persons with
    mental illness, 100
Mental health and substance abuse, xii
in adolescent populations, 63-64
and criminal behavior, xii
prevalence assessment, 61-62
Mental health treatment in correctional
    setting, 130-31; see also Mental health
    services coordination with
    criminal justice
addiction treatment, 131
anger management, 131
Bureau of Justice Statistics' report
    on, 100
case management, 131, 135
counseling or therapy, 131
domestic violence counseling, 131
group therapy, 131
life skills, 131
medications, 131
New Jersey Department of
    Corrections, 130-31
post release, 130
psychiatric evaluation, 131

psychotropic medication, 131
reentry assistance, 131
screening at intake, 131
sexual offender treatment, 131
and substance use disorders, see
    Mental illness and substance use
    disorders tiered approach, 130-31
twenty-four hour care, 131
Mental illness in prisons and jails
criminal behavior of people with
    mental illness, 101-04
in 1980s, 100
nuisance offenses, 101
prevalence, 101, 156
training for work with, 159
treatment impact, 105
Mental illness and substance use disorders
civil commitment criteria, 99
in criminal justice system, 99-101
"criminalization," 99
treatment and criminal deviance, 99
Mental retardation is not mental illness, 158
Mentally ill
class bias, xii
crimes committed by, 101-03
and criminal justice system, 109-25
delinquent girls compared to boys, 91
diversion from criminal justice
    system, 125-28
ethnicity of, 158
fear of violence from, 119
gender of, 158
good behavior of, 159
lead chaotic lives, 108
live in impoverished communities, 108
medication cost, 132
and mobile crisis teams, 115
not mentally retarded, 158
procedural fairness, 127
punishment v. rehabilitation/
    therapeutic goals, 127
as result of abuse, 91
and responsibility for criminal
    deviance, 98
serious cases of, 108, 159
stigma of, 156-57
and therapeutic jurisprudence, 127
types of crimes committed by, 101
Meta-analysis, 167-68, 173-76
    Andrews et al, 169, 171-72
    Cohen, 169
    Dowden and Andrews (1999), 170
    Dowden and Andrews (2003), 170

Dowden, Antonowicz, and
Andrews, 170
Hettema, Steele, and Miller, 195-96
Lipsey, 169, 171-72
Lipsey, Chapman, and
Landenberger, 170
literature reviews, 54
MacKenzie, Wilson, and Kider, 169
Petrosino, Turpin-Petrosino, and
Finckenauer, 169
magnitude of effect of treatment in
reducing recidivism, 168
what it is, 168
Michigan Department of Corrections
prisoner mental health funding, 129
video teleconferencing for families of
inmates, 307
Millon Clinical Multiaxial Inventory-III
(MCM-III)
comprehensive mental health
assessment, 89
Minnesota Department of Corrections, 76
Substance Use Disorder Diagnostic
Interview-IV, 71-72
prisoner mental health funding, 129
Minnesota Multiphasic Personality
Inventory (MMPI)
comprehensive mental health
assessment, 89
Minor criminal risk factors, 55
fear of punishment, 55
lower social class, 55
personal distress, 55
related to recidivism, 55
verbal intelligence, 55
Minority families and criminal sanctions on
families, xv, see also Families
Mission of organization, 216
MMPI, see Minnesota Multiphasic
Personality Inventory (MMPI)
Monitoring of program delivery, 177
Moos, Rudolf
environment for offender change, 232
Moral Reconation Therapy, 175
Motivational Enhancement Therapy,
188, 195
Motivational Interviewing, xiii,
57, 177,193-201
with adolescents, 195
case managers use, 193
coding systems for, 201
and cognition, 57
in custodial settings, 195

definition of, 57
and ethnicity, 57
factors to facilitate change, 57
Four-Stage Model for Supervision,
196-97
Hettema, Steele, and Miller
meta-analysis, 195-96
and manuals, 177
in meta-analysis, 177
and motivation, 57, 194
as prelude to other treatment, 194
and responsivity, 34t, 46, 95
in substance abuse, 194-95
techniques of, 188
training programs for use of, 199-201
use in corrections, 193
Moving forward, 197t, 198

N
NA, see Narcotics Anonymous (NA)
Narcotics Anonymous (NA) in correctional
setting, 131
National Association of Probation
Executives, 378
National Commission on Correctional
Health Care, 128, 133
National Directory of Drug and Alcohol
Abuse (SAMHSA), 85
National Institute of Corrections
partnership with ICCA, 377, 380
training seminars with ICCA, 380
National Mental Health Association
advocates universal screening for
mental health and substance
abuse, 94
National Organization for Victim Assistance
(NOVA), 361
Native Americans
American call to service, 320
male inmates' alcohol dependence, 75
Nebraska and prisoner health care
funding, 129
Need, see also Criminogenic need; Risk,
Need, Responsivity
criminogenic effect, 172
definition of, 44, 46
target criminogenic needs, 5t
Neglect and being abused, 7t,
see also Abuse
Networks of collective support and
reasons for lessening of, 320
Nevada and prisoner health care
funding, 129

New Freedom Commission on
      Mental Health
   health/substance use disorders, 89
   Lehrman's horror stories, 89
   primary health care screening for
      mental disorders, 89
New Castle County, Delaware
   reentry court, 125
New Freedom Commission Report,
      disorder within behavioral-health
      system, 107
New Hampshire and prisoner health
   care funding, 129
New Jersey
   jail health care, 129
   mentally ill murderer, 138
New Jersey Department of Corrections
   C.F. v. Terhune, 130
   correctional health care treatment, 131
   mental health treatment, 130
   prisoner health care funding, 129
   prisoner mental health funding, 129
New Offenses by Service figure, 28
New York
   Brad H. v. City of New York, 130
   Vera Institute study of community
      service versus jail, 322
Norfolk, Virginia
   ICCA conference site, x
North Charleston, South Carolina, 351f5
Not effective correctional and treatment
      programs, see also What
      does not work
   alcohol and drug education, 227
   boot camps, 227
   case management, 227
   intensive supervision, 227
   non-directive counseling, 227
Nothing works is wrong, 214

O

Obsessive-compulsive disorder in
   British prison, 76-77
Occupational licensing
   formerly incarcerated face
      restrictions on, 316
Offender accountability, 295
   not rehabilitation, 293
   responsible behavior within social
      relationships, 293-94
Offender age and LSI and recidivism, 43
Offender assessment, see Assessment
      instruments for use on offenders

Offender reentry strategies, see also
      Restorative justice principles
      of reentry
   assistance in state correctional
      facilities, 130
   community role, 315
   family support for, 306
   for persons with mental illness, 125
   ICCA conference topic, x
   and parole supervision, 125
   rehabilitation—Todd Clear's idea, 109
   treatment system noncompliant with
   needs of community, 107
   restorative justice principles, 315-49
Offender responsivity
   in cognitive-behavioral programs, 170
   in skills-based programs, 170
Offenders
   and their communities, 302
   engagement in change process, 236
   as individuals, 294
   learn about victim trauma, 367
   as members of families and
      communities, 294
   telling their story, limits on, 365
   type and CPAI score, 17
Offenders Behaviour Programmes Unit of
      HM Prison Service, 187
Ohio Department of Rehabilitation and
Corrections
   community service and reduction in
      re-offending, 323
   incarcerated fathers and children
      united, 307
Oklahoma Department of Corrections and
      Bodega Model of case
      management, 308
Openness, warmth, and understanding, 186
Oregon and prisoner health care
      funding, 129
Organizations, 378
   culture of, 216
   infrastructure of, 216
   line personnel in, 217
   line supervisors in, 217
   mission of, 216
   staff supervision in, 217

P

PADDI, see Practical Adolescent Dual
      Diagnosis Interview (PADDI)
Palmer, Ted, 166-67
Paraprofessionals as trainers, 185

Parental incarceration rate, 302
Parental rights for formerly
    incarcerated restrictions, 316
Parenting, 307
Parole, see also Probation and parole
    parole revocation, 124
    reward for good behavior, 124
    rules, 348
    supervision abolished, 215
    without treatment ineffective, 167
Parole boards
    discretion on release, 158, 159
    role of, 122
Parolees' community service versus jail, 323
Pathways to crime for boys and girls, 203
Pennsylvania State Prison System, 90
    and alcohol abuse and
        dependence, 90
Personal
    distress as minor criminal risk
        factor, 55
    and noncriminogenic needs, 27-28
Personality assessment
    and responsivity research, 46
    and illness, 106-07
Perspectives, 381
Petersilia and MacKenzie
    boot camp research, 167
Petrosino, Turpin-Petrosino, and
        Finckenauer
    meta-analysis of Scared Straight, 169
Phone calls
    collect phone call rates, 307
    from prison, 280
    phone cards, 307
Physical abuse, 70, see also Maltreatment
    in homes of girls acting out, 91
    and sexual, emotional abuse as
        behavioral-health condition, 65
    underlying cause of female juvenile
        delinquency, 91
Pierce County, Washington
    pilot program/case management
        model for juvenile offenders, 198

Police
    culture of agency, 116
    discretion of, 158
    diversion, 118
    gatekeepers to criminal justice
        system, 109, 115-17
    medicalizing events, 116-17
    training in medical illness, 116

Politics and publicity about violence of
    mentally ill, 138-39
Portland, Oregon, 351f5

POSIT, see Problem-Oriented Screening
    Instrument for Teenagers (POSIT)
Post-traumatic stress disorder (PTSD)
    British prison, 76
    correlated with maltreatment, 70
    as result of abuse, 91
Posted rules and fairness component, 232
Poverty
    and opportunity in United States,
        157-58, 305
    poor families' involvement in criminal
        justice system, 302-04
Practical Adolescent Dual Diagnostic
    Interview (PADDI), 64-65, 68
    interview on maltreatment, 70
    screen for mental health problems and
        substance use, 88
Practitioner characteristics, 184
Pre-trial diversion's net widening, 135-36,
    see also Diversion
Predictive criterion validity estimates by
    assessment generation, 19-22
President's Commission on Law
    Enforcement and Administration of
    Justice, 99
Prevention from becoming part of the
    system
    education component, 93
    for girls and women, 93
Principles of Effective Human Service in
    Justice Contexts, 5t
Principles of Specific Responsivity, 30t
Prison-based educational services for
    adolescents and adults, 90
Prison Health Services (PHS), 132, 133
Prisons, see also British prisons; State
        correctional facilities
    different than jails, 142f2
    experiences in, 7t
    health care funding of, 128-29
        mental health funding, 129
Privatization of corrections and
        mental health, 139
    add coordination measures to
        contracts, 140
Pro-social interventions, 293, 337-39
    family often not recognized, 302
    positive informal affective
        relationships, 338

without treatment ineffective, 167
Probation
court cooperation, 124
without treatment ineffective, 167
Probation and parole, see also Parole;
Probation
agents have conflicting roles, 124-25
case management toolbox, xiv
Probation and parole *(continued)*
expectations of, 124
evidence-based practices, 214-15
facilitator of offender change, xiv
line officers to implement evidence-
based practices, xiii, 216
mission and purpose definition, xiii
and Motivational Interviewing, 197, 218
numbers of, 123
organizational infrastructure, xiii
role of, 217-18
staff supervision, xiii
skills set of officers, 218
synthetic officer, 217
training for agents, xiv
using evidence-based practices, xiii
Probation officer
deliver case management model for
juvenile offenders, 198
relationship and structuring skills, 189
reward for integration of mental health
and criminal justice, 140
role conflict of, 159
training for, 159
Problem-Oriented Screening Instrument for
Teenagers (POSIT) for youth
psychosocial functioning, 88
Problem-solving courts, 361
Procedural justice's environment, 232
Professional associations
advocacy role, 382
collaborative and strategic
alliances, 382
"communities of memory," 381
contacts made at meetings, 381
information network, 381
key value of, 381
relationship skills, 385
Professional discretion, 5t
Program assessment, 33-41
Correctional Program Assessment
Inventory (CPAI), 181
correctional treatment accreditation
process, 181-82
performance-measurement, 182-83

Program delivery management and
organization, 4
Program effectiveness and meta-
analysis, 178
Program implementation and Lipsey's
meta-analysis, 169
Program integrity, 204
component of successful recidivism
reduction, 203
quality of, 203-04
Promising correctional and treatment
programs
drug courts, 227
emotional skills, 227
moral reasoning, 227
Motivational Interviewing, 227
treatment with testing and
sanctions, 227
treatment accountability for safer
communities, 227
twelve step with curriculum, 227
Prosecutors, 118-22
discretion to indict mentally ill
or not, 158
informal handling of cases, 120
knowledge of mental illness and
treatment, 158
training for, 159
Psychiatric disorders
childhood sexual abuse of women, 92
and jail placement, 132
Psychoactive drugs
harmful use, 86
use, intoxication, abuse,
dependence, 86
or LS/CMI General Risk/Need
(from Andrews, Bonta, and
Wormith, 2004) 21t
Psychology of criminal conduct
empirical understanding of effective
correctional treatment, 16-19
empirical understanding of risk/need
factors, 12-16
general personality and social
learning/cognition, 45
theoretical understanding, 10-12
Psychotherapy outcome research, 183-84
characteristics of successful
therapists, 189
PADDI, 65
Psychotropic medications in state
correctional facilities, 130
PTSD, see Post traumatic stress

disorder (PTSD)
"Punishment works agenda" ineffective, 167

Q
Quick screens availability, 79

R
Racial disparities in arrests,
　larger significance of, 282
Reading problems in justice and clinical
　　adolescent populations, 90,
　　see also Education
Reasoning and Rehabilitation Program, 175
Recidivism reduction
　boot camps do not decrease
　　recidivism, 169
　cognitive-behavioral treatment, 170
　for community service versus jail '
　　participants, 322
　criminal sanctions not effective, 171
　effective correctional-treatment
　　impact, xiii
　family involvement in, 170
　girls and women, 93-94
　for juveniles, 170
　and LSI, figure, 15
　relapse-prevention techniques, 170
　research involvement, 171
　responsivity factors, 170
Reentry, see Offender reentry strategies
Reentry court in New Castle County,
　　Delaware, 125
Reintegrating formerly incarcerated
　　individuals, 348-49
Relapse-prevention techniques and
　　recidivism
　Dowden, Antonowicz, and Andrews
　　meta-analysis, 170
Relationship building, 233, 339-41,
　　see also Therapy relationship
Repairing harm, 332-37
Report on Women in Criminal Justice
　young women acting out for
　　self-protection, 91
Research-based practice and meta-
　　analytic findings, 172
Research involvement and recidivism
　　reduction, 167, 171
Researcher involvement, 175, 178-79
Responsivity, see also Risk, Need,
　　Responsivity
　in case management, 192-93
　cognitive-behavioral strategies, 5t

Motivational Interviewing, 195
principles of, 30t
specific, 7t, 29-33, see also
　　Specific responsivity
staff relationship and structuring, 4
Responsivity research,
　gains in personality assessment, 46
　and gender issues, 46
　Motivational Interviewing, 46
　stages of change, 46
Restorative community service
　criteria, 368-69
　emotional needs, 368
　financial needs, 368
　physical needs, 368
　reparation to meet needs, 368
　skill building for offender, 369
Restorative dialog
　compliance rate high, 368
　community service for victim-offender
　　recovery, 368
　between victim and offender, 367
　victim gains fear reduction, 368
Restorative justice model, 225-26
　accountability, 226
　basic skills, 226
　dialog, 367-68
　doing justice by repairing harm, 349
　emotional development, 226
　offender obligation to victims and
　　community, 349
　proposed model, xvii
　rejects punishment for its
　　own sake, 349
　service tied to pro-social
　　community groups, 349
Restorative justice as the norm
　adversarial process is
　　alternative, 369-73
　agency serves victims and
　　offenders, 369
　confidentiality guaranteed, 370
　current practices, 372-73
　meeting with surrogate offender, 372
　pre-sentencing work, 373
　results of this approach, 371
　team case-management system, 370
　victim outreach, 370
Restorative justice principles of reentry,
　315-49, see also Offender reentry
　strategies
　altering community's views of
　　previously incarcerated, 316

building community capacity for informal support, 316
reducing community barriers to reentry, 316
Restorative justice process
anger management skills, 369
communication skills, 369
conflict resolution skills, 369
Retribution and reintegrating formerly incarcerated, 348-49
Reviewing and supporting, 197t, 198
Rhine, Edward E., 392
Risk, see also Risk-Need-Responsivity
higher risk offenders, 172
match intensity of services with risk level, 5t
Risk and need factors, 7t-8t, 12-19
antisocial personality pattern, 7t
Risk-needs assessment
clinical value, 4
higher risk cases, 4
theoretical and empirical foundations of, 54
Risk-needs assessment tools, 4, 17, 182-83
mean effect size of adherence, 17
meta-analytic studies support, 45
practical utility of, xi, 56-57
and promising intermediate targets for reduced recidivism, 13
security level, 4
staff training and supervision, 4, 55
treatment planning and follow-up, 4
Risk-Need-Responsivity, 226 see also each item individually
actuarial risk of offender, 226
adherence and effect size by gender, 43
adherence to and recidivism, 55
adversarial and restorative justice system contrasted, 361
agency level need ongoing assessments for, 46
Andrews, see Andrews
assessment instruments need prompts for, 46
case closure, 4
case management, 4, 46, 192-93
challenges, 57-58
cognitive-behavioral strategies, 384
crimonogenic needs targeting, 384
critical criminologists' criticism, 42, 44-45, 46
custody, 4
dynamic need factors, 226

female offenders, 170
feminist criticism, 41-44, 46
high-risk individuals, 226
intensive treatment only for moderate and higher risk cases, 384
low-risk cases and intensive services wrong, 384
managers and supervisors heed relationship and structuring skills of delivery staff, 385
medical model interventions, 380
monitoring, feedback, and corrective action vital, 385
quality control in, 384
and restorative justice dialog, 385
staff monitoring for use of, 46
underused due to implementation problems, 46
validated risk/needs instruments, 384
what does not work, see What does not work
Risky sexual behaviors, 74
Robinson, Dr. David, xiii, xiv
Role playing and treatment effect relationship, 39
Roosevelt, Franklin Delano, 320
and formation of Civilian Conservation Corps, 320
Ruiz v. Estelle, 128

S
SAMHSA, see Substance Abuse and Mental Health Administration (SAMHSA)
Sanctions with treatment, 167
social-learning-based programs, 171
staff training, 171
technical supervision, 171
use of manuals, 171
Scared Straight programs and increased recidivism, 169
Screening instruments
for adolescents, 63-68
criteria for, 87
easy to use, 87
for mental health intake at state correctional facilities, 130
for mentally ill, 88
purpose of, 62-63
self or group administered, 87
short, 87
inexpensive, 87
universal screening for mental health

disorders, 89
versus diagnostic determinations, 62
versus diagnostic evaluations, 78, 79
Self-abusive behavior as result of abuse, 91
Self-esteem programs, 7t , 36-37
Self-help societies and American call
to service, 320
Self-image change process, 335-37
during activity or service, 335-36
examples of service activities, 336
new life goal, 336
prevention strategy for at-risk girls, 93
research questions, 336-37
service and community building,
344-45
Sentencing guidelines equate uniformity
with justice, 348
Sentence length of mentally ill versus
nonmentally ill, 142f9
Sentencing options' impact on
recidivism, 166
Sentencing reform
legislators examining, 295-96
number of yearly releases, 303
Service, 187
return on investments, 80
Risk, Need, Responsivity, xi
therapist behavior and style, 187
in United Kingdom, 187
Settlement houses and American call
to service, 320
Sex offenders,
cost-benefit analysis of programs
for, 169
Offenders Behaviour Programmes Unit
of HM Prison, 187
Sexual abuse, 7t, 70, see also Maltreatment
girls running away from, 91
in home of girls acting out, 91-92
and mental health disorders 91
precursor to criminal justice system
involvement, 92
precursor to mental health
disorders, 92
public health threat, 92
statistics on, 91
and substance use, 91
Sexual offending
risk factors, 7t
treatment in prisons, 131
Shapiro, Carol, xv, 393
family as natural support system,
xv-xvi

Shulman, Jerry, xii, 392-93
Substance abuse and dependence
confusion, xii
Simourd, Dr. David, xi
assessments, predictive validities of, xi
correctional knowledge, advances, xi
Skill-based methods, 203, see also
Cognitive-behavioral interventions
Social achievement and criminal risk
factors, 55
Social capital, see also Human capitol
development and community
service work
causes of decline, 320
of individuals, 306
Social health and personal well being, 7t
being abused, 7t
domestic violence, 7t
financial issues, 7t
health, 7t
self-esteem, 7t
Social learning/cognitive perspective
on crime, 11t-12t
Social networks and families as part of,
305-06, see also Families
Social relations as criminal risk factor, 55
Social skill building for girls, 203
Social work as correctional supervision component, xiv, 322. see also Case
management
Socio-economic status and LSI and
offender recidivism, 43
Special education in justice and clinical
adolescent populations, 90
Special needs offenders, xi, 61-161
Specialty court diversion, see Courts,
specialized
Specific responsivity
anxiety, 7t
ethnicity/culture, 7t
gender, 7t
mental disorder, 7t
motivation stages, 7t
psychopathy, 7t
Staff
certification, 182
monitoring for use of Risk, Need, and
Responsivity, 46
orientation toward treatment
model, 185
paraprofessionals, 185
psychotherapy research, 183-84
relationship skills, 5t

selection, see Staff retention
and training
skill, see staff skills
style, 183
supervision, see Staff supervision
training and supervision,
55, 181-82, 185
traits for success, 186
Staff selection and training, 5t, 180
and recidivism reduction, 171
Staff skills, 183
and client outcome, 177
and mental health background, 185
and staff certification, 182
and supervisory tenure, 182
user group symposia, 182
Staff supervision, xiii, 181-82, 185, 217
behavioral management approach to
supervision, xiv
staff training and supervision
considering Risk, Need and
Responsivity, 55
Staff training
cost of nationwide, 200
in effective correctional practices,
199-201
interdisciplinary training on mental
illness and criminal justice
coordination, 140
managers' supervised practice, 201
for dealing with mentally ill, 159
and ongoing supervision, 200
planning session for, 200-01
of program delivery staff, 175, 177
supervised practice, 201
supervisors' role in, 201
on social status of mentally ill, 158
on race, 158
and sentence length of, 159
and social status of offenders, 158
Stages of Change
and Motivational Interviewing, 34t
and responsivity research, 46
State correctional facilities, see also
Prisons mental health funding, 130
mental health systems inside
prisons and jails, 130
prison population-reduction
measures, 296-97
provide psychotropic medications, 130
provide reentry assistance, 130
screen for mental health
issues at intake, 130

substance use treatment in, 130
therapy or counseling provided, 130
Stimulants,
Caucasian male dependence on, 75
female dependence on, 74
Strength
assess to enhance prediction, 4, 5t
definition of, 44
and individualized case planning, 4
Substance abuse, 55, see also Alcohol
dependence; Substance dependence;
Substance use
and conduct disorder in boys, 91
and criminal risk factors, 13t, 55
and depression in girls, 91
different from dependence, 62
of inmates and mental health
status, 303
international perspectives, 76-77
and Motivational Interviewing, 194-95
National Directory of Drug and Alcohol
Abuse (SAMHSA), 85
situational opposed to chronic
disorder, 86
treatment in jails, 143f14
versus substance dependence, 83-85
Substance Abuse and Crime Prevention Act
of 2000
cost savings of, 296
Substance Abuse and Mental Health
Administration (SAMHSA), 85
Substance dependence, see also
Substance abuse; Substance use
comparison of juvenile justice
population,
state inmates, UK inmates, 77
distinct from abuse, 62, 63, 68
juvenile treatment needs, 71
women versus men in criminal
justice system, 92
Substance dependence disorder
screening, 79
UNCOPE, 78
Substance-dependent adolescents, 69-71,
see also Adolescents at high risk
age of first intoxication, 69-70
and CRAFFT, 87
ongoing treatment services needed, 71
similar to adults, 69
treatment strategy for girls with dual
diagnosis, 93
Substance-dependent individuals differ
from substance abusers, 72-74

Substance use, see also Substance abuse;
    Substance dependence
    in adult populations, xi
    and clinical services pre and post
        incarceration, xi
    and illness, 98
    in juvenile populations, xi
    as major risk factor for
        delinquency, 91
    medicalized response, 98
    and moral character, 98
    not meeting diagnostic criteria for,
        89-90
    responsibility for criminal deviance, 98
    and screening and diagnostic tools,
        xi, 77-78
    versus substance dependence,
        xi, xii
    treatment, 98, 130
Substance use screens
    quick screening instruments, 77-78
    Substance Use Disorder Diagnostic
        Interview-IV, 71-72
    UNCOPE screen, 77-78
Substance Use Disorder Diagnostic
    Interview-IV, 71-72
Successful service providers, 185
SUDDS-IV, see Substance Use Disorder
    Diagnostic Interview-IV
        sufficient dosage is component of
        successful recidivism reduction,
        203
Suicide as result of abuse, 91
Supervision, 177 see also Staff supervision
    Community service versus jail,
        322-23,

T
Tables
    Association of Childhood Sexual Abuse
    with Drug Contributions to
        General Class Origins: Mean
        Estimates from Eight
        Meta-Analyses, 14t
    Correlation (r) Between Criminal
        Behavior and the Central Eight,
        Personal Emotional Distress and
        Lower Dependence and
        Psychiatric Disorders in Adult
        Women, 92
    Examples of Fourth-Generation
        Assessment: Level of Service/Case
        Management Inventory (LS/CMI),

7t-8t
    A Four-Stage Model for
        Supervision, 196-97
    Major and Minor Risk/Need Factors in
        the Forensic Mental Health
        Construction Sample for VRAG,
        24t
    Major Risk/Need Factors and
        Promising Intermediate
        Targets for Reduced Recidivism,
        13
    Mean Predictive Criterion Validity
        Estimates (r) from Meta-Analytic
        Studies by Generation: Based on
        Andrews, Bonta, and Wormith, 20t
    Number of Positive Dependence
        Criteria for Dependent Cases, 77
    Personality and Social
        Learning/Cognitive Perspective on
    Crime, 11t-12t
    Predictive Criterion Validity Estimates
        (r) for LS/CMI General Risk/Need
        (from Andrews, Bonta, and
        Wormith, 2004) 21t
    Prevalence of Diagnoses by Gender of
        Adult Inmates, 75t
    Principles of Effective Human Service
        in Justice Contexts, 5t
    Principles of Specific Responsivity, 30t
    Proportion of Adult Inmates with
        Positive Criteria Given a
        Diagnosis of Abuse, 73t
    Proportion of Adult Inmates with
        Positive Criteria Given a
        Diagnosis of Dependence, 72t
    Proportion of Cases with Positive
        Indications for Behavioral Health
        Conditions, 67T
    Results from Meta-Analysis on
        Effective Correctional and
        Treatment Programs, 227
    Some Feminist and Critical
        Criminological Criticisms of Risk,
        Need, and Responsivity, 42
    Scorable Content of The Correctional
        Program Assessment
        Inventory (CPAI), 9t
    Specific Responsivity: Stages of
        Change and Motivational
        Interviewing, 34t
    Specific Treatment Recommendations
        for Women Assigned to Need and
        Responsivity Considerations,

31t-32t
Treatment needs for chronic
  conditions, 80
Task Force on Empirically Based
  Principles of Therapeutic Change,
  232-33
Taxman, Dr. Faye, xiv, 395
  behavioral management approach to
    supervision, xiv
Tazewell, Illinois, County State's Attorney,
  deferred prosecution program, 118
Techniques defined, 231
Terrorism, 7t
Therapeutic alliance, 187
  in therapeutic communities, 227
Therapeutic change, 232-33
Therapeutic communities,
  with aftercare for reducing criminal
    behavior, 227
  in correctional setting, 131
  for drug addiction and co-occurring
    mental illness, 131
Therapeutic jurisprudence, 119, 127
Therapist characteristics and relationships,
  184-85, 233
  alliance with client, 233
  cohesion in group therapy, 233
  confrontational approach, 188
  empathy, 188, 233
  feedback 233
  genuineness, 233
  goal consensus, 233
  open-ended questions, 188
  positive regard for client, 233
  Rogerian, 188
  style and skill traits, 189
Therapy or counseling in state correctional
  facilities, 130
Thinking for a Change, 175
Third Generation and Fourth Generation
  Increase in r Square, 27
Transportation to distant institutions, 307
Treatment dose (more treatment = better
  results), 175
Treatment effectiveness literature review,
  167-73
  meta-analysis, 173-76
Treatment inadequacy,
  behavioral health issues, 98
  substance use illness, 98
Treatment model and treatment effect
  relationship, 38
Treatment needs for chronic conditions, 80

Treatment and supervision relationship, 39,
  see also Therapist characteristics and
    relationships
Tuberculosis, 128

U
UNCOPE, 77-78, 87
  adolescent screen, 78
  adult population screen, 78
United Kingdom, 181, 187, see also
    British prisons
  alternative sentencing to community
    service, 322
  community service and reduction in
    re-offending, 323
  co-occurring conditions in prisons,
    76-77
  correctional treatment accreditation
    process, 181-82
  Offenders Behaviour Programmes Unit
    of HM Prison Service, 187
United Nations Alliance of Non
    Governmental Organizations, 378
Universal screening
  for mental health disorders, 89
  National Mental Health Association
    advocates, 94
  as prevention strategy for at-risk
    girls, 93f
  for substance abuse and mental health
    disorders, 93, 94
Urban America
  mass incarceration impact on, xv-xvi
  and networks of family and friends, 290
U.S. Department of Labor co-sponsorship
    for Civic Justice Corps projects, 352f14
Utah juvenile offenders
  community service and reduction in
    re-offending, 323

V
Van Dieten, Dr. Marilyn, xiii, xiv, 395-96
Vera Institute
  State Sentencing and Corrections
    Program, 295
  study of community service versus
    jail, 322
Verbal intelligence as minor criminal
    risk factor, 55
Victim-offender
  conferences, 367
  interconnectedness, 366-67
Victim's rights movement,

accountability of offender, 362-63
incarceration of low-risk offender
counterproductive, 364
input on civic service options, 362
notification, 362
repair for victim, 363
right to be heard, 362
victim's questions, 364
Victim's role, 361-62
Victimization, see also Abuse
assessment for, 63
and female offenders, 74-75, 202, 203
inmates prior problems, 74
services for juvenile justice population
needed, 71
Violence, see also Abuse
girls' mental reaction to
exposure to, 91
history of and criminal behavior, 203
related to substance use, 74
Violence Risk Appraisal Guide (VRAG), 56
forensic mental health assessment
using, 22-26
General Personality and Social
Learning Cognition, 56
Virginia delinquent girls suffered physical
and sexual abuse, 91
Visitation
extension of hours of, 307
improved conditions for, 307
Volunteer work, see also Community
service
by incarcerated, 320
value of for community, 345-46
vision of collective learning and skill
building, 347
Voting rights of formerly incarcerated
restrictions on, 316

W
Ward and Maruna rehabilitation theory,
44, 385
Washington State
juvenile probation uses
Motivational Interviewing, 197
mentally ill murderer, 138
multisystemic therapy failure in, 41
Pierce County pilot program/case
management model for juvenile
offenders, 198
Welfare reliance and recidivism figure, 43
What does not work, see also Not effective
correctional and treatment

programs
moderate-risk individuals, 226
nondirective client-centered
counseling, 380
programs for low-risk offenders, 380
and restorative justice dialog, 385
What works,
evolution and origins of, xiii, 166
ICCA work not over, 383
implementation improvement, 384-85
rehabilitative programming, xiii
What Works movement, 165
*What Works? Questions and Answers about
Prison Reform,* 166
*What Works: Reducing Reoffending—
Guidelines from Research and
Practice,* 173
When Work Disappears, 282
Wilson, Shifra, 343-44
Wilson, William Julius, 282
Wolff, Dr. Nancy, xii, 396-97
criminal justice and behavioral health
systems, xii
Women, see Female adolescents; Female
offenders, Females; Feminist
challenges
Wyoming and prisoner health care
funding, 129

Y
Youth Corps program, 321
Youth as resources, 351f6

Z
Zehr, Howard, 361

Other Titles Available from ACA-ICCA

What Works and Why: Effective Approaches to Reentry. 2005.

What Works: Risk Reduction: Interventions for Special Needs Offenders. 2002. Harry E. Allen, Editor.

What Works: Assessment to Assistance: Programs for Women in Community Corrections. 2000. Maeve McMahon, Editor.

What Works: Research to Results: Effective Community Corrections. 1999. Patricia M. Harris, Editor.

What Works: Strategic Solutions: The International Community Corrections Association Examines Substance Abuse. 1999. Edward Latessa, Editor.

What Works: Successful Community Sanctions and Services for Special Offenders. 1998. Barbara J. Auerbach and Thomas C. Castellano, Editors.